Impossible to Hold

American History and Culture
GENERAL EDITORS
Neil Foley, Kevin Gaines, Martha Hodes, and Scott Sandage

Guess Who's Coming to Dinner Now?
Multicultural Conservatism in America
Angela D. Dillard

One Nation Underground
A History of the Fallout Shelter
Kenneth D. Rose

The Body Electric
How Strange Machines Built the Modern American
Carolyn Thomas de la Peña

Black and Brown
African Americans and the Mexican Revolution, 1910–1920
Gerald Horne

Impossible to Hold
Women and Culture in the 1960s
Edited by Avital H. Bloch and Lauri Umansky

Impossible to Hold

Women and Culture in the 1960s

EDITED BY

Avital H. Bloch and Lauri Umansky

NEW YORK UNIVERSITY PRESS
New York and London

NEW YORK UNIVERSITY PRESS
New York and London
www.nyupress.org

Library of Congress Cataloging-in-Publication Data
Impossible to hold : women and culture in the 1960's /
edited by Avital H. Bloch and Lauri Umansky.
p. cm. — (American history and culture)
Includes bibliographical references and index.
ISBN 0–8147–9909–4 (acid-free paper) —
ISBN 0–8147–9910–8 (pbk. : acid-free paper)
1. United States—History—1961–1969—Biography.
2. Women—United States—Biography.
3. Women—United States—Social conditions—20th century.
4. United States—Social conditions—1960–1980.
I. Bloch, Avital H.   II. Umansky, Lauri, 1959–
III. American history and culture (New York University Press)
E841.I47   2004
920.72'0973'09046—dc22   2004017282

New York University Press books are printed on acid-free paper,
and their binding materials are chosen for strength and durability.

Manufactured in the United States of America

c 10 9 8 7 6 5 4 3 2 1
p 10 9 8 7 6 5 4 3 2 1

For our children
Amir and Amnon

~

Carenna and Wendy

Contents

Introduction   1

PART I Break

1   The "Astronautrix" and the "Magnificent Male":
    Jerrie Cobb's Quest to Be the First Woman
    in America's Manned Space Program   9
    Margaret A. Weitekamp

2   Building Utopia: Mary Otis Stevens
    and the Lincoln, Massachusetts, House   29
    Susana Torre

3   Life on the Cusp: Lynda Huey and Billie Jean King   43
    James Pipkin

4   Balancing Act: Ursula Kroeber Le Guin   65
    Zina Petersen

PART II Bridge

5   Ambassadors with Hips:
    Katherine Dunham, Pearl Primus,
    and the Allure of Africa in the Black Arts Movement   81
    Julia L. Foulkes

6   Take Everyone to Heaven with Us:
    Anne Waldman's Poetry Cultures   98
    Roxanne Power Hamilton

7   Joan Baez: A Singer and Activist   126
    Avital H. Bloch

8   "Ain't No Mountain High Enough": Diana Ross
    as American Pop-Cultural Icon of the 1960s   152
    Jaap Kooijman

PART III Confront

9   The Choices before Us: Anita M. Caspary and the
    Immaculate Heart Community   177
    Susan Marie Maloney

10 Shaping the Sixties:
    The Emergence of Barbara Deming   196
    Judith McDaniel

11 Yoko Ono and the Unfinished Music of
    "John & Yoko": Imagining Gender and
    Racial Equality in the Late 1960s   217
    Tamara Levitz

12 "Hanoi Jane" Lives:
    The 1960s Legacy of Jane Fonda   241
    Barbara L. Tischler

PART IV Connect

13 "I Feel the Earth Move":
    Carole King, *Tapestry*, and the Liberated Woman   261
    Judy Kutulas

14 Sonia Sanchez: "Fearless about the World"   279
    Michelle Nzadi Keita

15 A Beacon for the People:
    The Sixties in Dianne McIntyre   292
    Veta Goler

16 Judy Chicago in the 1960s   305
    Gail Levin

    About the Contributors   327

    Index   331

Introduction

The 1960s in America opened to the Cold War sputters of the
Nixon-Kennedy debates. Women hovered at the edges of the public
imagination in the early years: Jackie in pill-box hat; Marilyn
crooning to the president. They were not, by anyone's estimation,
at the helm of American culture. Then the sixties happened and
somehow, in the course of that fierce decade, women launched a
juggernaut that outpaced anything NASA could concoct. . . .

It happened that way and, of course, it did not. The story of
women in the 1960s remains as incomplete and enigmatic as every other
historical narrative in the making. More than thirty years past, an era that
has become as proverbial as it was real still inspires and confounds the
American imagination. We know more in hindsight about the complexi-
ties of a time rife with nuclear danger, war, rage, delight—revolution writ
large and small. We know, too, that *women's* lives changed, profoundly
and irretrievably, during those years. And more remains to be known.

This collection of essays enters two parallel, yet occasionally inter-
secting, conversations about the long decade of the 1960s: One is about
culture, the other about women. *Impossible to Hold: Women and Culture in the 1960s* aims to exemplify and encourage their convergence.

Of the many studies of 1960s culture, few focus on women. A smat-
tering of women make it into the pages of the major texts on the era.
They surface as incipient feminists suffering insult and gathering steam in
the Civil Rights, student protest, and antiwar movements. Hippie chicks
and Weatherwomen make an appearance, as do a handful of anomalous
popular culture figures. On the whole, however, sixties culture remains
synonymous with men and male-dominated movements.

1

In *Impossible to Hold*, sixteen authors examine a range of pursuits—from space exploration and sports to music, religion, literature, and the performing arts—through which women helped shape the cultural configuration known as "the sixties." Some of the figures featured here defined themselves as feminist, while others did not. Some achieved mass celebrity, while others made their mark principally among the avant-garde. Separately and in the aggregate, their cultural work helped to gender the sixties. These essays seek to retrieve and understand that work.

Just as accounts of sixties culture in general have downplayed women's importance, studies of women in that period have tended to give culture short shrift. With some significant exceptions, writers have traced a common path for women from the mid-1960s into the 1970s, a path of increasing self-realization and anger that passed, often, through the Civil Rights, radical, and countercultural movements of the day out onto the wide-open political plaza of second-wave feminism. For the most part, the story of the sixties for women has been the story of feminism's roots and routes, a tale that subordinates culture to the more recognizable formations of political activism. This is not an incorrect telling, only a partial one. Culture also mattered.

Working thematically along a jagged chronology of the 1960s, the essays here trace the activities of women whose lives and work intersected with the culture of the decade in significant ways. Women who sought to break into "male" fields of endeavor populate the first segment of the book. Margaret A. Weitekamp tells the story of Geraldine "Jerrie" Cobb's unsuccessful try to penetrate the male realms of NASA and space, respectively, in the early sixties. Susana Torre depicts architect Mary Otis Stevens's determination to reconfigure domestic space by literally removing the walls that enclose the nuclear family in its gendered and privatized roles. James Pipkin explores the ambivalent position athletes Lynda Huey and Billie Jean King occupied as aggressive competitors in the years when women were still consigned to the sidelines of track, court, and field. And Zina Petersen analyzes the deliberate embrace of ambivalence in the works of science fiction writer Ursula Kroeber Le Guin, the first woman to achieve spectacular success in a genre long considered the bastion of men.

The book's second section, titled "Bridge," features women whose work and personae helped connect earlier social and artistic movements or sensibilities to the more radical trends of the sixties. As anthropologists and dancers, Katherine Dunham and Pearl Primus made connections between the African and African diasporan experience and African American life in particular, presaging and contributing to the budding Black Arts movement of the 1960s. Dance historian Julia L. Foulkes makes a strong case for seeing roots of that movement in the work of Dunham and Primus, a view that puts women at the center rather than the extreme periphery of black-cultural nationalist artistic activism, where many scholars locate them. Roxanne Power Hamilton shows how poet Anne Waldman straddled two "generations" of writers—the Beats and the second-generation New York School poets. Waldman's centrality to the New York poetry scene of the sixties complicates its reputation as an almost entirely male-dominated realm in which any woman could be dismissed, in poet Ted Berrigan's words, as "just a girl." Like Waldman, folksinger Joan Baez carved out an artistic space for women without defining her stance as "feminist"; connected to the style and values of the pre-countercultural folk music scene, committed to the political causes of sixties-generation radicals, and grappling with her own image as a "feminine" performer and activist, Baez typified the "bridge generation" who, in Avital H. Bloch's analysis, helped to gender the sixties as much by default as by intent. Motown diva Diana Ross also occupied an ambiguous cultural space, as she bridged or "crossed over" racial schisms in the music scene, in part by deploying an exaggeratedly "feminine" image that audiences devoured, gender stereotypes intact. At the same time, as Jaap Kooijman argues, Ross grew beyond the limitations placed on "good girls" of the early sixties, as she, like thousands of other young women finding their voices later in the decade, began to speak out about racial injustice.

The book's third section, "Confront," presents four women who consciously confronted cultural and institutional power structures, with the express desire to effect radical change. To varying degrees, these women staged their protests *as women*, if not as self-declared feminists. Susan Marie Maloney chronicles Anita M. Caspary's bold departure from the Catholic Church to form the ecumenical Immaculate Heart Community, devoted to "a faith-based life based on individual preference and not institutional affiliation." Poet and activist Barbara Deming took a sharp turn toward the left in the 1960s as she committed herself to peace and antiracist activism. As her biographer Judith McDaniel shows, Deming's early Quaker education in pacifism and her lesbian identity informed her willingness to break rules for the cause. Yoko Ono, already an avant-garde artist who had fought personal demons of parental expectation and racial stereotyping long before she met John Lennon, took on the music industry and former Beatle John's listening public when she worked as an equal with her husband to create music that liberated her authentic voice; as Tamara Levitz explains, the raw pain and urgency in Yoko Ono's vocalizations troubled listeners who expected more mellifluous sounds from a female performer. Actress Jane Fonda, too, moved toward authenticity in her life as she shed the sex-goddess image on which she had risen to fame in films such as *Barbarella* to challenge U.S. involvement in Vietnam. Fonda's widely publicized 1972 visit to Hanoi, where she championed the liberation struggle of the Viet Cong, drew unending ire from portions of the American public, according to historian Barbara L. Tischler, not simply for its perceived "treasonous" tenor but also because, as woman and celluloid sex object, Fonda had stepped out of line.

The fourth and final section of the book, "Connect," focuses on women whose music, poetry, dance, and art fully incorporated the values and insights of the sixties, and did so in a gender-conscious fashion. Over the course of the decade, Carole King transformed herself from a composer of mainstream pop music to a singer-songwriter nonpareil of works that examined the minutiae of young, liberated women's psyches. Judy Kutulas analyzes the countercultural and feminist appeal of King's acclaimed *Tapestry* album. Michelle Nzadi Keita furthers the discussion of the Black Arts movement in her study of activist poet Sonia Sanchez. A major figure in a movement that can no longer be seen as the exclusive province of men, Sanchez produced terse, in-your-face poetry about black women's pain and dreams, with the intention of inciting revolutions both personal and political. Dancer Dianne McIntyre, Veta Goler writes, similarly incorporated the energy of the Black Power movement into her choreography and performance. A direct artistic descendant of Katherine Dunham and Pearl Primus, McIntyre is an important artist whose work belongs in any reckoning of the art and culture of the 1960s. Finally, art historian Gail Levin traces the activities of Judy Chicago, perhaps the best-known woman artist of the long decade of the sixties. Chicago's signal shows of the period, especially her famous "Dinner Party," cast women, quite literally, as the centerpiece of a wide-ranging celebration of genius and generativity.

By the time the long decade of the sixties ended—sometime in the mid-1970s—women's involvement in American culture, and conversely, the centrality of culture to American women's lives, could no longer be questioned. The essays in this volume offer insight into how and why the *gendered* cultural revolution of the sixties occurred. We hope, in the process, to offer fresh takes on some of the era's better-known figures and to raise from obscurity a few who deserve to be known more widely. By any estimation, women by the end of the proverbial sixties were at the helm of American culture. Perhaps Carole King, describing the texture of her own life in the title song of the *Tapestry* album, said it best:

> My life has been a tapestry of rich and royal hue
> An everlasting vision of the everchanging view
> A wondrous woven magic in bits of blue and gold
> A tapestry to feel and see, impossible to hold.
> —*Tapestry*, Epic Records, 1970

PART I

Break

1

The "Astronautrix" and the "Magnificent Male"

Jerrie Cobb's Quest to Be the First Woman in America's Manned Space Program

Margaret A. Weitekamp

In 1962, Lucille Ball's new television series, *The Lucy Show*, featured an episode in which Lucy's friends tricked her into thinking that she had been tapped to be a "lady astronaut." In "Lucy Becomes an Astronaut," Ball's character, who was terrified by the dangers of space flight, tried everything to escape the assignment, pleading, "How much does that man in the White House want me to do for my country anyway?" The comedy reached its climax when Ball uncomfortably donned a silver spacesuit, knees knocking but nonetheless willing to do her part for the space program. In the episode's conclusion, much to her relief, her friends revealed the joke. During the same season, *The Jetsons* premiered in primetime. In "Jane's Driving Lesson," the space-age mother introduced in each show's opening as "Jane, his wife" decided that if her eight-year-old son Elroy had a learner's permit, then surely she could learn to drive the family spacecraft. Instead, she scared the driving instructor so badly that he went back to a less dangerous job: hunting lions. In each case, the idea of a woman piloting a spacecraft—a female astronaut—provided the crux of the comedy. In the fall of 1962, an ongoing debate about whether women could be astronauts emerged in popular culture.[1]

As they wrote the episodes, both shows' writers drew inspiration from the real-life controversy sparked by Geraldine "Jerrie" Cobb, the first woman to pass the physical examinations developed for the National Aeronautics and Space Administration (NASA). When the privately funded program that tested her and eighteen other women ended because

Navy officials withdrew the permission to use their facilities, Cobb lobbied the federal government to support additional women's testing. Her campaign—and the broader debate that it inspired—exemplified what cultural critic Susan J. Douglas has called the "prefeminist agitation" of the early 1960s.[2]

Even before the modern women's movement created powerful advocates and widespread recognition for feminist issues, signs of women's discontent could be seen. In 1961, Women Strike for Peace organized a fifty-thousand-housewife walkout to protest above-ground nuclear tests. That same year, President John F. Kennedy tapped former first lady Eleanor Roosevelt to head the President's Commission on the Status of Women. Yet such actions remained but foreshadowing, harbingers of a consciousness poised to emerge in the coming years. By 1963, Betty Friedan published *The Feminine Mystique* and Congress passed the Equal Pay Act, setting the stage for the women's movement. In 1961 and 1962, however, Cobb struggled to get government officials and the mass media to acknowledge women's potential.[3]

Although her lobbying ultimately failed, Cobb's advocacy forced national decision-makers to grapple with women's physicality—and their potential role in the Cold War space race. In 1962 and 1963, NASA astronaut John Glenn and writer/ambassador Clare Boothe Luce represented the two opposing sides of the national discussion. Glenn's defense of the space agency's policies reflected its increasing emphasis on the astronauts' masculinity. Boothe Luce advocated passionately for women's full participation in the national space effort. Beyond the narrow question of female astronauts, however, their arguments revealed a dynamic struggle over gendering outer space and the space program. Ultimately, the two-year cultural and political debate that Cobb inspired highlighted the turmoil surrounding women's roles on the eve of the feminist movement.[4]

The "Astronautrix"

Cobb's life as America's first female astronaut candidate began when she met Dr. William Randolph Lovelace II, NASA's head of Life Sciences, and Brigadier General Donald Flickinger, chief of the Air Force's Air Research and Development Command (ARDC), in September 1959. In 1958, Lovelace's namesake foundation developed the physical testing regimen for NASA's first astronaut candidates, examinations later depicted in

Tom Wolfe's novel *The Right Stuff* (and Philip Kaufman's 1983 film of the same name). A visionary who anticipated orbiting space stations but still expected a gendered division of labor, Lovelace looked forward to multi-person space crews that included women—albeit in pink-collar jobs such as laboratory technicians, support staff, and telephone operators (communications officers).[5]

Lovelace and Flickinger wondered whether women also offered any physical advantages for space flight. In tests conducted in England, Canada, and the United States, women regularly outperformed men in enduring cramped spaces and prolonged isolation. Women had fewer heart attacks than men did. Scientists even speculated that women's internal reproductive system might be better protected from radiation or vibration than men's reproductive organs were. Moreover, women offered the same skills as men did, but in smaller physical packages since, on the average, women are lighter and shorter than men are. A smaller spacecraft for a more compact occupant would be easier to engineer and less expensive to fly.[6]

To investigate women's capabilities, the doctors recruited Cobb to be their first test subject. As a commercially licensed pilot who had ferried aircraft to Europe and South America, she offered impressive flight credentials, including several aviation records. Indeed, she had been recognized as the Women's National Aeronautical Association 1959 "Woman of the Year in Aviation" and the National Pilots Association's "Pilot of the Year." She jumped at the chance. Using names Cobb suggested, Flickinger sifted through pilot records from the Civilian Aeronautics Authority (CAA, the precursor to the Federal Aviation Administration) to select other potential candidates based on age, height, weight, and flying experience. By the end of November 1959, however, before they finished checking the CAA records, the Air Force canceled the program.[7]

Concerns about public reaction drove the decision. As Flickinger wrote to Lovelace, "The concensus [sic] of opinion . . . was that there was too little to learn of value to Air Force Medical interests and too big a chance of adverse publicity to warrant continuation of the project." The flight surgeons feared that investigating women's talents opened the service up to public criticism. Suggesting that women could be astronauts—a physically dangerous occupation—transgressed the accepted roles for women. As a result, the Air Force researchers concluded that Project WISE (Women in Space Earliest) could not continue without attention, and any such publicity would most likely be negative.[8]

The space research community's profound discomfort with female physiology hampered its investigation of women's potential. Despite medical data collected from various women's divisions during World War II, including the Women Airforce Service Pilots (WASP), aerospace scientists still considered themselves to know little about the particular workings of the female body. Moreover, the complete absence of a physiological baseline shamed no one. Like other medical researchers of the time who assumed that women's monthly cycles changed their bodies so fundamentally that they became unreliable as test subjects—and yet prescribed remedies for women based on all-male studies without any adjustment—aerospace scientists simultaneously declared women to be too complicated and largely irrelevant.[9]

Contemporary descriptions of an ideal woman astronaut also reflected the researchers' uneasiness. In a 1959 *LOOK* magazine cover story published under the title question "Should a Girl Be First in Space?" scientists offered a profile that focused on minimizing female traits. Because space suits had not been designed with women's curves in mind, the profile not only defined the prospective female astronaut as ideally "flat-chested" but also reiterated the requirement a second time: "She will not be bosomy." According to the physicians *LOOK* quoted, women's reproductive organs also posed problems. Scientists planned not just to manage but even to "eliminate" menstruation using medication. Furthermore, the woman astronaut had to be "willing to risk sterility from possible radiation exposure." In their view, men's biological needs had to be accommodated but women's physiology added unmanageable complications.

Concerns about introducing a fertile woman into close quarters with men remained unspoken but undeniably present in *LOOK*'s description. Scientists sought to assure themselves that the woman who would be locked inside a cramped spacecraft would be the boyishly built wife of one of the crewmembers, not a buxom single woman who might bring her sexuality on board with her. The close confines of a space capsule could not tolerate (hetero)sexual tension.[10]

These misgivings went from theory to reality when Flickinger and Lovelace resumed the canceled women's testing project. Instead of working under Air Force auspices, Lovelace conducted the experiment privately at his Lovelace Foundation in Albuquerque, New Mexico. Five months after they first contacted her, Cobb took the Project Mercury physical. Lovelace announced her success on August 19, 1960, at the Space and Naval Medicine Congress in Stockholm, Sweden. The Associated Press wire carried the story to hundreds of American newspapers. Although Lovelace cautioned that "no definite space project [existed] for the women," he also declared that "we are already in a position to say that certain qualities of the female space pilot are preferable to those of her male colleague."[11]

When Cobb raised the specter of potential female astronauts, the mass media reacted in ways that typified the transition occurring in the early 1960s: they both heralded and undercut women's coming empowerment. In a similar case, Susan Douglas has argued that popular early 1960s television shows telegraphed signs of American women's widespread discontent—and the concurrent need to suppress such agitation. Shows such as *Bewitched* and *I Dream of Jeannie* featured women whose extraordinary powers upset men's lives, but whose actions could always be neutralized in the end. In the case of *I Dream of Jeannie*, NASA itself symbolized the rigid hierarchy that fell apart when a woman intruded. The announcement of Cobb's achievements added a real-life dimension to the growing cultural turmoil about women's power.[12]

When Lovelace announced Cobb's success, newspaper and magazine articles touted her physical achievements while also attempting to reduce her to an acceptable female role. The *Washington Star* covered the news as if Cobb had won a beauty contest, not passed astronaut tests, reporting in detail on her weight and proportions: "Miss Cobb, who has a 36-26-34 figure, said she lost 7 pounds during a week of testing but regained them. She stands 5 feet 7 inches and weighs 121 pounds." *Time* magazine blended her measurements with laudatory traits but found it necessary to invent a feminized word for astronaut, "The first astronautrix (measurements: 36-27-34) eats hamburgers for breakfast, is an old hand at airplanes, with more air time—over 7,500 hours—than any of the male astronauts." Over the next three years, Cobb found herself being called everything from "astronautrix" to "astranette," "feminaut," and "space girl." The term *astronaut* apparently carried such masculine connotations that even a potential female candidate for space required a new label.[13]

Articles began and ended with descriptions that characterized the twenty-nine-year-old Oklahoma pilot as girlish. Reports emphasized her hairstyle, a ponytail, and her fears, "grasshoppers." An Associated Press wire story even reduced Cobb to her hair color: "A blonde who may become this nation's first spacewoman predicted today that men and women will make space flights together." Reflecting the pressure on

Fig. 1.1. Geraldine "Jerrie" Cobb, posing alongside a full-scale model of the spacecraft that McDonnell Aircraft built to carry the first United States space travelers for NASA's Project Mercury. The photograph was taken on May 27, 1961 at the First National Conference on Peaceful Uses of Space in Tulsa, Oklahoma. *NASA Photo*

women to marry, reporters identified her as "Miss Cobb, who said she had no matrimonial plans" and as "bachelor-girl Cobb." The coverage provided a striking contrast to what had been deemed newsworthy when NASA announced its first seven astronauts a year earlier.[14]

As a part of the cultural debate about women astronauts, the masculine ideal of the daring astronaut developed slowly during the early 1960s. Indeed, when NASA first recruited its space travelers, the assumption that astronauts would be men remained so unquestioned that no one mentioned it. When NASA presented the seven *Mercury* astronauts to the public in 1959, *Life* magazine's coverage included a separate article titled "Backing Up the Men, Brave Wives and Bright Children," but the article about the men themselves ("Space Voyagers Rarin' to Orbit") highlighted the group's quiet confidence in the space agency's rocketry, not their masculinity. The astronauts' willingness to fly did demonstrate courage—especially given NASA's public difficulties in launching large rockets without explosions. Yet the article primarily described the astronauts as a "clean cut," "eager" group of "seasoned test pilots." After Cobb's public campaign raised the question of whether women could be astronauts, however, the characterization of NASA's male astronauts began to shift.[15]

Cobb's Campaign

Throughout the first half of 1961, Lovelace developed a larger women's testing program, inviting twenty-four more women to take the examinations with expenses paid by Jacqueline Cochran, the world-famous pilot. After Cobb, eighteen other volunteers answered invitations to the "Woman in Space Program." Unlike the male candidates who took their examinations as a group, however, the women took Lovelace's tests either alone or in pairs.[16] In the meantime, having exhausted Lovelace's Albuquerque facilities, Cobb underwent additional testing at other sites. She also began operating as the group's unofficial leader, corresponding with each of the participants, whom she dubbed her "fellow lady astronaut trainees." As the list of successful candidates grew, Lovelace arranged to bring the group together for the first time at the Naval School of Aviation Medicine in Pensacola, Florida, later that summer.

As Lovelace's plans proceeded, President John F. Kennedy announced the United States' intention to land a man on the moon. The lunar landing decision made NASA even more conscious of controlling its public image. In the opinion of NASA officials, considering women as potential astronaut candidates risked a public relations debacle by distracting public attention from the new mission. NASA's aversion to considering female astronaut testing reflected both the space agency's new focus and its internal culture. The military ethos of the young civilian agency did not welcome women. Under tremendous political pressure to match Soviet space advances, NASA officials saw women as liabilities.

Ultimately, the inclusion of women in the space race would prove unthinkable for American decision-makers. In the early 1960s, the Kennedy administration evaluated foreign policy options by assessing whether they provided appropriately strong responses to the Soviet Union. In a real way, the need to keep the astronaut corps all-male grew out of the gendered conceptions of strength and weakness that policy makers used to justify the United States' role in the space race. Testing female astronaut candidates did not project the image of international strength that Kennedy wanted.[17]

Flying a member of "the weaker sex" into space evoked the old aviation assumption—usually wrong but nonetheless widespread—that if a woman could fly a craft, it must be easy to do. In contrast, the arguments went, NASA's *Mercury* spacecraft required skilled pilots with engineering backgrounds and military jet test-flying experience. The very qualifications required for astronauts proved the complexity of U.S. space achievements. Demonstrating that a woman could perform those tasks would diminish their prestige. Consequently, including women in the U.S. space effort undercut the rationale of international competition used to justify space flight itself.

After all, American women already had a role in the Cold War mobilization. In the oft-cited 1959 "kitchen debate," when Vice President Richard Nixon showed Soviet premier Nikita Khrushchev how the model kitchen appliances at the American National Exhibition in Moscow eased housewives' lives, Khrushchev answered that women contributed to the USSR as productive workers. American ideology depicted Soviet women as masculine, de-feminized by their work roles and lack of domesticity. In contrast, U.S. women advanced the cause by maintaining the American way of life at home. By offering her services to her country as an astronaut, Cobb ran afoul of the gendered limits on Cold War patriotism.[18]

Nonetheless, in the midst of the May 1961 lunar decision, Cobb reminded NASA Administrator James E. Webb about her growing interest in space. She informed him of her successful stress tests at the Pensacola, Florida, naval base and her upcoming spin in the Johnsville human centrifuge. "When that is completed I will have passed all the tests given [to] the Mercury Astronauts." The space agency responded by appointing her as an official NASA consultant, an attempt to placate her. Without any specific duties, the consulting position placed Cobb back in the role of witnessing and supporting male action. Much to Webb's chagrin, however, Cobb took the appointment as encouragement.[19]

She volunteered herself to fly a suborbital space mission. Attached to her letter, on a separate page, Cobb included a prayer: "God has given me the ability to fly—the unrelenting desire to traverse his skies—and the Faith to believe. I offer myself—No less can I do." Cobb's faith made her persistent. But her religious fervor also highlighted the contrast between her conviction and NASA's scientific rationality. On a number of levels, Cobb did not fit the idea of a female astronaut.[20]

As a woman in the early 1960s, Cobb struggled in an untenable position. If married, then a woman should be with her husband. On the other hand, as a single woman, she either should have been trying to get married or, if gay, she should not be in space at all. The cultural expectations for women left no room for her to succeed.[21]

Resolute in her faith that her goals advanced the nation's space effort, Cobb did not relent, pressuring NASA to justify its policies. During the summer of 1961, even the agency's own public relations department had trouble providing good answers. Facing three letters from citizens asking about women in space, a NASA official inquired up the chain of command about how to reply. As he wrote, women "fall within the physically qualified; therefore, there must be other valid reasons why or why not we are to use women in our space flight program." Because the public debate about women astronauts refused to die, the space agency needed a more plausible rationale for excluding women.[22]

Lovelace's upcoming Navy tests promised to complicate the issue even more. Cobb and the other twelve women who passed Lovelace's tests were preparing for two unprecedented weeks of advanced aerospace testing. When employers refused to approve vacation time, two women quit their jobs in order to participate. Then, five days before their scheduled arrival, each woman received a crushing telegram: "Regret to advise arrangements at Pensacola cancelled Probably will not be possible to carry out this part of program . . . W Randolph Lovelace II MD." The Navy had withdrawn its permission for women to use its equipment, effectively canceling the program.[23]

Soon thereafter, Webb concluded that Cobb, whom he had previously touted as "a great asset to any part of the [space] program," did not have much to offer NASA after all. He informed her that since the space agency had not found a way to tap her skills, "I am wondering if there is any advantage to continue the consulting relationship." Cobb refused to concede defeat. She criss-crossed the country, growing increasingly frustrated with her lack of progress. As she wrote to her fellow women pilots, "The answers I got were more of the same and typical of bureaucrats—not yes and not no." Without a definitive denial, however, Cobb kept fighting.[24]

As a standard bearer for women in the early 1960s, Cobb was an unusual member of the "bridge generation." She exhibited no interest in budding feminism. Instead, as a religious person, she wanted to combat godless communism by beating the Soviet Union to a space first. As a pilot, she wanted to take on the biggest challenge available at the time—space flight. Even after the women's movement began, she never identified herself as a feminist (to this day, she justifies her actions in terms of patriotism and a pilot's passion to fly). Nonetheless, as she campaigned to restart women's astronaut testing, she needed to find someone who took women's issues seriously.

A key meeting with Representative George Miller of California, chair of the House Space Committee, finally broke the logjam. Unlike other politicians who politely rebuffed her, Miller took her interests seriously. More important, he offered to help. In July 1962, a special subcommittee of the House Committee on Science and Astronautics held public hearings investigating whether NASA's astronaut qualifications discriminated on the basis of sex.

"It May Be Undesirable"

The House subcommittee hearings became the most public phase of Cobb's campaign. Significantly, the hearings investigated sex discrimination two years before it became illegal. (Such biases in hiring were not against the law until "sex" was included in Title VII of the 1964 Civil Rights Act.)[25] As Cobb's efforts to restart the women's astronaut testing became better known, however, powerful political opponents aligned against it. The hearings transcript reveals how gender roles became reinscribed, both through the reassertion of women's proper roles and the deliberate construction of the astronaut/jet test pilot as masculine.

On Tuesday, July 17, 1962, Republican Representative Victor Anfuso of New York called the subcommittee to order. Miller, the full committee's chairman, did not attend, leaving the hearings in the hands of his colleague. Cobb and Jane Hart, another successful Lovelace candidate and wife of Democratic Michigan Senator Philip Hart, opened the first day by testifying that women brought valuable talents to the space effort. As Hart stated, "I am not arguing that women be admitted to space merely so they won't feel discriminated against. I am arguing that they be admitted because they have a real contribution to make." Cobb reminded the committee that women had been a part of every new frontier; she hoped that resuming women's testing would allow the United States to score a significant space "first."[26]

Without the widespread recognition of women's participation as inherently valuable, however, Cobb and Hart struggled to make their case. In questioning the necessity of the engineering degree requirement or the required jet test-piloting experience, Cobb and Hart challenged NASA's judgment. Moreover, in describing how the Pensacola tests ended because of the lack of NASA's request for such testing, Cobb indirectly blamed the space agency. At that point, Chairman Anfuso chided her, "This committee has the assurances that NASA wishes to cooperate and is cooperating. . . . And I know that you don't criticize any branch of the Government." Throughout the first day of hearings, Cobb and Hart found themselves in the awkward position of criticizing the very agency whose cooperation they needed.[27]

On the second day of testimony, NASA brought in the agency's biggest stars to testify against continuing the women's testing. The presence of astronauts John Glenn and M. Scott Carpenter—each fresh from NASA's most recent flights—demonstrated how seriously the space agency took the House subcommittee. Along with George Low, NASA's director of spacecraft and flight missions, the three space agency representatives testified that women could not meet NASA's astronaut qualifications. Furthermore, they argued that a female astronaut testing program would impede other NASA projects.

Low, accompanied by astronauts Glenn and Carpenter, repeated NASA's contention that all astronauts must be jet test pilots first. Carpenter testified that the women's extensive private aviation experience could not possibly prepare them adequately for space flight. In the hierarchy of aviation technical knowledge, he argued, jet test piloting occupied a level that was inaccessible through any other type of flying. As Carpenter told the subcommittee, "A person can't enter a backstroke swimming race and by swimming twice the distance in a crawl, qualify as a backstroker. I believe that there is the same difficulty in the type of aviation experience that 35,000 hours provides a civilian pilot and the experience a military test pilot receives." Relying on military jet test-piloting schools as the standard allowed NASA to place the responsibility for excluding women outside of its own control.[28]

In 1962, no women could enter military jet test-pilot schools because after the WASPs disbanded in 1944, the military barred women from flying its aircraft. Cobb and the other female candidates, experienced pilots with commercial ratings, could not possibly have the experience that NASA required. Their access to such training had been blocked. Notably, the space agency refused to take any responsibility for establishing requirements that, although not discriminatory on their face, could not be fulfilled by any American woman at the time.

NASA wanted jet test pilots at least in part because the status associated with their ranks enhanced the astronauts' image. (Cobb and Wally Funk, another successful Woman in Space Program candidate, discussed buying a single-seat British jet until they learned that NASA accepted only military jet school experience. Privately obtained training would not suffice.) For NASA, having its public face associated with military aviation's elite reinforced its image as a cutting-edge aerospace agency. Conceding that women might be able to perform the same tasks with non-jet flying experience would undercut that status.[29]

The NASA representatives' testimony illustrated how the idea of outer space as a masculine preserve underlay the way that the space agency defined its astronaut requirements. In perhaps the most telling commentary during the two days of hearings, John Glenn testified about the space effort's broader context:

> I think this gets back to the way our social order is organized really. It is just a fact. The men go off and fight the wars and fly the airplanes and come back and help design and build and test them. The fact that women are not in this field is a fact of our social order. It may be undesirable.[30]

Despite the absolute nature of his description—"it is just a fact"— Glenn felt compelled to explain, and thus reassert, the appropriate gender roles in space exploration. His testimony also acknowledged signs of growing dissatisfaction, however. His admission that women's exclusion "may be undesirable" indicated some awareness that the rigid gender roles of this social order benefited some while limiting others. Glenn and the other NASA representatives tacitly acknowledged the unrest that Cobb's efforts represented while nonetheless doing their best to ignore the tremors caused by imminent social and cultural changes.

Women who could pass astronaut fitness tests challenged the social order that Glenn described. Tom Wolfe's famous description of the competitive fighter pilot/astronaut ethos as "the right stuff" resonated at

NASA. In his 1977 tell-all autobiography about life as an astronaut, Walter Cunningham described how he and the other astronauts resisted changes in " . . . our public image, which we enjoyed, as the John Waynes of the space frontier." Women whose flight journals listed commercial ratings and thousands of flight hours threatened that image. And women whose physical condition rivaled the men's challenged the inevitability of the male fighter pilot/astronaut.[31]

Throughout the two days of subcommittee hearings, congressional representatives and NASA officials alike used patronizing analogies to ridicule and thereby contain the threat that women posed. Glenn made the most famous of these jokes when he testified, "My mother could probably pass the physical exam that they give preseason for the [Washington] Redskins, but I doubt if she could play too many games for them." Even representatives who supported the women's cause suggested that women astronauts might be included on a flight crew because they offer good company or because women's natural roles as peacemakers might diffuse tensions between men, who apparently would be ashamed to argue in front of a woman.[32]

Notably, throughout the two-year debate over female astronauts, those who opposed women in space never voiced the most obvious rebuttal: because astronauts cannot be women. No one suggested that women were too weak or otherwise physically incapable of space flight. Public figures recognized that women's interests could not be dismissed outright. Cobb's campaign exemplified the way that increasingly, in the early 1960s, women's concerns got a public airing even though their advocates lacked the clout to effect real change.

The impact of Glenn's presence, only five months after his triumphant orbital flight, cannot be underestimated. Ten months after Yuri Gagarin's April 1961 launch, Glenn's single orbit demonstrated that the United States had finally matched the Soviets in space. The nation welcomed him back with a tickertape parade. Carpenter's late May mission demonstrated that NASA could duplicate the feat. The astronauts' presence at the hearings impressed the representatives. Anfuso, chairman of the subcommittee, complimented NASA's "great men" and fairly gushed about their heroic example as he observed "women here bring[ing] their children just to look at them." Glenn even wowed Representative James E. Fulton of Pittsburgh, who had argued on the women's behalf. Fulton ended his questions on the second day with "And I want to tell you, Col. John Glenn is a stellar witness before a congressional committee. You are excellent." Glenn's star power had thoroughly dazzled Cobb's most vocal advocate. In the end, the House subcommittee proved unwilling to challenge the newly successful space agency. Despite setting aside two days for public hearings, the representatives would not compel NASA to consider female astronaut testing.[33]

"The Magnificent Male"

In the aftermath of the hearings, NASA officials felt freer to ignore Cobb's continued lobbying. In her continued correspondence with the space agency, Cobb grew irritatingly persistent, refusing to acknowledge the brush-offs she received from the government. As the mutual antagonism became more open, the construction of the space program as masculine also grew more pronounced.

In contrast to how the press covered NASA's first seven astronauts, the descriptions of the nine astronauts selected in 1962—written after the congressional subcommittee hearings—significantly highlighted their masculinity. In fact, when *Houston Chronicle* reporter Warren Burkett prepared a six-part series about the second group's physical examinations, he titled it "Astronaut: The Magnificent Male." Doctors described how the jet test pilots enjoyed working with their hands: tinkering with cars and airplanes. One examining physician described a candidate asked to drink barium water as downing the mixture "as if it were a Scotch and soda."[34] In a period of turmoil about women's roles, during a cultural debate about whether women could be astronauts, the gendering of the space program took on another aspect: the assertion of the astronauts' masculinity.

By the fall of 1962, having failed to win support from NASA, Cobb began speaking out publicly about her frustrating relationship with the space agency. According to Cobb, her consultantship exemplified NASA's problems. As she told her audiences, "I assumed [that] my appointment had something to do with women in space. That was over a year ago and—believe me—I'm the most unconsulted consultant in any government agency today." In a *Washington Post* article, she accused the space agency of "bypassing the one scientific space feat we could accomplish now—putting the first woman in orbit." And, in a particularly pointed rebuke, she reminded readers that NASA had been chasing Soviet achievements since *Sputnik*: "With that kind of attitude, it's no wonder that we're second in the space race." Her complaint about being an "unconsulted consultant" became a regular refrain in her talks.[35]

Cobb's public denigration of the space agency finally elicited a reaction. In December 1962, a full year after the NASA administrator first suggested ending Cobb's appointment, Webb summoned her to NASA's Washington, D.C., headquarters. He scolded Cobb to stop referring to her NASA affiliation, threatening to tell the press that he never consulted her because he found her unreliable. Recognizing that the cultural debate over women astronauts lacked the support needed to make it a real threat, NASA officials began asserting the need to exclude women from space more directly.[36]

In a February 1963 speech at the YMCA, NASA's astronaut trainer Robert B. Voas responded to Soviet boasts about plans to fly a female cosmonaut by ridiculing women's potential advantages. He joked that you could save weight using a female astronaut only if you could persuade her to leave her purse behind. Since male astronauts had discovered space flight's excitement, he argued, women's capacity to withstand isolation no longer mattered. Voas reasoned that flying a woman offered no real benefits, only the risks of launching an unqualified individual. Although NASA refused to risk lives with unqualified astronauts, Voas argued, the space agency gladly employed women in other positions. In addition to secretaries, he cited female nurses, physiologists, and artists. Female "computers" plotted trajectories. Two women even worked as senior NASA astronomers. Furthermore, Voas reminded the audience, no one should underestimate the astronauts' wives. He informed the group that flying an unqualified woman would insult the women who already worked with NASA.[37]

In his conclusion, however, Voas revealed the assumptions about masculinity and femininity underlying NASA's policies. The astronaut trainer assured his audience, "I think we all look forward to the time when women will be a part of our space flight team for when this time arrives, it will mean that man will really have found a home in space—for the woman is the personification of the home." Not until space had been domesticated—rendered safe and routine, and no longer a front in the Cold War—would women participate fully. In fact, the very presence of a woman would indicate that space no longer remained a dangerous site for international competition. Launching a woman challenged the inherent masculinity of space itself.[38]

The Soviet Union proved willing to do it. On June 17, 1963, cosmonaut Valentina Tereshkova became the first woman in space, briefly reinvigorating the American debate about female astronauts. In response, Clare Boothe Luce used her stature and connections to publish an articulate commentary that heralded the coming women's movement. The former congresswoman, ambassador to Italy, noted playwright, magazine editor, and wife of Henry Luce (the *Life* magazine magnate) offered perceptive insights into how gender shaped space exploration.

Even before Tereshkova flew, Boothe Luce expressed an acute awareness of how gender influenced space policy. In a "Monthly Commentary" published in *McCall's* magazine a month before Tereshkova's mission, she wrote, "Actually, the most important reason men will not (for a long time) accept women in the astronaut program is that in this field (as in most others) men somehow think their virility and masculinity depend upon establishing and maintaining their intellectual and physical superiority in it." When she learned that the Soviet Union had launched the first woman in space, she used her influence to publish a scathing critique of American policy makers.[39]

Following a three-page spread in *Life* magazine that featured photographs of Tereshkova preparing for her historic mission, Boothe Luce offered a full-page condemnation of American inaction titled "But Some People Simply Never Get the Message." According to Boothe Luce, Americans dismissed Tereshkova's first as a propaganda stunt because they failed to acknowledge communism's practice of equality between the sexes. Flying into space represented more than just a job; the space traveler became "the symbol of the way of life of his nation." By allowing a woman to undertake a dangerous mission laden with international visibility, Boothe Luce noted that "the Soviet Union has given its women unmistakable proof" that it valued them. In the end, she argued, the United States' failure to match Tereshkova's feat indicated more than a space race lag.

She charged that American unwillingness to consider flying a woman indicated a weakness in gender relations that put the United States at a disadvantage to the Soviet Union. As she wrote, the "failure of American men" to understand the advantages that women's equality gave the Soviet Union "may yet prove to be their costliest Cold War blunder." Given Boothe Luce's history of staunch anti-communism, such praise for the Soviet system showed how outraged she felt.[40]

Although *Life*'s coverage of their achievements set off a flurry of publicity for the thirteen women who had passed Lovelace's astronaut tests two years earlier, political support for women's testing did not materialize. Cobb's faith that she could be accepted on merit was dashed. Indeed, her campaign for space illustrated why an organized feminist movement became necessary. Without widespread recognition of women's issues as important, and without the political clout to effect change, Cobb's appeals to government agencies and space policy failed. Working within the system and playing by the rules did not work.[41]

The more Cobb interrogated NASA's requirements, the more apparent it became that the biggest obstacle remained basic sexism. As NASA's Robert Gilruth admitted in a less-guarded moment in 1963, "Although they [NASA astronaut qualifications] do not specify that applicant must be male, this is the case. NASA does not expect that any women will meet the qualification or will be selected."[42] Two years earlier, NASA officials would never have mentioned gender. Faced with the wider turmoil over women's roles and pushed to defend their practices by Cobb's campaign, however, space policy makers began to construct the jet pilot/astronaut as a masculine cultural icon. For women, the opportunities that Cobb pushed for in the early 1960s would not come until the late 1970s, when a transformed social, political, and cultural climate—reinforced by the 1964 Civil Rights Act and equal employment legislation—persuaded NASA to recruit female and minority astronauts for the space shuttle.

In 1964, however, faced with the devastating realization that she would never go into space, Cobb finally conceded defeat. In her sorrow, she turned her life over to God and found a new purpose for her flying. In 1965, she left the modern world to head for the Amazon, where she began a life as a missionary. The end of her quest for space marked the beginning of a new mission: a vocation as a flying emissary to the indigenous peoples of the Amazon. When the "proto-feminism" of the early 1960s eventually blossomed into the modern women's movement in the United States, she was thousands of miles away.

NOTES

Cornell University, the American Historical Association, the National Aeronautics and Space Administration, the John F. Kennedy Presidential Library, and the

Lyndon B. Johnson Presidential Library supported research contributing to this article. Thanks to Richard Polenberg, Margaret Rossiter, and Roger Launius for their guidance, and to the Not Piss Poor Women's Studies group at Hobart and William Smith Colleges.

1. "Lucy Becomes an Astronaut," episode 6, season 1, *The Lucy Show*, original airdate 5 November 1962; "Jane's Driving Lesson," episode 18, 1962–63 season, *The Jetsons*, original airdate 20 January 1963. In the 1984–85 episodes, Jane can drive/fly.

2. Susan J. Douglas, *Where the Girls Are: Growing Up Female with the Mass Media* (New York: Time Books, 1994), 125.

3. Ruth Rosen, *The World Split Open: How the Women's Movement Changed America* (New York: Penguin Books, 2000); Betty Friedan, *The Feminine Mystique* (New York: W. W. Norton, 1963).

4. See also Margaret A. Weitekamp, *The Right Stuff, the Wrong Sex: The Lovelace Woman in Space Program* (Baltimore: Johns Hopkins University Press, forthcoming 2004).

6. Jerrie Cobb and Jane Rieker, *Woman into Space: The Jerrie Cobb Story* (Englewood Cliffs, NJ: Prentice-Hall, 1963), 130, 132; Tom Wolfe, *The Right Stuff* (New York: Farrar, Straus, Giroux, 1979); *The Right Stuff*, written and directed by Philip Kaufman, 3 hr. 13 min., a Ladd Company release, 1983.

6. "Woman Space Pioneer," *Philadelphia Inquirer*, 15 January 1959, National Air and Space Museum, Smithsonian Institution, Washington, D.C. Hereafter, the National Air and Space Museum will be cited as NASM. "Womanned Flight," *Christian Science Monitor*, 13 February 1959, NASM; "Women Best Men in Solo Space Tests," *Chicago Daily Tribune*, 2 October 1959, NASM; "Girl 'in Space' Six Days without a Hallucination," *Chicago Daily Tribune*, 6 November 1959, NASM; Lillian Levy, "Space Researcher Sees Female Solos Possible," *Washington Evening Star*, 31 October 1958, 2N, NASM; "Woman Space Pioneer," *Philadelphia Inquirer*, 15 January 1959, NASM.

7. Born 5 March 1931, Jerrie Cobb began flying at twelve, earning a private pilot license at sixteen. Rieker and Cobb, *Woman into Space*, 48; Jerrie Cobb, *Solo Pilot* (Sun City Center, FL: The Jerrie Cobb Foundation, 1997), 46, 139; Martha Ackmann, *The Mercury 13: The Untold Story of Thirteen American Women and the Dream of Space Flight* (New York: Random House, 2003), 6.

8. Donald Flickinger to W. R. "Randy" Lovelace II, "Action Memorandum," 20 December 1959, Jerrie Cobb Papers, Ninety-Nines International Organization of Women Pilots, National Headquarters, Will Rogers Airport, Oklahoma City, Oklahoma. Hereafter the Jerrie Cobb Papers will be cited as JCobbP.

9. Allowing women in a military auxiliary while excluding them from aeromedical research seems counterintuitive. Regarding the WASPs, see Molly Merryman, *Clipped Wings: The Rise and Fall of the Women Airforce Service*

Pilots (WASPs) of World War II (New York: New York University Press, 1998). After the war, aerospace researchers ignored women because they were barred from military and commercial flying, the source of most research contracts.

10. Ben Kocivar, "The Lady Wants to Orbit," *LOOK*, 2 February 1960, NASM, 113–14, 116, 119.

11. "Woman Qualifies for Space Training," *Washington Post*, 19 August 1960, clipping, NASA Historical Reference Collection, National Aeronautics and Space Administration, History Office, NASA Headquarters, Washington, D.C. Hereafter, the NASA Historical Collection will be cited as NASA. "A Woman Passes Tests Given to 7 Astronauts," *New York Times*, 19 August 1960, 13. See also "A Lady Proves She's Fit for Space Flight," *Life*, 29 August 1960, 72.

12. Douglas, *Where the Girls Are*, 126–27.

13. "Spacewoman Ready for Flights with Men," *Washington Star*, 24 August 1960, NASA; "From Aviatrix to Astronautrix," *Time*, 29 August 1960, 41; Donald Cox, "Woman Astronauts: Dubbed 'Astranettes' a Team of Women Pilots Is Now Training for Space Flight," *Space World*, September 1961, 37, 58–60; Donald Cox, "NASA Refutes Space Girl Story," *New York World Telegram*, 29 September 1960, NASA.

14. "'Spacewoman' Would Let Men Come Along on Trip," *Baltimore Sun*, 24 August 1960, in *NASA Current News*, 24 August 1960, NASA; "Woman Predicts Coed Space Trips," untitled New York paper, ca. 1959–60, NASA.

15. "Space Voyagers Rarin' to Orbit," *Life*, 20 April 1959, 22–23; "Backing Up the Men, Brave Wives and Bright Children," *Life*, 20 April 1959, 24–25.

16. The first gathering of the successful candidates came in 1996, by which time two of the thirteen women selected had died.

17. Robert D. Dean, *Imperial Brotherhood: Gender and the Making of Cold War Foreign Policy* (Amherst: University of Massachusetts Press, 2001).

18. Elaine Tyler May, *Homeward Bound: American Families in the Cold War Era* (New York: Basic Books, 1988), 16–19; Stephen J. Whitfield, *The Culture of the Cold War* (Baltimore: Johns Hopkins University Press, 1990).

19. Jerrie Cobb to James E. Webb, 16 May 1961, JCobbP; "Girl Astronaut?" *New York Herald Tribune*, 28 May 1961, NASA; "Jerri Cobb Is Set for Space," *Washington Post*, 30 May 1961, Jacqueline Cochran Papers, Dwight D. Eisenhower Presidential Library, Abilene, Kansas. Hereafter, the Jacqueline Cochran Papers will be cited as JCP.

20. Jerrie Cobb, untitled recommendations, 15 June 1961, NASA, 5.

21. For other analyses of postwar women, see Joanne Meyerowitz, ed., *Not June Cleaver: Women and Gender in Postwar America, 1945–1960* (Philadelphia: Temple University Press, 1994).

22. Dr. G. Dale Smith to Mr. George Low, 19 June 1961, NASA.

23. Sarah Gorelick (Ratley) worked in AT&T's engineering department. Gene Nora Stumbough (Jessen) taught flying at the University of Oklahoma. Both quit.

Telegram, W. Randolph Lovelace II to Sarah Gorelick, 12 September 1961, Sarah Gorlick Ratley papers, Overland Park, Kansas.

24. James E. Webb to Jerrie Cobb, 15 December 1961, JCobbP.

25. Jo Freeman, "How 'Sex' Got into Title VII: Persistent Opportunism as a Maker of Public Policy," *Law and Inequality: A Journal of Theory and Practice* 9 (March 1991): 163–84.

26. Congress, House, Committee on Science and Astronautics, *Qualifications for Astronauts: Hearings before the Special Subcommittee on the Selection of Astronauts*, 87th Cong., 2nd sess., 17–18 July 1962, 7.

27. Ibid., 19.

28. Ibid., 54.

29. Wally Funk, oral history interview, edited transcribed tape recording, Trophy Club, Texas, 24 September 1997, 3.

30. Congress, House, *Qualifications for Astronauts*, 67.

31. Walter Cunningham, with Mickey Herskowitz, *The All-American Boys* (New York: Macmillan, 1977), 245.

32. Congress, House, *Qualifications for Astronauts*, 64.

33. Ibid., 59, 75.

34. Warren Burkett, "Astronaut: The Magnificent Male, Brains as Well as Bodies Have to Rate with Best," *Houston Chronicle*, 6 November 1962, Vice-Presidential Papers, Lyndon Baines Johnson Presidential Library, Austin, Texas.

35. Jerrie Cobb, "Project WISE," 21 September 1962, JCobbP, 4; Cobb in *Washington Post*, 16 November 1962, NASA; Cobb, "Women in Space," n.d., JCobbP; Zonta Club of Cleveland, "Women in the Space Age," 28 November 1962, JCobbP.

36. Robert P. Young, 27 December 1962, Young, R. P. Memos, NASA.

37. Robert B. Voas, "Speech to Downtown YMCA," 1 February 1963, Robert Voas Papers, NASA.

38. Ibid. See also Jodi Dean, *Aliens in America: Conspiracy Cultures from Outerspace to Cyberspace* (Ithaca, NY: Cornell University Press, 1998); and Constance Penley, *NASA/TREK: Popular Science and Sex in America* (New York: Verso, 1997).

39. Clare Boothe Luce, "A Monthly Commentary," *McCall's*, May 1963, JCobbP.

40. Clare Boothe Luce, "But Some People Simply Never Get the Message," *Life*, 28 June 1963, 31. The cover read: "Clare Boothe Luce, Soviet Space Girl Makes U.S. Men Sound Stupid."

41. "The U.S. Team Is Still Warming Up the Bench," *Life*, 28 June 1963, 32–33.

42. Frank Macomber, "No Room in Space for Gal Astronaut," Joliet, Illinois *Herald News*, 12 June 1963, JCP.

2

Building Utopia
Mary Otis Stevens and the Lincoln, Massachusetts, House

Susana Torre

The built environment was both a literal and symbolic battle-ground in the mid–1960s, when Mary Otis Stevens and her partner and husband built a house that became and remains a model for rethinking domestic environments. It was a time of incipient ecological awareness, exemplified by Buckminster Fuller's concept of "Spaceship Earth" and of challenges to the boundaries between the public and private worlds. One of the most rigid of these boundaries was the one between the spaces for the daily lives of men and women, the city being defined as (men's) work place and the suburb as (women's) private residential haven. The suburban single-family house was both symbol and actual physical expression of enclosure of the women and their children. The mass-produced conformity of such houses made comparisons with "the Joneses" both possible and more invidious.

Two pieces of legislation from the previous decade had been largely responsible for the cultural, social, and racial segregation embodied in the suburban private dwelling. The Housing Act of 1949 had promised "a decent house and suitable living environment for every American family,"[1] while the Highway Trust Act of 1956 gave a 90 percent federal subsidy to state and local governments to build an interstate highway system, deemed a defense measure and intended to boost the economy. The first of these measures, coupled with the state's power to expropriate private property for public benefit, led to the fast-paced development of remote and inexpensive tracts of land into homogeneous residential suburbs. The second encouraged the ripping apart of huge areas in major cities, mostly inhabited by the urban poor, for highway construction. These so-called slum clearances spurred the creation of tenant unions and

29

neighborhood organizations to fight the massive displacement of people and the destruction of viable urban neighborhoods.

Meanwhile, architecture and planning, the disciplines responsible for theorizing the organization and form of the built environment, were also being challenged from within and outside academia. Buckminster Fuller, the maverick inventor, scientist, engineer, mathematician, educator, and philosopher best known for his invention of the geodesic dome, was becoming influential in architectural schools, while in California and elsewhere hippie communes sprouted "Drop Cities" made out of domes. White youth rebelled against the conformity symbolized and perpetuated by the suburban house and the nuclear family that inhabited it, while American blacks protested their exclusion from the "American dream" that the suburbs had come to exemplify. Critics such as Jane Jacobs and professionals such as Shadrach Woods, known for his designs for open city forms,[2] and Robert Goodman, who had called architects and planners the "soft cops" of oppression in his influential book *After the Planners*, challenged the authoritarian, top-down assumptions of planning.[3] Meanwhile, student activists at the Massachusetts Institute of Technology (MIT) and elsewhere were helping tenants threatened with relocation to build "Tent Cities" in empty parking lots and successfully managing to get neighborhood committees included in the planning process. Some architects were proposing small-town designs, precursors of the late-1980s New Urbanism, as alternatives to the design of isolated suburban communities,[4] while others promoted alternate forms of settlement influenced by Fourier, the garden cities movement, and the American utopian socialists.

Although many women were becoming more visible and audible in cultural and political debates, they were having a harder time in architecture, especially when they sought to go beyond helpmate roles. Thus, the unconventional house in Lincoln, Massachusetts, that Mary Otis Stevens designed for her family in equal partnership with her partner and husband, Thomas McNulty, constituted an exceptional incursion into the dominant practice and discourse of architecture, one that could be claimed by later feminist discourse on "critical domesticity."[5]

The Architect

Mary Otis Stevens was thirty-six years old when she started the design of the Lincoln house.[6] A maverick since childhood, she discovered that

Fig. 2.1. Mary Otis Stevens in 1965. *Courtesy of Mary Otis Stevens*

physical order could be achieved by design during her junior-year trip to France, where Baron Haussman's plan for Paris led her to "dream of an order suitable for Americans [. . .] one that was not just rational but emotional as well." Upon her return to Smith College she tried, unsuccessfully, to change her major from philosophy to architecture. After graduation in 1949, Stevens moved to New York City, where her drafting course instructor encouraged her to apply to the school of architecture at the Massachusetts Institute of Technology. Stevens's father and his friend Eric Gugler, the architect of the White House's West Wing renovation, conspired to discourage her from pursuing architecture, assuming that she would marry and soon forget her professional ambitions. But their effort backfired when one of Gugler's colleagues confided to her that he enjoyed seeing through walls, inspiring her to want to do the same. She was accepted at MIT in 1950, just as she had decided to marry a socially acceptable suitor. Stevens entered architectural school in 1953, after a brief interlude when she and her first husband, William Vaughn Moody Fawcett, both born to privilege, became blue-collar workers.

At MIT, as Mary S. Fawcett, Stevens thrived in the interdisciplinary environment and the creative problem solving fostered there. She rekindled her friendship with her childhood mentor, Buckminster Fuller, a friend of her father and frequent visitor to the institute, and reconnected with her relative Samuel Eliot Morison, the Harvard historian, who became a father figure and adviser until his death in 1976. MIT's Department of Architecture was then receptive to new ideas and experimentation, in sharp contrast with the Bauhaus-inspired orthodoxy of Harvard's architecture school under Walter Gropius. A number of innovative thinkers and designers taught there, including the planning theorist Kevin Lynch, who had just been hired, and regular visitors included such internationally known architects as Louis Kahn, Eero Saarinen, and Alvar Aalto. Aalto had completed Baker House, a new dormitory building for MIT.

Stevens continued to test the boundaries of permissibility at the school of architecture, just as she had at Smith College. This time, and in spite of the open atmosphere, she encountered stronger resistance. She was discouraged from pursuing formal experimentation with curvilinear geometries and from undertaking the design of a model maternity hospital—a birthing center *avant la lettre*—as her thesis project. Nor was the institute welcoming to women: some graduating classes had none at all, and, consequently, there were no dormitory accommodations for them. A women's lounge, with cots on which to get a few hours' sleep during extended "charrettes," or around-the-clock design work before project presentation deadlines, was all the institute offered. Stevens worked mostly at home, to be back in time to cook supper for her husband, and thus missed out on the camaraderie developed by her classmates in the late-night work.

When she graduated in 1956, Stevens became the first architect in her family, with a thesis for a World Trade Center to revitalize the Boston waterfront (before City Hall and the expressway had been built). However, urban design was not then an approved area of study, and the faculty review committee demanded that she fulfill the customary build-ing thesis's technical requirements, made more burdensome because of her project's size. The summer of her graduation, Stevens began her pro-fessional apprenticeship at The Architectural Collaborative (TAC) in Boston, an office established eleven years earlier by Walter Gropius and several young architects, including two women, Sarah Pillsbury Harkness and Jean Bodman Fletcher. These women, whose husbands were also TAC co-founders, managed their domestic lives and large families with ample domestic help and part-time presence in the office.

By the time Stevens started working for the firm as a lowly model-maker and draftsperson, TAC's early informality had morphed into a rigid corporate environment. There, Stevens had a hard time working on proj-ects that violated her sense of relevance and meaning, such as high-rise, high-maintenance buildings for the University of Baghdad, or the Civic Center of Tallahassee, Florida, patterned after the Piazza San Marco in Venice. "Where were the Doges?" Stevens wondered, as she looked at photos of the design team scampering for shade in the project's site.

Unable to reconcile such contradictions, Stevens left to work on Adlai Stevenson's presidential campaign, which he lost in 1956 to Dwight Eisenhower, the popular incumbent. After the unsuccessful campaign, she resumed her architectural career in the office of Thomas McNulty, a Midwestern "working-class genius"[7] and former MIT assistant professor whose ideas she respected and whose fledgling firm included several MIT graduates. Her proposal for a pre-fabricated house competition won the first prize, creating a buzz about the firm and attracting clients for houses designed on the same principles of her winning entry.

Stevens obtained a divorce from Fawcett in 1958 and married McNulty shortly thereafter, also becoming his professional partner. During 1961–62, enabled by her inheritance from her father, they took time off to work in Ravello, Italy. There they worked on a book of ideas that was published almost a decade later under the title *World of Variation*, and on the design of their future house for the property in Lincoln that Stevens had purchased just before leaving. In Ravello they lived at L'Epis-copio (Villa Di Sangro), a former bishop's palace with a great architec-tural library, including a collection of French nineteenth-century folio-size volumes documenting the great buildings Napoleon had found in his campaigns. This experience would become an inspiration for her incursion into publishing architectural books.

The House

Even before it was finished in August 1965, the house attracted polemics. Although hidden from view, this strange dwelling in their vicinity annoyed the neighbors, and banks, following standard practice of the time, denied a construction loan on the grounds of its unconventionality. Its predominant material—concrete—suggested lowly basement construction. Town folk resented the proclivity to use personal resources to flaunt social norms. They had barely gotten accustomed to the house that Walter Gropius, founder of the German Bauhaus and an exile, had built in Lincoln in 1938. Neighbors had nicknamed it "the chicken coop" for its unadorned white surfaces and flat roof. Over time, Gropius's deanship at Harvard and his house's conventionally bourgeois layout—with sewing room for the wife, a study for the husband, and servants' quarters—won his neighbors' acceptance. But Stevens's house was something else, for its open plan suggested a lifestyle lacking in propriety, where the conventional meaning of privacy was profoundly contradicted.

Lincoln, Massachusetts, was—and remains—a small, conservative, but predominantly Democrat residential suburb of Boston, steeped in the American Revolution's early history and still including a yearly open town meeting in its governance. It is a town that passed a resolution in 1968 against U.S. involvement in the Vietnam War and pioneered the private land trust to preserve the low density of its origins as a rural farming community. Lincoln's sense of place and its history resonated with the history of those of Stevens's own ancestors who had championed the American Revolution,[8] and it appealed to her as a setting in which to live, practice architecture, and raise her sons.

When Stevens and her family moved into the finished house in the summer of 1965, they were followed by a *Life* magazine photographic crew. First appearing in December of that year in *Life*'s series "Ideas in Houses," the house received worldwide attention.[9] What drew the media's interest was, first of all, the novelty of the house's open geometry. This was an inversion of the historic New England compact structures, tightly bound around a hearth to withstand the rigors of hostile winters. The expansive curves, with their asymptotes reaching out and opening onto the landscape, turned the house into a kind of built topography, a constructed landscape form. Instead of surrounding and cloaking interior space, the graceful walls were designed to embrace and shelter the out-

Fig. 2.2. Mary Otis Stevens and Thomas McNulty, exterior view, house at Lincoln, Massachusetts, 1962-65. *Photograph by Julius Shulman*

doors in its concave recesses, creating a place were Stevens could cultivate a "middle landscape"[10] garden as a transition to a landscape that had been historically shaped by farming, and then left untouched.

Then, there was the unorthodox use of reinforced concrete as a residential building material above ground. The cast-in-place concrete walls, floors, and roofs reinforced the idea of house-as-landscape. And, as in nature, sunlight altered significantly the perception of space inside the house. Every sunny day at noon "a line of light ran down the center" of the house's open long axis, oriented north–south, and light also entered through linear skylights and clerestories, animating the curved planes with a play of shade and shadow. Ordinarily, concrete does not come alive with sunlight as natural stone does, so Stevens and McNulty picked the kind of cement that is usually employed in basement construction, which has an unpredictably wide range of coloration. Surface variation was extended by allowing "leakage" lines—the result of pressure from the wet concrete onto the joints of the wooden form—to become a texture on the walls. Because of the lack of material differentiation in the interior planes, the house could feel like a cave, an igloo, a tent, or a topiary maze in different seasons and weather—qualities that required experience over time and thus were elusive to the casual visitor, and practically impossible to document in publications. Exceptional as it was, the house nonetheless shared an architectural language of materials, form, and the use of natural light with buildings by Louis Kahn, Alvar Aalto, and Eero Saarinen, the internationally acclaimed architects that had influenced Stevens at MIT, although far more evocative of the human body in its suggestion of a birth canal or maternal cave than most Modern architects would ever wish to acknowledge in their work.[11]

But the most radical aspect of the house's design and the most talked-about feature in magazine articles was its lack of doors and well-defined rooms. The interior space was actually a kind of indoor pathway off of which areas for different activities unfolded. It was not entered from one end, like the axial hallways of classically planned houses, with rooms to either side. Rather, like a bazaar in Istanbul or Isfahan, the main axis could be entered from many different places, the typical primacy of the "front" door barely acknowledged in the interior by a small fountain and skylight. The plan resembled a rhizome. The space for movement and the spaces for activities flowed into one another, with negotiable, changing boundaries. Only bathrooms and a small guest room were afforded the conventional privacy of lockable doors. The lower floor was used for gathering, cooking, and eating, and housed areas for the children. The upper floor was for the parents. A taller, cylindrical form created a more definite enclosure for the library and the architectural office above, spaces for introspective activities and sustained concentration, less forgiving of unwanted interruptions.

What disturbed some neighbors in Lincoln, and attracted the interest of the architects and students who frequently visited the house, was the vision of family life the house implied. It was a vision that seemed to be, and was in fact, subversive of the forced togetherness of families, not only in the typical suburban home but also in the alternative hippie dwellings during the 1960s. Nor did it support a patriarchal hierarchy. This was a house for chance encounters, where strategically placed obstacles would let intruders know not to trespass, where "privacy was a

Fig. 2.3. Mary Otis Stevens and Thomas McNulty, interior view, house at Lincoln, Massachusetts, 1962-65. *Photograph by Julius Shulman*

state of mind" instead of a physical isolation behind closed doors. Each individual's privacy required that other family members acknowledge invisible boundaries. Thus the children grew accustomed to forms of sharing and withdrawing they could not recognize in other houses with separate rooms. The drawback was that the house could not—without losing its basic premise—provide for multiple and simultaneous needs for separation as a means of identity building as the boys grew to become teenagers. Thus the oldest son claimed the guest room as his own, the only one with a door he could close.

The interior organization, a reverse of the typical suburban home, could be seen as driving the exterior form. The ideas informing its design were closer to the philosophical discourse of Guy Debord and the Situationists than to the prevalent architectural discourse, focused on the construction of a renewed Modern vocabulary that was regionally based. The house's "psychogeographical" topography seemed to be designed for the kind of experience described by Guy Debord in his 1958 theory of the *dérive*:

One of the basic Situationist practices is the *dérive* [literally: "drifting"], a technique of rapid passage through varied ambiances. *Dérives* involve

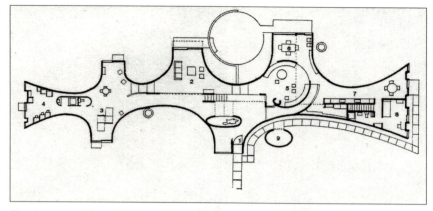

Fig. 2.4. Mary Otis Stevens and Thomas McNulty, lower level plan, house at Lincoln, MA, 1962-65. LEGEND: 1. Entry; 2. Living room; 3. Children's sleeping area; 4.Children's play area; 5. Library; 6. Dining area; 7. Kitchen; 8. Guest room; 9. Water tank. *Courtesy of Mary Otis Stevens*

playful-constructive behavior and awareness of psychogeographical effects, and are thus quite different from the classic notions of journey or stroll. In a *dérive* one or more persons during a certain period drop their relations, their work and leisure activities, and all their other usual motives for movement and action, and let themselves be drawn by the attractions of the terrain and the encounters they find there. Chance is a less important factor in this activity than one might think: from a *dérive* point of view cities have psychogeographical contours, with constant currents, fixed points and vortexes that strongly discourage entry into or exit from certain zones. But the *dérive* includes both this letting-go and its necessary contradiction: the domination of psycho-geographical variations by the knowledge and calculation of their possibilities.[12]

Like the Situationists, Stevens and McNulty were critical of the "society of spectacle"[13] and consumption, and this was reflected in the house's ability to support the erection of temporary props such as giant posters as backdrop for their children's rock guitar performances, while rejecting the display of possessions, which looked out of place on the austere, curved walls.[14]

Although it became a pilgrimage site for architects and students for many years, the house later faded from the discipline's memory. The critical inscription of women's architectural designs had not yet begun.

Architecture as a Multiplicity of Practices

The thirteen years between 1965 and 1978, when Stevens and her family lived in their Lincoln house, were bracketed by the escalation of the Vietnam War and the protest movement to end it, on the one hand, and the abrupt end of Nixon's presidency in the Watergate scandal, on the other. During this period Stevens adopted many public roles, while also raising her sons. In their architectural practice, she and McNulty were able, among other projects, to expand their experimental ideas in three additional concrete houses for sophisticated clients. One of these houses, the curvilinear Torf house in Weston, Massachusetts, is still inhabited by the original owner. As a political activist, Stevens joined others in her community to found an anti-war group and participated in the McGovern presidential campaign and promoting local low-income housing programs. And as a member of The New City, a project of the Cambridge Institute, she integrated a planning effort to create a new, alternative community. She also held Sunday salons attended by long-time mentors Buckminster Fuller and Samuel Eliot Morison, the heads and faculty of Harvard and MIT's architecture schools and their spouses, and the many prominent local and foreign architects who came to visit her house.

Her most enduring work during these years remains the creation of i press, which published, among other books, *The Ideal Communist City*, a collection of utopian plans by young Soviet architects and planners; Alexander Tzonis's *Towards a Non-Oppressive Environment,* a critique of the Bauhaus and its legacy; Doris Cole's *From Tipi to Skyscraper,* the first history of women in architecture; and Stevens and McNulty's theoretical book developed in Ravello, *World of Variation*. At the time, i press was the only American publishing house for books of ideas in architecture, similar to longer-established venues such as Il Saggiatore in Italy, under the direction of Gian Carlo de Carlo, a noted architect and frequent visiting professor at MIT. In spite of the good reception abroad and the translation of its books into other languages, i press failed to generate initial profits, and Stevens was forced to close it in 1974 when she could no longer support it from her dwindling inheritance. Within its short life, however, it had achieved the publication and dissemination in the United States of books that remain landmarks in the discourse on architecture and social issues. But the optimistic, risk-taking ethos of the 1960s had waned, and political and cultural moods, both in society and in the architectural academic and professional worlds, had turned conservative.

In 1978, Stevens and McNulty sold the house in Lincoln to its second and last occupant, Sarah Caldwell, the opera director and conductor who, at age twenty-nine, had founded the Opera Company of Boston and, at forty-eight, became the first woman to conduct at the Metropolitan Opera House in New York City.[15] They had had trouble attracting buyers for their unusual house, but Caldwell, who was Stevens's contemporary, liked its uniqueness and lived there with her mother, having previously requested from Stevens the design of an acoustical wood ceiling to dampen down the too-live sound of the house.

Mary Otis Stevens and Thomas McNulty went their separate professional and personal ways after the sale of the house, and she moved with her sons to Cambridge, near Harvard Square, where she remains today. In 1975, Stevens founded a new collaborative practice, Design Guild, with her former students at the Boston Architectural Center. Its clients were mostly non-profit organizations, with projects requiring historic preservation and the reuse of significant older buildings. Late in 1978 she married Jesse R. Fillman, a widower, former member of i press's board of directors, and a prominent lawyer who was a leading sponsor of civil rights and the arts in Boston. She remained active in political and sustainable design issues in the organization Architects for Social Responsibility. In 1991, Jesse Fillman died, and a major economic recession took a heavy toll on clients and architects alike. Stevens, then aged sixty-three, and her colleagues disbanded the Design Guild, and, as Mary Fillman, she started a new career as a musician and composer. After learning "how to see through walls" she has, forever inquisitive, learned to "see what one hears and hear what one sees," designing her musical compositions as an "invisible architecture."

In 2001, a newly wealthy owner, intent on amassing lakefront property for a faux-traditional estate, bought the Lincoln house and surreptitiously demolished it. Only afterward did the town start requiring permits for tearing buildings down.

NOTES

1. Wolf Von Eckhart, *A Place to Live* (New York: Delacorte Press, 1967), 291.

2. See Shadrach Woods, *The Man in the Street: A Polemic on Urbanism* (Baltimore: Penguin Books, 1975).

3. See Robert Goodman, *After the Planners* (New York: Simon and Schuster, 1972).

4. Among the better-known of these projects is La Clede Town, St. Louis, Missouri, designed by Cloethiel Woodard Smith & Associated Architects in 1967. See Ellen Perry Berkeley, "La Clede Town: The Most Vital Town in Town," *Architectural Forum* 129 (November 1968): 58.

5. Liane Lefaivre, "Critical Domesticity: An Interview with Mary Otis Stevens," *Thresholds* (an MIT student journal), no. 19 (2000): 22–25.

6. All the biographical references and sentences in quotation marks without attribution in this essay are based on an unpublished manuscript by Mary Otis Stevens, titled "Biographical Chronology," dated "10.7.02." It is based on an interview of April 2002 with Susana Torre and is available at the International Archive of Women in Architecture, http://spec.lib.vt.edu/spec/iawa/. For additional analysis of Mary Otis Stevens's work, see Jane McGroarty and Susana Torre, "New Professional Identities: Four Women in the Sixties," chap. 8 of Susana Torre, ed., *Women in Architecture: A Historic and Contemporary Perspective* (New York: Whitney Library of Design, 1977), 115–31.

7. The term was used by William Wurster, the MIT head of the Department of Architecture who had hired McNulty to teach there. McNulty was later denied tenure at MIT.

8. They were Ebenezer Stevens, who served under General Washington during the War of Independence; Mercy Otis Warren; and her brother James Otis.

9. See "A Sculpture for Living," *Life*, December 3, 1965, 122–29. The house was also published in the November 1965 issue of the *Architectural Forum* (U.S.A.), the February–March issue of *L'Architecture D'Aujourd'Hui* (France), the March 1966 issue of *Bauwelt* (Germany), and the October 1966 issue of *Domus* (Italy), among many other publications.

10. Leo Marx's expression refers to "the ordering of meaning and value around the contrast between two styles of life, one identified with a rural and the other with an urban setting." See Leo Marx, *The Machine in the Garden: Technology and the Pastoral Ideal in America* (London: Oxford University Press, 1964), 94.

11. See Christopher Reed, ed., *Not at Home: The Suppression of Domesticity in Modern Art and Architecture* (London: Thames and Hudson, 1996), a collection of essays examining the antagonism of Modernism toward domesticity and the human body as a sensuous entity.

12. See Guy-Ernest Debord, "Theory of the *Dérive*," at http://library.nothing ness.org/articles/SI/en/display/314.

13. See Guy, Debord, *Society of the Spectacle* (Detroit: Black & Red, 1967).

14. On this subject, Mary Otis Stevens wrote a book proposal on the topic of austerity, including references to different world cultures, and an unpublished essay entitled "Consumer Addiction and the Earth Culture," both available at the International Archive of Women in Architecture. See note 6, above.

15. From Sarah Caldwell's biographical notes at http://www2.worldbook.com/features/whm/html/whm068.html.

3

Life on the Cusp
Lynda Huey and Billie Jean King

James Pipkin

In the 1960s, as television coverage of sports events increased, the American living room became the nation's real sports arena. Although sports have always been woven into the fabric of American culture, before the 1960s those with inadequate incomes as well as blacks and women found their opportunities to participate in commercial sports severely limited. But the world of sports began to change with the tumult of the 1960s and 1970s—the anti-war movement, the civil rights movement, and the second wave of feminism. As many Americans sought freedom from a variety of cultural restraints, sports too began to open the gates for increased participation for women. The experiences of two women athletes in the 1960s—tennis star Billie Jean King and college sprinter Lynda Huey—reveal the personal and cultural ramifications of this shift. Although Huey was never to become a track star, while King was to achieve fame as the winner of twenty Wimbledon championships, they present similar stories of the role conflicts that women athletes of this period inevitably faced.

Women athletes' desire to enjoy full membership in the sporting world expressed aspects of the much longer and deeper political traditions from which second-wave feminism developed. As historian Ruth Rosen phrases it, the impetus to feminism included "the celebration of individual enterprise and initiative; a class politics expressed mostly through race and gender; . . . and a deep and abiding belief that in America, one can always reinvent oneself."[1] Women athletes rarely if ever engaged at the level of feminist public policy, but their pioneering efforts on the courts and playing fields reflected Betty Friedan's call for self-realization in her groundbreaking book *The Feminine Mystique*, published in 1963. While few of the prominent women athletes considered themselves feminists, their agenda and their activist spirit were clearly compatible with those of the self-defined feminists. In particular, because their efforts to pursue sports without any restrictions or barriers centered on the physical, their goals paralleled the feminist insistence on the rights of a woman to control and enjoy her own body.[2]

The leaders of the early women's movement in the 1960s had backgrounds very different from those of the leading women athletes. As Rosen points out, "feminism was resurrected by women whose ideas had developed in a deeply radical milieu"; she notes the important "continuities between labor union and Left activists of the forties and fifties and the origins of American feminism in the 1960s."[3] But a primary way the movement reached and affected the general public was through the media and popular culture. The exploits of women runners such as Wilma Rudolf, the unexpected star of the 1960 Olympics—the first post-*Sputnik* Olympics and thus the first opportunity for America to reassert its cultural dominance over the Russians—and the ratings success of Billie Jean King's victory over Bobby Riggs in 1973's televised "Battle of the Sexes" tennis match in Houston's Astrodome exemplify the role of sports in the spread of a feminist *Zeitgeist* to the popular consciousness.

The evolution of the liberated female athlete does not track perfectly the pattern of the larger feminist movement. Sports were placed far lower on the political agenda than issues such as equal pay and abortion rights. The National Organization for Women, founded in 1966, did not devote a workshop to sports until 1973.[4] Although their goals were often similar to those of many feminists, female athletes tended to be socially conservative and detached from the goals of women's liberation.[5] Most important, the crucial event in the revolution in women's sports did not occur until the 1970s: the passage of Title IX of the Education Act of 1972, the congressional legislation that outlawed discrimination on the basis of gender in schools receiving federal funding. This legal action led to a dramatic rise in women's participation in sports at both the high school and collegiate levels. Advocates for women's sports used its antidiscrimination position to advance the principle of equality for women athletes throughout amateur and professional sports, even though the federal law did not apply that widely.[6]

It is instructive to sketch the prevailing attitudes about women and sports before the great cultural divide that athletes like Billie Jean King and Lynda Huey straddled. As in other aspects of American life, women at best had performed on the margins of the world of sports. Sports were decidedly gendered cultural activities, and the history of sports was primarily a history of men and of masculinity. To speak of sports as a "male preserve" was to celebrate the masculine values of the hunter-warrior and to reinforce the traditional separation between the public sphere, where the male "performed," and the domestic sphere, which supposedly protected—and confined—the woman. If, during the nineteenth and early twentieth centuries, women were grudgingly admitted into the sports "sanctuary"—language appropriate for the sacred privileges of the initiates in the cult (including the "fans," a term derived from the Latin *fanum*, or "temple")—it was only to certain spheres within the sphere, activities such as calisthenics, walking, dancing, and horseback riding.[7] They were also permitted to play golf and tennis and to swim, but these sports were class-bound, available only to the wealthy, who could enjoy them in the secluded and protective world of the country club.[8]

Class and gender inflected the emphasis on sports found in the elite women's schools, primarily in the east, in the nineteenth century and the first half of the twentieth century. Educators at women's colleges advocated sports because of their health benefits and the socialization that recreation fostered. The underlying philosophy did not question accepted notions about women's place and role in society; women's sporting activities were not to be "ungraceful" or "unladylike."[9] Until the 1960s, many women's educators explicitly rejected the male model of sports, particularly its emphasis on competition. At the university level, for example, instead of the intercollegiate encounters enjoyed by men, women participated in "play days" and "sports days."[10] These activities emphasized intramural rather than intercollegiate sports and "play for play's sake" rather than prizes or awards. It was not until 1963 that varsity sports for women were accepted and 1967 before women were allowed to compete in national championships.[11] Between the two world wars there had been competitive women's teams in sports such as basketball, softball, and track and field, but most of these teams played in industrial leagues and the participants were working-class women.

While this general overview may blur some important particulars, it reveals that women's sports were, from their point of origin in America, shaped by the interplay of gender, social class, and the stages of the life cycle.[12] Underlying biological, aesthetic, and social issues continued to frame the experiences of women athletes in the 1960s. Although it was no longer the prevalent view, as late as the early 1960s some experts still

believed that strenuous participation in sports could harm women's reproductive organs. The biological and the social came together at puberty,
when peer pressure and physical changes caused many girls to abandon
their previous sports activities. For young women who remained active
in sports, an "aesthetic" question arose: athleticism and muscularity
violated society's conception of female beauty. Women who participated
in sport had always been the object of the male gaze—a newspaper
account of the first women's intercollegiate basketball game between
Stanford and California-Berkeley focused primarily on the players'
"pleasing appearance and becoming actions" rather than their athletic
ability[13]—and this "view," in both senses of the word, continued to be
an issue well into the 1970s.

The greatest women athletes of the era were probably the East Euro-
peans, who dominated swimming and field events in the Olympics, but
the "darlings" of the Olympic games were gymnasts such as the Russian
Olga Korbut, who won three gold medals at the Munich games in 1972,
and Romanian Nadia Comaneci, who won three gold medals at the
Montreal games in 1976. The American public viewed the muscular
East European women as "Amazons" who transgressed the boundaries
between male and female, while they found beauty in the childlike, girlish
physiques of the young gymnasts. The appearance of ease that gymnastics creates hid from the spectators the great strength the performances
required. The new audiences drawn to gymnastics preferred the "pixie"
bodies of these athletes to those of the mature women competing in many
of the other sports. At the Winter Olympics, the gymnasts' counterpart
was the skater: Dorothy Hamill, a gold medal winner at the 1976 Games
in Innsbruck, Austria, and other artistic dancers on the ice. Billed as the
latest in a long line of "America's Sweethearts," Hamill gained almost as
much fame for her trademark hair style as for her athletic ability, and she
cashed in on this aspect of her appeal with a series of Breck shampoo
commercials after her Olympic success. In contrast to sports that seemed
to be about feminine grace and beauty and choreographically delicate
aesthetics, sports that depended on strength, speed, and aggression,
which were considered "masculine" qualities, raised fears. Women who
competed in them threatened the social, if not the natural, order of things.
As Mildred "Babe" Didrikson Zaharias, perhaps the greatest American
woman athlete of all time, noted in her 1955 autobiography, "Well, with
almost any woman athlete, you seem to get that tomboy talk"[14]—that is,

the inevitable gossip about female athletes' masculine bodies and the related questions about their sexual orientation. If Teddy Roosevelt, baseball Hall of Fame player Ty Cobb of the Detroit Tigers, Coach Vince Lombardi of the Green Bay Packers professional football team, and other proponents who touted the character-building qualities of sports promised that sports "would make a real man of you," then the question loomed, "Could a real woman play sports?"

This, then, was the cultural reality in women's sports before Title IX and the changes it set in motion. The matters central to the history of women's sports had always pivoted on sexuality, female physicality, and the hegemonic control that men claimed over women's bodies.[15] But at the cusp between the era of the two world wars and the end of the "long decade" of the sixties as it extended into the seventies, a new focus on identity, role conflict, and the relativity of equality emerged. Sports historians John A. Lucas and Ronald A. Smith argue that in the 1960s and 1970s the question was no longer, as it had been in the 1890s, "Should a lady ride a bicycle?" or, as in the 1930s and 1940s, "Shall women compete in highly competitive athletics?" but "Shall women have equal opportunity with men to compete in athletics at all levels?"[16] The sexual politics of this question is a touchstone of the times. Women athletes who came of age in the 1950s and early 1960s arrived at this question only after battling deep tensions about their identities, their sexuality, and the way society "read" their extraordinary bodies. For these women athletes, the body was the site of deep-seated cultural beliefs and values as well as a site of identity. They describe their sporting experiences using terms such as "identity crisis," "schizophrenia," and "freak," all reminders of the cultural dissonance that accompanies what Billie Jean King describes as "life on the cusp."

Lynda Huey was born on May 13, 1947, in Vallejo, California. Her family moved to San Jose, where her father worked a variety of jobs, from carpentry to real estate and used car sales, while her mother took care of Lynda and her older sister. Growing up in a conservative suburb where she formed her views of sexuality and male–female relationships in part from poring over *Seventeen* magazine and "How to Be Popular" books, Huey did not have her first sexual experience until college. She recalls the death of John F. Kennedy as one of the few public events to distract her from a world of cheerleading and crushes on high school football heroes.

Her victories in track and basketball received no press, but she did get her name in the paper for winning the "prettiest statistician" award from the boys' baseball team.

After high school, Huey became a nationally competitive sprinter at San Jose State University and later taught physical education and coached at Federal City College in Washington, D.C., Cal Poly–San Luis Obispo, Mira Costa College, and Oberlin College. After pursuing opportunities as a writer for top sports magazines and hosting a television sports program, she became interested in working with injured Olympic athletes in the early 1980s. Today, she directs Huey's Athletic Network, a Santa Monica, California fitness consulting firm specializing in water exercise, aquatic therapy, and related services, and boasting a celebrity-studded clientele.

The subtitle of *A Running Start*, Huey's autobiography, baldly inscribes the dilemma she and others of her era faced; it reads "An Athlete, a Woman." A great gender divide separates the two words, and Huey spends much of the book exploring the "female–athlete dichotomy" that shadowed her aspirations.[17] She describes her life as "a series of identity crises" that caused her to develop a "split personality" bordering on "schizophrenia."[18] This trope of the divided self haunted other women of the 1960s who sought to enter the public sphere of sports. Women were allowed to enter the male sanctum sanctorum of sports only as decorations, the purpose served by cheerleaders like Huey in her high school years. Participation in sports was not intended to bring women public achievement or recognition but to contribute to their identities as social or domestic beings.[19]

Huey cites Marty Liquori, a champion runner of the time, and his theory of "the survival of the ugliest" to explain the plight of women athletes. Liquori argued that attractive girls have so many options and pressures that they eventually drop out of sports, leaving the "ugly girls," for whom sports is one of the few avenues for success and recognition. Huey absorbed the social and cultural constructions of gender underlying this thesis. The feminine ideal at the time was the skinny, pale model, not the strong, muscular, healthy woman who was in touch with her body. Huey admits that, like most adolescents, she wanted to conform. Although she had always been an active, energetic athlete, in high school she gave up a number of activities—riding her bike to school, running around the park, skateboarding down the street—that she feared would detract from her femininity.

Although she ran track, she was much more caught up in the limelight of cheerleading, the acceptable province of athletic girls who were also considered conventionally pretty. Cheerleading represented for her an attempt to move from the private to the public arena. She loved public attention: "The football players were masters of the game; I was mistress of the crowd. I had no doubt that I was every bit as important as they were. I was every inch a star."[20] But, as her language indicates, even when a girl managed to enter the public arena, she could not escape the gendered role of "mistress" who served the male "masters," the primary actors in the drama of the games. In her diary for October 23, 1962, she wrote: "Kennedy's jazz about Cuba sure has me scared. I want to live. I just can't die before I really get to be a cheerleader. . . . "[21] Only later, as she reread her diary, did she understand that the attention the cheerleaders received was only reflected glory from the male athletes. Cheerleaders only reacted, she finally realized, an example of the social dynamic that prepared women for marriage roles that may have worked in the 1950s but were to be dramatically changed by the social revolutions of the decade in which Huey would come of age.

Even as a high school girl, she knew that she "wanted both the pom-poms and the spikes,"[22] yet she did not believe she could ever have both. She had accepted the reality that girls' athletics were second-class. Instead of real uniforms tailored distinctively for each sport, the girls wore the same homemade green shorts and white blouses for every sport. The domestic origins of the girls' apparel suggested that they could only pretend to authenticity, as did the uniforms' plainness, the lacking of heraldry and icons that adorned the vestments of males and marked the ritual significance of their activities. More troubling than the lack of social status was the social pressure about the feminine body. One of the "song girls" who was almost as fast as Huey refused an invitation to join the girls' Amateur Athletic Union (AAU) track team, explaining, "My calves are too big already. They might get bigger."[23] Huey's own experience when she received no media recognition for winning the outstanding player award for both basketball and track, but got her name in the paper for winning the trophy for "prettiest statistician" for the boys' baseball team, underscored these issues. The girls continually received clearly encoded messages.

At the same time, Huey reveled in her athleticism. Unlike cheerleading, which she needed for its social status, running was still pure fun for her. She enjoyed being in shape, wearing spikes that she thought "proved that

[she] was a *real* runner,"[24] and engaging in serious competition with her AAU team. The result of these conflicting messages, one from the outside, the other from within, was the "schizophrenia" that dominated her view of her childhood and coming of age in the 1960s. In the 1970s, when she reviewed her high school diary and scrapbook, she discovered hundreds of pictures of herself in her cheerleader's uniform but not a single photograph of her high school athletic career. She had learned to deny a crucial aspect of who she was.

When Huey entered San Jose State University, she was confronted with a similar cultural message. She found a campus world divided into "Sorority Sals" and "Hercs" (short for "Hercules"). If women athletes were mannish Herculeses and divided by "natural selection" from attractive and social sorority girls, this further proved the "survival of the ugliest" theory. The Physical Education Department repeated the same pattern. Huey observed that most of the female students majoring in the discipline were overweight and unattractive according to the ideals of the time. Only two of the twelve women on the faculty were married, which underscored the suspicions about the sexual orientation of female athletes. Equally troubling to a serious athlete was that the department saw its mission as preparing the students to teach, not to compete or coach.

Huey recognized the department's philosophy as a "cookies and punch" mentality, which treated women's sports as a recreational rather than a competitive activity. Tennis, golf, and other historically "genteel" activities contributed to the socialization process for upper-class women who had the leisure time not generally available to lower-class women. If, as a Marxist analysis would have it, team sports promote in the masses the social acceptance and accommodation the capitalist system requires of the working class, individual sports are designed to foster the qualities of leadership essential to the ruling class; the costly lessons, expensive equipment, and extensive tracts of land made these sports attractive to those who sought class exclusivity. These were also considered acceptable sports for women because they did not allow physical contact and were played, originally, in modest clothing.[25]

While second-wave feminism did lead to changes in the world of women's sports, Huey's career took place on the cusp of this cultural divide. The San Jose State campus still mirrored traditional attitudes about the role of sports in the life of a woman and about women who attempted to enter the public world of competitive sports. Huey, like most other women athletes of her era, felt torn by conflicting desires. On the one hand, she had been informally training with the school's world-class male runners, such as Tommie Smith and John Carlos, athletes who were later to become ignominious icons to many conservative Americans when they raised the "black power" salute as they stood on the victory stand at the 1968 Olympics in Mexico City. But Huey was also pleased when an article by a local male sportswriter stressed her physical attractiveness more than her talent. Although she was emerging as a national-caliber sprinter, the writer emphasized how she contradicted the image of the big, burly Russian shot-putter that hung over women's track and field.

The tension between Huey's identity as an athlete and her identity as a "feminine" woman continued as the recurring motif of her life in the late 1960s. Because she subconsciously associated sports with masculinity, she adopted a "male" attitude toward many subjects—sports, sexuality, even other women—and at the same time compensated by "overstress[ing] my own attractiveness to conquer the self-doubts that other people planted in my mind."[26] In high school, emulating the male athletes sometimes caused her not to be selected for the girls' teams because she acted like a "loud-mouthed, cocky, know-it-all,"[27] but the other half of her consciousness spoke loudly in its own way: she was the worshipful girl who saved the Coke the football hero gave her and kept it in the freezer for over a year. In college, she saw herself as "one of the boys" when she worked out with the men's track team, and she carried that mentality with her off the track by acting with as much "machismo as the piggiest of the sports stars."[28] She later realized that she had internalized male attitudes that she emulated on the track to such an extent that she even disliked other women. Yet she perceived herself as an "imitation athlete,"[29] ineffectively trying to enter the public sphere of athletics by imitating the behavior of the natural inhabitant of this domain.

The masculine swagger Huey adopted did not mean that she neglected her needs as a woman. As much as she wanted to be treated as an equal athlete on the track, on Saturday night she wanted to revert to "eligible girlfriend."[30] But although she "play[ed] 'female'" to her male heroes, she assumed that she, too, could engage in "sex as sport" and adopt the men's attitude of "lov 'em and leav 'em."[31] She was, in a sense, living the life of the "new woman" described in Helen Gurley Brown's 1962 book *Sex and the Single Girl*. Yet thinking that a woman could be a female Hugh Hefner was like assuming she could be a serious athlete—a sign of cultural dissonance that led to a painful recognition of society's double standard. Because she entertained men, many of them black, at her apartment in San Jose, it became known as "Huey's Whorehouse," and in the early 1970s she was fired from her faculty position at California Polytechnic State University in San Luis Obispo because of her "fast" and "loose" lifestyle, the university administration's characterization of her interracial dating and multiple sex partners.

In *A Running Start*, Huey placed her struggle to find a wholeness that reconciled her identity as an athlete with her identity as a woman in the context of the cultural changes of the 1960s and 1970s. Her romance with Tommie Smith and friendships with the other black members of the San Jose State track team brought her close to the civil rights and black power movements as they affected the world of sports. She was a college student in the charged atmosphere of those days when "a new Afro almost always meant that a black militant had been born."[32] Sociologist Harry Edwards, who was soon to publish *The Revolt of the Black Athlete* (1969) about the systematic exploitation of the black athlete at predominantly white colleges, was on the faculty of San Jose State at that time. Huey had a firsthand look at his attempts to start a revolution in sports on the campus and to lead a boycott of the 1968 Olympics in Mexico City as a way of protesting racial injustice in America. Her chapter on this major political issue asks astutely, "Meanwhile, Where Were the Women?" The outstanding black female Olympic athletes were appalled to discover that they were excluded from participating in the boycott by Edwards and the committee planning the protest. Edwards offered only the weak excuse that the exclusion of the women was unintentional, the result of limited resources of time and money. Yet, when she was a student, Huey lacked a perspective on the cultural orthodoxy about femininity and the social construction of gender roles, and "never considered the need for another revolution to help women athletes."[33]

Huey's time at Oberlin College gave her the ideological support she needed to confirm the intimations of her own experiences, and she "never again saw sport with the same eyes."[34] She taught at Oberlin in 1973–74, when Jack Scott was director of athletics there. His book *Athletics for Athletes* (1969) presented the Marxist theory that sports were abused as another opiate of the people. He argued that sports should be taken away from the tyrannical control of the coaches and commercial interests and returned to the athletes. Scott's approach to athletics helped to demystify what Huey called her belief in "the rah-rah athletic scene."[35] She understood more conceptually now that sports were male-identified and that she had internalized that male orientation even though she was a woman.

Fig. 3.1. Lynda Huey finishes third in her first cross-country race while representing the newly-formed Wilt's WonderWomen Track Club (formerly La Jolla Track Club) in Fall, 1974. *Photo by Micki McGee Scott, courtesy of Lynda Huey*

She now wanted to see women strike out and make sport their own. Scott's academic department housed a radical world filled with portraits of Martin Luther King Jr. and Chairman Mao and telephone calls from migrant labor organizer Cesar Chavez and comedian–turned–black activist Dick Gregory. This environment helped to shape her philosophy when she taught at several California colleges after leaving Oberlin.

But perhaps the most significant shift in Huey's awareness centered on her sense of her body. Her autobiography both begins and ends with accounts of the "peak" experiences she often found in running when her "body and mind . . . totally expressed themselves."[36] At a dramatic cusp in cultural history when, as Huey believed, "millions of females . . . [had] lost all touch with their own physical beings except as objects on view,"[37] she experienced on the track moments in which her body became fully alive and transported her to what she called a feeling of "beyondness." This "beyondness" is not an out-of-the-body sensation; it is a feeling that takes her to the deep self that lies within the body. It is what the Greeks called the "daimonic," a vital energy that expresses itself in physical performance, in imaginative activity, and in sexuality. Indeed, Huey emphasized her sexual activities in her autobiography to show that her sexual assertiveness, like her athletic ability, was essential to her being. At a time when feminists were arguing that each woman must take control of her own body, Huey drew upon her experience as an athlete to insist that "every woman must control her body before she can control her mind and her life."[38] Her life is the story of someone who channeled the power of her body to her mind and freed herself from the traditional feminine stereotype. Clearly, she resisted following the pattern of "the survival of the ugliest." She had lived to see a health-conscious society with a new image of the female body, a body characterized by fitness, strength, and stamina rather than the old image of fragility and passivity. Her story foreshadows the larger society's awakening to the potential of the female body.

Tennis player Billie Jean King was perhaps the best-known woman sports star during the 1960s and is considered one of the most influential athletes in American history. In 1990 *Life* magazine named her as one of the "100 Most Important Americans of the Twentieth Century," and in 1994 she was ranked number five on *Sports Illustrated*'s "Top 40 Athletes" who had altered or elevated sports in the last four decades. In her career she won seventy-one singles titles and holds the record for the most Wimbledon titles. She was the top-ranked woman tennis player in the world from 1967–72 and ranked in the top ten for seventeen years. She was, in addition, the first woman athlete to earn $100,000 a year in tournament winnings and the first woman to coach a professional team (the Philadelphia Freedoms of World Team Tennis).

King's athletic prowess alone, however, could not have made her one of the "100 Most Important Americans of the Twentieth Century." For many people, she epitomized the second wave of feminism as it found expression in women's sports. She demanded that sponsors reduce the huge disparity between what men and women players were paid in the tournaments; she was the pioneer in establishing a separate women's tournament circuit, the Virginia Slims Tour, in 1971; and she brought increased visibility to female athletics when she launched *Women's Sports* magazine in 1974. Today, she is active in publishing and in promoting tournaments and tennis exhibitions. She serves on the boards of directors of the Elton John AIDS Foundation, the National AIDS Foundation and the Women's Sports Foundation, and is a tennis commentator for HBO.

Despite King's fame and Huey's relative anonymity, both women athletes share the perception that their lives were "schizophrenic" in a crucial respect. A better title for King's autobiography than the prosaic *Billie Jean* would have been the metaphor she used for one of the chapter headings: "Always on the Cusp." Saying that she was "born on the cusp" and "lived on the cusp," she uses this idea as a symbol for her life and her identity.[39] She sees her life as symbolic in many ways. As the pioneering leader of the women's professional tennis tour, King epitomized the sport, but she was also viewed as the sports equivalent of Betty Friedan, Gloria Steinem, Bella Abzug, and Jane Fonda—as she puts it, "the Feminist Athlete Doll."[40] She was the "tough bitch" who beat male chauvinist pig Bobby Riggs in the tennis "Battle of the Sexes" in the Houston Astrodome, on Mother's Day in 1973, before 30,472 fans (still the largest crowd to witness a tennis competition) and millions more on national television. She was one of the "new women" who threatened men in a variety of ways; their fears seemed justified when she not only beat a man but also admitted to an affair with another woman.

Born Billie Jean Moffitt in Long Beach, California, on November 22, 1943, King grew up in a conservative, lower-middle-class family. Her father, Bill Moffitt, after whom she was named, was a fireman and her mother, Betty, ran the house, then later earned money on the side selling Avon products and holding Tupperware parties to help pay for the children's sports activities. (King's younger brother Randy Moffitt became a major-league pitcher for the San Francisco Giants.) King's first love was softball, but she realized at an early age that there was no future in it and took up tennis when she was eleven. She developed her game on the public courts of Long Beach, becoming one of the top junior players in Southern California.

When she was seventeen, she broke into the national women's rankings for the first time at number four. King enrolled at Los Angeles State College in 1960. Although she was the best tennis player on campus and already one of the best female players in the world, she received no scholarship, yet her future husband, Larry King, the seventh man on the six-man men's tennis team, was on full athletic scholarship. In 1964, King dropped out of school to accept a businessman's offer to finance a trip to Australia to train with an important coach and devote herself full-time to a tennis career. In 1965, when she made the finals of the U.S. Open Championship in Forest Hills, her career dreams had become a reality. That same year she also married Larry King, who later became her business partner and manager.

King spent her childhood in a very structured society that she compares to *The Life of Riley*, a 1950s television situation comedy about a blue-collar workingman whose life of leisure was one of the "peace dividends" of the Eisenhower years. At home, everyone called her "Sis." The Moffitts saw themselves as the typical family living the American Dream. Her family was very religious (their pastor was Bob Richards, the former Olympic gold medalist in the pole vault), and King participated in her school's Youth for Christ organization and read the Bible faithfully every night. She even considered seriously becoming a Christian missionary. Then came the 1960s: "all of a sudden," King found that "the rules all started to change, and it seemed there weren't any rules left. I tried to go with the flow, but always seemed to find myself out in front and on the line."[41] Significant social change, King remembers, was "everywhere, [and] as I approached something, it turned, it changed. Nothing really happened as I had plotted it." The result was a life in which "it always seemed I was also on the cutting edge of that change."[42]

The edge cut both ways, however, and she struggled with some of the consequences of her aggressive ambitions. As a young amateur, she played a sport controlled by conservative men—she calls them, in the parlance of the times, "male chauvinists"—who treated the young women as second-class "bush league" players. Because she was a woman in a traditionally male world, a part of her identified as an outsider. Although sports brought her fame, she understood that "much of the reason why I've always felt that I was out of place was because of sports."[43] At the time, any girl who wanted to excel in athletics was considered strange, and being the daughter of a fireman, trying to break into a country club game, only compounded the feeling.

King's class-related discomfort was certainly not the product of self-consciousness. For example, she was not allowed to be in the Southern California Junior Team photograph because she did not have the required tennis dress. In addition to the social class problem, she had to confront the same issue that Lynda Huey did: "I have often been asked whether I am a woman or an athlete. The question is absurd. Men are not asked that. I am an athlete. I am a woman."[44] The problem was even more painful for King than for Huey because she was not considered attractive in the way American society defined beauty at the time. One of her first coaches hurt her deeply when he predicted, "You'll be good because you're ugly."[45]

As the co-founder of the women's professional tennis tour, King felt that the players had to market their bodies. She and the other leaders of the Women's Tennis Association wanted to take advantage of the fact that tennis is a "very sexy sport" played by young women with excellent bodies, wearing relatively little clothing, and so they "encourage[d] [their] players to be as attractive and as feminine as possible."[46] Tennis was the main women's sport to benefit from the increased television coverage of sports in the 1960s, and most of the angles were close-ups. Women golfers, who were often not in good shape, wore long Bermuda shorts and head visors; swimmers' suits flattened the natural curves of their bodies; and it would be almost twenty years before track, which drew television attention primarily only every four years at Olympics time, would feature the erotically appealing spandex and "Speedos" clothing. But in the 1960s the Women's Tennis Association's marketing strategy turned out to be effective, and the tour initially received a disproportionate amount of media coverage because male writers were attracted to "the sex angle."[47]

This proved to be an important strategy for developing the commercial opportunities of women's tennis, but King struggled with her own body image. She bemoaned her fat legs, bad eyesight, and flat "bahoolas," as she called her breasts in the title of one of the autobiography's chapters. She was keenly aware of the public perception of women athletes as "mannish freaks,"[48] the phrase that almost all women athletes of the 1950s, 1960s, and 1970s use in their autobiographies to describe the stigma they confronted. Women athletes' bodies seemed to transgress the accepted boundaries between male and female, drawing disquieting reactions from the American viewing public.[49]

Like Huey, King also felt torn by what she called a "split personality."[50] One side was clearly gendered as female; she described it as "that nice, polite me."[51] The other side consisted of those qualities necessary for victory on the court, qualities considered by the culture to be masculine rather than feminine. She viewed herself as an aggressive person who was not afraid to take risks in her life, and this style was reflected in her tennis. She played the serve-and-volley game (rushing the net and hitting the opponent's shot before it bounced) that was typical of men's tennis but not of the women's game of that era. The women generally played a baseline game (standing behind the back line of the court and waiting to return the opponent's shot until after it bounced) that made for long rallies and often was decided by the opponent's mistake rather than the victor's winning shot. King, however, described herself as an "attacking" player and sometimes referred to victories as "tak[ing] scalps."[52]

She was also blue-collar in the way she had to "grub it out,"[53] the expression she used to characterize the forceful, sweaty, non-aesthetically beautiful style of her game. The press coalesced gender and class in describing her play, never suggesting that she was a "lady." She was a "tomboy" named for her father. As she looked back on her childhood, she thought that even her class-driven dreams were too aggressive for a girl. It was taboo at that time, she felt, for a girl to aspire to a career that involved a lot of money. Her views imply that the construction of femininity entails class as well as aesthetic issues.

Her public image was reinforced by the opposing style, both on the court and off, of her chief rival, Chris Evert. Beginning with their first major confrontation in the semifinals of the 1971 U.S. Open, Evert served as a foil to King's character; she became the "fair heroine," the darling of conventional society and its gendered assumptions about women's roles. Evert brought to tennis what the pretty gymnasts and ice skaters did to their sports: the traditional concept of femininity. Fans and journalists often referred to Evert as "Chrissie." In fact, Evert chose *Chrissie* as the title of her autobiography. The diminutive expressed the fans' response to what they saw as "endearing" qualities, but it also infantilized her as a non-threatening child. If King was the tough feminist bitch, then Chrissy was the girl next door. When Evert summarized her legacy in her own memoir, she did not emphasize all the championships

Fig. 3.2. Billie Jean King's intense focus is one of the defining traits of a champion. *Photo provided by World Team Tennis*

she won but the femininity she brought to the sport. King, on the other hand, did not feel she could compete with Evert in this respect. King may have recognized the importance of marketing the women players' sexual appeal, but it is revealing that she never suggested that her own appearance and identity lent themselves to such a makeover. The challenge for the great women athletes of this era continued to be overcoming the assumption that sports and femininity were incompatible. Even the openly gay tennis player Martina Navratilova confessed in her autobiography about the change she made in her image when she dyed her hair blonde, had a makeup lesson at Vidal Sassoon's, and began to care about how she was photographed.

King's relationship with Evert reflected many of the conflicts of her own "cusp-like" identity. She admired Evert's star qualities, but she made pointed remarks about the discrepancy between Evert's image and the reality. The complexity of what Evert meant to King's own identity is suggested by the following confession:

> [s]ometimes I can't completely disassociate myself—not when Chris is playing, anyway. I'll never feel for any of the others the way I do for her. It'll always seem a little more painful when she loses, for she became some part of me on the court, and no matter who won, each of us needed the other. . . . [54]

King was sensitive to the subtle dynamics between them as they enacted the drama of the "fair" and "dark" heroines of cultural romances. They were foils, but each came as "a shadow self," embodying some of the other's deepest desires and wishes.

King's divided sensibility pervaded her life off the court as well. One of the key questions she asked herself in her autobiography was "Do you fit in anywhere?"[55] The situation went well beyond being a woman in a man's world. One of the most dramatic parts of her life was her affair with her secretary Marilyn Barnett. She admitted, "Obviously, I must be bisexual."[56] Again on the cusp, here the cusp of sexuality, she insisted that she was not comfortable in either the world of heterosexual marriage or the gay world. She strove to present herself as a complex person who defied the labels imposed upon her by others. But there is something disingenuous about her insistence that the affair had "nothing to do with my feelings, my perceptions of who I am."[57] She confessed, in fact, that one of the meaningful aspects of the relationship was that it made her feel soft and feminine. Here again is the "schizophrenia" that many women athletes of the 1960s felt. When she was in bed with another woman, King could be something that she could not be in sports. The complexity of the affair, which she acknowledged, belies the implicit casualness and passivity of saying, "[o]ne morning I woke up, and where was I? I was in another woman's bed."[58] The revealing question—"Where was I?"— restates one of the recurring dilemmas of King's life: her confusion about the role of women caught in the sudden cultural shift.

Sports historian Allen Guttmann argues that when the second wave of feminism began in the 1960s and 1970s, feminists were not particularly interested in women's sports, and women athletes often held conservative views about social issues. He emphasizes, however, that in the mid-seventies, when many feminists discovered the importance of sports and many women athletes became feminists, Billie Jean King played a major role in that process.[59] King's own perspective about her role as a feminist cultural icon mirrors her characteristically divided sensibility. She wrote in her autobiography that, despite the pomp and ceremony of her victory over Bobby Riggs in the "Battle of the Sexes" in 1973, she was not comfortable beating a man. She was also troubled that she achieved greater stardom in sports than her brother Randy Moffitt, a relief pitcher for the San Francisco Giants. She furthermore resisted accepting the mantle that women political activists would have had her wear, insisting that she is a traditionalist and that some of her attitudes are the "prejudices" of "a girl in a boy's world."[60] Even for women of the 1960s who broke the mold and dared to enter the public sphere traditionally reserved for the male, their stance was Janus-like. The Roman god of gates and entryways had a face on both sides of his head, but for Billie Jean King this double consciousness was as much a burden as a privilege.

The lives of Lynda Huey and Billie Jean King shed light on an important aspect of American culture in the 1960s and 1970s. Their stories coincide with the rise of the women's movement and to a certain extent mirror it. But King is more precise when she includes on the jacket cover of her autobiography a blurb that says her life is "tangled" with the rise of feminism. Most American women played no active role in the movement. While they realized that the great social changes of their times situated them in the midst of two worlds, it did not mean that they were prepared to assume the title of feminist. Many felt uncomfortable with an ideology that was not flexible enough to include black women as well as white women, working-class women as well as women from privileged backgrounds. Most important, they were uneasy about embracing a political and social agenda that opponents characterized as a rejection of femininity or an implicit embrace of lesbianism.

Billie Jean King explicitly took this stance, a position on the cusp. A self-proclaimed controversial figure, a maverick who was no longer willing to do what was expected of her and other women, she took great pride in leading women's tennis into the spotlight and demanding equal prizes for women contestants in tournaments. But her conflicted feelings about her femininity and her sexual orientation, as well as other reservations about goals and means, made her defiantly reject being seen as "the

Feminist Athlete Doll." It is significant that she entitled the last chapter of her autobiography "Vulnerable at Last," a final emphasis on her desire to be seen as feminine.

Huey's self-proclaimed identity crisis, her "schizophrenia," reflected the cultural schism in which she came of age. She was not an avowed feminist in the 1960s, but by the mid-1970s she had begun to question the relationship between gender, sports, and identity. Once she became aware of the cultural cusp on which she stood, Huey clearly identified with what she called "the new woman." She was no longer willing to be a woman whose own story would be subsumed in that of more "worthy" male athletes with whom she had been associated. Huey now understood that "a woman who is strong is not masculine; she is a *strong woman*."[61]

Like other women of the older generation whose lives overlapped with those young feminists who took the lead in the 1970s, King and Huey rebelled against the power of the feminine mystique, the 1950s cultural icons of domesticity and motherhood. But their legacy lies not in what they rejected but in the new models they embodied. As King confidently claimed: "Whatever, I made myself what I am."[62] Working within the realm of sports, they helped to transform American culture. By the late 1970s, women stood a chance, at least, to appear strong without being labeled as masculine. Competitiveness, aggressiveness, and muscularity seemed slightly less antithetical to femininity than they had in the 1960s. It had become possible, just possible, to be an athlete and a woman.

NOTES

1. Ruth Rosen, *The World Split Open: How the Modern Women's Movement Changed America* (New York: Viking, 2000), p. xiv.

2. Susan K. Cahn, *Coming on Strong: Gender and Sexuality in Twentieth-Century Women's Sport* (New York: Free Press, 1994), p. 252.

3. Rosen, *World Split Open*, pp. 69 and 355, n. 15.

4. Deborah Hiestand, "Women in Sport in the United States: 1945–1978," in Reet Howell, ed., *Her Story in Sport: A Historical Anthology of Women in Sports* (West Point, N.Y.: Leisure Press, 1982), p. 296.

5. Allen Guttmann, *Women's Sports: A History* (New York: Columbia University Press, 1991), p. 209.

6. Cahn, *Coming on Strong*, p. 251.

7. William Beezley and Joseph P. Hobbs, "'Nice Girls Don't Sweat': Women in American Sport," *Journal of Popular Culture* 16:4 (Spring 1983), p. 42.

8. Allen Guttmann, *A Whole New Ball Game: An Interpretation of American Sports* (Chapel Hill: University of North Carolina Press, 1988), p. 145.

9. Beezley and Hobbs, "'Nice Girls Don't Sweat': Women in American Sport," p. 42.

10. Guttmann, *Women's Sports*, pp. 135–42.

11. Guttmann, *Whole New Ball Game*, p. 149.

12. Guttmann, *Women's Sports*, p. 1.

13. This excerpt from the newspaper account is quoted in Beezley and Hobbs, "'Nice Girls Don't Sweat': Women in American Sport," p. 43.

14. Babe Didrikson Zaharias and Harry Paxon, *This Life I've Led* (New York: A. S. Barnes, 1955), p. 103.

15. Helen Lenskyj, *Out of Bounds: Women, Sport and Sexuality* (Toronto: Women's Press, 1986), p. 14.

16. John A. Lucas and Ronald A. Smith, *Saga of American Sport* (Philadelphia: Lea & Febiger, 1978), p. 342.

17. Lynda Huey, *A Running Start: An Athlete, a Woman* (New York: Quadrangle, 1976), p. 11.

18. Ibid., pp. 11, 16, and 232.

19. Donald J. Mrozek, "The 'Amazon' and the American 'Lady': Sexual Fears of Women as Athletes," in S. W. Pope, ed., *The New American Sport History* (Urbana: University of Illinois Press, 1997), p. 205.

20. Huey, *Running Start*, p. 20.

21. Ibid., p. 22.

22. Ibid., p. 36.

23. Ibid.

24. Ibid., p. 38.

25. Guttmann, *Whole New Ball Game*, pp. 145–47. For a more detailed discussion of the Marxist thesis, see Paul Hoch, *Rip Off the Big Game* (Garden City, N.Y.: Doubleday-Anchor, 1972).

26. Huey, *Running Start*, p. 45.

27. Ibid., p. 33.

28. Ibid., p. 16.

29. Ibid., p. 137.

30. Ibid., p. 31.

31. Ibid., pp. 17, 204, and 130.

32. Ibid., p. 108.

33. Ibid., p. 126.

34. Ibid., p. 179.

35. Ibid.

36. Ibid., p. 7.

37. Ibid., p. 12.

38. Ibid., p. 211.

39. Billie Jean King and Frank Deford, *Billie Jean* (New York: Viking, 1982), p. 18.

40. Ibid., p. 161.

41. Ibid., p. 18.

42. Ibid.

43. Ibid., p. 12.

44. Ibid., p. 16.

45. Ibid., p. 191.

46. Ibid., pp. 146, 147–48.

47. Ibid., p. 123.

48. Ibid., p. 89.

49. For a further discussion of this concept of the freak, see Leslie Fiedler, *Freaks: Myths and Images of the Secret Self* (New York: Simon and Schuster, 1978). Interestingly, with respect to the cultural construction of the body, other freaks were presented as having bodies that transgressed the natural boundary between human and animal, and many of these freaks were people of color. Certain black athletes had to deal with the stigma of being viewed as freaks because their bodies were "read" as unnatural in this respect.

50. King, *Billie Jean*, p. 199.

51. Ibid.

52. Ibid., pp. 205, 1.

53. Ibid., p. 127.

54. Ibid., p. 185.

55. Ibid., p. 18.

56. Ibid., p. 27.

57. Ibid., p. 12.

58. Ibid., p. 19.

59. Guttmann, *Women's Sports*, p. 209.

60. King, *Billie Jean*, p. 136.

61. Huey, *Running Start*, p. 237.

62. King, *Billie Jean*, p. 43.

4

Balancing Act
Ursula Kroeber Le Guin

Zina Petersen

In the 1960s, Ursula Kroeber Le Guin, a forty-something housewife from the Northwest, did intentionally what American culture did by default in those years: she trafficked in dichotomies. Working within such marginalized genres as science fiction, fantasy, and children's literature, Le Guin brought together disparate, even contradictory ideas and sought ways to balance them. Drawing on her early exposure to the philosophy of Taoism, and anticipating the sweeping interest young Americans would soon have for such far-flung ideas as androgyny, anarchism, and environmentalism, Le Guin crafted fiction that probed current societal problems by imagining the unlikely. In her radicalism, her willingness to take systems up by their roots for analysis, she tapped into the revolutionary ethos that led many in the cultural left to reject the "establishment" in favor of the "exotic."

What made Le Guin exemplary in this endeavor was her unique saturation in an "exotic" thought system—Taoism—and her ability to communicate through a popular culture medium that resonated with American youth, who both reveled in and rejected the technological milieu in which they had come of age. That Le Guin stood to the side, as a woman, in a genre itself pushed to the side of the literary meritocracy, only increased her power to reach the disaffected but yearning young people who devoured her writing.

She used her medium well. Ursula Le Guin was the first person to win science fiction's two most prestigious awards in the same year, for the same book: *The Left Hand of Darkness*.[1] And then she won the same awards again later, with her novel *The Dispossessed*.[2] In a genre traditionally associated with technology—rivets, space ships, laser guns—and seasoned liberally with competition and machismo, Le Guin's science fiction contributions were driven more by the considerations of cultural anthropology, mythology, and other social sciences. A concern with the balancing of difficult dualities replaced the drive for conquest as a theme. The recurring motif of balance in Le Guin's fiction stems directly from her spiritual groundings in Taoism, one of the Asian philosophies that were becoming popular in America as many young people became disillusioned or disappointed with Judeo-Christian mores.[3]

In fact, Le Guin's upbringing placed her in a unique position to anticipate the trends and ideas that would dominate the social thinking of the 1960s and 1970s. A self-professed "congenital non-Christian," Le Guin grew up under the tutelage of educated and open-minded parents, who encouraged her to learn and explore. Born the last child and only girl in the family, Ursula knew she was wanted and valued as a female. In her 1985 foreword to her mother's collection of Native American stories, Ursula writes, "Theodora had a firm heritage of female independence and self-respect. Her sense of female solidarity was delicate and strong. She made her daughter feel a lifelong welcome, giving me the conviction that I had done the right thing in being born a woman—a gift many womanchildren are denied."[4]

Ursula's parents were ahead of their time in many ways. Her father was a well-known anthropologist at the University of California at Berkeley. Fascinated with cultures of all kinds, and himself a mix of Victorian mores, academic discipline, and almost protohippie sensibilities, he and his wife kept their house stocked with books from many traditions, finding value in them all, justification for any form of disrespect, dismissal, or bigotry in none. Her mother, Theodora, after rearing the children, collected and published Native American legends and stories and also wrote both children's and adults' versions of the story of Ishi, the last Yahi, whom Alfred Kroeber had befriended in the 1910s.

The Kroebers' home was a haven and gathering place for international students and scholars, and during the World War II years it was a refuge for European political dissidents. The Kroebers embraced and lived ideals that would take another half-century to reach widespread popular consciousness. They were and remained radically open-minded through decades when the political climate was not welcoming of such far-reaching cultural tolerance. There was a multicultural, feminist, and experiential bent to their thinking, born of academic training and modern rationalism, that would permeate the air their children breathed growing up, allowing them and encouraging them to find in the world what they would.[5]

One influence Ursula found, and loved, was the poetry of the *Tao Te Ching.* Taoism's well-known symbol of the yin and the yang represents its tenet of the natural beauty of balance. Yin and yang are in balance, and the aim of the philosophy is to observe how each integrates into each, achieving complementarity. Such complementarity was what was sorely missing in the unrest of the social upheavals of the 1960s. When there was one, Le Guin's social "agenda" as revealed in her fiction was concerned with promoting not single causes but underlying thematic shifts in consciousness; she was cracking open and exploring areas of Western thinking that had been and were still pushing life out of balance, and she was considering the dynamics of individual response and responsibility toward that encroaching imbalance. How could we (or *could* we) reattain the balance being lost in so many facets of contemporary life?

Gender Issues

The most deeply embedded duality in the human mind is arguably that of male/female. In 1967, Le Guin was working on a book that would contribute to many discussions of gender issues; using the laboratory of science fiction, she distilled the problem by eliminating it. She set *The Left Hand of Darkness* in an androgynous society. Though this was not an idea entirely new to science fiction (or speculative fiction, or "magical realism," if we may include Woolf's *Orlando* in that genre),[6] Le Guin's lyrical novel challenged its readers, more deeply than had previous efforts, to consider the social and personal implications of gender and genderlessness. Her work both anticipated and furthered conversation about the issues central to the growing women's and gay rights movements. Again, balance formed the core of the story, and not just in the "ooh golly" factor of hermaphroditism, or in the pastoralist drive to get away from rivets as an end in itself: Le Guin won her awards for a substantial and soulful consideration of humanness.[7]

The premise of *The Left Hand of Darkness* differs from its plot: the plot involves a diplomat and an Earthborn "alien" struggling to prevent the first war ever to occur on the planet Gethen. The premise, however, was a thought experiment in gender sociology. Le Guin speculated to herself about what a society would be like if it had existed to the point of technological advancement capable of space travel, but had never had any wars as a part of its history.[8] Though there are many possible ways to account for such a culture, Le Guin settled on androgyny as an explanation. Her thinking regarding pacifism, in this book, inextricably links the personal and sexual to the literally and deeply political. In her essay "Is Gender Necessary? Redux" she explains her motivation in creating the Gethenians: "I eliminated gender, to find out what was left. Whatever was left would be, presumably, simply human. It would define the area that is shared by men and women alike."[9] What she identified as the three most interesting implications of this predominant asexuality in a human species are the absence of war, the absence of exploitation, and the absence of sexuality as a continuous social factor in human relations.

The absence of war would follow both from the ways permanent sexual identity relates to territoriality and genetic ownership and from such a society's lack of nation-states large enough or inclined, as yet, to foment wars. She points out that androgyny does not eliminate human problems any more than it eliminates human joys:

> The people [of Gethen] seem to be as quarrelsome, competitive, and aggressive as we are; they have fights, murders, assassinations, feuds, forays and so on. But there have been no great invasions by peoples on the move, like the Mongols in Asia or the Whites in the New World: partly because Gethenian populations seem to remain stable in size, they do not move in large masses, or rapidly. . . . Nor have they formed large, hierarchically-governed nation-states, the mobilizable entity that is the essential factor in modern war.[10]

Le Guin's novel presented a less-than-subtle condemnation of war and violence, demonstrating that if the balance of one part of experience teeters out of control, its undeniable connection to other systems will endanger *them* as well.

For Le Guin's novel to work as an experiment in the absence of war, it has to presuppose that in cultures driven by conquest and competition for property, desirable territory and the rights to genetic offspring are under the control of the victor in conflict. The victor is both the most aggressive and strongest physically. Thus, in warring societies one segment of the species (the adult males) competes for the role of victor, the other segments of the population becoming the territory (adult females) and genetic property (children) of those in power.[11] Eliminate, as Gethen does, the predictable and continuous physical disparity between male and female, and the culture presumably would develop no drive in this particularly toxic direction. The culture would lack the territorial tensions and also not develop the scope of conflict that comes of nationalism.[12] Thus one result of social genderlessness is simply to limit the scope of social conflict possible. Le Guin's commentary on the phenomenon puts it this way:

> The "female principle" has historically been anarchic; that is, anarchy has historically been identified as female. The domain allotted to women— "the family," for example—is the area of order without coercion, rule by custom not by force. Men have reserved the structures of social power to themselves (and those few women whom they admit to it on male terms, such as queens, prime ministers); men make the wars and peaces, men make, enforce, and break the laws. On Gethen, the two polarities we perceive through our cultural conditioning as male and female are neither, and are in balance: consensus with authority, decentralizing with centralizing, flexible with rigid, circular with linear, hierarchy with network. But it is not a motionless balance, there being no such thing in life.[13]

Similarly, without exploitation of specific populations of the culture, exploitation of resources would never develop to the extent it has and does in gendered societies. Le Guin says her Gethenians have coped with technology more patiently than we have on Earth:

> They have absorb[ed] their technology rather than letting it overwhelm them. They have no myth of Progress at all. Their technology is slow to advance and carefully considered, rather than competitive or driven by a new-is-best mentality. This is why it has taken Gethen so long to reach the technological parity with the other planets in the novel, but it is also why their uses of and attitudes toward technology differ, and largely why they have resisted exploiting their natural resources.[14]

The last implication—lack of a fixed sexuality-as-integral-to-identity —was possibly the most disquieting for many readers: it raised the specter of homosexuality. Though she avoided dealing overtly with homosexuality in the book (a decision she later regretted and remedied in a short story), the possibility of being both male and female went beyond the scientifically interesting. She was writing within a culture that had historically condemned androgyny as perversion; her invented Gethenian culture viewed permanent sexual identity as perversion.[15] In removing gender, Le Guin's novel foregrounded the dominance it has for us gendered creatures, forcing us to consider the implications of our sexuality and of our humanity.

Civil Responsibility, Anarchy, Utopia

To many 1960s activists, the gap between rich and poor marked one of the decade's most obscene "imbalances." Le Guin's fictional response to the issue of material inequality presented as extreme a political and economic postulate as the creation of a culture without permanent sex: working anarchy. The anarchist leanings of elements of the counterculture found expression in several of Le Guin's works from the last part of the decade, most profoundly in her long novel *The Dispossessed: An Ambiguous Utopia*.[16] A tenuous balance in *The Dispossessed* is achieved by a culture of anarchists who live in a system of absolute trust, honesty, and contribution. The novel explores social and economic systems that force the reader to reconsider material inequality from the point of view of there being a possible alternative. The two sister planets in the book are both populated by humans, but one planet maintains economic and political systems like those on earth, while the other has been settled by anarchists. Le Guin describes her view of anarchism as a much more thoughtful, idealistic, and considered philosophy than the popular imagination would have it:

> Not bomb-in-the-pocket stuff, which is terrorism, whatever name it tries to dignify itself with; not the social Darwinist economic "libertarianism" of the far right; but anarchism, as prefigured in early Taoist thought, and expounded by Shelley and Kropotkin, Goldman and Goodman. Anarchism's principal target is the authoritarian state (capitalist or socialist); its principal moral-practical theme is cooperation (solidarity, mutual aid). It is the most idealistic, and to me the most interesting, of all political theories.[17]

Anarchism as a system could achieve balance rather than voracious continual economic growth, and it would work if it worked, Le Guin asserted. In other words, like any utopian dream, her invented world of

Fig. 4.1. Ursula Le Guin, circa 1974. *Lisa Kroeber*

anarchistic peace would work through the actualized idealism of its adherents. The truly moral participants in this system are conscious of the deep psychic impossibility of property and ownership (you can't take it with you). Freedom, real freedom, as well as education, has to be allowed in order for such a utopia to work. Hers is an "ambiguous utopia" because Le Guin recognizes that the idealization of absolute sharing would also have to rely on absolute trust in the community. As many 1960s communards would realize, communities built on trust, morality, and idealism can be fragile. As in real-world attempts at utopia, Le Guin's society suffers from human frailty, tendencies that draw characters back to self-centeredness and away from the ideal.

Le Guin expressed anarchist sentiment in other works as well. In the one story in which the culture *has* achieved balance, the particular balance is not a good one. In her fantasy short story "The Ones Who Walk Away from Omelas,"[18] Le Guin posed an experiment on the words of William James in his essay "The Moral Philosopher and the Mortal Life" (of which she comments that "the dilemma of the American conscience can hardly be better stated"):

> If the hypothesis were offered us of a world in which Messrs. Fourier's and Bellamy's and Morris's utopias should all be outdone, and millions kept permanently happy on the simple condition that a certain lost soul on the far-off edge of things should lead a life of lonely torment, what except a superficial and independent sort of emotion can it be which would make us immediately feel, even though an impulse arose in us to clutch at the happiness so offered, how hideous a thing would be its enjoyment when deliberately accepted as the fruit of such a bargain?[19]

Le Guin's story answers James. "The Ones Who Walk Away from Omelas" tells a deceptively simple parable of the times, beginning with a description of a beautiful and blissful society in which everything is perfect, as the narrator summarizes:

> A boundless and generous contentment, a magnanimous triumph felt not against some outer enemy but in communion with the finest and fairest in the souls of all men everywhere and the splendor of the world's summer: this is what swells the hearts of the people of Omelas, and the victory they celebrate is that of life.[20]

But the voice of the narrator intrudes after the delectable description: "Do you believe? Do you accept the festival, the city, the joy? No? Then let me describe one more thing."[21] The catch for this utopian society is the unspeakably horrific suffering of a single child, kept locked in a closet in one of the government buildings. Everyone in Omelas knows it is there, and everyone knows it is the reason for the happiness of everyone else. Omelas thrives because of its pain.

This is not a transparent scapegoat story of willing sacrifice, as a Christian interpretation would allow: in the Bible, Jesus knew that he would suffer and accepted his "bitter cup," even if reluctantly. In Omelas, the child is merely a random victim, the hideous balance of suffering and happiness completely arbitrary. The societal blame is much more stark and challenging than that in a story of a willing scapegoat, and the only moral response to such a system is to leave. And yet, a simple departure does not release the tormented child, just as the exodus of the idealistic to communal removes in the American wilderness does not solve the problems of social and economic injustice.

Environmentalism

By the turn of the decade Le Guin had become completely disgusted by the U.S. war in Vietnam, a war she perceived as useless wholesale destruction, both of human life and of the environment. Environmental concerns were also gaining a foothold in the cultural consciousness of the time. Rachel Carson's landmark book *Silent Spring* had had a decade of influence on the environmental movement; Greenpeace had been established for over a year; and issues of pollution, imperialism, overpopulation, industrialization, and environmental violence were paramount when Le Guin published her 1972 novella *The Word for World Is Forest*.[22] Her stance in this work was both antiwar and proplanet, telling the story of a pristine planet under siege by Earth-descended invaders.

At the heart of the story was what Le Guin saw as a complex of destructive attitudes and ideas in our culture, once again stemming from dualistic imbalances. In the very year that the term *ecofeminism* was coined, Le Guin anticipated and illuminated its concerns with this story. Ecofeminism's main claim is that the environment is oppressed by the same agents of social thinking that oppress women; in other words, that in a patriarchal struggle for conquest, both Nature and Woman are perceived as the Other to be subdued and conquered by Man.[23]

In *The Word for World Is Forest*, Le Guin contrasts the worldview of conquest of the land versus a worldview of harmony with it. The inhabitants of the planet in the story are not only deeply enmeshed in their natural world but also have an attachment to their unconscious, through dreams, that the Western culture she criticizes has lost. A culture that would make war not only against its political enemy but also against vegetation, as the United States was doing with its herbicides in Vietnam, could not belong to the nature it was fighting, and thus had lost touch with its own true nature as well. There is thus something profoundly out of balance in a dualism that considers "civilization" superior to "nature." In her essay "Women/Wilderness," she says that those who are truly aware of our dependence on the environment distrust that word, Nature. Nature as not including humanity, Nature as what is not human, that Nature is a construct made by Man, not a real thing. . . . [T]he misogyny that shapes every aspect of our civilization is the institutionalized form of male fear and hatred of what they have denied and therefore cannot know, cannot share: that wild country, the being of women.[24]

The Word for World Is Forest relates a bitter coming of age for the inhabitants of the planet, who learn to hate and kill from their new enemies and thus forever lose their innocence, as well as their home. Le Guin's concern with the environment when she wrote it was personal, recognizing the urgency of environmental crisis wherever it occurred. Neither nostalgia nor sentimentalism, but rather common sense and a deep-seated commitment to Taoist principles, prompted her to call in her fiction for peace and a sustainable lifestyle on this planet, for if a lifestyle is not in some sort of equilibrium, some sort of sustainability, what can it be but self-destructive?

The environmentalists of the 1960s and 1970s were giving further voice to what many indigenous peoples had been saying for centuries: an economy that relies on war for growth is dangerous; but less obviously, an economy that is dying if it is *not* growing is just as sick, for it forces a relationship with the environment that is pathological, and ultimately will lead to war, consciously or not:

Most nations have been using the lion's share of their state budgets for weapons, both to guard against one another and to control their own poor. Weapons also become one of the major exports of wealthy nations to poor nations. Poor nations grow increasingly indebted to wealthy nations while buying weapons to repress their own impoverished masses.[25]

Insistence on expansion is the strategy of a virus, leading to the death of the host, Le Guin recognized. Having lived in the Pacific Northwest most of her life, she witnessed the destruction of old-growth forests and the encroachment of urban sprawl into once-healthy ecosystems. Like contemporary ecofeminism, Le Guin's fiction would argue that human-versus-human war is symptomatic of, but not separate from, the human war against our environment, and that both reflect deeply entrenched and deeply gendered traditions of oppression.

Marginalized Genres

In the early sixties, the literary canon, as accepted by the literary "establishment," was beginning its long crumble into the postmodern. Le Guin consciously—though not calculatedly—used science fiction, fantasy, young adult and children's literature, and other genres traditionally relegated to literary ghettos to express her ideas during this period. She confesses that at first she wrote in the "ghetto" genres in order to be free from the scrutiny to which "Great Lit'richah" is subjected:

> It took me years to realize that I chose to work in such despised, marginal genres as science fiction, fantasy, young adult, precisely because they were excluded from critical, academic, canonical supervision, leaving the artist free; it took ten more years before I had the wits and guts to see and say that the exclusion of the genres from "literature" is unjustified, unjustifiable, and a matter not of quality but of politics.[26]

Le Guin felt that, in addition to its potential for being well-wrought and insightful literature, science fiction as experimentation could also clear the palate of expectation and offer a laboratory setting for logical (or illogical) possibilities in situations outside the real.[27] The "what if" question posed by the suspension of reality in science fiction and fantasy provides a space for some answers, in much the same way as the utopian and communitarian experimentation of the sixties era did. As Margaret Atwood points out, Le Guin worked so successfully within the genre that she burst it asunder: "'Science fiction' is the box in which [Le Guin's] work is usually placed, but it's an awkward box: it bulges with discards from elsewhere . . . [but] the membranes separating [its] subdivisions are permeable, and osmotic flow from one to another is the norm."[28]

By writing in a genre marginalized by the mainstream, writing as a woman in that heavily male genre, and melding the ancient philosophy of Taoism to futurist imaginings, Ursula Le Guin was able to address the most cutting and important issues of the day. Her work exposed society's implicit assumptions and pointed out, gently or harshly, the insanity of oppression, of destruction, of imbalance.

NOTES

1. Ursula K. Le Guin, *The Left Hand of Darkness* (New York: Ace Books, 1991). This won the Hugo and Nebula Awards for 1969.

2. Ursula K. Le Guin, *The Dispossessed: An Ambiguous Utopia* (New York: HarperPrism, 1974). This was the Hugo and Nebula Awards winner for 1972.

3. Taoism joined other Eastern religions in a faddish abandonment of what was perceived as the failure of Western traditions to resolve problems. Aldous Huxley's explorations into drug-induced mysticism, Norman O. Brown's expansion of Freudian ideas, and even the arrival of the gurus in Oregon illustrated how people wanted a reliable spiritual identity and were not always able to find it.

4. Ursula K. Le Guin, "Introduction," in Theodora Kroeber, *The Inland Whale* (Covelo, Calif.: Yolla Bolly Press, 1985), 4.

5. Kroeber's work on the daily lives of the California Indians, much of which he learned from his friendship with Ishi, was to become a popular sourcebook for the counterculture's efforts to lead a simplified life. See Allen J. Matusow, *The Unravelling of America: A History of Liberalism in the 1960s* (New York: Harper and Row, 1984), 298.

6. Virginia Woolf, *Orlando: A Biography* (New York: New American Library, 1960).

7. It is also the best known of the early feminist utopia/dystopia novels that began to chip a niche for women writers in the science fiction genre generally; an examination of woman-friendly or woman-inclusive science fiction reveals that the real explosion of this type of work occurred during the seventies and early eighties, especially anticipating and participating in overtly feminist "cyberpunk" fiction. See Tonya Browning, "A Foray into History: A Brief Historical Survey of Women Writers of Science Fiction" (http://www.cwrl.utexas.edu/~tonya/Tonya/sf/history.html), 1.

8. Ursula K. Le Guin, *Dancing at the Edge of the World: Thoughts on Words, Women, Places* (New York: Grove Press, 1989), 10–11. This essay was originally published as a discussion of *The Left Hand of Darkness* in *Aurora* in 1976; later, she revised her thinking on a few of its points and republished it with new commentary in 1987.

9. Le Guin, *Dancing*, 10. See also Carolyn Heilbrun's 1964 discussion *Toward a Recognition of Androgyny* (New York: W. W. Norton and Co., 1973).

10. Ibid.

11. Rape as an actual policy of war is documented as recently as the Serbo-Croatian war of the 1990s—its "rationale" being the barbaric notion that since a woman impregnated by a man carries that man's genetic inheritance, she has become his territory and her children his possessions. See Martina E. Vandenberg, "Kosovo: Rape as a Weapon of 'Ethnic Cleansing,'" *Human Rights Watch* 12.3 (March 2000): 1–39.

12. Le Guin, *Dancing,* 11.

13. Ibid., 12.

14. Ibid.

15. After all, when her Gethenians are in their reproductive phase, their only function is sexual gratification. It makes sense to them that a person permanently sexed is a person permanently aroused, and thus not entirely rational. ("Have you ever lived in a small apartment with a tabby cat in heat?" asks Le Guin by way of comparison.) Le Guin, *Dancing,* 13.

16. Le Guin, *The Dispossessed.*

17. Ursula K. Le Guin, *The Wind's Twelve Quarters* (New York: Harper and Row, 1975), 260.

18. Ibid., 262.

19. Ibid., 263.

20. Ibid., 264.

21. Ibid.

22. Ursula K. Le Guin, *The Word for World Is Forest,* (New York: Putnam, 1972).

23. See *Ecofeminism and the Sacred*, ed. Carol J. Adams (New York: Continuum, 1995).

24. Le Guin, *Dancing*, 163.

25. Rosemary Radford Ruether, "Ecofeminism: Symbolic and Social Connections of the Oppression of Women and the Domination of Nature," in Adams, ed., *Ecofeminism and the Sacred*, 13–24.

26. Le Guin, *Dancing*, 234.

27. See Ursula K. Le Guin, "Introduction," in *The Norton Book of Science Fiction: North American Science Fiction, 1960–1990*, ed. Ursula K. Le Guin and Brian Attebery (New York: W. W. Norton and Co., 1993).

28. Margaret Atwood, "The Queen of Quinkdom," *New York Review of Books*, Sept. 26, 2002, 23–25.

PART II

Bridge

5

Ambassadors with Hips
Katherine Dunham, Pearl Primus, and the Allure of Africa in the Black Arts Movement

Julia L. Foulkes

In 1959, William Tubman, the president of the West African nation of Liberia, invited the African American dancer-anthropologist Pearl Primus to establish a performing arts center in Monrovia, the capital city. Just a few years later, the president of Senegal sought out Katherine Dunham, also an African American dancer-anthropologist, to perform a similar task for his country. These invitations came to Dunham and Primus at the end of their performing careers and at the beginning of a new stage in their careers as educators and community leaders. By the 1960s, Dunham and Primus had reached the top of the dance profession, securing fame by putting visions of Africa and the Caribbean on American stages. Interaction with newly independent nations in Africa in the early 1960s resonated back in the United States as the fight for civil rights for African Americans increased in intensity. Dunham, Primus, and the cultural traditions of Africa helped define a new surge of activity among black artists and intellectuals that came to be known as the Black Arts movement.[1]

Katherine Dunham and Pearl Primus influenced the Black Arts movement so that dance itself created a bridge in the 1960s between the United States and Africa. As educators and community leaders promoting dance, Primus and Dunham extended their knowledge of Africa and the Caribbean beyond theatrical stages to the streets of East St. Louis, Illinois, and New York City, thereby deepening ties within the African diaspora. And, as women in a Blacks Arts movement known for its masculinist tenor, they altered the message of the movement from one of racial exclusivity to a more universalist ethos.

The study of anthropology directed Dunham and Primus in defining their contributions to the African diaspora and the Black Arts movement. Born outside Chicago in 1909, Dunham pursued both dance and anthropology when she attended the University of Chicago in the early 1930s. She sought to combine her interests, learning not just *what* people dance but *why* they dance. When she received a grant from the Rosenwald Foundation, she got a chance to investigate just that by traveling to the Caribbean in 1935–36, spending most of her time in Jamaica and Haiti. There she observed secret rituals in rural areas and social dancing in the main cities and came back to Chicago bursting with choreographic ideas. She presented *L'Ag'Ya*, named for a Martinique fighting dance, in January 1938, under the auspices of the Chicago unit of the Federal Theatre Project, one of the divisions of the New Deal's Works Progress Administration (WPA). This success brought her to New York City, where she was hailed as black America's leading dancer by the NAACP's magazine, *The Crisis*, when she graced its cover in 1941.[2]

Attention in the dance world soon shifted from Dunham, however, to a newcomer, Pearl Primus. Born in Trinidad in 1919, Primus grew up in New York City from the age of two and early on set her sights on becoming a doctor. Like Dunham, Primus sought a path beyond racial discrimination through education, one of the few avenues open to African American women. Primus attended Hunter College, majored in biology, and began preparing for medical school soon after she graduated. She encountered discrimination in looking for jobs as a medical technician, however, and found instead a job at the National Youth Administration (NYA), another program of the New Deal. First working backstage repairing costumes for the show *America Dances*, Primus landed onstage when a dancer failed to show up one night. The event prompted Primus to take dance classes, and she ended up receiving a scholarship at the New Dance Group in the early 1940s. In 1943, she walked away with the honor of being picked by John Martin, the influential *New York Times* dance critic, as the most promising new dancer of the season.[3]

The careers of Dunham and Primus converged in their combining of anthropological fieldwork and choreography. Like Dunham in the 1930s, Primus received crucial financial support from the Rosenwald Foundation and, in 1948, chose to go to Africa. Born in the United States, Dunham focused more on the Caribbean; Primus, born in Trinidad, focused more on Africa. Each woman looked back one step: Dunham to great-grandparents from Haiti and Primus to West Africa, the home of long-ago relatives. Their choices reflected the searching for roots that many African Americans began to undertake in the twentieth century and encompassed the migratory patterns of enslaved laborers, from the shores of Africa to the Caribbean and, eventually, the United States.

Armed with DDT and a gun, Primus stepped beyond her birthplace of Trinidad to travel to West Africa, including the Gold Coast (now Ghana), Angola, Liberia, Senegal, and the Belgian Congo (first Zaire, now the Democratic Republic of the Congo).[4] Thinking the culture of African cities distorted by jitterbugging and commercial influences, Primus journeyed to the more remote areas of each country to live, work, and dance with various tribes. She soon was braiding her hair in their styles, going barefooted and bare-breasted, and consolidating her connections to various Africans with her dancing abilities; the Watusi dancers of the Congo renamed Primus "Omowale," meaning "child returned home."[5] Primus's experiences in Africa were similar to Dunham's earlier experiences in the Caribbean, where she too had been accepted into the societies she was observing. When Dunham returned to the United States, she committed herself to promoting the beauty and clarifying the meaning of Caribbean rituals and dances; Primus returned from Africa with a similar purpose. Her performances became more like lecture-demonstrations in which she would explain the significance of certain rituals before dancing them.

Anthropology strengthened these women's beliefs in the forceful ties binding together the peoples of the African diaspora, revealing both the distinctiveness of various peoples within the diaspora and the common gestures and movement that they believed stretched from Africa through the Caribbean to the United States. During this same period, anthropology also attracted the writer Zora Neale Hurston, who primarily investigated the religious beliefs, folklore, and language of black Americans in the South in the 1930s and wrote both fiction and non-fiction based on this research. All college graduates who pursued graduate education in anthropology, Hurston, Dunham, and Primus used anthropology as a legitimizing force for their explorations of the peoples of the African diaspora. By the beginning of the twentieth century, following the path-breaking insights of Franz Boaz (who served as a mentor to Hurston), anthropologists promoted the belief that cultural traits were acquired and learned, not innate. Some, like Margaret Mead, applied this idea to understandings of male and female roles; others, like Melville Herskovits, focused on the cultural roots of racial distinctions. This represented a radical leap in regard to common understandings of race: refuting the biological determinism of eugenics, cultural relativity overturnè the idea that skin color signified fundamental dissimilarities (and, for many, in-equalities) among people. Anthropology—and cultural relativism in par-ticular—aided Dunham and Primus in combating their marginal status in America, in addition to that of black peoples around the world, by explaining and defending various cultural patterns.[6]

Performances around the world in the 1950s extended their anthropo-logical insights worldwide. Dunham began touring after World War II, first in a tour to Mexico, on to particular acclaim in London and Paris, and then for the next ten years through South America, Australia, New Zealand, Asia, and back to Europe. Primus also toured worldwide in the 1950s, including an appearance before King George IV of England in 1951, and often went back to Africa. During a European tour in the late 1940s a critic called Dunham an "ambassador with hips," a label that recognized her worldwide impact but also modified it with an attribute of much African dancing—movement propelled from the hips.[7] This modi-fication reinforced certain stereotypes of black peoples (particularly their supposed "natural" lack of inhibition and increased sexual appetite) but also functioned as a way to allude to these dancers' status as women operating on the international scene. The epithet "ambassador with hips" reveals the particular role Dunham and Primus carved in their interna-tional careers: they worked outside conventional political and diplomatic channels most often reserved for men, and they used bodies in motion as a way in which to create ties between the disparate peoples of the African diaspora.

They did so in their writings and interviews, in their consultancies in African countries, but especially in their performances. Dunham's perfor-mances, for example, featured dances from a variety of traditions next to one another. A typical program started off with *Afrique*, what she called a "native air"; *Brazilian Suite*, a collection of dances to various Brazilian rhythms followed; then came *Barrelhouse Blues*, set in an American blues club; and a piece about Havana in the 1910s ended the evening. Not only the stories and settings formed links between Africa, Brazil, Cuba, and the United States; her company did as well. On tour, Dunham lost and then picked up dancers and musicians along the way. So Sighè Vitale, a young Italian woman of indeterminate heritage whose father was the superintendent of the Museum of the Italian Africa (about Ethiopia, which had been annexed by Italy in 1935), danced next to Mamadou Badiane, a female Senegalese dancer who joined the troupe in Paris; the Haitian drummer Jean Marie Durand played next to the Brazilian drummer Jairo.[8]

"Cubans, Brazilians, Trinidadians and recently Haitians have invaded Paris, London, Buenos Aires, Mexico City, in fact every great world Capitol, diffusing their rhythms and songs, providing perfect patterns of acculturation," Dunham wrote in typewritten notes in 1955, and she took some credit for that because of "the impact of a theatrical company such as ours." To her this meant that "each year brings more evidence of the interchangeability of cultures and of the universality of true rhythms."[9] Although Dunham did not specify what kind of rhythms were "true," her statement reflected both her and Primus's belief in the universality of artistic impulses and the necessity of including African music and dance into the "higher" realm of art recognized in the United States and Europe. To do this they stressed the narrative and ritualistic aspects of the rhythms and movements specific to sites within the African diaspora; that is, they emphasized the meanings and relatedness of dance and music to life cycles such as birth, marriage, and death and, most important, the ties that bind a community.

These attempts to show the universality and commonality of African-derived music and dance were less than smooth, however, despite Dunham's exhortation in 1955. Dunham's *Southland* demonstrated the tenuousness of the links. A dramatic piece that premiered in January 1951 in Santiago, Chile, *Southland* was the most overt political piece Dunham ever choreographed. She took as her subject the lynching of a black man accused by a white woman of a crime he did not commit. Lynching was not a new subject in dance or song, given dramatic effect most famously by Billie Holiday's rendition of "Strange Fruit"; Primus gave a bold dramatization in her own *Strange Fruit*, a 1944 solo. Dunham's *Southland* was prompted by continued lynchings in the United States and the failure of Congress to pass an anti-lynching bill, a battle that the National Association for the Advancement of Colored People (NAACP) had been spearheading since 1918.[10] But events in South America also impacted on Dunham's choreography. Earlier in her tour of South America, Dunham had been denied a room in the Esplanade hotel in São Paulo. She ended up filing a suit against the hotel, an act that prompted the passing of Brazil's first law prohibiting racial discrimination in public accommodations. Even though Brazil had a larger population of dark-skinned peoples than the United States, and a constitution that guaranteed equality for all its citizens, racial segregation persisted. Dunham brought attention to these issues in Brazil because she had suffered similar discrimination in the United States and spoke out against it there. She followed the same strategy in Brazil.

Dunham's immersion in these global issues of race reveals just how spotty inclusion of black peoples into the great capitals of the world was. And while she helped bring attention to the disgrace and unfairness of racial policies, she lost diplomatic favor. *Southland* roused immediate criticism from the U.S. State Department and prompted Dunham to perform the piece only once more, in Paris, a few years later. Dunham continues to insist that the piece resulted in her never receiving funds for her world tours and in the snubbing of her performances by American embassies in the years following the initial performance.[11]

In the mid-1950s, when the U.S. State Department began sending American artists abroad as cultural emissaries, Dunham was not selected. She continued, however, being an ambassador of the African diaspora by her own management and determination. She retreated to Haiti often, developing a number of projects, from the establishment of a museum of cultural and fine arts to the creation of a medical center.[12] When she received little support from the Haitian government for her many projects, she turned her attention to Jamaica. In late 1960, Dunham suggested starting a cultural and educational institute there that combined her technique and choreographic ideas with native Jamaican dance and dancers. As in Haiti, the plan received little support, primarily because native dancers claimed that her international prestige upset their domestic fame and created unfair competition.[13] These situations reveal that Dunham remained an outsider in Haiti and Jamaica, a status aggravated by her international success and despite her knowledge and pivotal role in bringing more attention to the traditions of the Caribbean.

These conflicts arose even more when Dunham and Primus turned their attention to Africa. On Primus's first trip to Africa in 1948, for example, Nigerian dancers thought she was there to "steal" their dances and return to the United States and make money performing them. This rumor prompted her to write an editorial in the leading paper there, defending her visit and the "exchange of cultures throughout the world."[14] This did not deter Primus from continuing her trip and going back often in the 1950s, a decade she spent traveling to Europe and Israel as well as Africa, holding only occasional performances in the United States.

Fig. 5.1. Afi Kong, Percival Borde, Pearl Primus, and Chief Fagbemi Ajanaku in Nigeria, early 1960s. *Photograph courtesy American Dance Festival Archives*

Primus also intermittently worked toward a doctorate in anthropology at New York University and married Percival Borde, a Trinidadian dancer and musician, in 1954; she bore a son a year later. Her family accompanied her to Liberia in 1959, when she accepted President Tubman's invitation to establish a performing arts center there. (She received a similar offer from the presidents of Ghana and the Sudan but turned them down because she did not have the time to do those as well).[15] Primus went off to Liberia viewing the venture as the climax of her career, combining her talents as dancer, choreographer, and anthropologist.[16]

Primus's relations with Liberia and Dunham's with Haiti were part of an interaction of African Americans with other parts of the African diaspora that had been growing throughout the twentieth century. Proponents of Pan-Africanism, the name of a movement that sought to gather intellectuals and politicians to work together to end colonialism in Africa and advance the interests of peoples of the African diaspora, met first in 1900 and again four more times in the first half of the twentieth century. Figures like Marcus Garvey, C. L. R. James, and W. E. B. DuBois promoted linkages between peoples of the African disapora, even though they held differing views on what those linkages should be—from Garvey's advocacy of return to Africa to DuBois's attempts to coordinate efforts against oppression and poverty worldwide.[17]

These politically focused efforts paralleled the kinds of cultural activities that Dunham and Primus spearheaded. In fact, the split between these activities demonstrated the different roles men and women had in the larger movement to define an African diaspora. Dunham and Primus offered cultural visions, and their successes spoke to the limited yet influential role these women carved out for themselves. Although they may not have spoken before the United Nations or at Pan-African congresses, they had far more contact with some African leaders than many male politicians had. Conforming to gender stereotypes that suggested that women excelled in education and the arts, Dunham and Primus pushed those arenas to have worldwide political impact.

Primus's activities in Liberia were a good example of what could be accomplished. Unlike most African nations, Liberia had been an independent state since 1847 and was originally set up as a place where freed slaves could return. The population consisted of settlers with European-African lineage, freed slaves from across the Atlantic, and indigenous peoples. William Tubman, the president elected in 1944, took as his mission to champion the tribes of the interior over the ruling elite in the coastal cities. His call to Primus was a part of this mission at a time when nations across the African continent were re-defining their national heritages to throw off colonial influences and celebrate native African traditions.

For Primus, the challenge was to preserve traditional arts against the encroachment of modern ways. She recognized that the *reasons* for traditional dances were disappearing; that is, the religious, tribal rituals preserved in dance were losing a battle against the secular, urbanizing influences of contemporary times. Her task, then, was to "find, encourage and train the folk artist and provide him with outlets through actual theatrical experiences—to make of him a performing artist."[18] This was quite a balancing act—to preserve indigenous dances within a foreign, Western model—for a "performing artist" was an imported role in Liberia, where traditionally there was no distinction between performer and audience. And yet Primus also stated that she was "not out to change Liberian dances or art forms, rather to give them unity."[19] Although she never defined exactly what that meant, her approach included some change, particularly in making the dances more suitable to a theatrical stage.

For almost two years, Primus remained in Liberia with her family and with the full support of the Liberian government, which gave her "carte blanche" to do what she thought needed to be done. Despite this endorsement, Primus encountered resistance to her leadership. Although specific evidence is spotty, in private notes Primus admitted to the jealousies, "misunderstanding, suspicions, anger, indifference, and confusion" that her efforts had aroused. Most prominently, she insisted that the first performances of this new troupe were not a recital by herself and her husband but of over one hundred Liberian artists.[20]

Dunham received a similarly ambivalent response in Senegal, where President Senghor invited her to advise him on the task of setting up a national dance company. Unlike Liberia, Senegal had just untangled itself from French colonial rule, in 1960, and declared itself a republic. President Senghor was a leading force in the renewal of Négritude in the 1950s, a cultural corollary to Pan-Africanism, primarily among French-speaking Africans. So Senghor's call to Dunham was similar to Tubman's call to Primus: to define and preserve the cultural contributions of his country. Like Primus, Dunham wanted to uphold indigenous arts and dances, and this was a position that the Senegalese government seemed to support.[21] But she encountered resistance to this idea from local dancers. An edge of defensiveness crept into Dunham's talks during this period, a devotion to "speak freely, whatever the consequence," and even in opposition to those present. Primarily, Dunham advocated training and education in the traditions of the past. While such Western traditions as ballet and modern dance could be included in training programs, they should be secondary and "taught within their historical context." All this was to avoid the presentation of "entertainment, or at most a superficial view of a trait of the culture of a people," which she believed fell into an exploitation that was yet another bond of colonialism. She recommended that African governments forestall this tendency, putting monies into training programs and managing the export of artists and companies with a control that "may border on dictatorship."[22] While this political control may have seemed antithetical to artistic expression, Dunham stressed the urgency of educating performing artists in this way so that the artist could serve "as an ideology within his country, as an ambassador outside."[23] Dunham's role in Africa, then, emphasized the political utility and impact of the arts and argued for worldwide broadcasting of past traditions to distinguish the new nations.

The consultancies of Dunham and Primus brought out the difficulties in creating ties between diverse groups of black peoples. Chosen because of their abilities to celebrate and unite the variety within the African diaspora, they were more successful at this on the stages of the United States than within the changing societies of Liberia and Senegal. In Africa, they encountered struggles with a growing urban, secular population trying to define a contemporary cosmopolitan ethos that went beyond traditions and rural heritage. And their efforts may have roused fears of continuing cultural imperialism and exploitative tourism for many Africans determined to run and define their own nations' destinies after years of harsh colonial rule.

Their work in Africa, however, had great impact on their reputations and in what they chose to do next: return to the United States. Relocating physically as well as mentally in the 1960s, Dunham settled in East St. Louis in 1967 and Primus in New York City in 1963, both determined to influence the communities in which they were living. They continued to celebrate the dance traditions of Africa, but they did so within specific American communities at a time when "black was beautiful" and Africa was heralded as the common mother of all black peoples. They brought home their attention to past traditions as a way in which to distinguish and unify the African diaspora.

Africa had served as a point of origin for other black intellectuals and artists but more often, as in the Harlem Renaissance, as a place to measure the distance that African Americans had traveled in cultural terms. Alain Locke, the rhetorician of the Harlem Renaissance, held up certain of the arts of Africa—especially sculpture—for their elegance of form, but did so to encourage African American artists to apply that elegance to their own artworks (as white modernists were doing), so as to be included in elite institutions.[24] In the mid–twentieth century, aided by the anthropological, artistic, and educational work of Dunham and Primus, artists and intellectuals embraced African arts as they were, not as a step toward "white" standards. This movement coalesced in the mid-1960s as the Black Arts movement, a cultural analogue to the Black Power movement. In 1965, LeRoi Jones (later Amiri Baraka) formed the Black Arts Repertory Theater in Newark, New Jersey, and in New York City, Chicago, Detroit, and San Francisco, other organizations such as presses and magazines devoted to publishing African American writers soon followed. An attempt to tie the arts firmly and wholly to black identity and the black community defined the movement. "Black art must expose the enemy, praise the people, and support the revolution," wrote Ron Karenga, one of the philosophers of the movement, in 1968.[25] Proponents within the movement saw Africa as the common origin for all blacks but also as a place where "art for art's sake"—a modernist credo—made no sense, where art instead was fused with life, embedded in communities, and served functional purposes.

This was a message that Primus and Dunham had long been promoting through the medium of dance. Returning from conflictual experiences in Africa in the early 1960s, they now delivered that message to a new audience and changed it in subtle ways to fit the new political context. Like the well-known writers associated with the Black Arts movement, such as LeRoi Jones and critic Larry Neal, Dunham and Primus focused on and criticized racism more overtly. Dunham, in fact, confronted racism in new ways when she moved to East St. Louis from Dakar. She was arrested early on, in July 1967, because she protested the arrest of a young black man on the suspicion of breaking windows. Darryl Braddix, who had taken classes at her school, was part of a crowd who had attended a lecture by H. Rap Brown and Stokely Carmichael, leaders of the Black Power movement, at Lincoln High School. Tensions between black activists and the police were common, and Braddix's arrest was part of the attempt to stem the brewing anger and frustration of the poor and discriminated-against in East St. Louis. Accustomed to being listened to, Dunham interrogated the police about the arrest and found herself arrested as well for insubordination. When police later found out who she was, she received an official apology.[26] But she had discovered what most blacks experienced in East St. Louis, and this thrust her into activism and, in particular, tied her to the young people of the community.

Primus also explicitly explained her work as a response to racism, saying, "[Dance] is the scream which eases for awhile the terrible frustration common to all human beings who, because of race, creed or color are 'invisible.' Dance is the fist with which I will fight the scheming ignorance of prejudice. It is the veiled contempt I feel for those who patronize with false smiles, handouts, empty promises, insincere compliments."[27] This more militant spirit infused most artists of the Black Arts movement, and male choreographers such as Eleo Pomare in *Blues Jungle* depicted the ravaged life of poor urban African Americans that demonstrated the effects of racism.

Fig. 5.2. Katherine Dunham teaching at Southern Illinois University, early 1960s. *Special Collections Research Center, Morris Library, Southern Illinois University, Carbondale, IL*

In contrast to rising African American male choreographers such as Pomare and Donald McKayle, Primus and Dunham continued to concentrate on African and Caribbean traditions in their performances, rather than on depictions of contemporary American scenes. In part, this was a continuation of earlier interests, but it also reflected the subtly different role Dunham and Primus had in the Black Arts movement. First of all, they initiated much of the interest in Africa and substantiated much of it with their anthropological fieldwork. Their diplomatic efforts in African nations also forced them to confront the difficulties in creating unified presentations of black peoples. Instead of emphasizing racial uniformity specifically, they hoped to bring out continuous strands within diverse cultural traditions. Unlike the political impetus that led other artists in the Black Arts movement to adopt an exclusive racial focus—and despite the resistance they encountered in Africa—the experiences of Dunham and Primus led them to hold on to a universal message for the arts. Primus, for example, in 1964 pronounced that dance—as best exemplified by its role in African life—communicated "the fundamental knowledge of the human race."[28] And in addition to speaking out against racism and for civil rights, she still maintained that a universalist message could be met: "I'm learning to deliberately reach beyond the color of the skin and go into people's souls and hearts and search out that part of them, black or white, which is common to all."[29] That universality may not have been specifically defined, and certainly was refracted through the brittle shards of racism, but it was a goal and hope that differed from the "estrangement" advocated by the poet and musician James Stewart, who argued that black artists remove themselves entirely from "white" institutions and standards of art.[30]

This commitment of Primus and Dunham to universality came from their workings with African peoples, their reconciliation with and use of "Western" theatrical standards, and their attempt to create a diasporic vision of African traditions of dance. And these goals and experiences may be attributable to their role as women—and older women at that—in a movement dominated by young African American men. In contrast to the more narrow, politically virile thrust of many of the male artists of the Black Arts movement, Dunham and Primus offered a mediated position, one that incorporated current political issues in the United States but looked, with hope, toward a broader international movement.

To accomplish this, they turned away from consultancies in Africa, where they received resistance to these ideas; returned to communities in the United States; and centered their activities in education and community outreach. Dunham developed the Performing Arts Training Center (PATC) in East St. Louis as an outgrowth of a Southern Illinois University project. Located at an old high school across the street from her home, PATC strived to reach young people on the streets, in gangs, in violent situations, and to re-direct their frustration and anger into the arts. For Dunham, the emphasis needed to be on African arts, because she saw this as the key to survival, growth, and pride—knowing where you come from.[31] To that end, she invited Mor Thiam, a drummer from Senegal, to teach in the program. She choreographed works that had direct relevance to the community, including *Ode to Taylor Jones* in 1968, a tribute to a local civil rights leader, and coordinated a memorial concert to Martin Luther King Jr., with the reminder that "our way . . . of honoring a fallen hero has been the way of Africa, of drums, of verse, religious dance."[32]

In New York City, Primus concentrated on exposing elementary-school children to different cultures via dance. Funded by the U.S. Office of Education in 1965–66, Primus worked on a project combining dance and anthropological content to teach children, ages six to eleven, about world cultures. She traveled to various schools around New York—from privileged private schools such as the Little Red School House in Greenwich Village, catering predominantly to white children, to a public school in East Harlem, populated by African American and Latino students. In language reminiscent of more recent times, Primus argued that "all teachers improve their capabilities to the degree that they are able to express themselves non-verbally as well as verbally." For children, this pedagogical approach would not only enhance motor skills and expressiveness but foster identification with children "in other areas of the world through an understanding of and creative participation in their dance."[33]

If one of the transformations of the 1960s was the growth of black pride, increasingly centered on a common homeland of Africa, Dunham and Primus deserve credit for promoting the link, a phenomenon more often attributed to the male artists and intellectuals of the Black Arts movement. Adding these women to the lexicon of this movement that has mainly been understood by looking at writers alters our understanding of it and its influence on 1960s culture. The accomplishments of Dunham and Primus shift the timeline of the movement to include cultural exchanges that preceded the mid-1960s, to re-claim the overlooked role of women in initiating and shaping the movement, and to reveal messages other than racial exclusivity that were a part of the movement.

Dance linked these contributions by its inescapable focus on bodies. If a person's skin color held such significance, dance showcased what was at stake—the finite limits of appearance. This led to an embrace of dance by leaders of the 1960s, from Ron Karenga to Malcolm X, both of whom claimed that "all Blacks can dance."[34] Malcolm X went further, interpreting his plunge into dance at a pad party in the 1940s as the final step to complete harmony with his African heritage.[35]

As finite as the appearance of bodies may be, however, dance also offered the possibility of altering what we see by moving. James Baldwin once described the power of performance as "the unmistakable silence in which [the performer] and the audience re-create each other."[36] Dance then served as a way in which to affirm the blackness of someone's skin and at the same time offer a new way of seeing that body. Primus's gravity-defying leaps exemplified the possibilities. Muscular, confident, and volitional, she soared above the ground as a self-sufficient woman not bound to any man, as a black person in defiance of racism and "white" standards, and across borders from Africa to the United States. Dancing, choreographing, and educating as "ambassadors with hips," Primus and Dunham connected Liberia, Haiti, and the streets of East St. Louis. They created a part of the Black Arts movement led by women, the power and magnetism of bodies, and the hope of the arts as a link among diverse peoples.

NOTES

1. James H. Meriwether, *Proudly We Can Be Africans: Black Americans and Africa, 1935–1961* (Chapel Hill: University of North Carolina Press, 2001), is the best synthesis of the relationship between African Americans and Africans during this period, although he does not cover cultural exchange. See also Mary L. Dudziak, *Cold War Civil Rights: Race and the Image of American Democracy* (Princeton: Princeton University Press, 2000); and Penny M. von Eschen, "Who's the Real Ambassador? Exploding Cold War Racial Ideology," in *Cold War Constructions: The Political Culture of United States Imperialism, 1945–1966*, ed. Christian G. Appy (Amherst: University of Massachusetts Press, 2000), 110–31. The foundational texts of the Black Arts movement are Addison Gayle Jr., ed., *The Black Aesthetic* (New York: Doubleday, 1971); and LeRoi Jones and Larry Neal, eds., *Black Fire: An Anthology of Afro-American Writing* (New York: William Morrow & Co., 1968). For a recent interpretation of the movement that recognizes the gender dimensions but does not include an analysis of that within its agenda, see James Hall, *Mercy Mercy Me: African American Culture and the American Sixties* (New York: Oxford University Press, 2001).

2. For more biographical information on Dunham, see Joyce Aschenbrenner, *Katherine Dunham: Dancing a Life* (Urbana: University of Illinois Press, 2002); Julia L. Foulkes, *Modern Bodies: Dance and American Modernism from Martha Graham to Alvin Ailey* (Chapel Hill: University of North Carolina Press, 2002), chap. 3; John O. Perpener III, *African-American Concert Dance: The Harlem Renaissance and Beyond* (Urbana: University of Illinois Press, 2001), chap. 6.

3. For more biographical information on Primus, see Foulkes, *Modern Bodies*, chap. 7; and Perpener, *African-American Concert Dance*, chap. 7.

4. Doris Hering, "Little Fast Feet: The Story of the Pilgrimmage of Pearl Primus to Africa," *Dance* 24, 7 (July 1950): 21–23.

5. Pearl Primus, "Earth Theatre," *Theatre Arts* 34, 2 (December 1950): 40–43; "Pearl Primus" (no author), *Ebony* 6, 3 (January 1951): 54–58.

6. On the history of anthropology in the 1920s and 1930s, see George E. Marcus and Michael M. J. Fischer, *Anthropology as Cultural Critique: An Experimental Moment in the Human Sciences* (Chicago: University of Chicago, 1986); James Clifford, *The Predicament of Culture: Twentieth-Century Ethnography, Literature, and Art* (Cambridge: Harvard University Press); George Stocking, *Race, Culture, and Evolution: Essays in the History of Anthropology* (New York: Free Press, 1968); and Philip Gleason, "Americans All: World War II and the Shaping of American Identity," *Review of Politics* 43 (October 1981): 483–518.

7. "Ambassador with Hips," *Our World*, n.d. [Sept 1947?], box 89, folder 8, Katherine Dunham Collection, Special Collections, Morris Library, Southern Illinois University, Carbondale, Illinois (hereafter SIU).

8. Correspondence and programs in SIU.

9. Katherine Dunham, "Personal Notes," July, 31 1955, box 49, folder 8, SIU. This appears to be a draft of liner notes for an album of Caribbean music, and I have corrected simple spelling and/or typographical errors in the quote for easier reading.

10. For a more in-depth analysis of *Southland*, see Constance Valis Hill, "Katherine Dunham's *Southland*: Protest in the Face of Repression," *Dance Research Journal* 26, 2 (Fall 1994): 1–10.

11. Aschenbrenner, *Katherine Dunham*, 150–51.

12. Katherine Dunham, "Haiti" [1951?], box 15, folder 9, SIU.

13. Fred [Alsop?] to Dunham, August 23, 1961, box 28, folder 6, SIU; "Plan for Establishment Katherine Dunham Activities in Jamaica," n.d. [ca. 1960], box 28, folder 1, SIU. About dissent in Haiti, see Katherine Dunham to Syvilla Fort, May 15, 1961, box 28, folder 4, SIU.

14. Copy of article included in State Department letter about the incident from the American Consul General in Lagos, Nigeria, to the Secretary of State in Washington, D.C., February 21, 1949. National Archives, State Department Decimal File 1945–49, Record Group 59, 250/34/24/03.

15. Walter Sorell, "Conversation with Pearl Primus," *Dance* 33, 10 (Oct. 1959): 17.

16. *Amsterdam News*, October 3, 1959.

17. For a general overview of these efforts, see Penny M. von Eschen, *Race against Empire: Black Americans and Anticolonialism, 1937–1957* (Ithaca: Cornell University Press, 1997).

18. Primus quoted in Sorell, "Conversation," 15.

19. *Amsterdam News*, August 20, 1960.

20. See handwritten notes in folder "Notes—First African Performing Arts Center (Konama Kende)" and folder "Notebook Africa, 1961," box 4 (Subject Files), Pearl Primus Collection, American Dance Festival Archives, Duke University.

21. Katherine Dunham, "Recommendations for Program of Cultural Expansion in Three Areas" [draft of Ford Foundation proposal?], January 3, 1964, box 50, folder 9, SIU. Dunham wrote, "[What is] indigenous is too often taken for granted," yet serves as an important resource for cultural exchange.

22. Katherine Dunham, "La Danse Negro Africaine Moderne" [ca. Dec. 1965] and "The Performing Arts of Africa Preface to the Future" [ca. Dec. 1965], box 50, folder 10, SIU.

23. Katherine Dunham, "The Performing Arts of Africa Preface to the Future."

24. See Alain Locke, ed., *The New Negro* (1925; reprint, with an introduction by Arnold Rampersad, New York: Atheneum, 1992), esp. his essay "The Legacy of the Ancestral Arts," 254–67.

25. Ron Karenga, "Black Cultural Nationalism" (1968), reprinted in Gayle, ed., *Black Aesthetic*, 32–38; quote 33–34.

26. *St. Louis Post-Dispatch*, July 31, 1967; Aschenbrenner, *Katherine Dunham*, 179–80.

27. Primus quoted in Ric Estrada, "Three Leading Artists, and How They Feel about Dance in the Community," *Dance* 42, 11 (Nov. 1968): 56–60; quote 58.

28. David Leddick, "Everyman's African Roots," *Dance* 38, 10 (Oct. 1964): 20–21; quote 21.

29. Primus quoted in Estrada, "Three Leading Artists," 56.

30. James Stewart, "The Development of the Black Revolutionary Artist" (1966), reprinted in Jones and Neal, *Black Fire*, 3–10; quote 6.

31. Aschenbrenner, *Katherine Dunham*, 174.

32. Dunham, "Memorial Service for Martin Luther King," box 52, folder 2, SIU.

33. Primus quoted in Nat Hentoff, "An Inheritance Comes to P.S. 83," *American Education* 2, 2 (Feb. 1966): 28–32; quotes 31, 32.

34. Ron Karenga, "On Black Art," *Black Theater* 3 (1969): 9–10; quote 10.

35. Malcolm X, with Alex Haley, *The Autobiography of Malcolm X* (New York: Grove Press, 1965), 57–58.

36. James Baldwin, *Tell Me How Long the Train's Been Gone* (New York: Dell Publishing, 1968), 332.

6

Take Everyone to Heaven with Us
Anne Waldman's Poetry Cultures

Roxanne Power Hamilton

> Poets had always been oppositional, liberated, angry about the
> right things or at least tuned in to where the energy, power was.
> Witnesses drawn to the flames. Witty too. Were poets dangerous?
> The FBI thought so. And yet as an artist I never felt lost in the ver-
> sion of that particular time. Poetic lineage went further back. In
> retrospect I think as activists we were politically naïve. As poets we
> were working hard to save the world.[1]   —Anne Waldman

Most poets in the 1960s responded to the particular vortex of
the Vietnam War, the peace movement, the civil rights struggles, and the
worldwide revolutions by writing poems that sought to transform culture
by raising the poet's own consciousness. Even poetry that responded to
the various struggles to politicize or liberate one's identity was still understood to be a largely individualistic and solitary endeavor that prioritized
"the personal," even when it was in the service of "the political." Poet
Anne Waldman has written that she is interested in "extending the written word off the page into a ritual vocalization and event, so that 'I' is no
longer a personal 'I.'"[2] A poem may be "a complete little universe," as
William Carlos Williams wrote, but Waldman's work as an infrastructure
poet in the sixties helped explode the concept that the poem's universe is
restricted to the self. In an era when communitarian values were on the
ascent, Waldman helped build entire poetry *cultures*, including two of
the largest such communities in history: St. Mark's Poetry Project in

New York City and the Jack Kerouac School of Disembodied Poetics in Boulder, Colorado. And as director of the country's largest poetry center from 1968 to 1978, Waldman was positioned to shape poetry culture as no other woman had before her.

The sounding cry of postmodern poetry came in 1950 with the publication of Charles Olson's "Projective Verse" and found collective voice and energy in Donald Allen's gathering of "outrider poets" in his ground-breaking 1960 volume, *The New American Poetry*.[3] Waldman claims she became a life-long votary of poetry during the Berkeley Poetry Conference in 1965, where she witnessed a huge gathering of "New American poets" read. Moved by new currents on both the East and the West Coasts, Waldman returned with Lewis Warsh to New York City to co-found the influential *Angel Hair* magazine, which they expanded into a book-publishing venture. She was only twenty. Three years later, in 1968, she was the director of the St. Mark's Poetry Project on the Lower East Side, bringing together a community of poets to read, publish, and activate a physical space devoted completely to the advancement of poetry. Her affiliation with the "second-generation New York School poets" led to other projects that helped define a community and a generation of experimental poets in the 1960s and 1970s. She was editor of the literary magazine associated with St. Mark's, *The World*, as well as the three award-winning anthologies that collected the work from *The World*; she and roommate Allen Ginsberg entered a "spiritual marriage" and co-founded the Jack Kerouac School of Disembodied Poetics in 1974; and her troubadour poet travels put her in contact with shamanic performance traditions, such as Maria Sabina's, that led to her widely acclaimed book *Fast Speaking Woman* (1975).

A "fast-speaking woman" poetics naturally emerges from Waldman's culture-work and literary endeavors in the sixties. In an era characterized by unprecedented speed—in the growth and expansion of the nation's economy, technologies, and subcultures—Waldman was able to capitalize on a national culture and an emerging poetry culture that favored what Donald Allen called "instantism."[4] As poet, editor, and administrator, her work embodied qualities associated with the second-generation New York School: speed in composition and publication, and a preoccupation with orality, both in the presence of a conversational speaking voice and the poetry's orientation toward performance. The fact that she was in a position of leadership as a woman poet in a male-dominated New York avant garde genders her fast-speaking aesthetic in ways that create an overlapping "third space" between two distinct literary groups of the sixties. These two groups—the so-called avant garde and the feminists—often defined themselves against each other, even though their shared preferences for "open field" and "projective" poetry point to poetic revolutions that were grounded in distinctly sixties cultural revolutions. In both cases, and particularly in Waldman's case, a performance-based aesthetic emerges from highly ritualized spaces where it is possible for entire communities to take a "vow to poetry" and to sustain it together.

Waldman's impulse to nurture a self-contained universe of poets similar to that of Sappho's "Moisopolon Domo," or house of muses, may have begun early in her life. "I am drawn to the view of Sappho as leader and chief personality in an institution of poetry and aesthetics because it activates a paradigm in my own life."[5] Waldman's mother, Frances Le Fevre, provided an early model for her work in building arts communities. As a young woman, Le Fevre dropped out of Vassar, married the son of poet Anghelos Sikelianos, and moved to Greece to participate in Sikelianos' Delphic Idea, an ambitious project that sought to provoke a resurgence of Classical Greek arts through arts festivals in Delphi. After writing and translating poetry in Greece for ten years, Frances married Anne's father, John Waldman, a jazz pianist turned professor. Coming from working-class backgrounds, both of her parents were the first in their families to attend college. As a young girl growing up on MacDougal Street in the West Village, Anne was steeped in a bohemian universe where bluesman Leadbelly was a guest in their house, folk singer Pete Seeger's child was her playmate, and poet Gregory Corso was a regular sight on the streets in her neighborhood. Unlike so many in her generation who felt disaffiliated from their parents' brand of affluent liberalism, Waldman felt a deep respect for her parents and, to this day, is committed to creating non-competitive poetry communities that support the creative initiative of youth without "stomping on the corpses" of the elders.[6]

As an adolescent, her spiritual leanings were nurtured at Grace Church School and Friends Seminary, where Anne became familiar with Eastern spirituality and meditated regularly in the Quaker silent meetings, a practice that may have influenced her decision to take Buddhist refuge vows in the early 1970s. Waldman enrolled in Bennington College in 1962, where she studied poetry, edited the literary magazine *SILO*, and performed in college theater productions. She wrote her senior thesis on Theodore Roethke under the tutelage of poet Howard Nemerov, but by then she was reading Gertrude Stein and emulating John Ashbery, forever moving away from certain formalities of academic poetry.

> As a woman I was increasingly interested in a break-down of semantics. . . . I wondered where to place myself as a female. What were my rites of passage, rituals? Envying the freedom of the male protagonist, the male poet, I was still a daughter yet carried a lot of male energy. . . . If you listened to the men, and stayed in love with the classics, you were intimidated, crippled, but if you could hold them at a distance, steal their secrets, look them in the eye, you were safe.[7]

While Waldman admired her mentor Nemerov, she felt stifled by the academic poetic tradition he represented, and she held her ground as they argued about the merits of Beat poetry and Frank O'Hara. O'Hara, a New York School poet who was curator for the Modern Museum of Art, wrote spontaneous, witty poetry in a poetic style he called "Personism."[8] O'Hara would influence the second-generation New York School poets perhaps more than any other single figure. Prior to her direct engagement with the city's avant garde poetry cultures, Waldman's Bennington-era poems were usually layered and metaphorical; "Hostility 1 for H.N." is uncharacteristically direct in its indictment of the traditions that she felt were "drowning her."

> I try to make your water my own,
> Your three levels of water,
> A looking into it.
> A dipping into it.
> Your reflection from it.
> I had seen water rising, filling the room,
> Drowning, containing us, for you. . . .
> I've tread too far on your settled mind. . . .[9]

Waldman began exploring a world outside of settled academia when she attended the Berkeley Poetry Conference in 1965, the summer before her senior year. There, she saw Charles Olson perform his poetry, she met her husband-to-be and poet-comrade Lewis Warsh, and she took LSD for the first time. In Berkeley, Waldman witnessed a broad range of poets, from Lenore Kandell to Ted Berrigan to Ginsberg, whose poetry emerged

from immediate context and responded to the phenomena in the surrounding environment. Certainly, the leap from reading the New American
poets to feeling included in the rituals of this new poetic tribe influenced
Waldman to make her famous vow to poetry: "I remember vowing then
and there that, beyond the practice of my own writing, I would work for
and be part of a literary community that would honor its members and
provide a network for their ongoing writing. . . . Poetry needed a larger
arena; the community needed it as well."[10]

It was at the Robert Duncan reading that she met Lewis Warsh. She
noted Duncan's arms dancing above him as he read and made the connection that such an embodied poetry could be a liberating art for women in
particular, who could be "empowered, more in touch with their bodies as
landscapes for writing, not imprisoned by hope and fear of being desirable, feminine."[11] Even more than Duncan's reading, Charles Olson's
vulnerable and spontaneous performance showed her how poetry could
transform lives if it were embodied live. "There's something very 'on the
line' and naked about the whole experience [of poetry readings]. . . . So
this all struck me full-force at Berkeley, and I could really see the poet as
a tribal shaman, speaking and moving and being embarrassing not just
for himself or herself, but for you, the audience."[12]

In urging poets to conceptualize the units of poetic form (the syllable
and the line) as having their origin in the *body* (the ear and the breath,
respectively), Olson's revolutionary manifesto, "Projective Verse," relo-
cated the "field" of the poem in the poet's entire body, rather than the
mind alone. "Projective poetry," also known as "open field poetry," dic-
tated radical openness, speed, an organic relationship between form and
content, and an immediacy of speech. Soon Waldman would put her own
spin on Olson's "fast-speaking" poetry and her own poetry would
become more projective, both in composition and performance. "I get up
& dance the poem when it sweeps into litany. I gambol with the shaman
& the deer. It is a *body poetics*."[13]

Before she herself experimented with performance, Waldman's
community-building efforts focused mostly on publishing and editing
projects. Shortly after the conference, during her senior year at Bennington, she and Warsh started a glamorous and arty magazine called *Angel
Hair*. Anne and Lewis were part of a "little" revolution, where "little"
was code for "little magazine" or "small press publications." Hugely
popular with the counterculture, they gave underground, working-class,

and activist groups an affordable public voice and played an indispensable role in the formation of social movements and upstart literary projects of the sixties. Within a few months, *Angel Hair* poetry magazine branched out to become a press, publishing early works by talented friends and poets including Gerard Malanga, Clark Coolidge, Tom Clark, and Bernadette Mayer. In all, Angel Hair Books published over sixty books by writers who were less likely to find homes for their work with mainstream publishing presses.

By the summer of 1966, Lewis and Anne were living together in a floor-through apartment at 33 St. Mark's Place, a location that fast became famous for their literary salons and late-night parties following readings at the Poetry Project. During the same summer, Waldman was offered a job at the new St. Mark's Poetry Project as assistant to then-director Joel Oppenheimer. In less than two years, Waldman became the director and built up what many have described as the liveliest and most significant poetry center in the United States.

Her work at the Poetry Project was contiguous with her social life and artistic life. After Ted Berrigan began showing up nightly following the second issue of *Angel Hair,* the apartment became the home base for the social alliances and creative collaborations of the so-called second-generation New York School poets. In a recent important study of the Lower East Side poetry cultures of the 1960s, *All Poets Welcome,* Daniel Kane writes, "The social world surrounding Waldman & Warsh's apartment at 33 St. Mark's Place and its relationship to the Poetry Project just two blocks away is articulated in a kind of insider's code, and tends to have a far greater presence in the magazine [*The World*] than any other interrelated systems of friendships and literary allegiances."[14] Not only poets but visual artists, musicians, and actors began coming over to their apartment every night—a culture-forming ritual informed by the fact that many of the regular visitors had no jobs. The apartment was also chosen to celebrate special events such as gala readings, art exhibits, book publications, and album releases. The Velvet Underground, for example, chose 33 St. Mark's to hear the master of their first record for the first time.[15] Led by Lou Reed and John Cale, the Velvet Underground was a short-lived band who achieved cult status. Beginning in 1966, they played in Andy Warhol's mixed media shows at the "DOM" on St. Mark's Place, helping to make the street Manhattan's center for the bohemian avant garde.

Fig. 6.1. Anne Waldman in her apartment at 33 St. Mark's Place, the social epicenter of Lower East Side avant garde poetry in the late sixties. *Photo circa 1972, copyright Sy Johnson*

Waldman's home and work nurtured a poetry culture composed of what she has called "outriders." Riding well outside the bounded territory of elite poetry cultures, typified at the time, by Robert Lowell's poetry of "white male, heterosexual angst," the outrider poets were "characterized by wild mind, spontaneity, a less secure lifestyle, political opposition, experimentation of form, and other unspeakable acts and digressions."[16] Waldman was an outrider among outriders and thrived among the notoriously male-dominated second-generation New York School poets. Both she and other members of the group point to her confidence at a time when it was difficult for women to break into print.[17]

Writer Stephen Koch remarked that, for years, Waldman was the only woman with stature and sway over this notoriously contrary group. The entire scene seemed to depend on her. Waldman was inclusive and egalitarian, renowned for her competence and self-possession: "a cultural grand dame Henry James would have been interested in."[18] Anne describes her relationship with one of the more assertive and well-known members on the scene, Ted Berrigan, who shared her gift for building community: "We shared a love and empathy for others, a need to be in charge, a fast wit, always wanting to be at the center of things, up on every book and situation, bossy. Take everyone to heaven with us."[19] Their community, centered on Tulsa "expatriates" Berrigan, Ron Padgett, and Dick Gallup, as well as Waldman, Warsh, and other "locals," made poetry accessible and sexy to a progressive youth culture. They found themselves empowered to set alternative arts agendas because the economy was flush and President Lyndon B. Johnson's Great Society initiatives made available unprecedented arts funding beginning in 1965. The agenda this group set was decidedly "hybrid," influenced by the inter-arts experiments of Andy Warhol and the poets' social and artistic interactions with painters, musicians, and filmmakers of the day. The poem was its own universe, but it "contained multitudes" of expanding universes typical of the fringe arts and social scenes of the sixties.

A typical poem published in *The World* or *Angel Hair* referenced a mix of mundane and exciting details from the day-to-day life of this group of friends. This preoccupation with everyday life was an inheritance from beloved New York School poet Frank O'Hara, whose popular "I do this, I do that" poetry certainly influenced Waldman and her group. On a cultural level, this deceptively superficial concern with the quotidian was churning up from deep dissatisfactions with institutional control over personal time. This widespread discontent would erupt in three years in the worldwide, youth-led revolutions of May 1968, the most salient demand of which was the improvement of everyday life. Waldman's own preoccupations with dailiness can be seen in her concise but abundant documentation of details related to her intermingling social and artistic lives. A 1967 journal entry records the non-stop stream of social interactions with poets at 33 St. Mark's Place.

> As I was writing this, the doorbell rang. It was Ted. . . . Then the doorbell rang again and it was Dick [Gallup]. . . . Then Michael [Brownstein] came again. And then Rene [Ricard] who told us that John Weiners was coming with Gerard Malanga. Then John Weiners came in with Gerard Malanga. It was exciting to think of seeing a new person before we came. Then we were all sitting around and turned on. Then Ted was talking a lot. Then a lot of things would happen at once.[20]

Waldman's poems and journal entries share a documentary inclusiveness, an incitement to record the fascinating minutiae of a small culture in formation. The members of this small culture wrote poetry that included the banal and friendly details of their own lives, lightly side-stepping the pressure to record monumental history or serious, weighty themes in closed-form verse. A good example of this kind of poem is "80th Congress," a collaborative poem by Berrigan and Dick Gallup, published nearly as quickly as it was written—a typical practice of a group who favored "instantism"—in the third issue of *The World* magazine.

> It's 2 A.M. at Lewis & Anne's, which is where it's at
> On Saint Mark's Place, hash & Angel Hairs on our mind
> Love is in our heart (what else?) dope & Peter Schjeldahl
> Who is new and valid (in a blinding snow storm)
> . . .
> Yes, it is now, 1967, & we've been killing time (with life)
> But at Anne & Lewis's we lived it up
> Anne makes a lovely snow-soda, while Lewis's watchamacallit
> warms up this Happy New Year's straight blue haze. . . . [21]

Collaborations among these poets and artists covered the gamut from extremely informal to formal, including spontaneous poems, numerous handmade books, illustrated poems and books, poetry book covers, and classic volumes of co-authored poetry such as Ron Padgett and Ted Berrigan's *Bean Spasms* and Berrigan and Waldman's 1970 book, *Memorial Day*. Of *Memorial Day*, Waldman states that "it was a cohesive elegiac piece, interestingly toned (we seem to hit a stride together) done through the mail. . . . I remember I was the final 'assembler' of the poem, had all the pages spread out before me on floor in Long Island and sort of danced around them, scissors and glue in hand or was it scotch tape?"[22] Sections in the collage poem resemble an oblique call and response between the narrators and between the living and the dead. Playing off a line that Berrigan probably wrote in the preceding section, Waldman wrote: "I woke up / as he typed that down: / 'Girl for someone else in white walk by' & then, / so did I. / So my thanks to you / the dead. / The people in the sky." A later stanza that appears to have been written by Waldman could be read as a formal and thematic blueprint for "Fast Speaking Woman," from the perspective of a fast-riffing girl: "I'm the girl in the rain the girl on the street / the girl in the trance the girl at your feet the / girl who just got off the girl who plays the piano."[23]

At 33 St. Mark's Place, Waldman moved away from her Bennington-style poems, which were more opaque and serious in tone and toward poems that broke down narratives and shrugged off message: "Words were things as Gertrude Stein proclaimed. . . . I got looser, dumber, more playful, writing down things I overheard, read, places, snippets from the radio, the street."[24] Instantaneous compositions were often valued over carefully rewritten ones. In her book *O My Life,* she even includes a hand-written page from her journal, dated April 20, 1969. In the lower corner she has glued a xeroxed photograph of herself lying nude on the couch with a caption that reads, "I like living this way."[25] Following Olson's commands in "Projective Verse" to "USE IT," that is, to work off of the phenomena in the immediate environment to inspire an instant response in writing, Waldman's inclusive approach to writing broke many staid rules about what kind of language was appropriate for poetry. "I was writing nightly, completely charged by the constant activity—artistic, political—of the Lower East Side environment. . . . Use it! An immediacy and urgency took hold to write all waking and sleeping details down quickly—as witness, as eyeballer of phenomena—and accept whatever shape they took."[26] One such poem, appropriately entitled "Tape," was "written" by speaking into a tape recorder, giving her the speed necessary to capture the breezy mood of the time: "O my life! little political overcoats / ocean human hills valleys / & you breezy / la la la la la la la la Brooklyn. . . ."[27] Found and "borrowed" poems and art were made by inserting lines or images from other artists to make what Larry Fagin has called "a third voice, a third sound" in pleasurable and process-driven rituals.[28]

This group of poet-friends was inevitably influenced by the sixties explosion of mass media and its resulting informal idioms, where poems could be co-written, published, and enjoyed almost at the speed of conversation. Their passion for collaboration was also inspired by early-century Dadaist collage and the mood sparked by New York School painters and poets a decade earlier: Abstract Expressionist painters were moved to paint in the improvisational idioms of jazz, and poets were borrowing concepts such as "action painting" to encourage a focus on process over product, on instantaneous response rather than mimeticism and representation. In a culture of planned obsolescence, pop artist Andy Warhol inspired artists to recycle and reassemble the used parts and refuse of an affluent and throw-away society. Poets and artists who collaborated at 33 St. Mark's Place and the Poetry Project were trying, in Ezra Pound's words, to "make it new" by creating a recombinant art culture.

The historically recombinant populations of the East Village were a perfect setting for the artistic sensibilities of this group. In the early part of the twentieth century, European immigrants had flocked to the Lower East Side. During the 1950s, a migration of West Village artists and bohemians seeking less-expensive rent moved to the East Village and settled in with the politically subversive East European neighbors. In 1967 thousands of hippies swarmed into the blocks surrounding Tompkins Square Park. Just down the street from Anne and Lewis's apartment, Andy Warhol opened his Electric Circus with the multi-media "Plastic Exploding Inevitable." A few blocks away the Fillmore East opened in 1968 and featured acts such as Jefferson Airplane, Janis Joplin, and the Grateful Dead, played for the new immigrant population.[29] The neighborhood's St. Mark's Church was becoming radicalized overnight by this "exploding inevitable" influx. The countercultural newspaper, the *East Village Other*, described the church as "physically old, but . . . spiritually young. It awaits the painters, the writers, the photographers, pornographers, poets, and musicians who care to use its facilities towards their own ends. It is perhaps the very spirit of the Lower East Side."[30]

Waldman's connection to St. Mark's Church-in-the-Bowery had roots in her childhood when she first met the Reverend Michael Allen. The forward-thinking Episcopalian minister assisted artists into positions of leadership "because he felt they were among the few people in society that were really doing theology."[31] When St. Mark's was awarded a $200,000 grant in 1966 to help rehabilitate the young "subculture of the beat," the Poetry Project was born. Though the project was officially entitled "Creative Arts for Alienated Youth," it was widely understood by the savvy young staff, including Waldman, that the money would be used to support a complex experimental arts forum whose members—as editors, publishers, writers, and organizers—had already contributed significantly to various urban arts communities. In his grant proposal, Harry Silverstein described the "juvenile delinquents" who were to be resocialized by the projects: "Their participation in community life is little if any . . . in this 'subculture of the beat' as it is sometimes known."[32] Films such as Nicholas Ray's 1955 *Rebel without a Cause* depicted an American culture that was obsessed with proliferating and policing images of juvenile delinquents. In films, comic books, and poster-art, "America was mass-producing images of white youth on the move yet with nowhere to go. . . ."[33]

Countering the impression that the Poetry Project was an outpost of deadbeats, Maureen Owen, who worked many years at the Poetry Project, described an already venerable poetry institution where she met many exciting women writers.[34] Waldman indeed proved effective in attracting more women poets to contribute to the growing poetry community at the Poetry Project. She had been struck by the absence of women other than Lenore Kandell at the otherwise inspiring Berkeley conference and noted that only four out of forty authors in the Allen anthology were women. Waldman took this as a personal challenge to invite more women into the poetry community.[35] Ted Berrigan's early attitudes conformed to the general perception of women poets before the Poetry Project opened. Remarking upon the Berkeley Poetry Conference, he confessed, "I did not know who this Lenore Kandell was, but I figured since she was a girl she couldn't be too good. I mean at that time, it was that way, just to be straight about it. She was just a girl, she wasn't somebody specific. . . . I didn't know of any young and exciting women poets. . . ."[36] Ironically, Kandell's *The Love Book* became a cult classic in the manner of *Howl* after authorities seized it in 1966 for being pornographic. In general, however, women with the slightest affiliation with Beat authors found themselves stained by Kerouac's fatal description of them as "girls" who "say nothing and wear black."[37] Even Waldman, who was technically too young to be a Beat writer per se, has been both admired and belittled as a presumed "beatnik chick" because of her later affiliation with Ginsberg at Naropa.

Beyond balancing the scales of gender representation at the Poetry Project, Waldman's ten-year stint as the first long-term director produced a record of considerable achievement: she raised the funds necessary for survival following the expiration of the government grant in 1968; she oversaw the *The World,* which, after thirty-seven years, has outlasted all the other mimeograph magazines; she published three books collecting the poetry of *The World;* and she developed an incomparable reading series. Authors clamored to be on the yearly line-up of readers, even if it meant they did so at their own cost. Waldman said, "We decided to call our new venture a poetry 'project' because we saw it as an ongoing event requiring hard work and perseverance. We also had in mind the sense of an outward *projecting,* to 'direct one's voice to be heard clearly at a distance.' Public readings were at the heart of the plan."[38] There have likely been more poetry readings at St. Mark's since Waldman began working there than any other poetry series in this century.[39]

Waldman organized two popular weekly reading series: Mondays were open to everyone, and Wednesday nights were reserved well in advance for more well-known poets. In a list of Wednesday-night poetry readings projected for Fall 1970/Spring 1971, Waldman wrote the names of fifty-five poets, including Robert Bly, Gregory Corso, John Ashbery, Andrei Codrescu, Diane di Prima, Muriel Rukeyser, Gary Snyder, and Diane Wakoski.[40] For readers as popular as Ginsberg and Burroughs, hundreds would pack the pews of the church. For the famous New Year's Marathon readings that Waldman initiated, close to a hundred poets would present their best three minutes' worth in an all-night reading that is, to this day, one of the East Village's largest ongoing maverick arts events. The Poetry Project newsletter recounts the highlights of the 1975 New Year's Marathon:

> Patti Smith wore a bra, wooed her fans with hip-swivelling blues poems, her right arm outstretched, leading an invisible charge. William Burroughs ignored the pushy *Time* photographer, plunged grim-faced through a sardonic text about institutionalized genocide. Gregory Corso arrived late, without cab fare, then brought down the house with an elegant poem retrieved from his back pocket. . . . Yoko Ono mesmerized the same throngs with a long mime of gradual speaking, reading. . . . Anne Waldman rocked back and forth with the relentless incantations of "Battery." . . . [41]

Under Waldman's watch, the Poetry Project welcomed artists working at the intersection of several art forms. In particular, poets who were influenced by so-called experimental music and by rock 'n' roll enlarged the cultural presence of poetry in an American culture increasingly tuned in to live performances, especially rock concerts. The cross-pollination of experimental music and poetry at St. Mark's grew as borders between popular and high culture collapsed and poets like Patti Smith moved into music. According to Ginsberg, "Patti Smith, Jim Carroll, William Burroughs, Laurie Anderson, Lou Reed, Philip Glass, Steven Taylor—were all at one time either apprentice poets at St. Mark's or . . . performed occasional work. So it had tremendous impact on the centralized progression of rock 'n' roll intelligentsia."[42] Waldman described a host of memorable poetry events that exploded the concept of the sedate poetry reading. Perhaps the most famous "reading" was performance poet John Giorno's bacchanalia in 1969, during which he staged one of his then-famous multi-media poetry events with music, fog and light machines, a punchbowl of acid-spiked punch, and hundreds of joints to "relax the audience," since poetry readings were notoriously stiff affairs.⁴³

Collective artistic practices were on the rise at the Poetry Project and were doubtless influenced by political practices in an era when the term *collective* could hardly be divorced from the quasi-socialist organizing principles of the New Left. One of these principles was the focus on *action*, a term that conjures Olson's action-focused Projective Poetry, as well as the *direct action* techniques associated with civil rights and anti-war activists. These do-it-yourselfers created their own reading and publishing apparatus without waiting for those in positions of established authority, such as big house presses, to "discover" the poets, one by one. By creating a community identity and community-made art based on the ideal of "action in common,"⁴⁴ they were able to side-step some of the frustrations and competitive fall-out of a purely self-driven culture.

The interest in collaboration and communal projects in Waldman's circle points to broadening interest in communitarian over individualized expression in poetry. Indeed, the poetry of self-expression was on the rise in many groups whose communitarian values were strongest—including feminists and participants in the Black Arts movement—as a way to counter conventional discourses of sexism and racism. The feminist rallying cry "The personal is political" found expression in their political and their poetical strategies. Consciousness-raising groups were formed to motivate women to give expression to, hence awaken to, their own oppression. Self-expression would lead to collective action to shift the power structure that lay beneath the indignities of everyday life.

In Waldman's poetry from the sixties and early seventies, it is nearly impossible to find evidence of her disgruntlement with her everyday life as a woman. Even when her poetry turned more deliberately toward gendered themes in *Fast Speaking Woman,* her claims about her experience of gender were mostly affirmative. One female genealogy she did not belong to was the "terminally unhappy hippie girl," and "given the public's fascination with tortured and depressed artists, especially female artists (Plath, Sexton, Holiday, Joplin, etc.),"⁴⁵ one wonders whether her perpetual good mood and strong self-esteem were a hindrance or a boost to her career. Waldman claimed that, in the sixties, she tended to write out of "some high energy place."⁴⁶ There was certainly the sense that an upbeat persona was de rigueur among those following in the footsteps of O'Hara and Berrigan. In "Hi Everyone!" the opening poem in her debut book published by a major press, *Baby Breakdown,* she opens cheerily: "Hi everyone! How do you do? / hello there!"[47]

While identity politics rarely played a role in Waldman's poetry, it is interesting to note that she did refer to her 1970 book *No Hassles* in her journal as "a feminine work dedicated to women."[48] Though she may not have claimed the title "cultural feminist," if she was developing a kind of "embodied poetics" over the years, one way in which she embraced this concept was through her gendered body. "I was an artist first, but also informed by a female physicality which unleashed, at times, a vivid imagination out of a 'pulsing cervix.' . . . And as an artist, my body represented every woman's."[49] One senses these pulses on the level of the line when she begins to write longer poems. In particular, in "Fast Speaking Woman," her rhythmic repetitions create a spiraling sense of movement, circling about the same space—"woman"—a space that is at the same time constantly in transition: "I'm a mobile woman / I'm an elastic woman / I'm a necklace woman / I'm a silk-scarf woman / I'm a know-nothing woman / I'm a know-it-all woman / I'm a day woman / I'm a doll woman."[50]

Waldman's claim that "as an artist [her] body represented every woman's" insinuates an essentialist view of the female body that Wald-man disavows in other writings. She has, in fact, written repeatedly of her identification with both masculine and feminine energies and of her desire to transcend the dualistic meanings inherent in a system that defines one gender against the other. In some writings she asserts that bisexuality is the psyche-gender of the artist, and elsewhere she seems to desire to escape gender altogether. "I propose a utopian creative field where we are defined by our energy, not by gender."[51]

Transformation of a gendered self-in-language is perhaps more interesting to Waldman in this early period of her writing than transformation of a gendered self-in-society. As such, her poetry was not aligned with the feminist poetry movement, which was more often than not identified with radical feminism and its insistence that women be identified as a "class" whose identity stabilizes around the fact of historical sexual oppression. Though Waldman did not self-identify with the feminist poetry movement, there were certain commonalities between this move-ment and the schools affiliated with the New American poets, including open form and an emphasis on performance.[52] The widespread transfor-mation of values that accompanied the interlocking cultural revolutions of the sixties were bound to create some common social values between otherwise dissimilar groups. New American poets and feminist poets both created a substantial network vis-à-vis small press publishing and frequent readings in coffee houses, bookstores, bars, living rooms, and eventually, universities. Both "movements" capitalized on the fact that "poetry was easier to write with limited time and money, numerous interruptions, and crude publishing equipment."[53] Both groups engaged in creative forms of "intertextuality" by referring to one another in their poetry and valuing community ideals over those of the individuals.[54] If feminist poets embraced the label "political poetry," however, the second-generation New York School poets felt less comfortable adopting that stance, even though most of them responded in their poetry, and in Waldman's case as an organizer, to the intensification of political events in the late sixties.

> I'd look out my window on St. Mark's Place and there was a "revolution" going on and I was part of it. We were angry about the war in Vietnam, about police brutality, strict drug penalties, racism, social injustice everywhere. I felt like an antennae, receiver, conduit for "my time." I was reeling—like so many of us in the sixties—from the intensity of a passionate vision of a better world and from all the sweet and painful informations that sang in my ear. Drug induced? Not entirely. More appropriately, poetry induced.[55]

By the spring of 1968, the world was spinning in a vortex of national and cultural liberation struggles that had been building throughout the polarizing politics of the Cold War. If the student-led revolution of May 1968 sparked new generations of European activist-intellectuals, progressives in the United States were experiencing serial shock and the collective sense that their best options for changing the world were going down in defeat to a culture of violence. Waldman's usual descriptive journal reads like an obit column: "'June 3: Andy Warhol is shot & critically wounded. What's happening?' 'June 5: Robert F. Kennedy shot in the head in LA after winning primary & in critical condition. . . . Feel a bit numb.' 'Friday: RFK dead.'"[56]

As if to foreshadow a year equated in the national imagination with assassination and the loss of "the dream," in early January 1968 a group of young activists showed up at St. Mark's Church during a poetry reading by Kenneth Koch and staged a "fake assassination" to protest the recent arrest of LeRoi Jones for the possession of illegal firearms. A round of "blanks" were fired at Koch, who recovered his composure enough to comment that perhaps he should not have opened with a poem whose first line was "My audience of camel dung and fig newtons," which he followed up with the wry observation, "Poetry is revolution."[57] Waldman wrote in her journal on January 22 that she was still shaken by the ritual fake-shooting of Koch.[58] When the Weather Underground inadvertently bombed their own headquarters in 1970, Waldman would write: "N.Y. is crazy. The 11th St. incident is really strange & creepy. I know one of those girls—Kathy Boudin—who escaped. . . . Our generation. And the other bombings! Spoke to folks in NY who say it's a state of emergency . . . I wonder. Seems like it was bound to happen sooner or later. Blow it up."[59]

Waldman claimed that, as poets, they were more effective than they were as activists at saving the world. At the Poetry Project, they were doing their part by organizing benefits and readings in support of the Committee for Non-Violence, the draft card-burning Catonsville Nine, the Chicago Seven, the Berkeley Defense League, among others. Events supporting the Black Panthers, the Trotskyites, and Motherfuckers' Soup Kitchen were held at St. Mark's Church.[60] Yet Waldman did not imply that the typically radical poets of the Poetry Project were saving the world by holding benefit readings on behalf of other activist groups whose work was more valid or efficacious than writing poetry. They were working hard to save the world by *changing the language*, and this activity, she believed, was even more effective than changing the debate, the outcome of an election, or the minds of politicians.

Though St. Mark's was a "hotbed of political activity" Waldman and the Poetry Project poets weren't writing "political poetry" per se; didactic poetry that contained slogans or dogma seemed counter to their purposes of reinfusing the language with genuine spontaneity. "Message poetry can be most tedious. You might communicate better by telephone, by an embrace, by sending your money to a worthy cause."[61] Poetry, as a genre, was viewed as a space where permission was given to avoid the limitations of formulaic speech and to invent new, more plastic forms suitable to the unexpected content of the age. Though most of her poems from the early collections are collage-style meditations on everyday life, commentary on political or countercultural issues can be seen in poems such as "Non-Stop," "Gun Power," "The Revolution," "Young People & Life," "How the Sestina (Yawn) Works," and "Dispersal of It," a poem that responds to a tear-gassing episode in Tompkins Square. As poet, she claimed the role of "antennae" bearing witness to the world outside the self without directly prescribing a cure for its shortcomings. In "Gun Power," Waldman insinuates that both violence and clichéd political rhetoric can be fought, or perhaps merely escaped, through poetry.

> Coming down hard on America
>
>   you've got to have a heavy typewriter
>   strength & power
> & superhuman energy to back you up
> Already you're exhausted & planning your escape (in this poem)
> Without words you're well on the way
>   to being an evolutionary trend
>
>   . . .
>
>   DECLARE WAR
>   BEWARE SINCERE WHITES
>   are interesting words, I think
>   which carry a certain weight like
>   GREAT SHACKLES do
>
>   . . .
>
> ALL OR NOTHING   LIFE OR DEATH
>   DECIDE NOW
> But you'd better be yourself or Bang!
>   you aren't going to last thru the summer
>   (& missing something if you do)[62]

These sections of the poem use humor and a subtle form of concrete poetry—capitalized political clichés are the loud visual counterpart to gun reports—to show that the poet needs "a heavy typewriter" and "superhuman energy" to survive the violence of the obvious.

Even without overt political agendas or intentions, the poets associated with the second-generation New York School were part of an action-oriented generation who, in the words of Patti Smith, were "totally ready to go."[63] This generation's uncanny confidence is evident in lines from Waldman's poem "Auguries of Speed": "But we feel terrific / nevertheless /

because we take over / the world tomorrow / We ask you to cooperate / you may not understand / we don't ask you to / We ask you to / give us your open mind / as open as space travel."[64] The explosive growth in economic, educational, and technological opportunities in the sixties produced a generation whose expectations of their culture and of themselves were greater than ever. Inspired by the May 1968 uprisings in Paris, the Italian "hot autumn" of 1969 produced a slogan that said it all: "*'tutto e subito,'* we want it all and we want it now."[65]

And yet despite, or perhaps because of, this global climate of youthful self-assurance, there were ominous signs of regression and the beginnings of a powerful political backlash at home. The rightward swing of 1968 was felt by the Poetry Project when their grant ran out that year, and Waldman, facing an uncertain future, redoubled her efforts to creatively raise the funds and good will of the poet-volunteers to keep the beloved project afloat. Amazingly, during this lean period, the Poetry Project drew on the formidable fund of community energies and prospered. "The room that had been taken up by fed funds & ultra-scam was now wall-to-wall poets & poverty, breathing energy, pencils sharpened, nothing but wits about them, vital."[66] The reading series expanded and the popular free poetry workshops continued to be offered. The tight and legendary community that had established itself at 33 St. Mark's Place did not fare as well as the Poetry Project, however. In 1968, Ted Berrigan accepted an academic job in Iowa; then Anne and Lewis separated. The apartment ceased to be the social center of the literary community. But the poetry *culture* this community created together continued to grow; it was one of the enduring cultural revolutions of the sixties that has survived to this day.

After nurturing a poetry institution that was virtually synonymous with "oral poetry," Waldman began to explore in earnest the relationship between her own poetry and performance in the late sixties and early seventies. She worked on performance projects with John Giorno such as "Dial-a-Poem" project and Streetworks, a series of poetry performances on the city streets, some of which were political actions. In a Streetworks event in 1969, Waldman—dressed as a human advertisement—donned a sandwich board on which she had written a poem entitled "Kind Days" for a street performance on Sixth Avenue that protested the war. A line in the poem addresses the expectations of the passerby with light irony: "HAND OVER THE MONEY / isn't my idea of what it's like to be a poet." Distinguishing the role of the poet from others who might accost you for money—salespeople, thieves, or beggars—as you hurry down the Avenue of the Americas, Waldman encourages a kind response with her title and her low-key appeal in the final lines about war: "that way madness lies / no more of that / let's have no more of that."[67] Such an appeal might very well have been more effective with a streetwise New York crowd than the more predictable and haranguing anti-war chants. Finding the right balance between originality, message, and street presence required an astute reading of audience. As Nuyorican Poets Café co-founder Miguel Algarín says about reading poetry outdoors, "When a New York street poet recites on Sixth Street and Avenue A, he cannot afford to sound pale and unengaging, because the principles are different. People are on the move."[68]

As Waldman read more, her confidence grew and was manifest both in the strength of her poetry and in her performance style. By the early seventies she began to grow into a more "kinetic" relationship to her written text. "'Performance' interested me in that it expanded text off the page. . . . I'd felt from my first reading at St. Mark's Church, where I sat, head bowed to page, that the voice coming out of me was only partial, and that I had a bigger sound to exhibit and explore. A sound that I would literally 'have to grow into.'"[69] She has made numerous recordings of her readings over the years and staged some fairly elaborate poetic collaborations with musicians and dancers; even so, Waldman hesitates to embrace the term *performance poet* in the same way she is reluctant to fully embrace other labels, such as an affiliation with a single school of poetry. For her, "performance poet" as a label is problematic because it presumes that a new art form has recently been discovered or popularized, when in fact lyric poets have been performing their words for centuries. More often, she refers to her poetry performances as "sprechstimme" or "speech singing."[70]

When Waldman read the long list poem "Fast Speaking Woman" in San Francisco, Lawrence Ferlinghetti found her after the reading and declared he wanted to publish it in a City Lights Pocket Edition. Waldman corresponded with City Lights Books in early 1975 about the title of her book. "I'm afraid the title of the book is absolutely FAST SPEAKING WOMAN—I know TALKING is more direct but I have this theory about poetry being poetry & *speech*—speech being weightier than talk, especially with this poem-chant. It's grander, less casual."[71] In a later letter to Ferlinghetti, she suggested the subtitle "and Other Chants."[72] This choice more firmly placed the book within the spiritualist tradition of Mazatec

Fig. 6.2. In a 1969 "Streetworks" event in Manhattan, Waldman wears her anti-war poem, "Kind Days." *Photo courtesy of Sidney B. Zamochnick*

shamaness Maria Sabina, who had inspired its composition, and within the chanting practices of Tibetan Buddhism, a spiritual path Waldman had already chosen. She and her partner, poet Michael Brownstein, traveled to South America in 1972, where she began writing a "list-chant telling all the kinds of women there are to be, interweaving personal details (how I see myself: 'I'm the impatient woman,' 'The woman with the keys') with all the energetic adjectives I could conjure up to make the chant speak of/to/for 'everywoman.' Chant is heartbeat. Chant is an ancient efficacious poetic practice."[73]

It was popular among spiritual-seekers from the counterculture to make the voyage to Sabina's home in Huatla to partake of the mushrooms (*hongos*), which Sabina called "saint children."[74] "In some way the impetus for the poem came out of intoxicated experiences—with mushrooms and peyote—particular extended moments or eternities where one becomes universal woman and also quixotic and protean woman, face constantly shifting and changing, shape-changing, entering everything around her."[75] Waldman went on to teach courses on shamanic poetries at Naropa and to lecture on "the poet as shaman" in Munich. Waldman never related to Sabina as would an initiate to a guru, nor has her tendency been to seek gurus of any stripe. Her attraction to Buddhism stemmed from the same place as her attraction to a literary life: both involved a disciplined practice of prostrating to the mind rather than a deity.[76]

Waldman's "vow to poetry" in 1965 was similar in spirit to the vow she took to Buddhism in the early seventies: in both cases, the vow acknowledged the sacred nature of imagination and community; community with all its passionate, chaotic, and complex relationships fed the imagination. When she prepared to take Buddhist refuge vows, she was informed she would have to give up all attachments, including her attachment to the imagination. "Imagination! Was I hearing this properly? . . . What had I gotten myself into? . . . I kept my fingers crossed symbolically as I took the vow. I would not surrender my imagination. But I got 'serious' about Buddhism nonetheless. And the imagination problem was like the woman problem, something you were expected to put up with."[77] She also observed that the tantric tradition, like the Judeo-Christian tradition, accorded respect to female *principles,* such as "wisdom," but real women challenged the lama-driven patriarchal structure.[78] "One didn't swallow Buddhism with its sexism whole, or the poetry scene of the sixties with its sexism whole."[79]

Fortunately, the lama who founded the Naropa Institute, Chogyam Trungpa Rinpoche, was himself a poet. Upon his arrival in the West, he reportedly asked a question Americans rarely ask themselves: "Where are the poets? Take me to your poets!"[80] In 1974 in Boulder, Colorado, Trungpa founded the country's first institution of higher learning influenced by Buddhist traditions. At a meeting that summer with Allen Ginsberg, Anne Waldman, Diane di Prima, John Cage, and others, Trungpa requested that Waldman and Ginsberg design a poetics program at Naropa where poets and meditators could learn each other's practices.[81] Almost immediately, the Jack Kerouac School of Disembodied Poetics emerged, an apparitional Moisopolon Domo dreamt up by Waldman and Ginsberg during an August all-nighter where the friends and roommates tossed out fanciful names for chairs, such as the "Emily Dickinson Chair of Silent Scribbling" and the "Frank O'Hara Chair of Urban Gossip."[82]

The one fantastical name that stuck was the name of the school itself. Kerouac's name was chosen because, in his beatific literary visions and journeys, he had himself realized and found a continuous mind-stream language to compassionately express a culture's *samsara*, its wheel of suffering: the First Noble Truth. Waldman came up with "disembodied," a spur-of-the-moment inspiration that grew layered meanings as the school evolved. The first layer of significance involved the Tibetan Buddhist notion of "lineage" as applied to the poet ancestors, not all of whom were alive, who were still "hovering on the tongues of young contemporaries, and we were still feeding on these elders with a sense of continuing the lineage."[83]

In order to simultaneously direct the Poetry Project and be the chief administrator of the Kerouac school, Waldman's energy had to increase commensurate to her growing status in popular culture. *People* magazine, focusing on Waldman's worldly presence, ran an article on her in August 1975: "In the rarefied world of avant-garde poetry, Anne Waldman is queen, a vampish one at that, cool, chic with long cigarette and Campari and soda. Her court is in Manhattan's ratty East Village. . . ." It goes on to describe her new court in Boulder, where "Waldman, 30, has made ankle-length silk sheaths, heels, designer scarves and clanking jewelry the last word in mountaineer mufti."[84] Waldman's perceived glamour in no way detracted from the serious academic mission at the Naropa poetics school. In 1975, during its first full summer of classes, two hundred students arrived to study with luminaries including Gregory Corso, Ted Berrigan, Dick Gallup, Larry Fagin, Diane di Prima, Joanne Kyger, Meredith Monk, Philip Whalen, Ed Sanders, W. S. Merwin, and many others. Serious but not stifling, the summer program opened up with William Burroughs "lecturing on the word as virus, time-travel through cut-ups . . . & how to become invisible simply walking down the street—an old Mafia trick."[85] Referring to Ginsberg's, di Prima's, and her own vision for the Kerouac school, Waldman emphasized that the study and writing of poetry should be taught as an ordinary, everyday practice that encouraged sanity.[86] For the past thirty years, the Jack Kerouac School of Disembodied Poetics has made good on the promise to cultivate a sane poetry culture that broadens the practice beyond the careerist focus of most traditional M.F.A. programs. Naropa Institute has become Naropa University and offers M.F.A. degrees in poetry and fiction through the Jack Kerouac School.

In the end, the lasting legacy of the Jack Kerouac School, the Poetry Project, and the ongoing poetry networks that formed around these two communities, or *sanghas*, is the evidence they provide that the vow to *community* is a much worthier vow than one made on behalf of one's own success, alone. Among poets, it has been fashionable—at least since the Romantic period—to cultivate the self-image of the solitary individualist who remains distinguished from the community rather than defined in relation to it. The paradoxical identity of poet-administrator, however, carries with it the risk that one's standing as "poet," pure and uncorrupted by the prosaic business of business, is diminished. Bernadette Mayer understood, when asked to direct the Poetry Project, that "although here was one of the most worthwhile tasks in the universe, there was the embarrassment among other poets of running a poetry 'institution'!"[87] Waldman may have struggled in the early years to overcome the suspicion of a few skeptics that, as a poet, she was not a purist. She may also have encountered the latent, if not express, attitude that community service is related to domestic and familial work. Care-taking professions have been feminized, hence culturally disempowered, in comparison to the grander pursuit of one's own place in Eliot's tradition of talented poet-individuals.

When Waldman took her vow to poetry, it was like the Buddhist Mahayana vow: a vow to enlightenment on behalf of others. "The practices as I understood them . . . were shamanistic and communal as well. You benefited not only yourself but others in the process."[88] Many historians have lamented the failure of the sixties experiment to make the counterculture's ten-year experiment in communitarian values the lasting values of the culture at large. The success of two progressive poetry institutions in an American culture that actively devalues poetry shows that progressive arts communities can succeed without the financial and ideological support of mainstream culture. In the years since the end of the Great Society funding, increasingly conservative federal administrations have mounted successful attacks on what remains of the threatening counterculture by slowly killing off the National Endowment for the Arts and linking its funding decisions to the perceived moral character of the artist or institution. To witness the results of the past thirty years' spread of global capitalism and fundamentalism is to appreciate deeply Anne Waldman's visionary labor in cultivating poetry cultures where non-competitive, non-aggressive principles are the prevailing values of the entire community.

NOTES

I gratefully acknowledge the thoughtful assistance of Anne Waldman, Laura Perkins, and the Special Collections librarians at the University of Michigan, Alice Notley, Ron Padgett, Daniel Kane, Sy Johnson, and Sydney Zamochnick.

1. Anne Waldman, "Anne Waldman: 1945– ," *Contemporary Authors Autobiography Series* (Gale Research Series 17, 1993): 270.

2. Anne Waldman, "'I Is Another': Dissipative Structures," in *Vow to Poetry* (Minneapolis: Coffee House Press, 2001), 194.

3. Donald Allen, *The New American Poetry* (New York: Grove Press, 1960). In his preface to the second edition, *The Postmoderns: The New American Poetry Revised* (New York: Grove Press, 1982), Donald Allen writes of the postmodern post–World War II poets he includes: "They have been called variously by literary critics and observers projectivists, the poetic 'underground,' the New York School, the Beat Generation, the San Francisco Renaissance, the Black Mountain Poets, or, most generally, the avant-garde. . . . [Charles Olson] was the first . . . to use the term 'postmodern' in its present significance" (9–10).

4. Allen, *The Postmoderns*, 9. In his preface, Allen wrote of the New American poets, "Their most common bond is a spontaneous utilization of subject and technique, a prevailing 'instantism' that nevertheless does not preclude discursive ponderings and large-canvassed reflections" (9).

5. Waldman, "'I Is Another': Dissipative Structures," 195.

6. Anne Waldman, personal interview, 18 April 2002.

7. Waldman, "Anne Waldman," 272–73.

8. Frank O'Hara, "Personism," in *Postmodern American Poetry,* ed. Paul Hoover (New York: Norton, 1994). O'Hara writes in his manifesto, "I don't believe in god, so I don't have to make elaborately sounded structures. I hate Vachel Lindsay, always have, I don't even like rhythm, assonance, all that stuff. You just go on your nerve. If someone's chasing you down the street with a knife you just run, you don't turn around a shout, 'Give it up! I was a track star for Mineola Prep'" (633).

9. Anne Waldman, "Early Work," Unpublished poem, *Anne Waldman Papers*, Special Collections Library, University of Michigan.

10. Anne Waldman, introduction to *Out of This World: An Anthology of the St. Mark's Poetry Project, 1966–1991*, ed. Anne Waldman (New York: Crown, 1991).

11. Waldman, "Anne Waldman," 275–76.

12. Anne Waldman, "My Life a List," in *Vow to Poetry*, 27.

13. Anne Waldman, introduction to *Iovis I: All Is Full of Jove* (Minneapolis: Coffee House Press, 1986), 2.

14. Daniel Kane, *All Poets Welcome: The Lower East Side Poetry Scene in the 1960s* (Berkeley: University of California Press, 2003), 156.

15. Lewis Warsh, qtd. in Kane, *All Poets Welcome*, 174.

16. Waldman, "Anne Waldman," 272.

17. One member, Ron Padgett, claimed "she could easily hold her own in this group of male poets" (personal interview, 12 Aug. 2003).

18. Stephen Koch, telephone interview, 11 Aug. 2003.

19. Anne Waldman, e-mail to the author, 17 Aug. 2003.

20. Anne Waldman, "Journals and Notebooks," journal entry, *Anne Waldman Papers*, Special Collections Library, University of Michigan, 9 Jan. 1967.

21. Ted Berrigan and Dick Gallup, "80th Congress," in *The World Anthology*, ed. Anne Waldman (New York: Bobbs-Merrill, 1969), 81.

22. Waldman, e-mail to the author, 17 Aug. 2003.

23. Ted Berrigan and Anne Waldman, *Memorial Day* (New York: Poetry Project, 1971).

24. Anne Waldman, introduction to *The Angel Hair Anthology*, ed. Anne Waldman and Lewis Warsh (New York: Granary Books, 2001), xxiv.

25. Anne Waldman, "Sunday/Monday, April 20/69," in *O My Life* (New York: Angel Hair Books, 1969).

26. Waldman, "Anne Waldman," 277. Indeed, Waldman was prolific during these years, publishing four books in three years: *Baby Breakdown* (New York: Bobbs-Merrill, 1970); *Giant Night* (Corinth Books, 1970); *No Hassles* (Kulchur Foundation, 1971); *Life Notes* (Bobbs-Merrill, 1973).

27. Anne Waldman, "Tape," in *Baby Breakdown*, 20.

28. Kane, *All Poets Welcome*, 157–58.

29. Ibid., 124.

30. Ibid., 125.

31. Steve Facey, qtd. in ibid., 124.

32. Ibid., 132.

33. Todd Gitlin, *The Sixties: Years of Hope, Days of Rage* (New York: Bantam, 1987), 31.

34. Maureen Owen, in Waldman, ed., *Out of This World*, 668.

35. Waldman, introduction to *Out of This World*, 2.

36. Ted Berrigan, qtd. in Kane, *All Poets Welcome*, 140–41.

37. Maria Damon and Ronna C. Johnson, "Recapturing the Skipped Beats," *Chronicle of Higher Education* 46.6 (1999): B4–B6.

38. Waldman, introduction to *Out of This World*, 4.

39. Kane, *All Poets Welcome*, xviii.

40. Anne Waldman, "Poetry Project," handwritten memo, *Anne Waldman Papers*, Special Collections Library, University of Michigan, 1970.

41. *Poetry Project Newsletter*, no. 22, 1 Feb. 1975.

42. Allen Ginsberg, foreword to *Out of This World*, xxix.

43. Kane, *All Poets Welcome*, 185.

44. Gitlin, *The Sixties*, 85.

45. Alice Echols, *Shaky Ground* (New York: Columbia University Press, 2002), 215.

46. Waldman, "My Life a List," 31.

47. Waldman, "Hi Everyone!" in *Baby Breakdown*, 1.

48. Waldman, "Journals and Notebooks," Aug. 1969.

49. Anne Waldman, "Take Me to Your Poets," in *Vow to Poetry*, 85.

50. Anne Waldman, "Fast Speaking Woman," in *Fast Speaking Woman: Chants and Essays* (San Francisco: City Lights Books, 1996), 3.

51. Waldman, "Feminafesto," in *Vow to Poetry*, 24.

52. Kim Whitehead, *The Feminist Poetry Movement* (Jackson: University of Mississippi Press, 1996), 4.

53. Ibid., 23.

54. Ibid., 44.

55. Waldman, "Anne Waldman," 277.

56. Waldman, "Journals and Notebooks," June 1968.

57. Kane, *All Poets Welcome*, 172–73.

58. Waldman, "Journals and Notebooks," 22 Jan. 1968.

59. Anne Waldman, qtd. in Kane, *All Poets Welcome*, 180–81.

60. Waldman interview, 18 April 2002.

61. Anne Waldman, "Vow," in *Vow to Poetry*, 135.

62. Anne Waldman, "Gun Power," in *Baby Breakdown*, 6–7.

63. Echols, *Shaky Ground*, 107.

64. Anne Waldman, "Auguries of Speed," in *Baby Breakdown*, 107.

65. Albers, Goldshmidt, and Oehlke, *1971: Klassenkampfe in Westeuropa* (Hamburg, 1971), 59, 184, qtd. in Eric Hobsbawm, *The Age of Extremes: A History of the World 1914–1991* (New York: Vintage, 1996), 324.

66. Bob Holman, qtd. in Kane, *All Poets Welcome*, 182.

67. Anne Waldman, "Kind Days," in *Baby Breakdown*, 10.

68. Miguel Algarin, "Volume and Value of the Breath in Poetry," *Talking Poetics from Naropa Institute* 2 (1979): 326.

69. Waldman, "Anne Waldman," 280.

70. Anne Waldman, "Oppositional Poetics," in *Vow to Poetry*, 61.

71. Anne Waldman, letter to Nancy Petersen, TS, 1 Nov. 1974, "City Lights Books Records," The Bancroft Library, Berkeley.

72. Anne Waldman, correspondence: Waldman to Lawrence Ferlinghetti; "City Lights Books Records," The Bancroft Library, University of California, Berkeley, 12 Jan. 1975.

73. Anne Waldman, "Fast Speaking Woman & the Dakini Principle," in *Fast Speaking Woman*, 35.

74. Ibid., 39.

75. Anne Waldman, "'Fast Speaking Woman' & the Dakini Principle" (undated typescript predating published draft), *Anne Waldman Papers*, Special Collections Library, University of Michigan.

76. Waldman, "Vow," 47.

77. Waldman, "Take Me to Your Poets," 83.

78. Ibid., 84.

79. Ibid., 8.

80. Ibid., 82.

81. Waldman, "Anne Waldman," 282–83.

82. Anne Waldman, "The Kerouac School of Disembodied Poetics at Naropa Institute," *Anne Waldman Papers*, Special Collections Library, University of Michigan, 1975.

83. Waldman, "Take Me to Your Poets," 86.

84. "A Priestess of New York Poetry Brings a Glamorous Anthology of Pros to a Colorado High," *People*, Aug. 1975

85. Waldman, "The Kerouac School," 3.

86. Ibid.

87. Bernadette Mayer, in Anne Waldman, ed., *Out of This World*, 660.

88. Waldman, "Take Me to Your Poets," 82.

7

Joan Baez
A Singer and Activist

Avital H. Bloch

National organizations, from the American Civil Liberties Union to the American Institute of Public Service and Americans for Democratic Action, have bestowed honors on Joan Baez in recognition of her role in radical and pacifist politics since the early 1960s. Baez played an important role in the promotion of peace, civil rights, and other social causes, yet most Americans have known, and still remember, her primarily as a folk singer at the height of her popularity during the 1960s and 1970s. Six certified Gold Albums and four Grammy nominations affirmed her artistic and commercial success. But arguably, Baez's greatest accomplishment was in combining a philosophy of nonviolence, civil rights ideology, and the anti–Vietnam War cause with her artistic career, in the spirit of the radical movements of the 1960s. These movements dissolved conventional boundaries between politics and culture, blending art and activism, style and theory, body and spirit, private and public. Adopting this attitude, numerous artists took radical views about the era's most controversial political issues. Unlike most of them, however, Baez could not separate her art and her politics. Through the multilayered complexity of her life as an artist, activist, and woman, Joan Baez became a cultural and political symbol of the turbulent era known as "the sixties."

Before Baez rose to any distinction as a singer, she had already encountered radical politics. The first ideal she absorbed as a child from her parents was the philosophy of nonviolence, which would become the principal passion guiding her political consciousness and activism throughout the 1960s and subsequent decades. Joan (Joanie) Chandos Baez was born in 1941 as the middle of three sisters.[1] Her mother, Joan

Bridge Baez, was born in Edinburgh, Scotland, daughter of a man who was both an Episcopalian minister and a drama professor. Bridge Baez was reared in the United States, where she studied dance before marrying Albert Vinicio Baez. Albert grew up in Puebla, Mexico. Converting from Catholicism, he become a Methodist minister, arrived in the United States, and trained as a physicist. Motivated by spirituality, a sense of social justice, and pacifist ethics, in the early 1950s the Baez family became Quaker. Unlike other Stanford University Ph.D.s recruited at that time for atomic research, Albert Baez rejected the cold war ideology that supported such work. He chose academic teaching, research, and consulting and became an anti-nuclear activist. In 1957, he was among the founders in California of the Peninsula Committee for the Abolition of Nuclear Tests, a group active against the policies of atomic development and testing. At home, at Quaker meetings and camps, and at the American Friends Service Committee First Day School she attended, his daughter assimilated pacifist beliefs.[2]

In the Quaker environment, two individuals especially exercised early influence on Baez and in the years to come would continue to provide ideological illumination and political collaboration.[3] Ira Sandperl was a Jewish radical and Gandhi scholar who preached social change through nonviolent means. Much older than Baez, Sandperl became her "bearded Guru," comrade, and close friend, who reinforced in her the ideal of nonviolence. In a Friends Service Committee conference in 1956, Baez also encountered another figure who would become a source of ideological inspiration and a personal friend: Martin Luther King Jr. In the first encounter, the leader of the civil rights movement spoke about "injustice and suffering, and about fighting with weapons of love." Nearly three decades later, she reported in her memoir *And a Voice to Sing*: "When he finished his speech, I was on my feet, cheering and crying: King was giving a shape and a name to my passionate but inarticulate beliefs."[4]

While she took part in the political excitement of the Quaker and anti-nuclear groups, Baez also began to express her aesthetic talents in drawing and, especially, singing. In 1957, she first attended Weavers and Pete Seeger concerts and also discovered Odetta, Harry Belafonte, and the Kingston Trio. All were known as the biggest names of the era's "folksong revival." After accepting a job at MIT in 1958 and moving with the family from Palo Alto, California, to Belmont, Massachusetts, Albert Baez introduced Joan to the clubs and coffeehouses in nearby

Cambridge. In the areas of Boston populated heavily by students, those spots became centers of the emerging "urban" folk revival, which was concentrated in the larger cities and campuses across the country. Baez, who was shifting away from her youthful taste for pop, country-western, and R&B, instead chose Seeger as her "second living idol" after Martin Luther King.[5]

The folksong revival of the late 1950s to the mid-1960s extended an ideology that originated in the revival's first wave back in the 1920s and 1930s. Also promoted by the socialist labor movement and the Communist Party, radical scholars of that period surveyed, collected, and documented traditional songs with roots in rural America, the South, black communities, and the urban working class. The movement's leaders idealized what they perceived as the authentic singing of the "folk" or the "people" about hardships, the sorrows of life, and social injustice. The music was understood as the true expressions of American roots and community life, giving "us a consciousness that the rhythms of our hearts and minds are those of countless others as well."[6] In addition to theory about the role of culture in progressive politics, the founders of the revival passed to their followers what would be defined as the official folk material. The assortment included old Anglo-Saxon and southern Appalachian Mountain ballads, black gospel and spirituals, Native American songs, and bluegrass country music, as well as work songs, union hymns, and political broadsides. Foreign traditional material—Creole, Caribbean and Latin American, Hindu, African, Israeli, and Yiddish— also was included in the repertoire.[7]

The new appeal of folk singing took place in a shifting context since the late 1950s. The Beat artists had manifested cultural individualism in response to the inflexible society of the cold war, blacks were struggling for civil rights, and soon the political new left would emerge. Songs that could be associated with industrial labor battles and the fight for racial equality served as a fertile base for a new generation yearning for ideological transformation. The new revival removed the songs and music from their original loci to the culturally and economically dominant parts of the country and introduced the folk material and the political message attached to it to new audiences and musicians. The "citybillies" and "folkniks" directed the music to the radicalized white youth and students, as well as to committed older members of the left and the labor movements, for a while uniting the two generations engaged in progressive

politics.[8] Baez's fascination with Seeger as a bridge figure between the generations reflected her attraction to the political flavor in the art of folk singing.

As a high school student, Baez had already developed her own "standard" and "pure folk" repertory, and singing that revival variety, she rose to fame at the age of seventeen. While she was a first-year student at Boston University, studying drama, she began appearing in the Cambridge student folk establishments, of which the best known was the Club Mt. Auburn 47. There in Harvard Square, she learned from other artists additional folk tunes, bluegrass, and hillbilly songs, so that her selection now included a diversity of ballads, African American and work songs, and music from cultures outside the United States.[9] Her appearance in 1959 at the first Newport Folk Festival won the crowd and marked the beginning of her great success. In 1960, by then quitting college and also singing in New York City clubs, she recorded her first album. She began a decade-long contract with Vanguard Records, the label that prided itself as the place "where music in its purest form could have a chance." Its co-owner, classical musicologist Maynard Solomon, became the "shepherd" and the "architect" of Baez's formative recording career, along with her manager Manny Greenhill. In 1961, with best-selling records and with performances in concert halls, festivals, and campuses attracting audiences of up to ten thousand people at a time, Baez "ruled the folk wave."[10]

Baez's claim to "pure" folk singing appealed to the young generation. Her singing seemed to provide a political message about roots, equality, and simplicity that meshed with the emerging new left's protest against middle-class values, an alienating urban environment, the toughness of the cold war, and an unresponsive political system. Unlike revival singers with an explicitly critical message, in the first years Baez lacked political directness in her lyrics, but her admirers yearned for the emotional messages of universal love, beauty, and suffering in her singing. Such content in her singing fueled a political spirit, even if not presented in a self-evident textual form.[11]

Part of Baez's success may be attributed to the "feminine" image she presented to her audiences. Her early persona blended such traditional, and stereotypical, traits as sensitivity, sentimentality, gentleness, and innocence, which her hallmark songs, the love ballads, transmitted. Traditionally sung by women, according to Baez, these "tragic ballads" were

Fig. 7.1. Joan Baez, drawn by Steven Alcorn. *The Alcorn Studio & Gallery, www.alcorngallery.com*

"unrelenting in their plots of death, misery, and heartbreak" mixed with "joy, loss, and tenderness." The songs romanticized innocence and virginity, just as she herself was then, in her words later, "a sentimental kind of a goof" with a "young and fragile heart," constantly wishing to fall in love. In the eyes of her female fans she was, as journalist Joan Didion described Baez, "the girl who 'feels' things, the girl who has hung on to the freshness and pain of adolescence, the girl ever wounded, ever young," and who "understands . . . beauty and hurt and love."[12]

Through her singing, Baez managed to convey a wide range of expression and empathy. She narrated stories with a minimalist singing approach, offering familiarity even when singing foreign songs. She could impart this sense of familiarity because the music itself conformed to known Western musical traditions and meshed with the contemporary urban "rockabilly" sound.[13] But perhaps the most important component was her voice, which conformed to traditional ideals of women's beauty and "purity." As one historian commented, her image was "virginity-centered," based on the "aching" and "penetrating pure soprano voice" many critics commented on. Poet Langston Hughes wrote in liner notes that Baez's vocal expression reminded one of "the sound of a light, flawlessly cast bell." He and other critics perceived the purity of a voice, which was "as clear as air in the autumn," "like rippling, cool as a mountain stream, [and] clear as the Colorado sunlight in the morning."[14]

Simplicity and innocence balanced the excesses in Baez's presentation. Her voice was not operatic. She avoided chromatization and flirtatious virtuosity. For a long time, she accompanied her singing only with acoustic guitar, the instrument of choice in folk music and increasingly played by women. Reminiscent of the lyre and the lute in early times, the guitar added to Baez's performances a flavor of traditionalism and rural simplicity.[15] She maintained the delicacy of sound even later on, when she incorporated more string plucking into the song arrangements.

Baez's performance style conveyed a certain intimacy, honesty, and naïveté as well. Wearing peasant-style outfits and handwoven accessories suggested a rejection of bourgeois style.[16] Motionless, with long straight hair, no makeup, and sometimes no shoes, she became, as various commentators have said, an "unassuming girl," an "honest personality," communicating "distilled emotion . . . with no irrelevant furbelows of gesture." "She sings with an astounding intimacy," commented folk musician John Cohen. And her body, in Hughes's words again, was "warm . . . And feet with toenails . . . Feet touching earth . . . Human feet with toes—like yours and mine . . . sweet singer of herself—and us."[17]

Baez also appealed to a sense of unifying American patriotism through her music. Maynard Solomon commented: "Joan and her songs give us this sense of common ground, of roots in the past and present of the shared fund of experience which links us . . . to each other, to our history." She related current protest to the national heritage through songs about those "scraping a bare life out of the Appalachian hills or the Alabama cotton-fields or West Virginia slagheaps or the Oklahoma flatlands or California orange-groves."[18] This evocation of common national heritage was significant in relationship to Baez's ethnicity as half Mexican, with dark hair and complexion and a last name Americans had trouble pronouncing properly. By avoiding typical Latin songs and publicly shunning her origins, Baez could moderate both romanticized and racist perceptions of her as an exotic "other" and identify herself as belonging to white mainstream America.[19]

The availability of the new socially critical "topical songs" in the folk style and the emerging grassroots political ferment of the early 1960s urged Baez to further articulate her pacifist worldview and combine singing with politics.[20] Her personal contact with King and his philosophy of nonviolent resistance first drew her to the civil rights movement. She first went to the South in 1961, and in 1962 she conducted a concert tour of southern colleges, insisting on a nondiscrimination policy for audiences. Her first participation in a civil action confronting the police took place in 1963 in Montgomery, Alabama, to which two years later she marched in the freedom ride from Selma.[21]

In the South, Baez experienced the force of African American "freedom songs" as they were sung in their authentic environment and communities. The movement used these songs to weld individuals together and mobilize them through moral support. Baez felt that singing in gatherings at churches and campuses helped her learn what makes people "become a community," so that she could touch people with their own songs. She later said: "I sang in a voice very different from the pure white one. . . . I sang with the soul I was adopting right there in that room." The audience "rose and held hands, swaying back and forth. . . . The singing was soft and tentative and many people were crying." Even more remarkable to Baez was her participation in the March on Washington in August 1963. She remembered her "knees were knocking" while she was leading a crowd of over 250,000 people in singing the civil rights movement's anthem "We Shall Overcome." And she acknowledged the honor to be "near my beloved Dr. King . . . when he let the breath of God thunder through him" during his "I Have a Dream" address. In 1966, Baez was marching at his side in Grenada, Mississippi, accompanying a group of black children toward an all-white school, once again encountering a hostile police force. She mentioned fear but emphasized: "I would be right next to King and quite happy to die there."[22]

The protest politics of the early 1960s motivated Baez also to adopt politically implicit topical songs. That is, she preferred those that asserted "that everything is completely screwy and there just doesn't seem to be much reason to anything," but without using "pamphleteering lyrics." For example, she often sang Melvina Reynolds's allegorical anti-nuclear "What Have They Done to the Rain." "It doesn't protest gently but it sounds gentle," she explained. In Bob Dylan's topical songs that "seemed to update the concepts of justice and injustice," Baez found the right political metaphors for herself. When she met him, not only did she fall in love with him but she also became his greatest admirer. On "Blowin' in the Wind" she commented: "If Bob had never written another song this contribution would be enough for a lifetime."[23] Using her fame, Baez helped Dylan's early career by introducing him in her performances as her guest performer. Before long they were praised together as "purveyors of . . . social consciousness and responsibility."[24]

On many occasions, Baez and Dylan sang together those "fresh and unique" songs Dylan wrote, and which she added to her permanent repertoire. Baez also sang occasionally with her sister Mimi and recorded songs written by Mimi's husband Richard (Dick) Fariña, a close friend of Dylan and himself a figure in the bohemian folk scene until his death in a motorcycle accident in 1966. The four conjoined in a "complex web of romance and musical association," but the stormy romantic relationship of Dylan and Baez was its most publicized part. Her artistic admiration for Dylan and her emotional attachment to him seemed to some observers of the relationship one-sided, suggesting that to Baez, Dylan became a man to look up to, while she often depreciated herself.[25] In a world where men dominated the music industry and talent and ideas were thought of as belonging to them, Baez was still accustomed to think of males as superior, as people from whom she had to learn. A documentary on Dylan's 1965 tour of England, on which he was joined by Baez, showed the media's attention to him, her accomplishments and a solo concert at the Royal Albert Hall notwithstanding.[26]

Gender inhibitions, however, did not limit Baez's political courage. Her artistic and financial success allowed independence and motivated her to expand her range of political protest. "I was in a position now to do something more with my life than just sing," she later wrote. In 1963, she was one of few singers to boycott ABC-TV's folk-singing program *The Hootenanny Show*, protesting the network's blacklisting of Pete Seeger for charges of contempt by the House Un-American Activities Committee (HUAC). In 1964, Baez spoke and sang at the Free Speech Movement (FSM) demonstration at the University of California at Berkeley, close to Carmel, where she had settled since late 1960 after moving back from the East Coast. Baez prided herself for convincing the angry students to claim Sproul Hall at the center of campus "with as much love as they could muster" and to join Ira Sandperl and her for a seminar on civil disobedience. She perceived the new model of campus rebellion as a form of protest that lent itself to nonviolent tactics, the beginning of broader peaceful change in American society.[27]

The year 1964 marked the first of a decade during which Baez, following a pacifist tradition, refused to pay large portions of her income tax. In a public statement to the IRS titled "I Do Not Believe in War," she argued that 60 percent of the taxes went to "build weapons that can take thousands of lives in a second, millions of lives in a day, billions in a week." Warning that the national security principle would eventually blow the world to pieces, she stated: "I draw my own line now." When the issue of the Vietnam War arose, she justified withholding her taxes with the declaration: "This country has gone mad. But I will not go mad with it. I will not pay for organized murder. I will not pay for the War in Vietnam."[28] In later years she would continue by reclaiming portions of her income taxes in federal courts as a conscientious objector to the Vietnam War.

Social issues also made up part of Baez's political agenda. In 1965, she demonstrated with the Assembly of Unrepresented People outside the White House. In 1966 she performed at a benefit for striking farm workers in California, and at a Christmas vigil at San Quentin Penitentiary, she called for the commutation of death sentences. Yet the expanding American intervention in Vietnam replaced the nuclear issue and some of the social themes for peace activists and the old left. Now they were joined by the new left, organized under Students for a Democratic Society (SDS), in protesting the war. The cause quickly presented to Baez new opportunities for public action. And as the disapproval of the war grew, the practice of using music for political opposition expanded. In addition to demonstrations, Baez performed at the "Sing In for Peace in Vietnam" at Carnegie Hall, and she even took the anti-war cause overseas. She lead the 1966 Easter Day anti-war march in West Germany, and in 1967 in Japan, her Hiroshima concert was dedicated to local peace groups.[29] While such events during the early phases of the anti-war movement lacked the dangerous aspect of civil disobedience seen in the civil rights confrontations, they still gave her music and ideology public exposure, as they publicized her determined spirit and political conviction.

Baez's political maturity and commitment to nonviolence peaked with the founding of the Institute for the Study of Nonviolence in Carmel in 1965. "To just feel like doing something good" without knowledge "was not enough," she said of her sense of political duty and the institute's mission of nonviolence training. The school recognized civil disobedience as effective and dignified at a time when anti-war sentiments were intensifying and the political climate radicalizing. Events in Berkeley had demonstrated the force of radicalism in California, just as the San Francisco Bay Area became a center for the emerging counterculture. Thus, what started with Sandperl personally tutoring Baez to complete her political education ended in Baez investing $40,000 in land for the institute. Concerned about the value of their property, however, neighbors attacked the Institute soon after it was initiated, arguing that it attracted "hippies and free-love subversives." The place closed after one month but re-opened later with Baez as its vice president and teaching aide to Sandperl, its president and intellectual leader.[30]

Engaged in the institute, Baez further articulated her pacifist worldview and applied it in the anti–Vietnam War movement. The fundamental principle of nonviolence that transcends all values, as she learned from the teachings Sandperl borrowed from Gandhi, is "the sanctity of life." No person has the right to kill or harm another person since human beings are all equal. Nonviolence instructs people "to be able to feel love for, sensitivity to, and awareness of . . . your fellow men"; therefore no such notion as "enemy" exists to justify use of force against people defined as inferior. Baez recognized that "just causes" exist but believed that even noble objectives never justify violent acts. It is not simply that only peaceful means are legitimate. Since "the means would determine the ends," nonviolent conflict-resolving mechanisms generated by understanding, kindness, caring, and love would better human societies.[31]

Hence, although it embraced emotions instead of physical power, nonviolence was never intended to be passive or submissive. What seemed to critics of nonviolence as surrender to Baez was active, potent, and pragmatic. "You cannot just sit by and ignore the daily horrors that take place in the world," she asserted. Rigorous engagement in civil resistance was needed to inspire the passion of love in adversaries. Baez stressed that such militant spirit lived inside her female body, which was "no more than a breakable twig." She declared herself a "nonviolent soldier," a person "who chooses to be a fighter but not to use weapons" and "aggressive force" to achieve the "nonviolent revolution."[32] Her terms reflected a traditional set of beliefs about violence and gender. Soldiers, aggression, and force were commonly believed to belong to the masculine realm, while love, care, and acceptance were attributed to women. Baez herself did not speak in terms of gender concepts but presented a genderless notion of "human nature," in which she observed two sides: the vicious and violent along with the soft, kind, and trusting. In Baez's utopia, nonviolence intended to attain a world in which the peace-loving "soft, beautiful side," traditionally associated with the female spirit, would triumph, so that all humans viscerally could emerge as equal.[33]

Such utopian objectives did not permit Baez to accept nonviolence as merely a tactical method. Her conviction became so righteous that when the era of civil disobedience gave place to the Black Power movement's more extreme rhetoric, she condemned African Americans who were losing patience with nonviolence. With hatred and destruction as their means, she claimed, theirs was not a real revolution. Baez became disillusioned even with Dr. King. She claimed that his nonviolence turned "petitionary" instead of remaining a force against all forms of oppression. Two years after his death, Baez defined the man she had long held in high esteem for nonviolent heroism as "an American first, a good citizen and a preacher second, a black man third and an exponent of nonviolence fourth."[34]

The forms in which the Institute for the Study of Nonviolence promoted Gandhian nonviolence also revealed the growing interest in "Oriental" philosophies and spiritualism among young Americans. Many of them took up such practices as silent meditation, which was included in the institute's program. Baez also took up meditation. She applauded its power to reduce fears and confusions, "attach people to the love in themselves," and connect to "people and life and death and everything that's just very, very real." Practicing meditation, Baez believed, strengthened her while it intensified her spiritualism and aspiration for love.[35]

In the early part of the 1960s, Baez was considered a folk performer, her music and style fitting into the contemporary definitions of folk authenticity. From mid-decade on, however, commercialization, large music festivals, and the mass distribution of records affected the revival. While the music was shifting away from its earlier "purity" and losing its immediate intimacy, it was also reaching more people, of different ages and with various political and aesthetic expectations. The assortment of "taste groups" represented a complex ideological scene consisting of the new left, its countercultural and student variations, feminists, and the broader anti-war generational mix.[36] This was the audience for Baez to touch as she expanded her repertoire and added new elements to her performance and image.

Yet, in the complex cultural and political climate of the late 1960s, the musical challenges Baez faced were difficult. When neither "pure" nor topical folk singing sufficed to express the generation's feelings of alienation, and sophisticated rock 'n' roll spread, folk music gave way to "folk rock."[37] This new sub-genre of rock dared singers like Baez to take musical risks. She chose to preserve her hallmark ballad selection, but added to it contemporary songs and more elaborate arrangements. The new songs were by young writers such as Dick Fariña, Paul Simon, and Tim Hardin and also included adapted Beatles and Rolling Stones songs. On the 1968 collection *Any Day Now*, she presented her interpretations of Dylan's earlier songs; in Nashville, she recorded music in a country-western style; and finally she chose to sing with a band. Scored poetry, mainly by classic European poets, added novelty to the artistic course Baez was taking, while it contributed to the folk legacy of meaningful texts and non-American sources. And finally, following the example of a growing number of female singers in the folk and singer-songwriter traditions, such as Buffy Sainte Marie, Janis Ian, and Carole King, Baez felt she "should give [songwriting] a try" too. Her first song was released in 1969, but it was not until 1971 that *Blessed Are . . .* came out with nine original songs. In the next two years, more were featured on *Come from the Shadows* and *Where Are You Now, My Son?* Baez's songs continued mostly to focus on personal themes, written from a woman's perspective. "Sweet Sir Galahad," for example, was a metaphoric ballad about Mimi's stream of emotions during her second wedding, while "Blessed Are" echoed the painful tragedy of Janis Joplin's death. "Love Song to a Stranger," about Baez's "transient love affairs," explored her thoughts about liberated female sexuality.[38]

These changes in musical direction did not indicate a radical transformation. Still tied to folk in sound and form, and centered in women's concerns in theme, Baez's music reflected only the necessary adjustments to a turbulent time. Rock 'n' roll, which came to rule popular culture, remained to her a disconcerting phenomenon because in various ways it developed as a force contradictory to her folk singing and politics. Musically, rock protested through the electric guitar. Its capacity to produce high volume, noise, and a combination of tones destabilized the familiar organization of sound and established new musical structures. The electric technology and powerful metallic sound diffused in immense outdoor spaces especially threatened the female folk-singing aesthetics of nature, tranquility, and intimacy. Furthermore, the electric guitar in the rock singer's hands, in addition to his outrageous outfits and motions onstage, displayed overt male sexuality and masculine supremacy, which were much reduced in the more affectionate and gender-egalitarian realm of folk, in which Baez was involved.[39]

While Baez may have felt uneasy with those aspects of rock culture, she specifically cited rock music's failure to address the major political questions of the time. Although Baez was an activist and a radical, the hostility she expressed toward rock culture mirrored her critique of the new left's extremes. As a nonviolence advocate, she rejected the left's late-1960s rhetoric of violent revolution, while in the counterculture she despised the political apathy and anti-social attitudes she saw in the flower children's "mystique of passivity." She also had no patience for the infatuation with drugs that take people "out of this sphere" and "do great violence to the spirit." Only addressing the personal concerns of indifferent youth, rock lyrics, Baez thought, lacked ideological content. Those attitudes seemed a far cry from the sense of political duty, discipline, and activism that characterized the folk generation.[40] One of the reasons she began writing songs may have been to provide some political message rock lacked, especially against the war, but also to criticize rock 'n' roll's celebration of drugs.[41]

Baez understood that the counterculture's idea of revolution was no longer political, as she would wish it to be, but a cultural rebellion through rock music. She commented that the Woodstock Festival, the highlight of rock music in 1969, had nothing to do with political revolution. Indeed, she saw rock 'n' roll as the music of false and dangerous revolution. She maintained that the music to which she was committed could express "a whole other level of being which rock doesn't come close to."[42] Thus, as the rock style became especially foreign to Baez as a singer and a politically conscious woman, her performance at Woodstock carried great symbolic weight. At a massive "electric" concert celebrating youth rebellion and free love, this "Madonna-like" woman, a "tangible Sibyl," and eight months pregnant at that, arrived with her mother. Trying to speak to the communal needs of thousands, she supported her rendition of the tender folk classic "Joe Hill" just with her acoustic guitar.[43]

Against such a background, Dylan's music became an issue for Baez. Much was said about his provocative appearance in 1965 at the Newport Festival, where he replaced the acoustic guitar with an electric one. The romantic split at that time between Baez and Dylan also signaled a widening ideological gap.[44] Dylan's apocalyptic poetry, nasal voice, and harsh guitar chords more easily fit into the rock culture than with Baez's folk music and style. When Baez recorded Dylan's earlier songs, they lacked his expression and meanings. She stated that she chose none of the "nasty, hateful, ugly songs," of which her interpretations, one critic wrote, sounded like "pale renditions."[45] As Baez matured and became increasingly independent, she dared to denounce even the men she had looked up to. Because Dylan was walking away from social commitment, like King, he had become a disappointment.

The frustrations with rock 'n' roll even caused Baez to distrust music's power to transcend mere pleasure. She still held that "singing is a joy" and "it's beautiful and it's neat to have beautiful things in a world that's falling apart and deteriorating and ugly." But disillusioned with the capacity of songs to convert people, she confessed that singing to her had become "more a diversion than a vocation." "I don't think that I could pretend that I could save the world with music," Baez explained in 1966. In 1970, she declared, "All those sounds . . . are irrelevant to the only real question of this century," which to her was the possibility of the nonviolent revolution. She began to believe that spoken words could effect political persuasion, and more frequently she included direct political commentary in her concerts, as in her appeals for draft resistance. Many people, however, rejected her "pompous intellectualizing" and "emotional oration." Preferring her as an artist, they wanted the music through which "shines a love of humanity and peace."[46]

Baez knew the limitations of rhetoric: "I wouldn't expect there to be more than about five people at any of my concerts who agree wholeheartedly with what I say." Indeed, because of her bold political critique in the late 1960s, and also perhaps because she defied the cultural mandate that women act frail and obedient, some Americans disapproved of her. In 1967, the CIA tried to silence her in a Tokyo television show by convincing the interpreter to erase an anti-war statement, and CBS-TV's *The Smothers Brothers Comedy Hour* censured her comments on the draft. In the press that same year, cartoonist Al Capp created the *Joanie Phoanie* strip, lampooning Baez as, in her words, a two-faced rich "show-biz slut." And because of "unpatriotic activities," the conservative Daughters of the American Revolution denied Baez the Constitution Hall in Washington, D.C., as a concert venue.[47]

Yet none of these reactions seemed as difficult to face as those Baez confronted after she was introduced to draft resistance. In 1967, she twice picketed the Armed Forces Induction Center in Oakland with the draft-resisting group The Resistance, whose radicalism was based on nonviolence as the source for social revolution. These actions ended in publicized arrests of Baez, along with her mother and her sister Mimi, who joined her in a display of the ideological solidarity of the family's women. The second encounter with the authorities brought Joanie and Joan Sr. to Santa Rita Rehabilitation Center for forty-five days.[48] Through their participation in the public action, the Baez women offered a model of intergenerational cooperation. In an era known for the "generation gap" between conservative parents and rebellious youngsters, that model constituted a metaphorical message about the extension of emotional and political commitment from one's immediate relationships to wider humanity.

In those risky acts of civil disobedience, Baez indeed played the role of a "soldier," a role typically associated with the male hero who fulfills a high duty through bodily strength and sacrifice. Despite the courage she demonstrated, however, Baez regarded the male draft resisters as the real heroes. She dedicated her 1968 "philosophical autobiography" *Daybreak* "with love, admiration, and gratefulness to the men who find themselves facing imprisonment for resisting the draft."[49] Baez also used her concerts for encouraging draft resistance. In the activist-oriented performance she developed, she blended the artistic and the political in a routine in which young men went on stage and handed her their draft cards while making an anti-war statement.

In 1968, Baez's anti-draft involvement resulted once again in a controversy. It centered on a poster The Resistance issued, which photographed her, together with sisters Pauline and Mimi, sitting on an elegant antique-style couch in a crossed-legged, ladylike fashion but barefoot and touching a woven straw rug, under the caption "GIRLS SAY YES to boys who say NO." Enraged and unimpressed by the poster's parodic chic, women's liberationists interpreted the message as one of sexual submission. Baez, however, asserted that the poster intended to object to the exclusion of women from anti-draft activism, and to inspire in them a sense of responsibility for peace. She defended the poster, saying that women "can help if they change their . . . conception of what 'hero' means" and "what qualities in a man they can really respect."[50]

Baez certainly responded to the controversial call of saying yes to men who say no when, in March 1968, she married David V. Harris, the student leader at Stanford University who founded The Resistance. To Baez, Harris may have embodied the man "feminized" enough in his commitment to nonviolence yet masculine in the revolutionary eloquence of his new left style. They married in a service performed by the director of the Episcopal Peace Fellowship, following the *Canadian Book of Prayer* as a tribute to war resisters exiled in Canada. The wedding took place in the middle of a speaking and singing campus tour Baez and Harris did together, to which the FBI attached a surveillance agent, and which the couple continued after the event. The press defined it as "the political marriage of the year" of "Mr. and Mrs. Peace." To Baez it meant that the "two halves of a circle" became "a whole." It was a metaphor about the merging of private and political lives, but it also represented a sacred commitment to peace. Harris's arrest in 1969 for refusing induction into the military underlined the political commitment they felt as a couple and the price they paid for the anti-war cause. For the twenty-two months of his imprisonment, she waited for him with their baby Gabriel Earl, the "child of peace." She felt "torn and suffering and estranged" but obligated to live up to her "established name, and his, and the image society had of us together."[51]

Although Baez asserted some new understanding of gender, the media exposed conservative gender relations in the couple's interactions with one another. In the privacy of their house and kitchen, Baez appeared as a warm mother and housewife. She stated in an interview to *Playboy*: "I've learned how to cook and I love it. No women's liberation front is going to take that away from me." Harris, meanwhile, appeared as the inspiring ideologue, while she was positioned behind him, merely echoing his words. He made authoritative political pronouncements, while she offered intimate and personal comments.[52] Baez faced difficulty adapting to the mores of feminism, as she repeated the pattern of deference to the "great men" in her life.

Following Harris's return from prison in 1971, Baez divorced him. It seems that she could find independent public expression only when she was on her own and in control of her space. Now, her early "aura of warmth and beauty" began to give way to a more mature and sophisticated style. She cut her hair short and wore "more expensive and sedate" clothes, creating an image of a woman, as various observers mentioned, "less angelic and more human," "firmly rooted in the insistence of inner and outer peace as a way of life." With "uncommon grace," one critic wrote, she projected "a portrait of a woman . . . from which anyone . . . ought to be able to draw strength and comfort." In creating a new public image, Baez highlighted motherhood and family, often connecting her role as mother to her anti-war politics. In an interview in 1970, for example, she said: "There is me . . . mother of a nearly-three year old boy . . . thinking about children dying in Vietnam."[53] Her child and other family members occasionally joined her performances, making these concerts, as one journalist described, like "a reunion of people with shared feelings . . . who . . . wanted to be kept up to date on the political activities of her family."[54]

As Baez acquired competence and activist skills, her political work assumed a broader scale. In 1971, she played a major role in organizing Amnesty International on the West Coast, and in 1972 she again devoted energies to ending the war in Vietnam. With Coretta Scott King and Women Strike for Peace (WSP), an organization of mothers for peace resolutions, with which Baez had collaborated since 1967, she organized "Ring Around the Congress." In this demonstration, women and children from across the country surrounded the Capitol, demanding that Congress stop funding the war. For the first time Baez experienced racially divisive politics and opposition, when members of Washington's black community, led by Marion Barry, tried to stop the anti-war action, insisting on the priority of anti-racist activism instead. King's wife resigned the organizing committee, while Baez kept fighting against the hurdles. At the event, Mimi sang with her; the participating women were playing with their children; and messages to Vietnamese children were tape-recorded.[55] Along with WSP's maternalist rather than feminist viewpoint, Baez helped reinforce the notion that the struggle for peace required "feminine" sensibilities and mores. She also conveyed a message to the larger peace movement to adopt the rhetoric of family belonging, to wage unity among all the members of the vast "family" that comprised the nation.[56]

In December 1972, Baez visited Hanoi. With ex–Brigadier General Telford Taylor, who was sent to investigate suspected war crimes, she represented the Committee of Liaison with Servicemen Detained in North Vietnam and was a guest of the North Vietnam Committee for Solidarity with the American People. She went with what she defined as a "deep-seated opinion that war itself is a crime; that the killings of one child, the burning of one village, the dropping of one bomb sinks us into such depths of depravity." What she witnessed there only confirmed to her the urgency of ending the war. In Hanoi, Baez wrote, she was "at the receiving end of the sixty percent of our taxes that go to the euphemism known as the Defense Department," referring to the terrifying experience during her stay of the aerial bombing by the United States called the "Christmas bombing." "The things that I felt and saw and thought and smelled were to me outrageous, heart-rending, and terrifying," she wrote about the fear for her own life and the devastating scenes of human suffering.[57]

In Baez's accounts of the visit, she once again conveyed anti-war sentiments from a motherist point of view. Most emotional were the encounters with women, children, and old people who lost loved ones in the bombings. She revealed a capacity to reach out, to show solidarity, and to mourn with these grieving people through physical contact and gestures. "Let me share your agony" was the motto of the song she wrote about Hanoi, "Where Are You Now, My Son?" "Where are you, my son" were the words of an old woman whose son lay dead in the mud, who "like a wounded old cat, could only tread back and forth over the place she'd last seen him, moaning her futile song *Where are you now, my son?*" The song was also an apology: "And I can only bow in utter humbleness and ask / Forgiveness and forgiveness for the things we've brought to pass." "As long as I see one kid's face a day, that will be enough to remind me that I can't take part in killing," she wrote when she returned.[58] Her endeavor to tell the American public about the horrors she witnessed signaled her passionate desire to see the war end.

True to her leftist politics and her rather unexamined gender stance, Baez developed the most powerful weapons in her own arsenal toward the goal of peace. She had, by the end of the 1960s, learned to direct the "feminine" qualities that had once defined and sometimes limited her, to the very causes that the movement had deemed "masculine": war resistance and unequivocal condemnation of U.S. foreign policy. Like many woman of the pre-feminist or bridge generation, Baez held on to traditional gender notions, in her politics as in her music, even as she in fact lived the life of a radicalized, indeed liberated, woman.

Baez became a symbol of the sixties, yet she must be assessed as a transitional figure, living both in and between eras. While she represented the continuity of the postwar peace, civil rights, and folk movements into the 1960s, she simultaneously symbolized the difficulties the 1950s generation experienced in bridging over to the new generation. Through a complex and constantly re-created web of cultural, artistic, political, and gender values, Baez responded to a shifting political-cultural atmosphere. The mix of protest and utopianism, together with tradition and pragmatism, offered a "something-for-everyone" package, making it possible for Baez to serve as "ambassador for youth" even as she appealed to segments of the adult "shirt-and-tie audience."[59] During a period when cultural paradigms were shifting and politics was in turmoil, she personified both transformation and continuity as the essence of the sixties. That not only made Baez a mediator between generations but also an icon of the era.

NOTES

1. The older sister is Pauline. The younger sister, Mimi, passed away in 2001.
2. Robert Cooney and Helen Michalowski, eds., *The Power of the People: Active Nonviolence in the United States* (Philadelphia: New Society, 1987), 132; Joan Baez, *And a Voice to Sing With: A Memoir* (New York: Summit Books, 1987), 23–24, 39; Joan Baez, *Daybreak* (New York: Dial, 1968), 36–52; Albert V. Baez and Joan Baez Sr., *A Year in Baghdad* (Santa Barbara, Calif.: John Daniel, 1988). See also Brian Easlea, *Fathering the Unthinkable: Masculinity, Scientists and the Nuclear Arms Race* (London: Pluto Press, 1983); Thomas Raymond Wellock, *Critical Masses: Opposition to Nuclear Power in California, 1958–1978* (Madison: University of Wisconsin Press, 1998).
3. Baez, *Voice to Sing*, 24–25, 28, 38.
4. Baez, *Voice to Sing*, 41–42; Joan Didion, "Just Folks at a School for Nonviolence," *New York Times* magazine, 27 February 1966, 17–19, 36, 40; Baez, *Daybreak*, 56–67; David A. De Turk and A. Poulin, Jr., "Joan Baez—An Interview," in *The American Folk Scene: Dimensions of the Folksong Revival* (New York: Dell, 1967), 235, 239.
5. Baez, *Voice to Sing*, 34–39, 42–44, 60; Robert Cantwell, *When We Were Good: The Folk Revival* (Cambridge: Harvard University Press, 1996), 5; Benjamin Filene, *Romancing the Folk: Public Memory and American Roots Music* (Chapel Hill: University of North Carolina Press, 2000), 183–204; Ellen J. Stekert, "Cents and Nonsense in the Urban Folksong Movement: 1930–66," in *Transforming Tradition: Folk Music Revivals Examined*, ed. Neil V. Rosenberg (Urbana: University of Illinois Press, 1993), 84–106.
6. Maynard Solomon, liner notes to *Joan Baez in Concert* (Vanguard, 79598-2, 2002). On the first revival, see Ronald D. Cohen, *Rainbow Quest: The Folk Music*

Revival and American Society, 1940-1970 (Amherst: University of Massachusetts Press, 2002), 8–66; R. Serge Denisoff, *Great Day Coming: Folk Music and the American Left* (Urbana: University of Illinois Press, 1971); Robbie Lieberman, *"My Song Is My Weapon": People's Songs, American Communism, and the Politics of Culture, 1930–1950* (Urbana: University of Illinois Press); John A. Lomax, *Adventures of a Ballad Hunter* (New York: Macmillan, 1947).

7. Peter D. Goldsmith, *Making People's Music: Moe Asch and Folkways Records* (Washington, D.C.: Smithsonian Institution Press, 1998), 101–289; Theodore Bickel, *Theo: An Autobiography of Theodore Bickel* (Madison: University of Wisconsin Press, 2002), 152–83; Judith Tick, *Ruth Crawford Seeger: A Composer's Search for American Music* (New York: Oxford University Press, 1997), 233–351.

8. Cohen, *Rainbow Quest*, 93–156; Cantwell, *When We Were Good*, 13–47.

9. Eric Von Schmidt and Jim Rooney, *Baby, Let Me Follow You Down: The Illustrated Story of the Cambridge Folk Years* (Amherst: University of Massachusetts Press, 1994); David Hajdu, *Positively 4th Street: The Lives and Times of Joan Baez, Bob Dylan, Mimi Baez Fariña, and Richard Fariña* (New York: Farrar, Straus and Giroux, 2001), 16–27, 54–55, 145–48; Archie Green, "The Campus Folksong Club: A Glimpse at the Past," in *Transforming Tradition*, 61–72.

10. Arthur Levy, liner notes to *Joan Baez, Vol. 2* (Vanguard, 79597-2, 2001) and *Joan Baez in Concert* (Vanguard, 79598-2, 2002); Baez, *Voice to Sing*, 50–65, Cantwell, *When We Were Good*, 342–43; Bob Rolontz, "Lass with a Delicate Air Slays Folk," *Billboard*, 4 May 1963, 12; John Tebbel, "The Hardy Independent: At Vanguard Records the Brothers Solomon Concentrate on 'Music We Like by People We Respect,'" *High Fidelity*, February 1964, 47–48.

11. Ron Eyerman and Scott Barreta, "From the 30s to the 60s: The Folk Music Revival in the United States," *Theory and Society* (August 1996): 520–23; Cantwell, *When We Were Good*, 325–28, 349.

12. Baez, *Voice to Sing*, 50, 55; Didion, "Just Folks," 41. For the early repertoire, see Joan Baez, *The Joan Baez Songbook* (New York: Ryerson Music, 1964). On ballads, see Bertrand Harris Bronson, *The Ballad as Song* (Berkeley: University of California Press, 1969), 243–56; Linda Phyllis Austern, "Love, Death and Ideas of Music in the English Renaissance," in *Love and Death in the Renaissance*, ed. Kenneth R. Bartlett (Ottawa: Dovehouse, 1991), 17–36; Christine A. Cartwright, "'Barbara Allen': Love and Death in an Anglo American Narrative Folksong," in *Narrative Folksong: New Directions*, ed. Carol L. Edwards and Kathleen E. B. Manley (Boulder: Westview, 1985), 242–58; Cantwell, *When We Were Good*, 217, 339–40; Peter Narváez, "'The Newfie Bullet': The Nostalgic Use of Folklore," in *Media Sense: The Folklore–Popular Culture Continuum*, ed. Peter Narváez and Martin Laba (Bowling Green, Ohio: Bowling Green State University Press, 1987), 65–76.

13. "Sybil with Guitar," *Time*, 23 November 1962, 54; Langston Hughes, "Joan Baez: A Tribute," liner notes to *Joan Baez/5* (Vanguard, VMD 79160, 1964); Cantwell, *When We Were Good*, 209–10, 315–16; Eyerman and Barreta, "From the 30s to the 60s," 528–31.

14. Cantwell, *When We Were Good*, 339–40; Nat Hentoff, "Folk Finds a Voice," *Reporter*, 4 January 1962, 40; Nat Hentoff, *Listen to the Stories: Nat Hentoff on Jazz and Country Music* (New York: HarperCollins, 1995), 89; "Sybil with Guitar," 54; Hughes, "Joan Baez"; Alice Echols, *Scars of Sweet Paradise: The Life and Times of Janis Joplin* (New York: Henry Holt, 1999), 48. On the sexual perception of the female voice, see Susan McClary, *Feminist Endings: Music, Gender, and Sexuality* (Minneapolis: University of Minnesota Press, 1991), 80–111; Leslie D. Dunn and Nancy A. Jones, *Embodied Voices: Representing Female Vocality in Western Culture* (New York: Cambridge University Press, 1994).

15. On the role of the female singer and their instruments in history, see Sophie Drinker, *Music and Women: The Story of Women in Their Relation to Music* (1948; reprint, with a preface by Elizabeth Wood and afterword by Ruth A. Solie, New York: Feminist Press, 1995).

16. Cantwell, *When We Were Good*, 323–24, 328. On clothing, see Diana Crane, *Fashion and Its Social Agendas: Class, Gender, and Identity in Clothing* (Chicago: University of Chicago Press, 2000), 1–25. See also Stephen B. Groce and John Lynxwiler, "The Silent Performance: Audience Perceptions of Musicians' Nonverbal Behavior," *Popular Music and Society* 18 (Spring 1994): 105–24.

17. Judith Milan, "On Stage: Joan Baez," *Horizon 5*, no. 1 (1962): 66; "Folk-Girls," *Time*, 1 June 1962, 39; Nat Hentoff, liner notes to *Joan Baez, Vol. 2* (Vanguard, 2097, 1987); John Cohen, "Joan Baez," *Sing Out!* 13 (1963): 6; Hughes, "Joan Baez." On women as the reproducers of roots and collectivity, see Floya Anthias and Nira Yuval, eds., *Woman–Nation–State* (New York: St. Martin's, 1989), 7–10.

18. Solomon, liner notes.

19. Baez, *Voice to Sing*, 28, 38, 40. On exoticism and women in music, see McClary, *Feminist Endings*, 60–67.

20. On topical songs, see Eyerman and Barreta, "From the 30s to the 60s," 527–28; Arnold Perris, *Music as Propaganda: Art to Persuade, Art to Control* (Westport, Conn.: Greenwood, 1985), 3–20; Jerome L. Rudnitzky, *Minstrels of the Dawn: The Folk-Protest Singer as a Cultural Hero* (Chicago: Nelson-Hall, 1976), 3–16; R. Serge Denisoff, *Sing a Song of Social Significance* (Bowling Green, Ohio: Bowling Green State University Press, 1983), 97–117; John Greenway, "The Position of Songs of Protest in Folk Literature," in *The American Folk Scene*, 112–129. Irwin Silber, "The Topical Song Revolution," in *The American Folk Scene*, 167–71; David A. Pichaske, *Generation in Motion: Popular Music in the Sixties* (New York: Schirmer, 1979), 51–69.

21. Baez, *Voice to Sing*, 104–5.

22. Baez, *Voice to Sing*, 103–5, 109; Joan Baez, interview on "Amazing Grace," in *Joan Baez: Rare, Live and Classic* (Vanguard, VCD-125/27, 1993), box collection brochure; Reebee Garafolo, "The Impact of the Civil Rights Movement on Popular Music," *Radical America* 21 (1992): 15–22; Robert Sherman, "Sing a Song of Freedom," in *The American Folk Scene*, 172–80.

23. Hentoff, "Folk Finds a Voice," 40; De Turk and Poulin, "Joan Baez," 244; Joan Baez, interview on "What Have They Done to the Rain," in *Joan Baez: Rare, Live and Classic*; Baez, *Voice to Sing*, 92; Levy, liner notes to *Joan Baez, Vol. 2*, and *Joan Baez in Concert, Part 2*; Joan Baez, interview on "Blowin' in the Wind," in *Joan Baez: Rare, Live and Classic*.

24. Richard Fariña, "Baez and Dylan: A Generation Singing Out," in *The American Folk Scene*, 251–52; Ralph J. Gleason, "The Times They Are a Changin'," *Ramparts*, April 1965, 36–37; Wade Hampton, *Guerilla Minstrels* (Knoxville: University of Tennessee Press, 1986), 209–18; Jerome L. Rudnitzky, "Popular Music as Politics," in *America's Musical Pulse: Popular Music in the Twentieth Century Society*, ed. Kenneth J. Bindas (New York: Greenwood, 1992), 3–8; Denisoff, *Sing a Song of Social Significance*, 118–34.

25. Hajdu, *Positively 4th* Street, 160–74, 183–91, 212–25, 239–42, 251–52; John Scaduto, *Bob Dylan: An Intimate Biography* (New York: Signet, 1973), 144, 170, 221–35; Patrick Morrow, "Mimi Fariña: Interview," *Popular Music and Society* 2 (Fall 1972): 62–73; Richie Unterberger, *Urban Spacemen and Wayfaring Strangers: Overlooked Innovators and Eccentric Visionaries of '60s Rock* (San Francisco: Miller Freeman Books, 2000), 239–55.

26. *Bob Dylan: Don't Look Back*, dir. D. A. Pennebaker (Virgin Vision, 1992), videocassette.

27. Baez, *Voice to Sing*, 75, 115–16, 118–19.

28. Joan Baez, "Joan Baez: Personal Statement," *Sing Out!* (1964): 57; De Turk and Poulin, "Joan Baez," 232–33.

29. Baez, *Voice to Sing*, 133–45; David Dellinger, *From Yale to Jail: My Life Story as a Moral Dissenter* (New York: Pantheon, 1993), 196–98, 211; Charles DeBenedetti, *An American Ordeal: The Antiwar Movement of the Vietnam Era* (Syracuse, N.Y.: Syracuse University Press, 1990), 100, 111–12, 120–22.

30. De Turk and Poulin, "Joan Baez," 235; Baez, *Voice to Sing*, 124–27; Alice Echols, "Hope and Hype in Sixties Haight-Ashbury," in *Shaky Ground: The Sixties and Its Aftershocks* (New York: Columbia University Press, 2002), 17–50.

31. Baez, *Voice to Sing*, 41; "Playboy Interview: Joan Baez," *Playboy*, July 1970, 64; Joan Baez, "Why We Began," *Journal: Institute for the Study of Nonviolence* (November 1966): 1–2; James Finn, "Joan Baez," in *Protest: Pacifism and Politics: Some Possible Views on War and Nonviolence*, ed. James Finn (New York: Random House, 1967), 454–62. See also Lloyd I. Randolph, "Gandhi in

the Mind of America," in *Conflicting Images: India and the United States*, ed. Soluchana Raghaven Glazer and Nathan Glazer (Glen Dale, Md.: Riverdale, 1990), 143–78.

32. Baez, "Why We Began," 2; "Non-Violent Soldier," *New Yorker*, 7 October 1967, 44; Baez, *Daybreak*, 122; "Joan Baez Harris," CDGA Institute for the Study of Nonviolence, box 1, Swarthmore Peace Collection, Swarthmore College; Robert Lewis Shayon, "Summer's Gain, Autumn's Loss," *Saturday Review*, 23 August 1969, 55; John Grissim Jr., "Joan Baez," *Rolling Stone*, December 1968, 12–14.

33. "Joan Baez," mimeographed interview, Institute CDGA, box 2, 15. On pacifism and the idea of the female morality of care, see Joan C. Tronto, *Moral Boundaries: A Political Argument for an Ethic of Care* (New York: Routledge, 1994): and Bernice A. Carrol, "Feminism and Pacifism: Historical and Theoretical Connections," in *Women and Peace: Theoretical, Historical and Practical Perspectives*, ed. Ruth Roach Pierson (London: Croom Helm, 1987), 3–28.

34. "Playboy Interview," 58.

35. De Turk and Poulin, "Joan Baez," 248; Baez, *Daybreak*, 122.

36. On taste groups, see George H. Lewis, "Cultural Socialization and the Development of Taste Cultures and Culture Classes in American Popular Music," *Popular Music and Society* 4, no. 4 (1975): 226–41; Holly Kruse, "Subcultural Identity in Alternative Music Culture," *Popular Music* 12, no. 1 (1993): 33–41; Tom W. Smith, "Generational Differences in Musical Preferences," *Popular Music and Society* (Summer 1994): 43–59.

37. Richie Unterberger, *Turn! Turn! Turn! The 60s Folk-Rock Revolution* (San Francisco: Backbeat Books, 2002); Perris, *Music as Propaganda*, 187–93.

38. Joan Baez, *Any Day Now* (Vanguard, VSD 79306/7, 1968); Joan Baez, interviews on "Sweet Sir Galahad," "Love Song to a Stranger," and "Blessed Are," in *Joan Baez: Rare, Live and Classic*—"Sweet Sir Galahad" in *The First Ten Years* (Vanguard, 6560/1, 1970); "Blessed Are" in *Blessed Are . . .* (Vanguard, VSD 6570/1, 1971); "Love Song to a Stranger" in *Come from the Shadows* (A&M SP4339, 1992); Noel Coppage, "Troubadetts, Troubadoras, and Troubadines . . . or . . . What's a Nice Girl like You Doing in a Business like This?" *Stereo Review*, September 1972, 58–61; John Potter, "The Singer, Not the Song: Women Singers as Composers-Poets," *Popular Music* 13, no. 2 (1994): 191–99; Sheila Whiteley, *Women and Popular Music: Sexuality, Identity, and Subjectivity* (New York: Routledge, 2000), 73–77.

39. Steve Waksman, *Instruments of Desire: The Electric Guitar and the Shaping of Musical Experience* (Cambridge, Mass.: Harvard University Press, 1999), 1–13; Rebecca McSwain, "The Power of the Electric Guitar," *Popular Music and Society* 19, no. 4 (1995): 21–40; Whiteley, *Women and Popular Music*, 22–31.

40. "Playboy Interview," 53–58; Baez, interview on "Blessed Are"; Peter Rossinow, "'The Revolution Is about Our Lives': The New Left's Counter-

culture," in *Imagine Nation: The American Counterculture of the 1960s and 70s,* ed. Peter Braunstein and Michael William Doyle (New York: Routledge, 2002), 99–124; Martin A. Lee and Bruce Shlain, *Acid Dreams: The Complete Social History of LSD: The CIA, The Sixties, and Beyond* (New York: Grove Press, 1992), 119–286.

41. On the Vietnam War and music, see Kenneth J. Bundas and Craig Houston, "'Takin' Care of Business': Rock Music, Vietnam and the Protest Myth," *Historian* 52 (November 1989): 1–23; David R. James, "Rock and Roll in Representations of the Invasion of Vietnam," *Representations* 29 (Winter 1990): 78–98; Terry H. Anderson, "American Popular Music and the War in Vietnam," *Peace and Change* 11 (July 1986): 51–65; E. Lee Cooper, "I'll Fight for God, Country, and My Baby: Persistent Themes in American Wartime Songs," *Popular Music and Society* 16 (Summer 1992): 95–99; Christine Scodari, "Johnny Got His Gun: Wartime Songs of Pacifism, Patriotism and Life Style in 20th Century American Culture," *Popular Music and Society* 18 (Spring 1994): 10–13.

42. Baez, *Voice to Sing,* 163; Larry McComb, "Broadside of Boston," *Sing Out!* (April–May 1967): 49.

43. "Sibyl with Guitar," 54; Cohen, "Joan Baez," 9; Didion, "Just Folks," 34; John Garrity, "David Harris: First Views from the Outside," *Rolling Stone,* 15 April 1971, 6; Joel Makower, *Woodstock: The Oral History* (New York: Doubleday, 1989), 194; Reebee Garofolo, "Understanding Mega-Events: If We Are the World, Then How Do We Change It?" in *Rockin' the Boat: Mass Music and Mass Movements* (Boston: South End Press, 1992), 15; Jonathan Eisen, ed., *Altamont: Death of Innocence in the Woodstock Nation* (New York: Avon, 1970).

44. Baez, *Voice to Sing,* 94–98; Hampton, *Guerilla Minstrels,* 157–66, 175–200; Rudnitzky, *Minstrels of the Dawn,* 137–51; Thomas O. Beebee, "Ballad of the Apocalypse: Another Look at Bob Dylan's *Hard Rain,*" *Text and Performance Quarterly* 11 (1991): 1834; Hajdu, *Positively 4th Street,* 235–36, 254–63, 276–82.

45. Susan Lyndon, "The Spirit of Gandhi Rules Her Life," *New York Times* magazine, 16 January 1969, 17–19; Scaduto, *Bob Dylan,* 256.

46. Grissim, "Joan Baez," 13; Lyndon, "Spirit of Gandhi," 17; "Playboy Interview," 55; De Turk and Poulin, "Joan Baez," 245; "Joanie against the System," *Melody Maker,* 8 August 1970, 21; Joe Radcliffe, "Joan Baez Stages Sing-Out for the Young Generation," *Billboard,* 23 August 1969, 19.

47. Baez, *Voice to Sing,* 127–28, 143–45; Don Heckman, "Joan Baez: 'I Was in a State of Guilt,'" *New York Times,* 18 June 1972, sec. 2, 5; Al Capp, "LiL Abner," cartoon, *Boston Globe* 31 December 1966, 17, and 2 January 1967, 15.

48. Michael Ferber and Staughton Lynd, *The Resistance* (Boston: Beacon, 1971), 78–147; David Harris and Joan Baez Harris, *Coming Out* (New York: Pocket, 1971), chap. 4; Joan Baez Sr., *Inside Santa Rita: A Prison Memoir of a War Protester* (Santa Barbara: John Daniel, 1994); John T. McGreevy, "The

Northern District of California and the Vietnam Draft," *Western Legal History* (Summer 1989): 255–80.

49. Baez, *Daybreak*, dedication page.

50. Jim Marshal, poster, 1968; "Playboy Interview," 6; Leslie Cagan, "Women and the Anti-Draft Movement," *Radical American* (September–October 1980): 9–11; Michael S. Foley, *Confronting the War Machine: Draft Resistance during the Vietnam War* (Chapel Hill: University of North Carolina Press, 2003), 191; Alice Echols, "'We Gotta Get Out of This Place': Notes Toward a Remapping of the Sixties," in *Shaky Ground*, 69; On gender and the war, see William B. Breuer, *War and American Women: Heroism, Deeds, and Controversy* (New York: Praeger, 1997); Susan Jeffords, *The Remasculinization of America: Gender and the Vietnam War* (Bloomington: Indiana University Press, 1989); Jean Bethke Elshtain, *Women and War* (New York: Basic Books, 1987), 139–241.

51. David Harris, *Dreams Die Hard* (New York: St. Martin's, 1982), 233–34; "Sacraments: Plighting of Protest," *Time*, 5 April 1968, 48; Baez, *Voice to Sing*, 146–48; Harris and Baez Harris, *Coming Out*, chap. 1.

52. *Carry It On* and *David Harris—Political Man*, dir. James Coyne et al. (New Film, 1970); Baez, *Voice to Sing*, 152–53; "Playboy Interview," 157; Harris and Baez Harris, *Coming Out*, chap. 2; Joan Baez Harris, introduction to *Goliath*, by David Harris (New York: Richard W. Baron, 1970), v–vi.

53. Lyndon, "Spirit of Gandhi," 17; Grissim, "Joan Baez," 12; Didion, "Just Folks," 25; "Non-Violent Soldier," 44; Richard Schickel, "A Gentle Plea for Pacifism," film review of *Carry It On*, dir. James Coyne et al., *Life*, August 1970, 18; Ellen Sander, "Joan Baez: 'One Day at a Time,'" *Saturday Review*, 28 March 1970, 61; Baez, *Voice to Sing*, 152–53; "Playboy Interview," 58.

54. "Garden Gathering," *New Yorker*, 23 August 1969, 23. Songs about family members were "A Song for David," in *One Day at a Time* (Vanguard, VSD 79310, 1970), and "Gabriel and Me," in *Blessed Are.* . . . See lyrics in Joan Baez, *Songbook* (n.p., n.d., mimeographed), 77, 86.

55. Baez, *Voice to Sing*, 184-92; Don Heckman, "Joan Baez," 2; Amy Swerdlow, *Women Strike for Peace: Traditional Motherhood and Radical Politics in the 1960s* (Chicago: University of Chicago Press, 1993), 142; Tom Wells, *The War Within: America's Battle over Vietnam* (Berkeley: University of California Press, 1994), 550.

56. On maternal and female values of peace and care, see Sara Ruddick, *Maternal Thinking: Toward a Politics of Peace* (Boston: Beacon, 1989); Linda Rennie-Forcey, "Women as Peacemakers: Contested Terrain for Feminist Peace Studies," *Peace and Change* 16 (October 1991): 331–54; Elshtain, *Women and War*, 194–258. On the connection between family and nationhood, see Walter Benn Michaels, *Our America: Nativism, Modernism and Pluralism* (Durham, N.C.: Duke University Press, 1995).

57. Baez, *Voice to Sing*, 199; Joan Baez, "Under the Bombs: Hanoi, December 1972" (Palo Alto, Calif.: Institute for the Study of Nonviolence, 1972, pamphlet), Institute CDGA, box 1; Wells, *War Within*, 558–59.

58. Baez, *Voice to Sing*, 218; "Where Are You Now, My Son?" in *Where Are You Now, My Son* (A&M SP 4390, 1973); Baez, *Songbook*, 199; "Joan Baez Harris." On the ideas about motherhood in the 1960s, see Lauri Umansky, *Motherhood Reconceived: Feminism and the Legacies of the Sixties* (New York: New York University Press, 1996).

59. Levy, liner notes to *Joan Baez in Concert*; Aaron Sternfeld, "Joan Baez Goes Right to the Concert Heart," *Billboard*, April 1968, 16; Radcliffe, "Joan Baez Stages Sing-Out," 19.

8

"Ain't No Mountain High Enough"

Diana Ross as American Pop-Cultural Icon of the 1960s

Jaap Kooijman

> I recall an uneasy stirring among women during this time [1968].
> Housewives were no longer content to stand behind the stove and
> cook; they were moved and affected by the killings of our soldiers
> and our leaders. Women had become agitated. We had our own
> opinions. We began to speak out. . . . The tumultuous events of the
> sixties had an effect on my choices as a woman, as a human being,
> and as a professional. Women's liberation changed my way of
> thinking in every facet of my life, from how I handled my business
> affairs to my expectations in my personal life.
>
> —Diana Ross, 1993[1]

In her 1993 autobiography *Secrets of a Sparrow*, African American pop singer Diana Ross explicitly recognized the 1960s women's liberation movement as an important influence on her professional and personal development into a strong and independent black woman. Such a revelation may have come as a surprise to readers, as, in the popular press, Ross tends to be perceived as a rather superficial and glamorous pop diva whose interests are limited to fashionable outfits and big hair. "Really, all I wanted to do was sing and wear pretty clothes," Ross once told journalist Gerri Hirshey.[2] Diana Ross is not the first entertainer who comes to mind when one thinks of influential African American women of the 1960s. Aretha Franklin, the "Queen of Soul," the "natural woman's natural woman," seems to be the most obvious delegate of this particular decade in which racial and gender relations underwent fundamental changes. Unlike Diana Ross, who sang romantic pop songs about the heartache of love, Aretha Franklin was demanding "R-E-S-P-E-C-T"—and that she received. Like male singer James Brown ("Say It Loud: I'm Black and I'm Proud"), Franklin has been widely recognized as a champion of the 1960s civil rights and black liberation movements, and, though to a lesser extent, and unlike Brown, as a voice of women's liberation.[3]

No less than Aretha Franklin, however, Diana Ross too was a pop-cultural phenomenon, positioned at the nexus of cultural and political change in the 1960s. She was the lead singer of the black-owned Motown record company's most popular "girl group," and Motown—the acclaimed "Sound of Young America"—was the largest American independent record label of the 1960s. Motown artists and groups such as Smokey Robinson and the Miracles, Mary Wells, Marvin Gaye, the Four Tops, the Temptations, Martha and the Vandellas, Gladys Knight and the Pips, and Little Stevie Wonder dominated the pop charts. Of all these Motown stars, Diana Ross and the Supremes were without a doubt the most popular and commercially successful. Between 1963 and 1970, they released twenty-five albums and twenty-nine singles, including twelve number-one hits.[4] Moreover, the Supremes, and Diana Ross in particular, became a fixed presence on American national television, performing their hit singles and American standards on programs like *The Ed Sullivan Show*, Johnny Carson's *Tonight Show*, *Hullabaloo*, and *The Hollywood Palace*. With her sequined evening gowns, fashionable thin figure, and elaborate wigs, Diana Ross became not only the face of Motown but also, to many, the face of American 1960s pop.[5] As television critic Rex Reed wrote in 1968, "The Cotton Club is gone, but Diana Ross is here, with her tapping, swinging, swaying, undulating, hydroelectric-voltage-voiced Amazonians and if there is to be any record of history in the 1960s, the Motown sound of the Supremes is certain to be a major part of it."[6]

If Diana Ross served as a champion of the civil rights movement or women's liberation, she did so inadvertently, for the most part. Her 1960s persona did have broad significance, not in the traditional political sphere but rather in the glamour and glitter of mainstream American popular culture. Through a continuously evolving "star text," to use cultural critic Richard Dyer's term, Diana Ross played a meaningful role in the cultural history of the 1960s. The Diana Ross "star text"—including

actual performances, autobiographical accounts, promotional interviews, and critical reviews—engaged matters of race, class, and gender in
America in complex ways, despite the overwhelming superficiality of the
pop medium itself.[7]

Crossover into Mainstream American Culture

> I like to do everything. . . . I know how to curl hair with a hot curler, how
> to make a bed; I can sew and make jivey dresses. I can call a cab and
> carry a ticket on an airplane and travel all by myself. I'm a hardworking
> ham. I can be anything I want.   —Diana Ross, 1966[8]

The success story of Diana Ross and the Supremes has become a classic
example of the American Dream. Three young black women from the
inner city of Detroit rise up from the ghetto to become glamorous pop
stars adored by millions around the world. In 1959, the fifteen-year-
old Diana Ross, living in the Brewster Housing Projects, joined Florence
Ballard and Mary Wilson to form the singing group the Primettes, soon
to be known as the Supremes. As the liner notes from their first album
Meet the Supremes (1962) suggest, Motown did not want to sign "the
girls" to the label until they had finished high school. Between 1961 and
1964, Motown released eight Supremes singles, of which one, "When
the Lovelight Starts Shining through His Eyes," became a minor hit.
Then their ninth single, "Where Did Our Love Go," shot to number one
on the pop charts. At the end of the year, on December 27, 1964, the
Supremes made their debut on national television, performing their third
number-one hit single "Come See about Me" on the *Ed Sullivan Show*.[9]

In the academic literature on Motown and African American popular
culture, Diana Ross and the Supremes are often presented as an ultimate
example of a "crossover" into American mainstream popular culture.[10]
With their sweet pop songs and their elegant dresses, Diana Ross and the
Supremes proved that black young women from the inner city of Detroit
could be as beautiful, attractive, and successful as their white counter-
parts—or at least could be accepted by white audiences as such. They
presented a positive and attractive example of racial integration, becoming the sweethearts of America just a year after Martin Luther King
presented his "I Have a Dream" speech in Washington, D.C., and in
the same year that President Lyndon B. Johnson had signed the Civil

Rights Act into law. Moreover, Diana Ross and the Supremes were a show-case for Motown's founder and president Berry Gordy's belief in Black Capitalism. According to black capitalists like Gordy, commercial success was the key to achieving civil rights. Once prosperous black-owned companies had been established, legal and civil equality could no longer be denied.[11]

Although the crossover of the Supremes (and with them, the Motown label in general) tends to be perceived as a racial crossover into white American mainstream culture, the issue of class should not be overlooked. With the Supremes, Motown tried to challenge the existing racial and class-based prejudice that African American entertainers were "coarse" and "rough."[12] As entertainers from the Detroit inner city, the Motown artists were often considered to be lower-class, not only by white Americans, but also by some of the African American elite. In an interview with Lawrence Otis Graham, one member of the Detroit African American elite remembered:

> The Motown people were uneducated entertainers, so they were some-what coarse. We certainly asked them—as celebrities—to sit on the dais at our events—you know, for publicity purposes—but that's as far as things went. The best of them was Diana Ross because she wanted to improve herself, and just look how well she's done. . . . But then again, she was a bit coarse too, because you know she also grew up in the Brewster Housing Projects.[13]

To counter this class-based racial stereotype, Motown established its Artist Development Department to transform its artists from teenagers living in the Detroit public housing projects into elegant "ladies" and "gentlemen" who could dazzle the world. During the early 1960s, Diana Ross and the Supremes were taught by former model Maxine Powell how to move "gracefully" and to behave "correctly," both on and off stage. As Powell believed, showing a sense of class was the key to success. She insisted on correcting the Supremes' "naughty" moves, which she considered "unsuitable" for elegant young black ladies. "Instead of shaking their whole bodies, I showed them how to do a roll of their buttocks *with class*."[14] As Supreme Mary Wilson recalled: "Mrs. Powell took her job seriously, and she would make us walk up and down the mirrored room while she critiqued our every move. . . . I can remember feeling her eyes upon me as I walked around with books on my head. Were my shoulders straight? Was my posture good? Was my makeup—the little I wore then—feminine and flattering—not too brassy?"[15] Diana Ross claimed that Maxine Powell "greatly contributed to my increased self-confidence" by teaching the Supremes good manners, including the way to slide in and out of a car when dressed in a miniskirt. "We giggled a lot about this, but when we had finished her training, we could sit at the table with Princess Margaret or Princess Anne and feel at ease. We could look and feel as if we belonged anywhere."[16]

Motown's attempt to counter class-based racial stereotypes by grooming its artists into upper-class performers could be interpreted as catering to a white sensibility, resulting in a style of elegance that was defined by white terms. Alice Echols, for example, argues that "there was a limit to how much 'blackness' [Motown's Berry] Gordy would allow." Gordy's sensitivity to white sensibilities was not only shown by the grooming of the Motown artists but also by his "sweetening" of the music (turning R&B into pop) and his discouragement of politically controversial songs to avoid disturbing white audiences. Yet, Echols recognizes that such a perspective enables the also problematic claim that Motown was "too white" or "not black enough."[17] Indeed, in the 1960s, white music critics complained that Motown artists were selling out their "blackness" to become popular with a wider, and thus white, audience.[18] Rock critic Ralph Gleason singled out Diana Ross and the Supremes as an example of African American artists who were "on an Ed Sullivan/TV-trip to middle-class America," claiming that the Supremes were so eager to become part of white America that they dressed up like the McGuire Sisters.[19] In other words, white critics like Gleason argued that the Supremes (and other black performers) failed to live up to the white expectations of how African American artists were supposed to present themselves. In this way, critics not only failed to recognize the powerful presence of Diana Ross and the Supremes in American popular culture but also denied them an African American identity based on their own terms, claiming that Diana Ross and the Supremes were too "bourgeois" and thus not "black" enough.

The fact that Diana Ross and the Supremes were transformed into *ladies* meant that a class-based racial stereotype was being challenged by a gendered stereotype. Historian Gerald Early has pointed out that Berry Gordy deliberately used women to make a crossover into mainstream American culture, as "he felt that black women were less threatening and, in some ways, more comforting to the white public than a black man would be, especially with the intense sexuality and sensuality that the 'new' popular music of Rhythm and Blues and Rock and Roll suggested."[20] Early leaves out that female artists would also be less threatening and more comforting to older and middle-class audiences, of all colors. With the Supremes, Motown was able to present a singing group that could bring elegance and innocence to the "new" popular music, both in the way they presented themselves and in the material that they recorded. In 1965, the Supremes performed in front of an adult audience at the New York nightclub Copacabana, singing Broadway tunes and American standards in addition to their hit singles. Motown released concept albums such as *A Bit of Liverpool* (1964), which included the Supremes' versions of songs originally sung by the Beatles; *The Supremes Sing Rodgers and Hart* (1967); and *Diana Ross and the Supremes Sing and Perform "Funny Girl"* (1968). Diana Ross and the Supremes recorded commercials for Coca-Cola (on one, Ross sighs, "Ooh, these bubbles tickle"), showed their armpits in promotion of Arrid Extra-Dry deodorant, and gave their name to a brand of white bread. As the star of the Supremes, Diana Ross became a star product of American capitalist consumer culture. Motown's promotional material and interviews particularly emphasized how Ross had transcended her unprivileged social background. For example, in May 1966, *LOOK* magazine presented a photo-spread article on the Supremes entitled "From Real Rags to Real Riches." In one of the photographs, Ross is pictured on a balcony in the Detroit Brewster Housing Projects, gloomily looking out over the neighborhood. "I don't remember it being as awful as this," the caption reads. "To a kid, I guess everything seems bigger and nicer than it really was."[21] By showing that through commercial success an escape out of the "ghetto" was possible, Diana Ross had become a role model of racial integration and social mobility, though based on her transformation into an elegant lady.

Gender and the Star Image

> I'm not going to allow myself to be a loser. I want to be a strong woman and a good woman for a man, whichever man I choose—and if he chooses me. . . . I have only one life to live *and* lose—and I want to live it . . . as a good daughter, a good woman, a good wife, and someday, a good hostess in my married home.
> —Diana Ross, 1969[22]

When discussing the Supremes, music critics tend to focus on the assertiveness of lead singer Diana Ross, whose sheer ambition pushed the other Supremes literally into the background.[23] Diane Cardwell, for example, points out: "Diana Ross overshadowed her singing partners with her poise, savvy, and star-driven determination. She cultivated a persona that was at once ladylike and flirtatious, both glamorous and vulnerable."[24] As Cardwell's comment suggests, Ross used the image of a passive and restrained "lady" to act as an active and determined woman. A similar perspective is presented in the autobiographical accounts of female Motown singers such as Martha Reeves, Brenda Holloway, and Supreme Mary Wilson. They all have portrayed Diana Ross as a calculating competitor who would do anything to secure a successful career, including having sex with Motown's president Berry Gordy.[25] This dominant and widespread perspective about Diana Ross as an assertive and calculating woman who used her female sexuality to achieve individual success and stardom has become an essential element of her star image. As Susan Douglas writes in *Where the Girls Are*: "Ross has taken a lot of heat in recent years as the selfish bitch who wanted all the fame and glory for herself, so it's easy to forget her importance as a cultural icon in the 1960s."[26]

Paradoxically, Diana Ross is also often perceived as merely a product shaped by Berry Gordy, who used her to succeed in his crossover strategy. Moreover, musicologists tend to see Diana Ross as a vocal instrument in the musical production by Holland-Dozier-Holland, the male songwriting and producing team that was responsible for ten of the twelve Supremes number-one hit singles. Motown was a true hit factory, meaning that Motown used the assembly-line production technique by dividing the different segments of production between musicians, producers, and singers. Often, the producers tried one song on several artists before presenting the final product to Berry Gordy's Quality Control. Berry Gordy himself always stood at the end of the line, making the final decision as to whether or not a song would be released.[27] In his search for economic success, Gordy tended to favor those artists who proved to be the most commercially successful. Rather than a mere hit factory, however, Motown's publicity department presented the company as one big family, closely intertwined with Detroit's African American community. The Motown artists shared this view. "Maybe the Motown sound is just love and warmth," Mary Wilson of the Supremes told *Time* magazine in 1966; "like a family, we all work together, fight and kiss all day long."[28]

Fig. 8.1. Publicity shot of Diana Ross, 1971. *Photo by Harry Langdon*

Berry Gordy favored Diana Ross because she could make his ambitions to create a crossover superstar come true. As he remembered: "In the heyday of the Supremes I saw the butterfly emerge from the cocoon and I was dazzled. She was magic and *she was mine*. Diana was willing to let me make her a star and I knew she had the talent, drive and stamina to go the distance."[29] Ross herself has credited Gordy for supporting and encouraging her, yet, just as he emphasized his possession of her, Ross also revealed the extent of male domination over her by describing him as "at times my surrogate father, at other times my controller and slave driver."[30] Some degree of paternalism certainly marked Gordy's male control over Diana Ross's career. Indeed, as black culture historian Mark Anthony Neal has argued, instead of being a part of the "burgeoning black feminist movement," Ross's success should be interpreted as the result of a male-dominated production process. "Ultimately, Gordy's calculated control over Ross for much of her career represented little change from the standard uses of black women within popular culture. Ross's image as an independent black woman was as saccharine as her singing voice, while Gordy parlayed this imagery into a limited victory for black capitalist patriarchy."[31] As a product of male producers, the Ross image can be perceived as "saccharine" or superficial, yet that does not exclude the possibility to perceive the Ross star image as an embodiment of female empowerment and independence, from a consumer's perspective. As a commodity of production and consumption, the star text can contain contradictory and conflicting values.

To white male critics in the 1960s, Diana Ross seemed to present an unthreatening image of black female sexuality, both in image and music. According to music critic Jon Landau, Ross "oozes sex . . . and is a fine vocalist," but she stayed within the limits set by the male producers, resulting in a "safe" sound. "Consequently, she is the least jarring of Motown vocalists, the least disturbing, and the most able to reach a car-radio audience."[32] Comparing Ross to fellow Motown singer Martha Reeves, musicologist Richard Middleton noticed that Ross presented a "sweeter, prettier, more restrained vocal tone and delivery," resulting in "a slightly more controlled, more sober experience." Ross's vocals presented "less excitement and ecstasy, and instead an emphasis on a kind of sweet sensuality."[33] "She is sexy—yes—but very classy," wrote *New York Times* reporter Richard Goldstein of Ross: "It doesn't really matter what she says. Others shriek, she whispers: 'Baby love Oh baby love I need your love . . . ' And we are all soldier boys, hanging on an implication. She is our foxhole fantasy, but it is all distant, somehow untouchable passion, meant for an audience, but for no one individual in it. So it sounds clean."[34] These descriptions reveal an emphasis on female sexuality that is based on passivity and restraint. Ross's image as a black woman was perceived by these white male critics as so "clean" and "unthreatening" that she could break racial barriers, in terms of being accepted as a sex symbol to white men. As historian Charles Kaiser points out, "Even a Southern [white] boy who hated Martin Luther King might fall in love with Diana Ross."[35]

However, this white male perception of Diana Ross as an attractive but "clean" and "safe" sex symbol does not take away the possibility that Ross could function in other ways for other audiences. As Susan Douglas has described in her book *Where the Girls Are*, Diana Ross was an important cultural icon of the 1960s because she was one of the first African American female stars with whom white female teenagers could identify. As Douglas recalls: "As slim as a rail with those cavernous armpits, gorgeous smile, and enormous, perfectly made-up eyes, Diana Ross is the first black woman I remember desperately wanting to look like, even if some of her gowns were a bit too Vegas. I couldn't identify with her completely, not because she was black, but because when I was fourteen, she seemed so glamorous and sophisticated."[36] According to Douglas, Diana Ross was both girl and woman, both sexy and respectable, both black and white. Ross could function as an attractive black image for white female teenagers to emulate because her star image embodied these seemingly contradicting and ambiguous values of race, gender, and female sexuality.

To African American teenagers, both male and female, Diana Ross's elegance and style could function as a role model of empowerment. For example, television host Oprah Winfrey repeatedly has exclaimed in public that seeing Diana Ross perform on national television in the 1960s drastically changed her life and the prospects she envisioned for herself as a teenager. Referring to the Supremes' first performance on the *Ed Sullivan Show* in 1964, Winfrey stated: "When I saw the Supremes on TV that night, it was magical to me because I had never seen black women on television (although we were called 'colored' at the time) or anywhere for that matter who conveyed such glamour and such grace. . . . And for years I wanted to be like Diana Ross or just somebody Supreme."[37] To the African American and gay author Don Belton, Ross proved to be "the closest thing I had to a role model," as she "evoked for me a make-believe world of opulence and refinement, where style could conquer all, including racism, homophobia, and poverty."[38] African American fashion columnist Rod Stafford Hagwood also considered Ross to be a role model. "There were few blacks on television in those days, and Diana Ross was wearing beautiful gowns, had a pretty voice and a great deal of charisma. Instant role-model material . . . Ross beamed out a message through her glamour that said a lot about pride, class and the morphing effect of really good wigs."[39] As these observations show, to some African American teenagers—focusing on elegance, style, and flamboyant fashion rather than the music she sang—the "superficial" star image of Diana Ross proved to be a source of personal empowerment, providing a welcome alternative to the stereotypical representation of African American artists in American popular culture, particularly on national television.

The Commodification of Politics

> The business I'm in, it's glamorous—lights, pretty clothes, beautiful people—it's got a regular life pattern to it. All those things are nice, but the most important thing is that you get involved in current events. You have to take a part and be ready to help and to have opinions.
>
> —Diana Ross, 1969[40]

In 1967, the Supremes changed their name to Diana Ross and the Supremes, as Motown wanted to capitalize on the solo potential of the lead singer.[41] That same year, Cindy Birdsong replaced original Supreme Florence Ballard. The fact that the general public hardly noticed this change of personnel emphasized the dominance of Ross. Although Diana Ross and the Supremes continued to be popular, their music appeared outdated in the rapidly changing and politically charged music scene of the late 1960s. Moreover, television performances and Las Vegas–styled live shows had become Ross's main priority, targeted at an older—both white and black—middle-class audience. By then, with the rise of the cultural left, pop culture had not only become political, but political commitment also had become commercially fashionable. In 1968, Diana Ross and the Supremes recorded their first politically charged single, "Love Child," dealing with premarital sex and single motherhood. The social content of the song was emphasized by the "ghetto look" outfit Ross wore on the album's cover and during the performance of "Love Child" on the *Ed Sullivan Show*, consisting of cut-off jeans, bare feet, and an Afro wig. Ironically, the "ghetto look" on Diana Ross was merely another fashionable outfit—Ross was just as "natural" wearing a sequined evening gown as she was sporting a "natural" Afro wig. As Diana Ross remembered: "The lyrics were good, but those sweet romantic love songs like 'Come See About Me' were more real to me. It was the sixties. Life was moving, and everything had to change, our music included."[42]

Although he supported the civil rights movement, Berry Gordy had been reluctant to get Motown involved in politics. Motown did release the 1963 *The Great March to Freedom* album, containing Martin Luther King Jr.'s Detroit speech of June 23, 1963.[43] When he did want to show Motown's political commitment to the civil rights movement, Gordy tended to use Diana Ross as spokesperson—to many, because of her glamorous image, the least likely of all Motown artists to fulfill that role. In 1965, the Supremes performed in a CBS *War on Poverty* television special and recorded the single "Things Are Changing" for President Lyndon B. Johnson's Equal Employment Opportunity Campaign. The song, produced by the white Phil Spector, addressed black women who did not have "the kind of man everyone looks up to." The message of the song was clear: racial discrimination was no longer a barrier to a life of hard work that could produce respectable men. Thanks to the recent legislation that promoted racial equality in employment policies, un-employed African American young men could now find jobs, the song claimed. "Race or color won't stand in your way," Diana Ross sang. "Good jobs are out there just waiting to be found."[44] The Johnson administration continued to consider Diana Ross an appropriate role model for African American teenagers. When, in June 1968, the all-black Public School #192 from New York City came to visit the White House, the presidential staff invited Ross to look on as President Lyndon B. Johnson told these "affirmative Negro kids" to stay in school, obey their parents, respect the police, and care for "all the people of this nation that cares so much for you."[45] Moreover, Diana Ross and the Supremes performed at fundraisers of the Democratic Party, much to President Johnson's pleasure. Supreme Mary Wilson recalls being "thrilled" to meet with the president, particularly after he told her: "I was supposed to rush away from here and head back to the White House before the show was over, but I refused to leave until I got to talk to the Supremes."[46]

During the early 1960s, such presidential performances by the Supremes would have been considered an achievement of the civil rights movement. By 1968, however, African American artists who performed before the president or supported his programs were accused of selling out to the political establishment by the (predominantly white) cultural left. As the African American author Ralph Ellison stated in 1968, his support of President Johnson "caused a few of my white colleagues to charge that

I had 'changed' or sold out to the 'establishment,' and I lost a few friends."[47] And so, while Diana Ross was performing at the Lyndon B. Johnson fundraiser in Los Angeles, the Students for a Democratic Society were demonstrating outside. As one of the demonstrators would later remember, "Thousands of us marched to the Century Plaza Hotel where the Supremes were *serenading* LBJ."[48] As the use of the verb *serenading* implies, critics from the left did not consider Diana Ross and the Supremes merely providers of entertainment but active supporters of the political establishment.

On April 5, 1968, the day after Martin Luther King had been assassinated, Diana Ross and the Supremes performed "Somewhere (There's a Place for Us)" from *West Side Story* on Johnny Carson's *Tonight Show*. In the middle of the song, Ross addressed the audience and quoted from King's famous "I Have a Dream" speech, including the final plea: "Free at last, free at last, thank God Almighty, free at last!" Although in retrospect the performance may appear to be rather bombastic, the citation of King's words by a glamorous pop singer could have an unusually strong impact. When Ross repeated her plea for racial harmony in front of the British royal family in London, she explained her actions afterward by stating: "It's not a protest because I don't say anything bitter. It's more like a prayer. This is very hard for me to explain." Ross also expressed her belief in the "good philosophy" of Stokely Carmichael, the former civil rights leader of the Student Non-Violent Coordinating Committee and by then a spokesman of the Black Power movement. "If it wasn't for people like him, things wouldn't be happening today. I think the militants have their place because you need someone to be strong."[49]

In his article provocatively titled "How Diana Ross Became a Talking, Instead of Just a Walking, Doll," British journalist Chris Welch concluded, "Diana's simple expression of her beliefs, perhaps because they come from a rather unexpected source, have a greater strength and power for communication than from more forcible spokesmen."[50] However, most critics did not take the more "radical" political position of Ross seriously.[51] They considered the "newly empowered" Diana Ross as fake as her Afro wig. In the words of Ben Arogundade: "The new wigs offered 'instant-'fro-without-the-grow' for those too lazy or impatient to cultivate a bouffant of their own. They allowed blacks to live aesthetic double lives."[52] Diana Ross's endorsement of the Democratic presidential candidate Hubert H. Humphrey was also met with skepticism. On July 23, 1968, at a press conference in the New York Waldorf Astoria, Ross addressed political issues that were particularly of interest to African American voters, such as the need to rebuild the inner cities after the recent riots and the racial inequality of the military draft. Moreover, Ross called Vice President Humphrey "a courageous man" for his long commitment to the civil rights movement, as he, back in 1948, had been the first Democrat in the U.S. Senate to openly advocate the enactment of a civil rights bill.[53] Humphrey, in his turn, praised Diana Ross and the Supremes: "Tens of millions of fans respect you, not only as great entertainers, but as symbols of merit, of achievement, yes, of human rights."[54] The press, with the exception of a few African American newspapers, did not take Ross's endorsement seriously. Instead of addressing her actual speech, the press focused on her "shocking-pink silk suit and matching pill-box hat," reporting that Ross "leered at [Humphrey] from under her magnificent eyelashes."[55] Clearly, the fashionable image of Diana Ross disabled the critics to perceive her actions as belonging to the traditional political sphere, and subsequently they could dismiss them as superficial.

Solo Superstar

> And I love the cocky little new kids who come up to me and say, "Diane, I hear you leavin' The Supremes. How can I get your job as lead singer?" And I ask, "Wouldn't you just settle for being a Supreme?" and they say, "Nope, only lead singer." —Diana Ross, 1969[56]

On January 14, 1970, Diana Ross gave her farewell performance with the Supremes at the Frontier Hotel in Las Vegas. The fact that the concert took place in Las Vegas, rather than their hometown Detroit, was telling of the route that Ross and Motown had taken. No longer merely a pop singer, Ross had become an all-around entertainer. Before leaving the Supremes, she had starred in two popular NBC television specials: *TCB (Taking Care of Business)* in 1968 and *GIT (Gettin' It Together) on Broadway* in 1969. Although both specials also starred the Supremes and fellow Motown group the Temptations, the focus was clearly on Diana Ross. She performed in a modern jazz dance photomontage sequence entitled "Afro Vogue," dressed in fashionable costumes inspired by the traditional costumes of African tribes. Ross also starred in the "Leading Lady Medley," consisting of Broadway standards such as "People" from *Funny Girl*. Motown clearly used the opportunity to prepare Ross for the next step in Berry Gordy's crossover strategy: Diana Ross had to leave the Supremes behind to become a Hollywood movie star. The glamour and excess associated with Hollywood were already present in her first solo concert of August 1970. "Baby, Baby, Where Did Diana Go?" *Time* magazine questioned in its review. "Diana Ross makes her electric entrance, shimmering like a Broadway sign. She sports a frizzy Afro wig about the size of a boxwood hedge and a sequined sarong that looks as if it were cut from the Orion constellation."[57]

Diana Ross's first number-one hit single "Ain't No Mountain High Enough" (1970), a remake of the 1967 Motown duet by Marvin Gaye and Tammi Terrell, is a telling example of the flamboyant and larger-than-life Hollywood star image of Diana Ross. While the original version is a classic love song in which two lovers express their never-ending love to each other, the Ross cover version, more than six minutes long, is a slow, melodramatic, spoken account of a passing love, followed by an orgasmic rendition of the chorus. To some, Ross's version embodied the superficiality of the Ross star image. As Gerri Hirshey has stated: "In Ross's hands, Marvin Gaye and Tammi Terrell's soulful 'Ain't No Mountain High Enough' became a huge, saccharine production number. Licking a finger, laying it on a sequined haunch, she'd declare herself HOT with a well-miked *Tsssssssst!*"[58] Others, such as Richard Dyer, recognized the romantic quality of Ross's version, "with its lyrics' total surrender to love, its heavenly choir and sweeping violins." According to Dyer, Ross's "Ain't No Mountain High Enough" is "both a celebration of a relationship and the almost willing recognition of its passing and the exquisite pain of its passing," making the song an expression of a bittersweet experience and "perhaps one of the most extravagant reaches of disco's romanticism."[59] Moreover, the song seems to express Diana Ross's determination to reach for the highest goal in individual success, even if that meant leaving loved ones behind.

By starring in *Lady Sings the Blues* (Sidney J. Furie, 1972), depicting the life of legendary jazz and blues singer Billie Holiday, Diana Ross was able to transcend her status as pop singer. As black film historian Donald Bogle has pointed out, Berry Gordy (who produced the film) utilized the legendary status of Billie Holiday to transform Ross into a black Hollywood star by symbolically taking her "back to the holy waters . . . [to be] rebaptized and born again. Diana, the princess of ghetto chic, a girl/woman known as plastic, goes through Billie's horrors and humiliations.

By doing so, she acquires a certain depth and relevance."[60] In "real" life, the glamorous and triumphant star quality of Diana Ross was reaffirmed by her being nominated for a best actress Academy Award and receiving a standing ovation after a special screening of *Lady Sings the Blues* at the Cannes International Film Festival. "Diana Ross: Lady *Doesn't* Sing the Blues," the *New York Times* rightly noted.[61]

Even more than her performance in *Lady Sings the Blues*, Diana Ross's personal yet public life brought forward the contradictions contained within her star image. On the one hand, Ross personified the modern and independent black women. Her successful social mobility was expressed by a 1973 Blackglama mink coat advertisement. "What becomes a Legend most?" the slogan of the advertisement read, featuring a picture of Ross by photographer Richard Avedon. As Ross had become a legend in her own right, there was no need to mention her name.[62] On the other hand, Diana Ross continued to be the product of her male mentor Berry Gordy, who appeared to be omnipresent. In a four-page photo spread in *Life* magazine of 1972, Ross is shown at home in her luxurious Beverly Hills mansion, together with her (white) husband Robert Silberstein, her "mentor" Gordy, and her two young baby daughters. "Seated on the floor of her sunken living room, Diana relaxes with her husband, Bob Silberstein. Although elaborate wigs are her trademark (see cover), she often goes without one at home."[63] Again, the representation of Diana Ross emphasizes her successful social mobility, crossing boundaries of race and class, yet simultaneously, the photo spread suggests that beyond the glamorous star image, Ross could also fulfill the traditional gender role of being the "good hostess in [her] married home."

The complexity of the Diana Ross star image is perhaps best captured by a Motown publicity photo of 1971. The picture, taken by Harry Langdon as part of a photo shoot for the Diana Ross solo album *Surrender*, shows Ross's almost angelic face framed by a huge Afro. The result is an extraordinary combination of fashion and Black Power imagery. On the one hand, Ross is presented as a traditional 1950s Hollywood diva: her bare shoulder emphasizes the sensuality of the picture, while her heavily made-up eyes look up into the sky. On the other hand, Ross is presented as a fashionable version of Angela Davis, the Black Power activist, wearing big earrings and sporting a "natural" Afro. Like her star image, Ross's Afro is larger than life and "superficial"—after all, her Afro is a wig.

However, the power of the image, and in extension the Diana Ross star image, lies in its embodiment of the contradiction between fashion and politics, and its refusal to accept that those two cannot go together.

Conclusion

In 1972, Diana Ross recorded the song "When We Grow Up" for Marlo Thomas's popular children's album *Free to Be . . . You and Me*.[64] Starring a host of showbiz celebrities, the album intended to break with traditional gender roles—boys should be allowed to play with dolls while girls should be encouraged to excel in sports. With "When We Grow Up," Diana Ross questioned the importance for an adult woman to be pretty and to wear dresses and perfume, concluding that it really should not be necessary. The song is significant because, in contradiction to the content of the song, the power of the Diana Ross star image was based on elegance, style, and flamboyant fashion. All Ross really wanted to do was to sing and wear pretty clothes. By doing exactly that, she proved to be a powerful presence in 1960s American popular culture, challenging racial and class-based stereotypes through the appropriation of the gendered stereotype of the elegant lady.

The 1960s in American popular culture was a time of rapid change, particularly in race and gender relations. The contradictory values of the 1960s are embodied in the star image of Diana Ross. Both passive and assertive, Ross presented a mixed image of black female sexuality. She presented a gendered stereotype, transforming herself into a "lady" to enable racial integration and social mobility. Although (often white and male) cultural critics dismissed Diana Ross's role as Motown's political spokesperson, because of the glamour and glitter of her pop-star persona, that same glamour and glitter could provide an image to be emulated by some white female teenagers and a source of empowerment for some African American teenagers. The complexity of the star image made it possible that Ross could both be a product of a male-dominated production process and, at the same time, function as a model to be emulated. Here politics and fashion do go together. The evolving Diana Ross star text reveals that issues of race, class, gender, and sexuality are not only intertwined but can also be contested outside the boundaries of the traditional political sphere, namely, within the glamorous sphere of the allegedly superficial pop culture.

NOTES

1. Diana Ross, *Secrets of a Sparrow: Memoirs* (New York: Villard Books, 1993), 148–49. Regan Books has announced the publication of a second autobiography, entitled *Upside Down: Wrong Turns, Right Turns, and the Road Ahead*, to be published in 2004.

2. As quoted in Gerri Hirshey, *Nowhere to Run: The Story of Soul Music* (London: Pan Books, 1984), 162.

3. For a comparison between Diana Ross and Aretha Franklin, see Nelson George, "Two Detroit Sisters," in Nelson George, *Buppies, B-Boys, Baps and Bohos: Notes on Post-Soul Black Culture* (New York: HarperPerennial, 1992), 179–82.

4. The number-one hit singles are "Where Did Our Love Go" (1964), "Baby Love" (1964), "Come See about Me" (1964), "Stop! In the Name of Love" (1965), "Back in My Arms Again" (1965), "I Hear a Symphony" (1965), "You Can't Hurry Love" (1966), "You Keep Me Hangin' On" (1966), "Love Is Here and Now You're Gone" (1967), "The Happening" (1967), "Love Child" (1968), and "Someday We'll Be Together" (1969).

5. For a more extensive discussion of Diana Ross and the Supremes on American national television, see Jaap Kooijman, "From Elegance to Extravaganza: The Supremes on the *Ed Sullivan Show* as a Presentation of Beauty," *Velvet Light Trap* 49 (Spring 2002): 4–17.

6. Rex Reed, *Big Screen, Little Screen* (New York: Macmillan, 1971), 118. The quote is taken from Reed's review of the *TCB (Taking Care of Business)* television special, starring Diana Ross and the Supremes with the Temptations, originally broadcast by NBC on 12 November 1968.

7. Richard Dyer, *Heavenly Bodies: Film Stars and Society* (London: British Film Institute, 1987); Richard Dyer, *Stars*, new ed. (London: British Film Institute, 1998); Richard Dyer, *Only Entertainment*, 2d ed. (London: Routledge, 2002). Perhaps particularly in black popular culture, as Stuart Hall has suggested, such a recognition is necessary, as black pop is all about style, music, and the body, elements that often have been considered to be superficial by (white) mainstream cultural critics. See Stuart Hall, "What Is This 'Black' in Black Popular Culture?" in Gina Dent, ed., *Black Popular Culture*, a project by Michele Wallace (Seattle: Bay Press, 1992), 21–33.

8. Jack Hamilton, "The Supremes: From Real Rags to Real Riches," *LOOK*, 3 May 1966, 70–76, 72.

9. Biographies of Diana Ross and the Supremes include: Geoff Brown, *Diana Ross* (New York: St. Martin's Press, 1981); Sharon Davis, *Diana Ross: A Legend in Focus* (Edinburgh and London: Mainstream Publishing, 2000); James Haskins, *I'm Gonna Make You Love Me: The Story of Diana Ross* (New York: Laurell-Leaf Books, 1980); J. Randy Taraborrelli, with Reginald Wilson and Darryl Minger, *Diana* (Garden City, N.Y.: Doubleday, 1985); J. Randy Taraborrelli, *Call*

Her Miss Ross: The Unauthorized Biography of Diana Ross (New York: Birch Lane Press, 1989).

10. Donald Bogle, *Brown Sugar: Eighty Years of America's Black Female Superstars* (New York: Da Capo Press, 1980), 168–170; Gerald Early, *One Nation Under a Groove: Motown and American Culture* (Hopewell, N.J.: The Ecco Press, 1995), 117–119; Philip Brian Harper, *Are We Not Men? Masculine Anxiety and the Problem of African-American Identity* (New York: Oxford University Press, 1996), 84–88; Suzanne E. Smith, *Dancing in the Street: Motown and the Cultural Politics of Detroit* (New Haven: Yale University Press, 2001), 121; Brian Ward, *Just My Soul Responding: Rhythm and Blues, Black Consciousness, and Race Relations* (Berkeley: University of California Press, 1998), 266–268.

11. Nelson George, *The Death of Rhythm & Blues* (New York: Plume Books, 1988), 103–104; Elvis Mitchell, introduction to Ben Fong-Torres, *The Motown Album: The Sound of Young America* (London: Virgin Books, 1990), 18.

12. Ward, *Just My Soul Responding*, 232–252. See also Donald Bogle, *Toms, Coons, Mulattoes, Mammies, and Bucks: An Interpretive History of Blacks in American Films*, 3d ed. (Oxford: Roundhouse, 1994); bell hooks, *Black Looks: Race and Representation* (Boston: South End Press, 1992).

13. Lawrence Otis Graham, *Our Kind of People: Inside America's Black Upper Class* (New York: HarperPerennial, 2000), 305–306.

14. Kingsley Abbott, "Motown Style: The Charm School and Miss Powell," in Kingsley Abbott, ed., *Calling Out around the World: A Motown Reader* (London: Helter Skelter, 2001), 59–61, 60, emphasis in original.

15. Mary Wilson, with Patricia Romanowski and Ahrgus Juilliard, *Dreamgirl: My Life as a Supreme* (New York: St. Martin's Press, 1986), 151.

16. Ross, *Secrets of a Sparrow*, 121–122.

17. Alice Echols, *Shaky Ground: The Sixties and Its Aftershocks* (New York: Columbia University Press, 2002), 170–171.

18. Simon Frith, *Sound Effects: Youth, Leisure, and the Politics of Rock 'n' Roll* (New York: Pantheon Books, 1981), 22; Tony Palmer, *All You Need Is Love: The Story of Popular Music* (London: Book Club Associates, 1977) 158; Ward, *Just My Soul Responding*, 267; Wilson, *Dreamgirl*, 211.

19. Ralph J. Gleason, "Like a Rolling Stone," originally published in *The American Scholar* (1967), reprinted in Jonathan Eisen, ed., *The Age of Rock: Sounds of the American Cultural Revolution* (New York: Vintage Books, 1969), 61–76. Quotation on page 67.

20. Early, *One Nation under a Groove*, 117–118.

21. Hamilton, "The Supremes," 72.

22. Jack Hamilton, "The Supreme Supreme: Diana Ross," *LOOK*, 23 September 1969, 68–74, 73–74.

23. Hirshey, *Nowhere to Run*, 45–49; Lucy O'Brien, *She Bop: The Definitive*

History of Women in Rock, Pop, and Soul (New York: Penguin Books, 1995), 79–83.

24. Diane Cardwell, "Diana Ross," in Barbara O'Dair, ed., *Trouble Girls: The Rolling Stone Book of Women in Rock* (New York: Random House, 1997), 116–123, 118,

25. Martha Reeves, with Mark Bego, *Dancing in the Street: Confessions of a Motown Diva* (New York: Hyperion, 1994), 116–119; Susan Whitall (editor), *Women of Motown: An Oral History* (New York: Avon Books, 1998), 114–116; Wilson, *Dreamgirl.*

26. Susan J. Douglas, *Where the Girls Are: Growing Up Female with the Mass Media* (New York: Random House, 1995), 96.

27. Nelson George, *Where Did Our Love Go? The Rise and Fall of the Motown Sound* (Sydney: Omnibus Press, 1986), 50–147; Ward, *Just My Soul Responding*, 259–266.

28. "Singers: The Girls from Motown," *Time* 87, 4 March 1966, 83–84.

29. Berry Gordy, *To Be Loved: The Music, the Magic, the Memories of Motown* (New York: Warner Books, 1994), 195, emphasis mine.

30. Ross, *Secrets of a Sparrow*, 108.

31. Mark Anthony Neal, *What the Music Said: Black Popular Music and Black Public Culture* (New York and London: Routledge, 1999), 90.

32. Jon Landau, "A Whiter Shade of Black," originally published in *Crawdaddy!* 11 (September–October 1967), reprinted in Eisen, ed., *Age of Rock*, 298–306, 302.

33. Richard Middleton, *Pop Music and the Blues: A Study of the Relationship and Its Relevance* (London: Victor Gollancz, 1972), 222.

34. Richard Goldstein, "The Super Supremes: 'Stop in the Name of Love'," *New York Times*, 23 July 1967, D11.

35. Charles Kaiser, *1968 in America: Music, Politics, Chaos, Counterculture, and the Shaping of a Generation* (New York: Grove Press, 1988), 195.

36. Douglas, *Where the Girls Are*, 96.

37. Oprah Winfrey, *The Oprah Winfrey Show* (November 1993). On another *Oprah Winfrey Show* (April 2000), Winfrey told Diana Ross: "You presented that beauty, and more important—hope—for me. Hope that my life could be better, that I could do better."

38. Don Belton, "Miss Diana Ross: It's Time for More Than That 'Little Extra,'" *Equal Times* Minneapolis, August 1991, newspaper clipping.

39. Rod Stafford Hagwood, "Supreme Image," Broward Metro *Sunshine* magazine, 25 June 2000, newspaper clipping.

40. Hamilton, "Supreme Supreme," 74.

41. Although the name change is often mentioned to show how Motown singled out Diana Ross as the leading Supreme, the names of other Motown groups

were similarly changed for commercial reasons. The Miracles were renamed Smokey Robinson and the Miracles, Martha and the Vandellas were renamed Martha Reeves and the Vandellas.

42. Ross, *Secrets of a Sparrow*, 139.

43. Smith, *Dancing in the Street*, 21–23; see also Ward, *Just My Soul Responding*, 268–275.

44. The Supremes, "Things Are Changing," originally released in 1965, re-released on compact disc: Diana Ross & the Supremes, *Anthology* (Motown, 2001). Ironically, "Things Are Changing" is one of the few songs recorded by the Supremes that was written and produced by a white producer, namely, Phil Spector. The song was also recorded by two non-Motown groups: The Blossoms and Jay and the Americans, all released in 1965.

45. James Jones, memo to President Lyndon B. Johnson, "Talking Points: Public School #192, New York City," 24 June 1968, Diary Backup, 26 June 1968, Appointment File, box 103, Lyndon B. Johnson Library, Austin, Texas.

46. Wilson, *Dreamgirl*, 204.

47. Ralph Ellison, "The Myth of the Flawed White Southerner," in James MacGregor Burns, ed., *To Heal and to Build: The Programs of President Lyndon B. Johnson* (New York: McGraw-Hill Book Company, 1968), 207–216.

48. Paul Krassner, *Confessions of a Raving, Unconfined Nut: Misadventures in the Counter-Culture* (New York: Simon and Schuster, 1993), 151, emphasis added.

49. Chris Welch, "How Diana Ross Became a Talking, Instead of Just a Walking, Doll," *Melody Maker*, 30 November 1968, 16–17.

50. Ibid.

51. Ward, *Just My Soul Responding*, 267; Wilson, *Dreamgirl*, 211.

52. Ben Arogundade, *Black Beauty: A History and a Celebration* (New York: Thunder's Mouth Press, 2000), 75.

53. The entire text of the Diana Ross speech is printed in the African American newspaper *The Voice*, 31 July 1968, A4.

54. Press release, Citizens for Humphrey, "Acknowledgement by Vice President Humphrey to Supremes," 23 July 1968, Hubert H. Humphrey Papers, box 150.F14.7B., Minnesota State Historical Society, St. Paul, Minnesota.

55. Lewis Chester, Godfrey Hodgson, and Bruce Page, *An American Melodrama: The Presidential Campaign of 1968* (New York: Viking Press, 1969), 417; Mary McGroy, "Supremes Sure of Humphrey," *Evening Star* Washington, D.C., 24 July 1968.

56. Hamilton, "Supreme Supreme," 74.

57. "Baby, Baby, Where Did Diana Go?" *Time* 96:7, 17 August 1970, 30–31.

58. Gerri Hirshey, *We Gotta Get Out of This Place: The True, Tough Story of Women in Rock* (New York: Atlantic Monthly Press, 2001), 94.

59. Richard Dyer, "In Defense of Disco," originally published in *Gay Left* 8 (1979), reprinted in Dyer, *Only Entertainment*, 151–160. Quotations on 156–157.

60. Bogle, *Brown Sugar*, 176–180.

61. Aljean Harmetz, "Diana Ross: Lady *Doesn't* Sing the Blues," *New York Times*, 24 December 1972, D4, D17. For a more extensive discussion of *Lady Sings the Blues*, see Jaap Kooijman, "Triumphant Black Pop Divas on the Wide Screen: *Lady Sings the Blues* and *Tina: What's Love Got to Do with It*," in Ian Inglis, ed., *Popular Music and Film* (London and New York: Wallflower, 2003), 178–192.

62. Peter Rogers, *What Becomes a Legend Most? The Blackglama Story* (New York: Simon and Schuster, 1979), 60–61.

63. "New Day for Diana: Now a Movie Star, Too, Diana Ross Has Everything—and Likes It," *Life* 73:23, 8 December 1972, 42–45.

64. Michael Jackson and Roberta Flack performed the song on the accompanying television special.

PART III

Confront

9

The Choices before Us
Anita M. Caspary and the Immaculate Heart Community

Susan Marie Maloney

Our Decrees pledge us to an unending search for personhood, relevance and Christian community. They deny the attainment or even the ideal of human perfectibility. They demand an asceticism we have never before been asked for—an unselfconscious devotion to the truth, a vigilant and constant concern with the destructive forces in our society, a sensitive response to the needs of others, a willingness to welcome diversity not merely to tolerate it, and a condemnation with the clarity of Christ of the primary evil—hypocrisy, especially religious hypocrisy.[1]

Spoken by Anita M. Caspary in 1969, these words were revolutionary for a Catholic nun. Caspary was the Mother General of the Immaculate Heart of Mary Sisters (IHMs) of California until she assumed the presidency of the Immaculate Heart Community from 1963 to 1973. As the only American woman to head a Catholic religious order of nuns[2] and relinquish her vows to create a new ecumenical community of men and women, Caspary articulated a new vision for Catholic nuns and religious women in the modern world. So prominent was she that *Time* magazine featured her on its cover on February 23, 1970.[3] Under Caspary's leadership during the 1960s, the IHM sisters rejected the interference of the Roman Catholic male hierarchy in their lives. In a democratically elected forum, they rewrote their religious rule. They were motivated by the liberal changes of the Second Vatican Council (Vatican II) as well as the American culture of the 1960s. The new rule the IHM sisters created in 1976 incorporated insights from modern psychology, with its emphasis on individual freedom; from humanistic philosophy, which eliminated the division between the sacred and the secular; and from the women's liberation movement. This new IHM rule and its accompanying practices, however, provoked the ire of the church authorities. James Francis Cardinal McIntyre, the local and internationally influential archbishop of Los Angeles, threatened the IHM nuns: If they did not stop the process of "modernization" of convent life, they would suffer.[4] As a punishment for lack of submission to the cardinal's demands, the IHM sisters were fired from the Los Angeles Catholic schools. Despite this economic reprisal and the continual refusal of McIntyre and Vatican representatives to approve their new rule, the IHMs chose to withdraw from canonical Catholic status and reconfigure as a new ecumenical order. During the 1960s, this decision became a cause célèbre.[5]

What prepared Caspary to lead over four hundred IHM nuns to change radically their commitment and lifestyle, and subsequently to reject the male religious authority of the Roman Catholic Church? What was the historical context that allowed Caspary and the IHMs to make such a choice? What role did the culture of the sixties play in this extraordinary event in American religious history? And what is the significance of Caspary and the Immaculate Heart story?

Anita M. Caspary—The Early Years

Born in 1915 in South Dakota, Anita was the third eldest of eight children of Jacob and Marie Bruch Caspary.[6] Raised in Los Angeles of a strong German-Catholic family, Anita was encouraged her parents in her inclination toward religion and literature. Surrounded by a strong extended family and Catholic environment of school and church, she developed her talents. She was valedictorian of her high school and college classes, the latter at Immaculate Heart College (IHC). "Stable," "traditional," and "conservative" would describe these formative years of Caspary's life. The questioning of authority formed no part of her early experience.[7]

After receiving her B.A. in English in 1936 from IHC, Caspary joined the Immaculate Heart sisters. The spirit of the order, a blend of respect for the religious rule and pragmatic common sense, attracted her. She writes, "The sisters who taught there struck me as unique individuals. . . . Something about the atmosphere delighted and challenged me. . . . It became clear to me that these sisters were genuinely human while at the same time following their Rule. So convent life did not demand mystery, and it could be a source of expansive love and understanding."[8] Caspary's desire to join the Immaculate Heart order was also highly influenced by her teacher and close friend, Mother Eucharia Harney.

Caspary's early years in the convent were peaceful. She was considered an "obedient nun."[9] She writes, "Although my values were not always those of the governing body in the community, I had not usually, as a young nun, questioned the system. . . . [I]t was my personal practice of the vow of obedience, how well I fulfilled the will of superiors, the legalistic rules . . . ," that was important.[10] Mother Eucharia encouraged Caspary's leadership qualities and assigned her to diverse ministries in order to familiarize her with the works of the community. She mentored Caspary's abilities to revere tradition yet adjust to cultural mores, according to the IHM legacy. An excellent teacher and adviser, Caspary quickly was selected for graduate studies. "Choosing which sisters would be selected for advanced training was a compromise between Immaculate Heart College department heads and authorities in the religious community itself."[11] Indeed, pursuing advanced studies represented an act of obedience for Caspary, not one of self-promotion. In 1942, she received a master's degree in English from the University of Southern California, and in 1948 a doctorate in English from Stanford University.[12]

Graduate studies introduced new worlds to Caspary. Learning the art of reasoned argument, experiencing a diversity of opinions, prepared her well for the life of a college professor. Returning from Stanford, she rose quickly in the ranks of academic leadership to become, in 1950, chair of the English Department and graduate dean of the college. Trained in the life of a nun and committed to teaching, she envisioned a scholarly life in English literature and Catholic intellectual life in the IHM community.[13] Little did she know what religious and cultural changes of the 1960s were in her future.

Anita Caspary and the Hollywood Nuns[14]

The Immaculate Heart sisters early on were known as a progressive—open and unconventional—order of nuns. Change was not a stranger to them.

Established in Spain in 1848, the order first sent members to California in 1871. By 1924, the sisters and their new American recruits found the European restrictions intolerable and separated from their Spanish origins. The legacy of a pioneer spirit plus leadership in the hands of non-Spanish nuns gave a unique American flavor to the community.

Mother Eucharia Harney headed the IHM sisters in the 1950s. While "Mother E," as she was fondly called, was respectful of the church traditions, she was vibrant, vivacious, and warm. She epitomized the flair, independence, and respectful but pragmatic approach to convent life.[15] More important, for her there could be an exemption from any rule as long as the motivation was the love of God or the love of neighbor. Her attitude toward convent life and her natural talents were embedded in an independent spirit and cultural sensitivity that characterized the IHMs as a community. Mother E's dynamic leadership was expansive and attractive to others. Her impact on Caspary's life cannot be overstated.

Women like Mother Eucharia were precursors of the sixties spirit, with their open attitude toward change, a healthy critical attitude toward rigid religious rules, and a strong commitment to excellence in education. "In retrospect," Caspary recalls, "the spirit of Vatican II was presaged by the spirit of Mother Eucharia. In the later fifties and early sixties, she created an environment unknown in traditional convent life."[16] This nontraditional atmosphere allowed for secular speakers at Immaculate Heart College, the education of IHM nuns at secular universities, and the education of the young nuns to articulate and hold a reasoned position even if it meant a "respectful disagreement" with those sisters in authority. In the early 1960s, the IHMs also welcomed eminent psychologists, theologians, and sociologists to their religious retreats in order to understand the relationship of the social sciences to their spiritual lives.

In sum, these "Hollywood" nuns possessed a predisposition to the culture of the 1960s. They were open to secular thought, accustomed to dialogue and disagreement, and committed to the education of women. They had leaders who schooled them to question authority, and they counted a majority of their members as critical thinkers willing to take risks. These historical and cultural factors set the stage for their conflict with James Francis Cardinal McIntyre, which led to the split in the IHM order of nuns and the eventual creation of a new ecumenical community.

Anita Caspary—College President and Mother General

In 1958, Caspary was appointed president of Immaculate Heart College. Known for excellence in the liberal arts, IHC was considered the progressive Catholic college in the west.[17] With a young and energetic faculty, the departments of art, music, education, and religious studies were gaining a national reputation for creativity and innovative methods. In retrospect, Caspary recalls two memorable incidents important for her evolving consciousness of the values of cultural and spiritual authenticity, and of responsibility to truth, so prominent in the culture of the 1960s. One was a public event, the other a private encounter.[18]

Mary's Day was a public religious feast held annually at IHC to honor Mary the mother of God. The traditional day of prayer ended with a solemn procession and the crowning of the statue of Mary with flowers. Caspary recalls this event: "The repetition of this ceremony year after year left the students of the young generation of the 1960s cold."[19] Headed by nationally recognized artist Sister Corita Kent, in 1964 the art department was asked by the college administration to create a feast day relevant to the students' experience. To honor Mary, Sister Corita, herself a significant artist in the countercultural and antiwar movement of the 1960s, incorporated art, posters, flowers, crepe-paper hats, bright garlands, modern music, and dance to create a general atmosphere of joyful celebration.[20] Mixing traditional elements used for religious ritual and culturally relevant symbols, the day gained notoriety as a 1960s religious feast day. The female flower children of the period were honoring the Catholic symbol of womanhood—Mary, mother of God. Since the new celebration was unusual for a Catholic college, Mary's Day at IHC attracted the press and TV.[21] This publicity expanded the college's reputation as a liberal institution that adopted new forms of worship; the attention also focused on the nuns, who showed a 1960s spirit. The IHMs' interpretation of Mary's Day represented a spirituality that united traditional Catholic symbols with an understanding of the age of Aquarius. Not surprisingly, the Mary's Day event brought about a clash with the conservative Cardinal McIntyre. The conflict raised hard questions for Caspary about the legitimacy of the authority the cardinal attempted to impose on the college when IHC chose lecturers who were liberal and culturally relevant. It was apparent that religion was meaningful even for the rebellious yet spiritually seeking youth of the 1960s.

Catholic Church authorities of Los Angeles were critical of the radical atmosphere of the 1960s and its impact on IHC. Caspary remembers well the negative response of the cardinal and the duty she felt to respond to his inquiries about Mary's Day.[22] Her task was to defend IHC's belief in the blend of religious commitment with the various cultural elements of the time. Catholics and others frequently construed this new imaginative interpretation as an affront to religious tradition. The 1960s was a period in which many young Americans searched for spirituality outside of traditional religions, and the protesting counterculture sought spiritual experiences in relevant rituals from a diversity of faith perspectives, originating both from the East and the West. Caspary understood that the 1960s exposed the spiritual desires of the "youth culture." Both students and nuns needed new devotional practices. She publicly defended the faculty and student organizers of the event. Years later, in an interview, she remembers the event: "By contemporary standards, this event of Mary's Day would not warrant any public attention. However, for me, it raised the continuing tension of McIntyre's critique of our new religious and devotional practices as manifested in Mary's Day."[23]

Caspary was aware of the debates over the principle of freedom in institutions of higher education during the 1960s in the context of student revolt on American campuses. Students demanded participation in decisions and pressed for socially and politically "relevant" teaching, which some faculty considered as violations of academic freedom. As an open-minded college president, however, Caspary responded to the wishes for cultural relevance by her Catholic female students. Moreover, she believed that the college's religious mission combined well with some of the surrounding society's intellectual and cultural trends: "I wanted to hold in creative tension the Catholic character of the college and the commitment to a liberal education."[24]

After years of reflection, Caspary recalls the progression of her thinking about the cardinal's exercise of his authority. "On a more personal level, I found myself questioning the authority of the archbishop in such matters. His continual complaints were not reasoned and I questioned the judicious use of his authority. At this point in my career these were daring thoughts for me."[25] Caspary continued to defend the progressive stance of IHC and the IHM sisters, which appropriated cultural symbols of the 1960s, particularly those dealing with women and youth. To her, the cardinal's traditional arguments were no longer justified. McIntyre continued to assert his authority and attempted to dictate curriculum, approve speakers, and supervise events at IHC.

Caspary was not unlike other women of the 1950s and early 1960s who were apprehensive about challenging male control in the years prior to the age of consciousness-raising groups which became so prevalent in the women's liberation movement. Yet, Caspary relates a second and more private encounter with Cardinal McIntyre in which she surprised even herself by confronting him. In this meeting, she was accused by McIntyre of heading a "liberal" college. She describes her emotional transformation from repressed feelings of rage to justified anger.

> As the minutes ticked on, the cardinal's face grew red with his failure to elicit a promise of change in policy from me. Suddenly, he turned from me, apparently about to leave the room in disgust with no closure. Like a flaming fire, my own repressed feelings about the community, the college, and the cardinal flared . . . my thoughts of the sisters who worked long hours to make our small liberal arts college an effective and prestigious Christian influence . . . all flashed before me. In a spontaneous response I demanded that he return to his chair and listen to me. Not yet startled by my own brash action, I made my final defense [of our aim] to become an outstanding Catholic college in California.[26]

Caspary describes this incident as etched in her memory: a pivotal turning point of speaking truth to power. For her, as a woman, to challenge a prelate of the church was shocking yet emancipating. After years of reflection, this incident remains a watershed moment for her. The encounter in which she "found her own voice" created in her an empathetic understanding for the experiences of other women confronted by dominating authority figures.[27]

Caspary's reaction to McIntyre in this incident was similar to the responses of many women to male authority figures during this period. Indeed, the 1960s era was rife with young people confronting authority figures, questioning tradition, and demanding rights. Todd Gitlin writes of the era: "[F]igures of authority were proprietors without a cause."[28] Ordinarily shy and deliberative, Caspary had not been conditioned by her upbringing and years in the church to challenge or dispute those in authority. Yet what she viewed as injustice and obvious condescension on the part of McIntyre forced her to make a choice: exert her presidential authority or be silenced. This encounter, although it took place in the context of a private meeting, represented for Caspary an assault on her community of students and teachers, their inspirations and ideals. She was more than herself in that moment; she felt she was speaking for the community and its values. This sense of a collective consciousness, of a communal spirit within oneself, was ingrained in Caspary. The tradition of the Immaculate Heart sisters as women of conviction and the 1960s ideals of truth and justice reinforced Caspary's determination to lead. She knew that she was not alone in the religious and cultural revolution before her.

Caspary and the IHMs, like most nuns of the Catholic Church, had a dual relationship with the cardinal. On the one hand, the IHMs were responsible to him for certain religious practices and teachings; on the other hand, they were academic leaders heading an independent college, and therefore not subservient to his demands. Caspary demonstrated the need for a delicate balance between these two positions. The Mary's Day incident and the personal meeting with McIntyre sharpened this distinction and the tension it created for her. In the context of the turbulent society and culture of the 1960s, it signaled the more "decisive encounters" with him that were soon to come.[29]

The Catholic Church Context and the Second Vatican Council

The radical changes of the 1960s, the inherited liberal thought of Immaculate Heart College, and the context of countercultural California were not the only significant influences on Caspary and the IHM order. A major source of the changes made by Caspary and the IHMs lay in the documents of the Second Vatican Council.[30] Urged by Catholic scholars to update the church from a medieval bulwark of conservatism to a church relevant to the modern world, Pope John XXIII called all Catholic bishops to the Vatican to discuss the spiritual renewal and modernization of the church. Not since 1870 had a pope called for a re-examination of universal church teachings. In 1962, John XXIII asked the bishops to engage the contemporary advances made in biblical studies, science, communications, human rights, politics, justice, and peace. His expectation for the entire church was to "read the signs of the times" and to interact with modernity. The principle of *aggiornamento*, or updating, characterized the new self-understanding as a church in need of renewal.[31]

The words *momentous, transformative,* and *cataclysmic* aptly describe the effects of Vatican II on the Catholic Church. In four years, the documents would eventually transform Catholic church life. Gone would be Mass in Latin, nuns in habits, priests alone at the altar, and Gregorian chant as the music of the church. Rather, Mass would be celebrated in the language of the people, nuns would be women religious in short skirts, lay ministers would preside at the altar, and guitars and modern music would supplant organs and medieval chant. The Catholic Church rejected an isolationist stance toward global events and opened up to the emerging world cultures of the 1960s in Europe, Asia, Africa, and the Americas.

Of the sixteen documents issued by Vatican II, only one dealt with the life of women and men in religious orders: Perfectae Caritatis.[32] During the period following Vatican II, Pope Paul VI issued a more pragmatic directive to accompany this document, *Norms for Implementing the Decree: On the Up-to-Date Renewal of Religious Life.* This revolutionary mandate granted a period of experimentation, which in effect suspended the rigid and legalistic way of life regulated by the church's code of law. This suspension allowed religious orders to return to the original vision of their respective founders. Further, the *Norms* gave the ultimate authority for renewal to the religious orders themselves. In effect, for women religious, the power to determine their renewed life was in their own hands, not those of the male hierarchy.

These documents created the possibility for a new—private and public—perception of Catholic sisters. With the antiquated habit as a public reminder of the rejection of the world, sisters had been public symbols of the church's ability to govern and sanctify. The call to adapt to modern reality and experiment challenged every facet of a community's and individual sister's life. For those in leadership, it became no small task to remain faithful to the original vision yet to adapt to the contemporary world.

As a prelate of the church and reigning archbishop of Los Angeles, Cardinal McIntyre was a conservative man in his religious perspective and remained such even after Vatican II introduced new ideas for renewal to the church. Despite his attendance at several sessions of Vatican II, he impeded within the archdiocese many of the mandated changes. His charitable works notwithstanding, his authoritarian stance and volatile disposition when approached with the new ideas of Vatican II became common knowledge.[33] For him, the prime duty of a cardinal was to be guardian and interpreter of the Catholic tradition.[34] Not surprisingly, he did not promote the experimental period that the pope allowed women religious.

The IHMs versus the Male Church Hierarchy: The Core Issues

McIntyre's negative attitude toward church renewal and the IHMs' determination to follow the dictates of Vatican II and update their lives set the stage for further conflict. With the culture of the 1960s, with its direct challenge to established authority, as the backdrop to this struggle of the IHMs with the male church hierarchy, who would define the lives of the IHM sisters?

> The key concepts in the way of life we visualize are relevance, responsible personhood and open community. The latter idea, that of open community means that we reconcile the tragic split in the religious vision, the split between the religious and worldly, natural and supernatural, the Church and human society. This theology of reconciliation means that Christ is to be encountered not only inside the visible Church, but also in a sin-scarred world, . . . in the midst of external misunderstanding or opposition . . . we are free to regulate our own lives, our own prayer-schedule. . . .[35]

Caspary spoke these words in 1973, ten years after she and her General Councillors launched the period of experimentation in 1963. Under a mandate from the General Assembly of that year, she and her General Councillors initiated a long-range study of all IHM documents, constitutions, policies, and procedures.[36] This study was to be guided by the Holy Spirit, the documents of the Vatican II, revisions of canon law, and the lived reality of the sisters.[37]

Years later Caspary wrote, "Although we [the General Council] were remarkably diverse personalities . . . we could see that the whole structure of religious life urgently needed redesign."[38] "The Immaculate Heart Sisters . . . would give enthusiastic reception to papal documents that authorized wide consultation of members, the updating of our Rule, and legitimate experimentation . . . [W]e needed to do much more than merely 'think' a new form of religious life to bring about a hoped-for transformation."[39]

To create a new form of religious life, a five-year plan of study and renewal was adopted by Caspary and the IHM sisters.[40] The study revealed that there were more underqualified sisters in administration and teaching positions in the 1960s than in the previous decades. These statistics rang an academic alarm to the IHMs, who prided themselves on being excellent educators. The decision, made by Caspary, her council, and the IHM study commissions, to educate these sisters in a systematic rotation plan meant that some sisters must be temporarily withdrawn from teaching in Los Angeles Catholic schools. This collective decision embraced by the community became a major source of conflict between Cardinal McIntyre and the IHM sisters.

During this period, other experimentation in religious practices and procedures also flourished. Local convents initiated new prayer rituals, and most important and symbolic were the changes in the women's appearance: The religious habit was abandoned for secular dress. In terms of organization and power, all the convents decentralized their decision-making processes, replacing the position of Mother Superior with communal decision-making bodies. In the spirit of experimentation, and reflecting the influence of humanistic psychology, Caspary and the elected delegates realized that a wider forum for community participation, debate, and discussion needed to be formed. The IHMs formed ongoing study groups and commissions based on the chief issues before the community, creating a democratic forum of total community involvement on a voluntary basis. The new Decrees of 1967 accepted by the IHMs stressed even more the significance of the women's movement, innovative liturgical practices, social justice involvement, individual responsibility for work, and ministry as service in the world rather than the cloister. The underlying concepts of relationships and values superseded the traditional convent model of organization and efficiency.

In spite of this overwhelming embrace for the period of experimentation and updating, a minority of members of the community dissatisfied with Caspary and her General Council alerted Cardinal McIntyre of their fear of change. Caspary writes, "Anyone aware of our past history of innovation and progressiveness, as well as of our difficult relationship with the cardinal, could predict a troubled future."[41] Because they had dared to respond seriously to Vatican II, the new IHM Rule and its practices evoked further scrutiny from McIntyre and other church officials. Between 1965 and 1969, the IHM sisters had three visitations. In this series of extraordinary church procedures, representatives of the pope, the Roman Catholic curia, and a committee of U.S. bishops made official visitations to the IHM convents in order to question each sister's allegiance to the new practices and Rule.[42]

Upon completion of these visitations, the IHMs were issued four directives: Adopt a religious habit, meet for daily communal prayer, remain committed to teaching in Catholic education, and submit to the authority of the local hierarchy. These famous "four points" sent shock waves through Catholic religious communities of women in the United States.[43] For the wider public, these four points challenged the legitimacy of the IHM innovations as inappropriate for Catholic sisters and unduly influenced by the counterculture of the 1960s.

Amid strong support and severe criticism, Caspary spent two years attempting to reconcile the differences between the IHMs' distinctive vision of religious life for women and that imposed by the hierarchy. In December 1969, Caspary addressed her sisters:

> The fact remains that the notion of self-determination and the ability of a community to listen to the word of God and to find an historically relevant response is not acceptable presently to the institutional Church. . . . To witness to integrity is a difficult role—it demands purification of one's motives, a rejection of all the means by which one can manipulate others; it calls for just anger without erratic outbursts of temper, for steadiness of purpose cleansed of stubborn immobility. . . . If we can make the idea . . . of "person in community" succeed, then, even though our numbers are small, we have in hand the Archimedes' lever that can move the world. Certainly such a group, Gospel-oriented, combining various types of membership in charity, can affect this impersonal, mechanized, technological world of ours which has become cruel and tragic even while it yearns for redemption.[44]

At a time of crisis, when American society was suffering cultural and political schisms between conservative and radical ideologies, a moment of crucial decisions for Caspary and the IHMs arose. In an emotional address to them, Caspary said: "I have felt for sometime that the IHM's . . . are being asked in a special way to read the signs of the times, to forge ahead, to begin with enthusiasm to work at a community of hope. . . . With confidence and peace, I choose to go ahead. If you believe that you can make this choice freely and willingly, I ask you to join with me."[45]

Fig. 9.1. Sister Mary Humiliata, IHM was the Mother General of the Catholic order of sisters (1963-70) and the first president of the new ecumenical Immaculate Heart Community (1970-73). *Courtesy of Anita M. Caspary, IHM*

The majority of the IHM sisters, over four hundred, including Caspary, signed dispensations from their vows.[46] They created the new Immaculate Heart Community. Members may be either married or celibate. They do not make vows but rather promise to give to the community from their time, talent, and treasure (financial resources). They must be Christian women and men, regardless of sexual orientation. Each member holds individual responsibility for his or her employment. The community, which continues to attract new members, currently sustains five nonprofit corporations dedicated to the homeless, retreat work, the elderly, and high school education. The ideals of voluntary communal bonds, gender equality, female leadership, commitment to community work, and a faith-life based on individual preference and not institutional affiliation have been the foundations of the new IHM community. Caspary and her followers created a concept of a religious community outside organizational church structures that combines some convent traditions as well as beliefs developed during the 1960s.

Anita Caspary and the Significance of the IHM Story

Many historians of the 1960s give meager attention to "mainstream" religion, considering it a cornerstone of traditionalism.[47] Caspary and the IHM story counter this historical perception. The confluence of an extraordinary woman leader, the principles of Vatican II, a community of educated women, the political and cultural ideals of the 1960s, and the women's movement transformed a century-old religious order of nuns into a modern Christian community of women and men.

The IHM story is significant also because it is about one woman and many women. In 1969, Jo Freeman, a prominent feminist activist, wrote: "Men will not liberate women, women must free themselves. They have waited too long as it is. Now the movement is growing, organizing, and becoming more militant. The largest minority group is getting angry. They are tired of working for everyone's liberation except their own."[48] Although they were Catholic nuns tied to the church's traditions and limited by its beliefs regarding their practical and symbolic role in the faith, Caspary and the IHMs understood their renewal as part of the secular women's movement, and they included female self-determination in the (new) Decrees of 1967. Similar to women in the wider society, Caspary "raised her consciousness" of her own oppressive situation. This was a disconcerting and shocking experience for her—shocking because, like many women of her generation, she and the IHMs believed that the religious ideals of women's perfectibility, obedience, and service underlying social relations and religious law were attainable goals.

For Catholic sisters, the IHM story holds particular import. Without relinquishing their vows, most women's orders have culturally modernized by adapting modern dress, diversifying their ministries, and engaging in innovative prayer rituals. Politically, they gave an equal place to men and democratized decision-making processes. Indeed, church scholars believe that the IHMs not only paved the way of modernization for their sisters in religion but demonstrated to Vatican officials the power of a women's community confronting Catholic authorities. Evidence indicates that the male hierarchy has not interfered to the same degree in the internal affairs of any American Catholic order of sisters since the Immaculate Heart Community was established in 1970.[49]

Caspary's leadership and the choice of the IHM women to withdraw from canonical status raise a significant issue for women in all organized traditional religions: the pressure to be recognized by the male hierarchy. The IHM women did not change their Christian commitment by integrating contemporary ideals and style into their faith; they changed only its form. The majority of members remained Catholic. In the creation of a Christian community, they demonstrated a collective understanding of self-recognition as sufficient for a Christian Catholic commitment. This cuts into the heart of Catholic patriarchal authority and exposes its institutional vulnerability. Who determines a legitimate Catholic commitment? How does the church struggle for its distinct place during times of radical cultural change and emergence of spiritual alternatives? How does male church recognition reward a community of women? As the history of Caspary and her sisters demonstrates, these questions were hotly contested during the 1960s. And the debates remain part of the legacy the IHM sisters have given to women in religion, and most particularly to Catholic orders of sisters.

Reflecting on the past, Caspary writes:

> In a way we were naive American women who believed that law was normative, concerned with the attainable. To be dispensed from its observance was viewed as a concession to weakness that was to be avoided. But the IHMs were not only American, they were generationally of the 1960s: they believed that one must "tell it like it is." . . . The insistence on truth without nuance was not the only sign of the sixties among us. We had suddenly engaged in the events taking place in the world around us. . . . [W]e were sharing, not a sense of "continuous lived history," but rather "a collage of fragments scooped together as if a whole decade took place in that instant."[50]

This sense of making history, taking in from a historical period its particular characteristics, represented a commitment to conjoin the feminist idea of women's empowerment with the best principles of the Catholic heritage.

As an academic as well as religious leader, Caspary initially approached the issue of renewal in religious life as a series of rational disagreements. As the male hierarchy revealed its contempt for women's spirituality and the collective authority of the community, these disagreements transformed into a moral crisis of grave proportion. A strong case can be made that the IHMs were the first nuns in the United States to "grow up" and be women and face the "fathers." The act of renunciation of the vows was not an act of "adolescent" rebellion, as some church leaders characterized it, but a deliberate adult choice.

As Caspary demonstrated, one role of a leader is to provide to her followers the clarity of the choices before them. Sociologist Betty Jean Bluth writes:

> Anita Caspary was the face and voice of the IHM sisters both externally and internally for the entire process of change. Taking all of the ideas and events, Anita Caspary reached into the experiences, discussions and arguments of the sisters, and saw a new order. She gave unity and new meaning to a myriad of expressions. She formed the dilemmas and issues into coherent paradigms, gave her sisters clarity so that every choice could be made with full understanding, one logical step at a time.[51]

Caspary's leadership propelled her to the forefront of the revolution of Catholic women's religious communities during the "long decade of the sixties." She symbolized the intellectual and emotional strength of women to resist male oppressive religious authority. Along with 1960s feminists who struggled to revolutionize society, she led women to transform gender power relations. Most important, she led women to define their own spiritual lives.

NOTES

1. Anita M. Caspary, IHM, *Witness to Integrity: The Crisis of the Immaculate Heart Community of California* (Collegeville, MN: Liturgical Press, 2003), 269.

2. The terms *nuns*, *sisters*, and *women religious* are used interchangeably in this essay.

3. "The Catholic Exodus: Why Priests and Nuns are Quitting." *Time* cover story, February 23, 1970.

4. Caspary, *Witness to Integrity*, 1.

5. Over two hundred news reports detail the conflict between the IHMs and Cardinal McIntyre. See the Archives of the Immaculate Heart Community, Los Angeles, California. See also Caspary, *Witness to Integrity*, xv. To date, the IHM community is the only ecumenical group in the United States with its origins in an established Catholic order of sisters.

6. Anita M. Caspary, IHM, interview with author, May 29, 2003.

7. Ibid.

8. Caspary, *Witness to Integrity*, 13–14.

9. It was customary for nuns, upon entry into the novitiate, to receive religious names. In 1937, Caspary accepted the name of Sister Mary Humiliata. With the changes adopted at the Second Vatican Council, she reassumed her birth (baptismal) name.

10. Caspary, *Witness to Integrity*, 47.

11. Ibid., 32.

12. Caspary preferred doctoral study in theology or philosophy, but these disciplines were not open to women at the time. Obediently, and with enthusiasm, she accepted the assignment to obtain a doctorate in English. Anita Caspary, IHM, interview with author, May 22, 2003.

13. Sr. Anita M. Caspary, IHM, ed., *Mauriac: A Christian Critic Book* (St. Louis, MN: Herder Book Co., 1968).

14. The Immaculate Heart sisters' motherhouse, college, and high school were located in Hollywood; hence the moniker.

15. One story is told of Mother Eucharia discussing the efficacy of grand silence (the Rule forbade conversations after nine P.M.) with the novices until three o'clock in the morning. Anita Caspary, IHM. Caspary interview, May 29, 2003.

16. Caspary, *Witness to Integrity*, 20.

17. Caspary interview, May 29, 2003.

18. Ibid.

19. Caspary, *Witness to Integrity*, 38.

20. See cover of *Newsweek*, December 25, 1967. With the support of Caspary and the IHM sisters, Corita Kent (1918–1986) became one of the most prominent antiwar artists of the sixties. Her works were available in various forms: posters, greeting cards, advertising, and billboards. *The Rainbow* in the Boston harbor is one of the largest copyrighted paintings in the world. Corita Kent, "The Artist as Social Activist amid Adversity: How the Job Is Done," in *Sacred Dimensions of Women's Experience*, ed. Elizabeth Dodson Gray (Wellesley, MA: Roundtable Press, 1988), 37. Kent's serigraph *Mary Is a Ripe Tomato* is an example of her use of the language and images of the sixties in religious art.

21. Caspary, *Witness to Integrity*, 38.

22. For McIntyre's response, see ibid., 38–41.

23. Anita Caspary, IHM, interview with author, June 18, 2003.

24. Ibid.

25. Caspary interview, May 29, 2003.

26. Caspary, *Witness to Integrity*, 37.

27. Caspary interview, May 29, 2003.

28. Todd Gitlin, *The Sixties: Days of Hope, Days of Rage*, (Toronto: Bantam Books, 1987), 31.

29. Caspary interview, May 29, 2003.

30. Also referred to as Vatican II.

31. Meaning "to bring fresh air to a situation," *aggiornamento* epitomizes the spirit Pope John XXIII wished for Vatican II.

32. *Perfectae Caritatis,* in *Vatican Council II: The Conciliar and Post Conciliar Documents,* ed. Austin Flannery, O.P. (Northport, NY: Costello Publishing Co., 1981), 611, 624, 903, 350. Two other documents shaped the new IHM Rule: the *Dogmatic Constitution on the Church* and the *Pastoral Constitution of the Church in the Modern World.* The former changed the traditional symbol of the church from the mystical body of Christ to the church as "people of God." The latter shifted the notion of the virtuous life and the understanding of the human person. See Caspary, *Witness to Integrity,* 85–108, 225–231.

33. See also Father George Barry Ford, *A Degree of Difference* (New York: Farrar, Straus & Giroux, 1969).

34. For McIntyre's background, see Caspary, *Witness to Integrity,* 55–66.

35. Anita Caspary, IHM, "The Making of a Servant Community" (unpublished speech given to Tacoma Dominicans, Washington, June 14, 1973), 8.

36. In religious orders of women, the General Assembly is the final authority. The General Council, which consists of the Mother General and her councilors, is responsible to the General Assembly for implementing decrees and policies. Caspary, in leading the changes, always had the support of the majority of the members of the General Assembly.

37. Caspary, *Witness to Integrity,* 51.

38. Ibid.

39. Ibid., 53.

40. Elizabeth Ann Flynn, IHM, was the coordinator and moving force behind this study and the demands it elicited. Caspary interview, June 18, 2003.

41. Caspary, *Witness to Integrity,* 53.

42. Ibid., chap. 8 and 12.

43. Ibid., 158–161.

44. Ibid., 267, 269, 270.

45. Ibid., 271.

46. Ibid., 210. Fifty members of the IHM sisterhood did not follow Caspary and remained as the Immaculate Heart Sisters, an order recognized by the Catholic hierarchy.

47. For example, Todd Gitlin in *The Sixties* does not address religion or spirituality.

48. Jo Freeman, "The Women's Liberation Front," *The Moderator* (November 1968); Web site http://womenshistory.about.com/cs/60s70s/index2.htm.

49. Anita M. Caspary, IHM, interview with author, May 27, 2003.

50. Caspary, *Witness to Integrity,* 48–49.

51. Betty Jean Bluth, Ph.D., "Anita Caspary, IHM and The Sisters of the Immaculate Heart" (unpublished paper, June 1, 2003). Bluth also wrote "A Convent without Walls" (unpublished diss., University of California, Los Angeles, May 1969). This sociological study deals with the organizational changes of the Immaculate Heart Community.

10

Shaping the Sixties
The Emergence of Barbara Deming

Judith McDaniel

Barbara Deming (1917–1984) was a poet and essayist whose first political writing appeared at the beginning of the 1960s. Her influence on the major discussions that emerged around issues of nonviolence, feminism, and lesbian and gay liberation was far reaching. Although she was not widely recognized as a "popular" writer, within the movements that occurred during her political life—civil rights, anti–Vietnam War, feminist, and lesbian/gay—Barbara Deming was considered a major force. Deming was a participant, and she was more. Her background, her intellectual training, her ability to make a personal connection with a vast range of people, all gave her a perspective on her times that was unique.

When Barbara Deming's writing was at its most powerful, she could make her readers feel sympathy for another's situation. Her intention for her writing was that what she saw and reported—and the moral judgments she made about what she observed—would have the effect of creating in her readers a more "free and active" sympathy.[1] If readers were also moved toward actions that were intended to change an injustice, she was pleased. And she knew that the combination of a deep moral sympathy with others and an action to change injustice could profoundly affect the lives of those taking the actions. It was this ability that made Barbara Deming one of the profound influences on the culture of the 1960s.

In March 1960, poet and film critic Barbara Deming made national news by confronting Fidel Castro publicly about human rights in the new revolutionary Cuba.[2] Within a few weeks of her return from Cuba, Deming was attending meetings of the Committee for Nonviolent Action

(CNVA), a pacifist group advocating unilateral disarmament of atomic weapons. "What am I doing here?" she asked rhetorically in an article published in *The Nation*. The conversation in this group, she wrote with apparent surprise, "is talk of revolution," and "I am the daughter of a well-to-do Republican lawyer."[3]

By the spring of 1963, Deming was in jail in Birmingham, Alabama, following a civil rights demonstration in which she and "a group of Negro demonstrators . . . were petitioning . . . for the right to be treated like human beings."[4] By the middle of the decade, she was in an Albany, Georgia city jail for walking through the center of the city on a racially integrated peace march.[5] During the sixties, as she learned her way in a variety of causes, she also found her voice and her subject as she wrote articles about politics and political activism.

If Deming's transformation into a revolutionary was surprising to her, it seemed shocking and inexplicable to the friends, family, and lovers who knew her best. And yet, seeds of this transformation had been planted by her family, her education, and her sexual identity and emerged in her early life. The non-acceptance of paternalistic authority, the absolute commitment to nonviolence, and her self-identification as a sexual/gender rebel were the themes that defined her political influence on the movements for political and social justice that spanned the next twenty-four years of her life, until her death in 1984.

Child of a wealthy professional family from New York City, a poet and film critic of literary repute in her own right, Deming did not outwardly resemble today's media-shaped image of either the "radical protesters" or the "flower-children" of the sixties. Though many of them were upper- or upper-middle-class, Deming was more than twenty years older than most of those protesters. Her peers in political activism were neither the young black civil rights workers nor the angry young college students threatened with the draft and military service in Vietnam. Deming's peers were thoughtful, committed, reserved middle-aged professionals such as Dave Dellinger and A. J. Muste who formed the 1950s response to the threat of atomic, and then nuclear, war.

Born in 1917, Barbara Deming was forty-three in 1960. The second of four children, she was the family's only daughter. Her mother was Katherine Burritt, who had been a singer before her marriage to Harold Deming, the "Republican lawyer." Raised in Chicago and Paris, Katherine was a free-spirited, independent woman, and she modeled that for her children—in her friendships and her affairs with men and women. Harold

Deming would have been an artist or a naturalist except that his father expected him to be a lawyer and Harold never disobeyed his father. This expectation of obedience to paternal authority was also part of Barbara Deming's family code; Harold Deming determined that his first son would be a lawyer, his daughter would be a teacher, and his next two sons a doctor and a writer. Only Barbara refused his direction, maintaining her intention to write. Harold never fully relented but did allow that she might find some work as an editor if she couldn't bear the thought of teaching.[6]

The Deming children all began school at the Friends Seminary on East Sixteenth Street in New York City. It was located only three blocks south of the Deming home on East Nineteenth Street. The catalog for Friends Seminary advertised—in 1923, the year Barbara Deming entered—a school that built up "traditions of Simplicity, Sincerity and Diligence." Like the progressive schools that would follow several decades later, Friends Seminary had "a personality peculiarly its own, a spirit which cannot be easily described, but which is the natural result of teachers' and pupils' working together in friendly companionship." In this curriculum, the school itself aimed to become a real and lifelike community in which students could face and address problems similar to the problems in the larger outside community. Rather than teaching any specific theology, Friends Seminary referred to "moral growth" and "religious feeling," which gives every person a sense "of kinship with a universal power upon which all life depends." In this school context, the Quaker tenet of "that of God in every person" emphasized a "sense of honor, the rights of the younger and weaker, the courtesy that does not forget, and the spirit of service."[7]

The Quaker commitment to nonviolence grew out of this belief in a non-hierarchical, non-authoritarian life in a community that is not just a collection of separate individuals but a living whole that is more than the sum of its parts. Spontaneous pacifism, Friends still believe, should arise in the context of such community, since to injure any part of it is to damage the whole. For twelve years, all during her school years, this system of thought and belief formed Barbara's constant environment. The school created an environment that Barbara Deming found completely compatible with her personality, her own natural bent. In fact, it was this community that she tried to recreate many times during her life, whether in prison, in feminist consciousness-raising groups, or, finally, in the lesbian collective she founded.

As a result of her upbringing, when Barbara Deming began to come of age sexually, she was able to freely confide in her mother. During the summer of 1933, when Barbara Deming was sixteen, she became sexually involved with Norma Millay, sister of poet Edna St. Vincent Millay, a woman twice Barbara's age.[8] We cannot know what exactly Barbara knew about sex and sexuality at the time, but she later wrote to her mother:

> I have always been grateful to you for the fact that when you first told me about homosexuality you spoke of it simply and did not condemn it as anything ugly. Because of this, when I fell in love with Norma I felt no hatred of myself. My first experience of love was free of that poison. I've always been grateful to Norma, too—for *she*, of course, taught me no shame.[9]

The record we do have of that first love affair is certainly "free of that poison." Young Barbara was distractedly, delightedly, exuberantly in love during that year, writing poetry that was equally unrestrained and unstructured. Her letters to her mother describing the affair and her feeling toward Norma are passionate, witty, and utterly revealing. "I go for walks," the young Barbara confesses. "I walk up to Norma's mailbox and touch it and come back." A few days later: "She's well—well I guess you know. I worship her—and mummy, she really likes me. I can never truly believe it. Oh, we've talked and—oh, I love her, I love her, I love her."[10]

At the end of that year, Barbara left home for Bennington College, a newly founded liberal arts college in Vermont. Almost immediately, Deming the poet was carefully changing the pronouns in her love poems from "she" to "he"; and one result of that change was that the poetry stopped flowing exuberantly.[11] Writing carefully, straining to find the exact word, being extremely reluctant to edit or change a single word and, at the same time, typing copy after copy of a single poem with a word or phrase changed, restored, changed again—this became Barbara Deming's writing process as she struggled to reconcile her sexuality with the social mores of her times.

Deming graduated from Bennington in 1938—during the Great Depression and before the outbreak of World War II. During the war, she worked for the Library of Congress National Film Library Project based at New York's Museum of Modern Art, reviewing war films. In the early fifties, a bequest from an aunt allowed Deming to spend time traveling in Europe, where she began writing the stories in the collection *Wash Us and Comb Us* (not published until 1974). During those years, Deming had men and women lovers, following perhaps the example of her mother or the necessity of her times and class.

Barbara Deming's emotional life finally began to settle in the mid-fifties after the death of her father. It was then she met painter Mary Meigs, an artist of similar age and social class. "My life changed very much at this time," Barbara wrote. "I began to live, and then lived for many years, with a woman who knew that she chose to be a lesbian."[12] Barbara was thirty-seven, and she and Mary had a home in Wellfleet, Massachusetts. Their friends and neighbors were intellectuals such as Edmund Wilson and Mary McCarthy. All their friends knew about their relationship, that these two women were lovers, but no one ever spoke aloud what they all knew.

Mary Meigs, the painter, and Barbara Deming, the writer, kept strict schedules in order to do their work. Most of the money they lived on was Mary's, from a family trust. Barbara sold some stories and poems to small journals such as *Voices* and to national magazines such as *Vogue* and the *New Yorker*; she was the regular film reviewer for *Vogue*, the *Partisan Review* and *The Nation*. While she had a national reputation and was accepted as an artist and intellectual in many circles, in March 1960 she was discouraged about her failure to publish more, and about the reception of her literary work in general.[13] When she visited Cuba in the early spring of 1960, Barbara Deming had never written a political poem or essay; she had never demonstrated for or against anything, nor engaged in electoral politics, nor named herself a lesbian to friends or family.

The Turning Point: Cuba, 1960

Early March 1960 found Barbara Deming vacationing in a guesthouse just outside Havana. She was one in a party of four and there were no other guests.

Only a year and a few weeks earlier, guerrilla rebel commander Fidel Castro had marched out of the mountains and into downtown Havana, marking the end of the Batista regime. Batista had been a ruthless dictator, which was well known by the U.S. government; but he was also staunchly anti-communist—a position that played well in Washington during the heat of the Cold War. Fidel Castro, supported by Cuban peasants, workers, and many intellectuals, waged a classic guerrilla campaign against Batista for years before the final victory. Washington watched from a distance, not sure what Castro's victory meant, refusing to recognize the new Cuban government. A year into the new government, Cuba was in the throes of a cultural, political, and economic transformation. Few traditional tourists were willing to chance the turmoil. Deming and her companions were all artists—writer Bessie Breuer; Bessie's husband, the sculptor Henry Poor; and their daughter Anne Poor, a painter, who was Barbara's age, forty-three. Bessie Breuer, an old friend of Barbara's mother, had been the first woman to hold an editorial position at the *Herald Tribune.*

In 1960 there was little unanimity of opinion about Castro's revolution, even among the intellectuals and artists who had been frequent visitors to Cuba. Barbara Deming's party, enjoying the unnatural quiet of post-revolutionary Cuba, had different understandings of what Castro meant and what he was doing. Anne Poor remembered that "every meal was a big political discussion," with Anne and Bessie arguing in favor of Castro and Henry and Barbara Deming playing the conservatives who "didn't think much of this revolution."[14]

Anne remembered that the sticking point for Barbara was the fact that Castro was executing some of the Batista officials who had been tried and found "criminal" under the revolutionary government. Barbara thought that was wrong, in Anne's memory of how it was, and she decided one morning to drive into Havana and tell him so. She found Castro coming out of a hotel, an old famous hotel, where he had been saying goodbye and thank-you to Herbert Matthews, the reporter from the *New York Times*, the only reporter Castro felt had been fair to the revolution while he was out in the jungle fighting. Anne wasn't there. But, she said, Barbara had told her about the encounter and she could imagine it all—"the great doctor came down and was getting in his car. He turned and a tall woman said, 'I'd like to speak to you Dr. Castro.' All the cameras and nobody else dared to come near him. And he said, 'What about?' And she said, 'I don't approve of you.'"[15]

Barbara's official account was different, of course, more deliberate. Her article describing the conversation with Castro was published by the leftist news magazine *The Nation* shortly after her return to the United States. The only obstacle she said she encountered in communicating with Cubans was that "they are so eager to talk to Americans about what is happening, that I sometimes found myself trying to listen to two or three people at once. No one was indifferent."[16] The soldiers she saw seemed young and Cubans were not afraid of them. Castro himself was not a threatening figure; his people referred to him as "our kid. 'That kid, he's working too hard,' we say. It's very, very strange; we feel responsible for him." As a result of having talked with Cubans for a week—or rather, having listened to Cubans for a week—she wrote that she found herself "stepping into a taxicab and telling the driver that I would like, please, to talk with Fidel Castro."

She didn't find him at once, although the cab driver was helpful and took her to an office where she could make her request. Another Cuban, an engineer, took her from desk to desk. She could not question, she said in her article, that while "Cubans may be loudly critical of the present policy of our government . . . they are not hostile toward the American people. . . . No Cuban with whom I spoke treated with scorn my determination to try and see Castro." And so, she finally did speak to him, just in the manner a number of Cubans had suggested to her, by "catching his eye in a public place" and asking if she could talk with him. Castro was standing on the sidewalk outside the Sevilla Biltmore Hotel when Barbara Deming stepped up to him and began to ask him questions.

> I introduced myself as an American distressed at the poor relations existing between our two countries. I did understand, I told him, that he had cause for bitterness; but, I said, his angry words were losing him friends in the United States—even those who might well be his friends. . . .

They spoke for over an hour. The conversation ranged from accusation and denial to mutual exploration. Castro never stopped insisting that when he made speeches, he was not speaking to Americans or to the U.S. government, but to Cubans. He spoke now at length and with feeling: "Don't you understand? I have to build up in the Cuban people a national conscience. I have to teach them what their true situation is. I have to make them aware of what lies before them, to be done and to be suffered. How did George Washington have to speak to his soldiers at Valley Forge?"

Cubans had two primary complaints against the U.S. government in 1960. They were furious that the U.S. government had given asylum to some of the most notorious torturers and murderers of the dictatorship. And they did not understand why the United States allowed Batista supporters—primarily the wealthy expatriates who had benefited from the regime—to mount air strikes against Cuba from U.S. territory. Deming began as an apologist: "Our government naturally deplores the raids," she affirmed, "but it wasn't easy to prevent them. How was one to keep a pilot from lying about his destination?" The Cubans knew better. If the planes had been bombing Canada, they asked her, don't you think your government would have stopped them?

Nor did the Cubans believe the U.S. government didn't know about the murders and tortures committed by the Batista henchmen who had been granted asylum in the United States. She learned the meaning of a particularly Cuban gesture,

> where the speaker touches the corner of his eye, meaning: I have seen it. This gesture was repeated for me many times. There is scarcely a person to whom one speaks whose family has been untouched by Batista's torturers. About 19,000 Cubans were murdered by them. In Havana alone they castrated 300 men and boys, so people said. Some of the tortures they perfected are almost unspeakable.

Reporters were there that day. After Barbara and Castro had spoken for quite a while, two men from NBC pushed through the crowd to ask Castro for an interview the next day. When he tried to decline, they began asking him questions, standing out on the street corner. There must have been a photographer with the reporters, for someone took a dozen photographs that day of Barbara Deming and Fidel Castro. One, published with her expanded "Dialogues in Cuba" in *Revolution and Equilibrium* (1971), shows a profile of Castro, hand raised, finger pointed in a gesture of admonishment. Barbara is watching him, listening carefully, with her characteristically intense gaze. In one of the unpublished photographs, a crowd surrounds the two, some men standing on tiptoes to see these two tall, striking individuals, but when these photographs were taken, they were clearly speaking only to each other.

Whatever verbal exchange took place between Barbara Deming and Fidel Castro that day, perhaps changing her mind about Castro or his revolution, the real transformation occurred once Barbara Deming returned to the United States.

Creating a Persona, Creating a Decade

"The way I remember her is being a very wealthy, upper class woman," said David Dellinger, one sixties radical commenting on another. "I might have made some comparisons with my own upbringing, but I thought maybe she was even more upper class than I was."[17] A few months after her article in *The Nation*, Dellinger met Barbara Deming in 1960 at a conference of the Committee for Nonviolent Action, perhaps the very one at which she heard "talk of revolution." He was surprised that she had come, because she didn't know anything about disarmament or leftist politics.

Deming, remembering herself at that time, agreed. She wrote:

> Before the 1960's, though I probably would, if asked, have called myself a liberal, I took no real political position—for I had given politics no real thought. Until I began to immerse myself in the writings of Gandhi,[18] after a trip to India in 1959, the subject had not captured my consecutive interest. I had accepted without exerting myself to question the many familiar myths about this country—like the myth that we are a uniquely generous state, incapable by our very nature of imperialism. . . . The shock of the trip to Cuba began my liberation—the profound shock of discovering that gap that lay between what I had been told was happening there, and happening between our two countries, and what I now learned for myself was happening.[19]

The shock of discovering the gap between what her government told her and what she learned from her own experience—and her willingness to credit her own experience against the "authority" of the government experts—brought Deming into an adversarial stance with most of the widely accepted assumptions of her generation: that war, specifically World War II, solved problems; that our leaders "knew best" and should be deferred to (in spite of the lessons of the Nuremberg Trials);[20] and that gender was immutable and sexuality a very private matter. These were the basic assumptions of a large portion of the U.S. population during the 1950s.

As a result of her early Quaker schooling, when Barbara Deming became an activist, she was, in her heart and mind, an advocate and practitioner of active nonviolent resistance. She always disliked the term *pacifists* as a way of describing those who practiced nonviolence. In one of her articles about the CNVA, written in the first year of her own political awakening, Deming clarified her own definitions of nonviolence and pacifism: "What soon became apparent about these people [from CNVA] was that they were above all people ready to act." Somewhere in the past, the term *passive resistance* had emerged, but Deming insisted, "It should be discarded. The 'pacifists' are the only freely active people I have met in a long time. Coming face to face with them was, in fact, like entering a new world."[21] Supporting nonviolence and unilateral disarmament during the height of the Cold War was certainly not a popularly held stance, but what appealed to Deming most directly was the freedom of those who chose to disobey. It is a theme from her earlier life with her father, and one that carried continuing resonance for her. She quoted a student at Columbia, who tried to board and disarm a Polaris missile-carrying submarine in harbor in New London, Connecticut:

I have been told that I must not refrain from learning to kill. I have also been told that I must prepare myself in every way for my annihilation. And I have been told that I cannot be present at the places where these conditions are set down. I have the right not to obey these conditions.[22]

Not obeying, said Deming, brings a certain degree of freedom to the individual who makes the choice. It is unclear whether the protestors' actions will change the conditions they are protesting, whether others will join them in their struggle. "But there is no question," she concluded, "their actions have changed *them*." As she observed the demonstrators, she began to see a certain similarity in them. "They all share an extraordinary spontaneity—the sense that an individual *can* act, and *has* weight."[23]

This belief motivated most of the movements for social justice during the sixties; and Deming defined another element of their effectiveness—they acted out of moral necessity. They were political in their intent and effect, Deming admitted, but that was not why the Peace Walkers walked or the anti-nuclear protesters protested. They would raise their voices "whether or not they have a chance of being heard. They raise them simply because the truth for them is the truth, and will not be mocked."[24]

Shaping the Sixties

For Barbara Deming, speaking her understanding of the truth became central to her self-definition and was the source of most of her influence on the sixties. Her articles on demonstrations, walks, internal peace movement struggles, and more were appearing every month in *The Nation*, *Liberation*, and small movement newsletters. After an exchange of letters with Martin Luther King Jr. in 1962,[25] Deming began to insist—in her published writings—that the peace movement and the civil rights movement needed to be joined—not by the civil rights activists all embracing pacifism and refusing to join the military, as some prominent peace activists had suggested.[26] Deming believed the peace activists and the civil rights activists shared a similar goal—respect for individual lives, human dignity, and self-determination.

Peace Walks were designed to raise awareness of the danger of war, particularly nuclear war. Walkers marched through towns and villages carrying signs and banners and handing out leaflets. During a "Nashville, TN, to Washington, D.C. Peace Walk," Deming and others in the walk met with some of the civil rights activists at Scarritt College for Christian Workers. "Two Negro leaders were among those present—James Lawson and Metz Rollins." Lawson chided the Peace Walkers for thinking the two movements were unconnected:

> There is a clear-cut relation between the peace walk and what some of us are seeking to do in the emerging nonviolent movement in the South. [Both] are constantly thinking not in terms of civil rights but in terms of the kingdom of God on earth, the brotherhood of all men. . . . What is behind it is an effort to build a community for all of us . . . "the beloved community." I say that this work is related to the work for peace. . . . And the peace walk is related to the task of building community here. . . . The movements are related to each other, in a sense are one and the same enterprise.[27]

As the walk continued, the dialogue with civil rights workers, marchers, and leaders also continued. Soon the Peace Walkers were being escorted by black college students, staying the night in black churches, and being attacked, black and white together, by Southern racists. At the end of her article about this walk, "Southern Peace Walk: Two Issues or One?" Deming made the connection that served her for the next twenty years of her activist career. Walking with an integrated group, she said, made the talk "more painful; but it also snatched it from the realm of the merely abstract. For the issue of war and peace remains fundamentally the issue of whether or not one is going to be willing to respect one's fellow man."[28]

Deming was able to use her writing and her personal activism to influence understanding of the uses of nonviolence in the civil rights movement and then in the anti–Vietnam War movement. That she took a committed stance, an activist stance, was important; but it may have been even more important that Deming herself was able to understand and write about the experience—the intention, the result, the personal and social elements of transformation.

Her book *Prison Notes*[29] exemplifies that process. Barbara Deming was arrested in Albany, Georgia, on January 27, 1964. She was a member of an interracial Peace Walk from Canada to Cuba, protesting nuclear weapons, when Sheriff Laurie Pritchett told the Peace Walkers that they could walk on a side street but not down Broad Street, the main thoroughfare. The main street in Albany is wide, with wide sidewalks, and there is no possibility that the fifteen or seventeen Peace Walkers could have obstructed traffic or even blocked shoppers going in and out of stores. They were stopped, Barbara writes in *Prison Notes*, for walking as an integrated group. Deming spent twenty-seven days in the Albany city jail, part of that time in a partial hunger strike. Her notes about the experience were made on long sheets of toilet paper, folded up and mailed to CNVA people who were not—at that moment—in jail with them.[30]

The civil rights movement in Albany, Georgia, was an integral part of the actions happening throughout the South after World War II. Albany's own history of black activism began with the founding of a "voter's league" in 1946, through the forming of the NAACP chapter in 1950, and the beginning of the Albany movement in November 1961. The Albany movement was a combination of local efforts for civil rights with several initiatives launched by the Student Nonviolent Coordinating Committee (SNCC). Charles Sherrod and Cordell Reagon from SNCC tested the federal interstate laws in 1961 and rode into Albany on a Trailways bus. By December, the Freedom Riders were out in Albany in full force. When, in January 1962, Ola Mae Quartermain was arrested on a city bus for refusing to give up her seat, the Albany bus boycott began. Black churches were burned in several counties around Albany. Finally, in 1963 the Segregation Ordinance was removed from the Albany City statute book, and in October 1964 six black police officers were hired—and not allowed to carry guns.

Barbara Deming's group was arrested on January 27, 1964. There was no mention of this incident in the headlines of the *Albany Herald*, nor in any stories. The Quebec-to-Guantanamo Peace Walk missed by several months the national news focus on Albany. There was one letter to the editor from Brad Lyttle, the walk coordinator. "Peace Walker Makes Appeal" was the heading and Brad told the citizens of Albany,

> . . . we would like to be on our way to Cuba, to talk to Fidel Castro about non-violence, forgiveness and compassion. It is difficult for us to leave Albany until we have enjoyed freedom of speech here, for how can we enjoin upon Castro that he grant rights we cannot exercise in the United States? We appeal to you and to the people of Albany to insist that freedom of speech, of public demonstration, be made a reality here.[31]

Two weeks later the *Herald* published a letter from Barbara Deming. She speaks to the issue of the potential for nuclear annihilation of the planet, noting that we have the power to destroy mankind because of a revolution in science. Her argument is one she will develop again and again in other situations, for other struggles:

> We believe that in this new age it has become absolutely necessary for us to begin to live with this care for one another—not only for those close to us but for all those we have been used to think of as outsiders. We believe that we must learn to struggle with each other, when we have differences, only as those in a true family do—by persuasion, but example, by refusing to co-operate with actions of which we disapprove, but never with violence, always unwilling to destroy each other, either in body or spirit.

Because of this terrible reality—of nuclear weapons—Deming says that we simply must learn to talk with one another and that is why they are refusing to give up their march, refusing to admit guilt and be released from prison. "We believe it is necessary, as it never was before in history, for people to learn to speak with one another—especially people with differences; and for them to be free to do this and for all barriers to this freedom to fall."[32]

A few days later, the marchers were released. They marched through town on one side of Broad Street. There was no notice of their departure in the local press; for Albany, this event (or non-event) was over. For Barbara Deming, it had just begun.

Prison Notes, Deming's first published book, appeared two years later. It was widely read and established Deming's reputation as an activist and leader. *Prison Notes* is a very personal, honest book. Barbara Deming hated being in jail; she suffered from poor health, a "weak constitution" in the best of times, and enduring a hunger strike in cramped quarters with no exercise was physically difficult and sometimes personally humiliating. But these experiences themselves are not the heart of *Prison Notes*; the book is about what Barbara Deming learned from these experiences—learned about herself, about human nature under pressure, and about the intersection of the laws of a city, or a country, with another code of moral justice. When Ray Robinson, an African American peace marcher, was singled out for separate punishment, Deming writes that she "heard the sound of his long body dragged across the cement floor of the passageway beyond our cells; and then with astonishment, felt the shock of the rough cement against the length of my own body." Weeping, and feeling at the same time an overwhelming love for Ray Robinson, Deming later speculated about the source, nature, and use of this depth of feeling:

> To feel within me a sympathy for others very much more free and active than usual is a little intoxicating. I wonder what the limits are to such sympathy, and how much it might be able to bring about—and how much it has brought about already, in history.[33]

Connecting the Personal

When Barbara was released from the Albany County jail, Mary came down to Georgia to get her. They had planned to go to Florida together for a few weeks while Barbara recovered her health. Mary had watched Barbara's transformation into a political activist with dismay. "By 1964, I was in mourning," Mary recalled. "I thought her new metamorphosis prevented her from being an artist any more. She actually stopped working on her stories." Barbara's withdrawal, the redirection of her attention away from the relationship and the work they had valued together, changed their life. Neither woman expected Mary's response to Barbara's political involvement—that she would feel threatened as an artist, that she would feel guilty about being an artist because that cut her off from "real life." By the time Mary went down to Georgia to get Barbara upon her release from prison, she took with her a new lover, Canadian writer Marie-Claire Blais.[34]

For several years, these three powerful women tried to make a mutual relationship work. Sometimes it did. Each of the three remembered times of happiness and connection. But as the years passed, Barbara left more and more frequently on her political trips and work. Still, she hid the nature of her personal, sexual relationships from most of the people she worked with politically. It seemed to her the price for being able to do this work.[35]

In early 1966, Barbara Deming responded to a general call made by the War Resisters League and the CNVA for volunteers to go to Saigon to mount a nonviolent protest against the war in Saigon itself. She and five others were chosen for the action. With A. J. Muste, Brad Lyttle, Bill Davidon, Karl Meyer, and Sherry Miller,[36] Deming went to Saigon in April 1966. They went without visas because U.S. citizens were allowed to visit South Vietnam for up to seven days without a visa. They waited until near the end of their stay before unfurling banners in a public place. They were promptly arrested, detained, and expelled from the country. Following that action, in December and January 1966–67, Barbara Deming and three other women went to North Vietnam for eleven days to see firsthand the parts of the country that had been bombed by American planes. They began in Hanoi and went into the countryside to rural villages, some of which had been completely destroyed:

> We stood, for example, in Phu Ly, which is a town that used to have a population of about eight thousand, and today it has a population of nobody; because the planes came in April, in July, in August, three times in October and finally the night before Christmas, and there is hardly a building in that town—if there is one; I didn't see one building—that has been left intact.[37]

Deming recounts for the reader the pattern of her visit to village after village, how they would learn the history of the place, see examples of the destruction, visit the wounded and maimed in hospitals, many of whom were children. After this account, Deming describes napalm and the damage repair tried by surgeons, often unsuccessfully. She catalogs the hospitals hit by bombs—the world-famous leper colony, run by the Red Cross and clearly marked as such, also bombed. So, she challenges

Fig. 10.1. Barbara Deming and A.J. Muste in detention at Tan Son Nhut airport, Saigon, April 21, 1966, just before expulsion from Vietnam. *Courtesy of the Barbara Deming Archives*

her audience and readers, "we are waging war in Vietnam even against children; and we are waging war even against the sick and utterly helpless—against lepers. WHAT ARE WE DOING? It seems to me that Americans must begin to take a very hard look at themselves, and at the role we are playing in the world today."[38]

Taking a very hard look at their government was one response of anti–Vietnam War protesters. For some, it was not easy to give up the assumption that the state was a benign paternal authority acting in the best interests of the communal whole; but a generation of college students seemed to be challenging that assumption. They could be dismissed as immature, as young people experiencing an age-related need to rebel for the sake of rebellion. But Barbara Deming was not young or immature, and she believed that "one of the primary tasks for those who hope to build a radical movement is the desanctification of authority."[39] She watched the courtroom sentencing of some of the demonstrators who had marched against the Pentagon in 1967 and observed that "the state wants obedience." The price of probation and a chance to walk out of jail was to promise the court "to behave themselves." According to Deming, for people who felt their behavior had been motivated by the highest moral and ethical demands, to desist from protest was not an option. And "behaving themselves" was what they had been doing in their protests.

It should, therefore, be no surprise that Barbara Deming, having seen the human damage of the war in Vietnam with her own eyes, was easily able to distinguish between symbolic and real violence. When Daniel and Phillip Berrigan and others poured blood on the draft records in Baltimore and burned draft records with napalm in Catonsville, Maryland, they were accused of committing violence themselves by the state and by some nonviolent activists.[40] Deming knew better. The goal, as she articulated it, was

> to hamper in any serious way the machinery of the warfare state. . . .
>
> I have heard the original action of these nine men and women discussed at length in the pacifist movement . . . as an act of sabotage—asking: Might it set a dangerous precedent? And in staring with anxiety at the act, some of them tended to abstract that one hypnotic aspect, "destruction of property," in the process, to speak like those who find civil disobedience of any sort a dangerous precedent encouraging others to disobey laws at random. What characterizes the Catonsville Nine is that they saw to it that their action would not be an act of mere sabotage. . . . In the first place, the property they destroyed was of a very special kind . . . [not] property that is in any sense the true extension of a person (as a man's house would be, or a work of art), but on the contrary, property that clearly diminishes other people, papers by which a life and death power over other men is held. The nearest parallel would really be the papers of ownership that once gave slave holders power over men. . . .[41]

In addition to choosing very carefully the kind of property they would destroy, with the symbolic use of napalm they communicated the reason for their feeling that it was urgent for them to take this action. Finally, the trial itself, attended by hundreds of supporters who created marches, vigils, and educational moments every day, made sure that more and more Americans became aware of the true nature of the warfare state and how it operates. Deming never stopped believing that if people really understood the suffering of others, they would go to great lengths to stop it.

Theoretically, Deming was moving closer and closer to an overtly feminist politic. From the early sixties, the second wave of feminism had been desanctifying the male hegemony of power. Deming's actions put her in a parallel course with many of those first feminists, but she did not find her life and politics converging until nearly the end of the sixties. In 1968, she became reacquainted with a classmate from Bennington College, Jane Verlaine, who was beginning to separate from her husband. By 1969 Jane and her two children were living with Barbara.

Creating a life with Jane was not simple. Barbara's life was very busy and very public. She was involved in political actions, discussions, and events. She looked at every issue as it arose. And finally, with Jane, she must confront her own oppression as a lesbian, because Jane's ex-husband threatened a custody suit, naming Barbara as the reason for his wife's disaffection and asserting that Jane was unfit to raise her own children as a result of Barbara's influence. In a letter to Dave Dellinger, she described how Oscar told Jane "right in front of the kids" that he "forbids them to have any more contact with her Bull Dike [*sic*] friend." Not sure how far Oscar wanted to take his anger, and yet quite sure how unfavorably the courts would look at lesbian mothers in 1969, both women were aware that Jane might have to give up "her plan to share a house with me. And then we will simply wait, until the kids are older, to make our lives together. And call this a war-time separation."[42]

During this period, Barbara experienced a growing separation from the anti-war, nonviolence movement. Letters from friends accused her of dropping out of the movement; Barbara explained over and over again that in fighting her way toward the right to live with the person she loved, she was not leaving the movement but expanding it. Ray Robinson, her companion on the Southern Peace Walk through Albany, Georgia, complained, "Well if you have never been to the bottom, complete bottom, no you cannot understand me. I can never forget the struggle."[43]

Deming had not forgotten the struggle; for the first time the struggle was about her own life. "I lie at the bottom of my spirit's well,"[44] begins a poem about this period. Stressed, afraid, attacked, Barbara Deming responds with a characteristic surge into action and writing. Her second book about the sixties, *Revolution and Equilibrium* (Grossman, 1971), is dedicated "to my sisters in the growing Women's Liberation movement—

and especially to Jane. May we find the right ways to insist upon new relations between all of us, in which not domination but equity is seen to answer the soul's need."[45] None of the essays in this collection is overtly feminist, but Deming's dedication lets the reader know the direction her political work will take for the remainder of her life.

NOTES

1. Barbara Deming, *Prison Notes* (New York: Grossman Publishers, 1966), 120. The Barbara Deming Archives are located primarily at the Schlesinger Women's History Library at Radcliffe College; some materials from the period of *Prison Notes* are at the Mugar Library at Boston College. Both collections are fully cataloged and open to researchers. Permission to quote from the archives can be obtained from Judith McDaniel, Deming's literary executor. All quotations from unpublished letters are taken from the Schlesinger collection. All quotations from Deming's friends and relatives are from unpublished interviews conducted by Judith McDaniel.

2. Barbara Deming, "Dialogue in Cuba," *The Nation*, May 28, 1960.

3. Barbara Deming, "The Peacemakers," *The Nation*, December 17, 1960.

4. Barbara Deming, "In the Birmingham Jail," *The Nation*, May 25, 1963.

5. Deming, *Prison Notes*.

6. Interviews with MacDonald Deming, 8 July 1992; Quentin Deming, 11 July 1992 and 1993, n.d.; and Angus Deming, 26 October 1992. Unpublished.

7. *Friends Seminary Catalog* (1922–23), p. 7.

8. Letters to Katherine Deming, March 1934.

9. Letter to Katherine Deming, 1974.

10. Drafts and revisions of early poems in the Schlesinger Library.

11. Interview with Mary Meigs, January 16, 1992.

12. Notes about her poems taken from comments Barbara wanted to make during a reading. Undated.

13. Interview with Meigs, January 16, 1992.

14. Interview with Anne Poor, March 17, 1992. Unpublished.

15. Ibid.

16. Deming, "Dialogue in Cuba."

17. Interview with David Dellinger, May 2, 1995. Unpublished.

18. Mohandas Gandhi (1869–1948). As the leader of the Indian independence movement, he defined the modern practice of nonviolence, wedding an ethic of love to a practical method of social struggle. His philosophy was rooted in a deep spirituality; for Gandhi, the struggle for peace and social justice was ultimately related to the search for God. His writings reveal a man whose life and message bear special relevance to all spiritual seekers.

19. Barbara Deming, preface to *Revolution and Equilibrium* (New York: Grossman Publishers, 1971), p. xv.

20. The first of its kind in history, the Nuremberg Trials judged twenty-two Nazi leaders for crimes committed in the framework of their policy. It sought, in an international legal framework, to try people for crimes against humanity. One of key points established that following "superior orders" was an unacceptable defense for committing a crime.

21. Deming, "The Peacemakers."

22. Ibid.

23. Ibid.

24. Ibid.

25. Unpublished letter from Martin Luther King Jr. to Barbara Deming, in the Barbara Deming Archives at the Schlesinger Library, Radcliffe College, Cambridge, Massachusetts.

26. Barbara Deming, "Southern Peace Walk: Two Issues or One?" *Liberation*, July–August 1962.

27. Ibid.

28. Ibid.

29. *Prison Notes* (1966) was reprinted by University of Georgia Press in 1994.

30. Among the papers of Bradford Lyttle in the Swarthmore College Peace Collection, Swarthmore, Pennsylvania.

31. Brad Lyttle, "Peace Walker Makes Appeal," letter to the editor, *Albany Herald*, January 27, 1964.

32. Barbara Deming, letter to the editor, *Albany Herald*, February 14, 1964.

33. Deming, *Prison Notes*, pp. 120–22.

34. Interview with Meigs, January 16, 1992.

35. In a letter written December 1, 1972, to Rita Mae Brown, for example, Barbara explains why she could not, for some years, be more public as a lesbian.

36. Barbara Deming, "We Are All Part of One Another," *Liberation*, May–June 1967.

37. Barbara Deming, "The Temptations of Power—A Report of a Visit to North Vietnam," in *Revolution and Equilibrium*, 166.

38. Ibid., p. 170.

39. Barbara Deming, "Desanctifying Authority," *Liberation*, November 1967.

40. "The pacifist writer Barbara Deming—who had blessed Catonsville even when secular antiwar critics, unmoved by the religious left's metaphorical symbolism, often dismissed them as clerical cowboys" Murray Polner and Jim O'Grady, (*Disarmed and Dangerous: The Radical Lives and Times of Daniel and Philip Berrigan* [New York: HarperCollins, 1997], p. 242).

41. Barbara Deming, "Interfering with the Smooth Functioning of the Warfare State," *Liberation*, December 1968.

42. Letter to Dave Dellinger, August 30, 1969.

216 | JUDITH McDANIEL

43. Letter from Ray Robinson, January 14, 1971.

44. In *I Change, I Change: Poems by Barbara Deming,* ed. and with an introduction by Judith McDaniel (Norwich, VT: New Victoria Publishers, 1996), p. 120.

45. Dedication page in Deming, *Revolution and Equilibrium.*

11

Yoko Ono and the Unfinished Music of "John & Yoko"

Imagining Gender and Racial Equality in the Late 1960s

Tamara Levitz

On 9 November 1967, at the height of the San Francisco flower power and rock-and-roll counterrevolution, *Rolling Stone* magazine released its first issue. Promising insider coverage of the antiestablishment music of the "electric generation," the editors included on its first page a photograph of John Lennon, a favored rock icon who appeared with his new granny glasses and army fatigues in a scene from Richard Lester's film *How I Won the War*. Lennon's engaged, "tuned in" stance contrasted dramatically with that of his wife Cynthia Powell, who was included in a second photograph, reproduced on page three. She joined the other Beatle wives (Patti Boyd Harrison and Maureen Starr) and Patti's sister Jenny Boyd in modeling psychedelic fashions from the Beatles' new Apple Boutique in London. Donning indistinguishable blond hairdos, makeup, and expressions, the four women looked exactly like Barbie clones or Stepford wives: interchangeable, vacuous dolls with identical Brigitte Bardot pouts.[1] Placed strategically in *Rolling Stone*'s first issue, these photographs attest to the gender inequality of late 1960s rock-and-roll culture. In rock-and-roll historian Gillian G. Gaar's words, women's "roles remained overwhelmingly conventional, a situation which was rarely challenged. . . . [They] were not encouraged to develop as songwriters, they were almost never instrumentalists, and they remained under constant pressure to appear 'feminine' in the public eye."[2]

Into this stifled world of peroxide, black mascara, and mini skirts stepped the Fluxus artist and intellectual Yoko Ono. Born into a noble,

217

educated, and wealthy Japanese family in 1933, Yoko could trace her father's family back to Saisho Atsushi, a viscount active in overthrowing the Japanese shogun system in the mid–nineteenth century. Her maternal grandfather, Yasuda Zenjir, had founded the Yasuda Bank and ran the most powerful Japanese *zaibatsu*, or financial combines, before World War II. Yoko grew up between Tokyo, San Francisco, and New York and suffered considerable hardship during the war, when her family had to seek refuge in the countryside and faced hunger and social ridicule. After studying philosophy briefly at Gakushuin University in Tokyo in 1952, and composition and art at Sarah Lawrence College, she had moved to Manhattan in 1956 with her newlywed husband, avant-garde composer and pianist Toshi Ichiyanagi. There and in Tokyo (from 1962 to 1964), she had built her reputation as a performing and visual artist, especially through a series of concerts in her loft on Chamber Street in New York (December 1960 to June 1961), and through her involvement with artists who identified with Fluxus and with the Japanese avant-garde.[3]

Inspired by Marcel Duchamp, John Cage, and the Dadaist rebellion of the 1920s, and by performers like Charlotte Moorman, dancers and film-makers like Yvonne Rainer, composers like Morton Feldman, La Monte Young and Richard Maxfield, and visual artists like Naim June Paik, Yoko set out to challenge societal norms and aesthetic standards through radically original conceptual art, music, and "events" (a word Yoko preferred over "happenings").[4] In 1964, Yoko published *Grapefruit*, her first collection of "instructional pieces": short texts intended to initiate or inspire events that could lead to musical, philosophical, or personal insights.[5] Her life took a dramatic turn when she moved to London in September 1966 with her second husband, Anthony Cox, and their child, Kyoko, in order to participate in the "Destruction in the Arts" symposium. There, she not only established herself as an artist through numerous high-profile events but also met John Lennon, with whom she became inextricably bound by 1968. Together they embarked on a musical collaboration that would challenge the gender and racial hierarchies of 1960s rock and roll.

Drawing on the traditions of Dadaism, futurism, and surrealism, as well as on the Japanese traditions of Kabuki, haiku poetry, and Zen philosophy, Yoko established a body of creative work in the 1960s that thematicized the female body, the role of women in society, relationships between men and women, the media, violence, and pain. She expressed her notions of female equality most explicitly in her music of the late

Fig. 11.1. Cover of *Unfinished Music No.1: Two Virgins*, photograph by John
Lennon, photograph of photograph by John Bigelow Taylor.
Courtesy of Yoko Ono

1960s, which she created at the height of her feminist activism, and in
collaboration with John Lennon, as part of their multimedia project
"John & Yoko." Reflecting on, but not equivalent to, Yoko and John as
actual people, this project encompassed a wide variety of cultural practices ranging from scores to instructions, objects, events, performances,
advertisements, films, and videos and drawings. The first phase of Yoko
and John's musical dialogue began in May 1968, when they made the
impromptu recording that would later be released as *Unfinished Music
No. 1: Two Virgins*, and ended six albums later, when they split in 1973.
Deeply committed to John Lennon, and philosophically attracted to the
revelatory potential of binary thinking, Yoko attempted on these albums
to establish forms of musical expression that could express female
equality within the framework of a heterosexual relationship. It was not
always easy for her to affirm this stance within the chauvinistic and racist
context of British popular culture in the late 1960s. In John Lennon's

presence, Yoko suddenly found herself defending her very right to creative expression, and faced with considerable pressure to conform to the model of a pretty, white, submissive Beatle wife.

Yoko and John escaped the social nightmare they experienced in England by moving to New York in 1971. There Yoko faced not only the prejudice of John's fans and the rock-and-roll establishment but also the very different and far less agonizing task of gaining acceptance by second-wave feminists, who frequently advocated separation from, rather than integration with, men, and who thus did not always understand why Yoko was with John. In this context, Yoko felt it necessary to defend her heterosexual stance by rejecting publicly the notion that lesbianism was the only choice for women seeking liberation and equality: "The ultimate goal of female liberation is not just to escape from male oppression. How about liberating ourselves from our various mind trips such as ignorance, greed, masochism, fear of God and social conventions?"[6] It is a tribute to Yoko's intelligence and willpower that she was able to persist with her feminist project within these two very difficult and conflicted contexts. In the process, she succeeded in reimagining the nature of popular music and offering a radical reinvention of women's place within it.

The groundbreaking cover of Yoko and John's first album, *Unfinished Music No. 1: Two Virgins* (November 1968), constitutes their first attempt to use the powerful "imaging recording process of the media" as a medium for changing people's thoughts about society and women.[7] First appearing in *Rolling Stone* as an advertising insert, this now infamous frontal and back image of Yoko and John nude caused an enormous scandal and was immediately confiscated as pornography in the United States and Britain.[8] Jann Wenner emphasizes that "by today's standards, [the cover of *Two Virgins*] might not seem remarkable, but in 1968, it was utterly astonishing. People did not pose naked, let alone famous people; and John was at the peak of his Beatles fame, a revered household icon around the world. Thus, these pictures were a revolutionary statement."[9] Contrary to what Wenner says, however, many women posed nude in the 1960s, even in almost every issue of his magazine, *Rolling Stone*. By emphasizing John's rather than Yoko's nudity, Wenner implicitly acknowledges that what most shocked him and others about this photograph is how it questioned the traditional practice of objectifying nude female bodies for the benefit of male spectators. In Kristine Stile's words, "Lennon had entered Ono's double articulated cultural space—the space of Woman and ethnic Other, the space of an Asian Woman."[10] Much of the "John & Yoko" project was about critiquing in this way standard media representations, or what Yoko called "odorless celluloid prince and princess images up there on the screen," for having too little to do with the reality of people. By giving the fans a more "natural" view of how a racially mixed couple might look when they had just gotten out of bed, without makeup, optical illusions, or camera tricks, Yoko, with John, offered a "piece of reality" to an "image driven culture," thereby creating, in Yoko's words, "a direct threat to our false existence."[11] In the minds of American youth and hippies, this message translated into a plea for sexual liberation: "[W]hoever you are, however ordinary your body, nothing to be ashamed of, be free."[12]

Yoko and John gave themselves identical exposure on *Two Virgins* in order to communicate the message that beneath the specific and evident markers of their gender and racial differences they possessed equal human cores, and thus the same right to exist in the world. Yoko was so convinced of the "fundamental parity that exists between substances whose outward form and material qualities differ" that she constantly reacted with amazement when people treated her unfairly or with prejudice because she was a Japanese woman.[13] "It's hard to remember your slanted eyes and your skin in the melting pot of a recording session," she later wrote, "but I suppose that is the first thing that hits them when they try to communicate. 'That Jap. You never know what she's thinking.' Next time you meet a 'foreigner,' remember it's only like a window with a little different shape to it and the person who's sitting inside you."[14] Although racial and gender differences were at the forefront of people's minds in the late 1960s, they were not widely represented in the media and rarely discussed in relation to Asian women. bell hooks reminds us that Yoko was making her media statements at a time "when there was no cultural studies, no focus on border-crossing, no Bennetton ads, no celebration of multiculturalism and definitely no accepted fascination with eating the other." As Yoko commented, "It was very hard for the fans. Too suddenly this woman, who is not even a pretty blonde white woman or something, was sitting next to their hero and occupying a kind of equal space."[15] As symbolic figures, she and John thus asked their viewers to see beyond their flesh and bones, toward the existential truth of their "transcendental love."[16] Drawing on Antoine de Saint-Exupéry's widely popular children's book *Le petit prince*, John and Yoko even gave a performance on 18 December 1968 in which they appeared on stage in a white bag in order to communicate the existential message that "the essential rests invisible to the eye."[17]

In her art, Yoko interpreted gender and racial differences as abstract polar opposites that were necessarily inseparable and unified in her mythological imagery. Long before she met Lennon, she had begun to think in terms of such binary opposites, describing herself as neither American nor Japanese but rather as an "amalgam" of both.[18] She and John had emphasized such an archetypal interpretation of gender and racial difference in their first collaborative event on 15 June 1968, "John" by Yoko Ono and "Yoko" by John Lennon, in which they planted two acorn seeds at Coventry Cathedral to represent both the union of two artists as well as the union of polar opposites—yin/yang, East/West, and man/woman—thereby bringing together the "dichotomous forces of life." In the art and music that followed, they played repeatedly on the notion of combining symbolic halves, hoping through this conceptual game to convince their listeners that spiritual and imaginative truth could be found in recognizing the two-sidedness of the one, or essential interrelation of opposites. Like many counterculture artists, Yoko may have drawn her understanding of the unity of polar opposites in mythological imagery partly from Alan W. Watts, *The Two Hands of God: The Myths of Polarity*.[19] John later described this principle as "the male and the female is better than a male or a female separately, that's what Yoko and I think. Being with her makes me free, you know. It makes me whole. I'm half without her. Male is half without a female."[20] These two halves could also be understood as the "self" and its "shadow," which Yoko interpreted in Carl Jung's sense as the "primitive and instinctive, negative 'double' of the body."[21] On the cover of *Two Virgins*, John suggests that he is the "shadow," for example, by wearing an unidentified necklace that seems to act like a totem, implying his connection to a ritualistic, magical, or mystical world. In his own words, he was enacting here "the primitive avant-garde."[22]

The challenge for Yoko and John in creating the music of *Two Virgins* was to find sounds that, like the two artists' images on the album cover, were "marked" by gender and racial differences, yet which could be unified to create a spiritual whole. We assume it is John who begins this musical experiment by toying around with taped and electronic sounds against a backdrop of his casual conversation with Yoko. Intimidated by the electric guitar "jamming" scene in London, which demanded of him a macho masculinity he felt uncomfortable with, John trades in his guitar here for the safety of his soundboard and for the comfort of working with Yoko.[23] Gradually, he adds electronically manipulated acoustic instruments, leading to a distorted piano vamp that Yoko accompanies with her distinctly female voice uttering dissonant melodic sighs. If Yoko is to be John's sonic equal, however, she cannot continue to mark herself as an accompanist or play any of the other subjugating musical roles common to women in late 1960s pop. She can neither imitate the angelic singing of rock muses like Marianne Faithful, play the tambourine like Michelle Phillips of the Mamas and Papas, lose herself in the excesses of victimization like Janis Joplin, nor dance to the beat like the dancers on *Shindig*. About four and a half minutes into the first side of the album, Yoko lets us know that she will not let this happen by letting out a sudden and terrifying vocal sound equal in volume, quality, and intensity to John's electronic noise. Barred ideologically from the male domain of electric guitar experimentation, she becomes a living electric guitar—a feminine embodiment of an instrument denied to most women in the 1960s. As the music intensifies, both John and Yoko scream and speak in reaction to each other, exploring a range of moods in an abstract framework that avoids a rhythmic accompaniment. Yoko seems encouraged to explore ever more experimental aspects of her vocal production, galvanized by the sounds of John's radio static, electronics, feedback, and excerpts of various genres of popular music of the twentieth century. While "their opposing cultural gestures forc[e] each other to grimace," Jonathan Cott commented, "what miraculously happens is that everything simply and unselfconsciously comes together."[24]

Creating abstract sounds that cannot be whistled, imitated, lip-synched, or remembered, Yoko's voice seems to function in *Two Virgins* and elsewhere as the sonic equivalent of her immobile body on the album's cover, emphatically proclaiming her physical being-in-the-world through its weighted presence. Like the character Lulu from Alban Berg's opera of the same name, to whom she frequently compared herself, Yoko establishes her presence through the sheer sonic quality of her female voice.[25] This voice is not beautiful, lyrical, or accompanimental, and thus does not easily inspire daydreaming or nostalgia. Rather, it forces an awareness of Yoko's very real existence, as it relates imaginatively with listeners' own inner sounds and the emotions attached to them. As John said, "She becomes her voice and you get touched."[26] Although Yoko did not record very much before meeting Lennon, there is evidence that she had developed this characteristic singing style long before.[27] Jill Johnston reported, for example, that Yoko concluded her performance of *AOS-To David Tudor* at Carnegie Recital Hall in 1961 with "amplified sighs, breathing, gasping, retching, screaming—many tones of pain and pleasure mixed with a jibberish of foreign-sounding language that was no language at all."[28] Yoko defined this unique vocal style specifically as female by telling reporters that she had discovered it while taping and playing backward herself imitating the sound of a woman giving birth.[29] By creating unfamiliar sounds from a very familiar source, she "avoided self-conscious subjective expression in favor of 'real' sound."[30] The result is curiously without agency, separated by degree from the personal expression of emotion, and thereby abstracted in a manner familiar in contemporary music yet utterly foreign to popular music at that time.

Yoko and John fuse their abstracted male and female musical identities on *Two Virgins* by rejecting closed form and a traditional compositional approach, based on developmental logic and organic continuity, in favor of an intense musical improvisation resembling a sexual act. Yoko had developed this musical approach in part as means of rebelling against her distant father, whom she had not met until she was two and a half years old. "My mother would show me his picture before bedtime and tell me 'Say good night to father,'" she remembered.[31] Later, her father tormented her by leading her to believe his love for her depended on whether she could play the piano well.[32] Yoko overcame this trauma by replacing the knowledge-based performance traditions of classical music that had caused her such existential loneliness as a child with a musical collaboration that celebrated the love between two human beings in its very expressive and spontaneous essence. On *Two Virgins*, she and John inspired each other to dig beneath the artifice and conscious techniques of classical music and pop in order to reach a point where they could explore self-indulgently their immediate, direct responses to each others' oral utterances, creating a music of "complete liberty and total surprise."[33] Yoko understood her singing in this context as a sexual act: "You're using your body and your mind as opposed to a translator, which is an instrument," she later commented. "It's total giving, it's something of you that you're giving on a direct level. It can be compared to giving sex with a vibrator. Getting high with a vibrator is like giving a high with an instrument. Whereas doing it with your voice is really giving it with yourself."[34] In conceiving of music as sexual union, they joined the hippies and others in promoting social and political revolution through sexual liberation. Their indulgence in themselves was crucial to their project of making the personal political through their art.

The relationship between the sounds on *Two Virgins* and Yoko and John's shockingly nude presence on its cover is not immediately evident, and is made explicit only in their film of the same name, which premiered at the Chicago International Film Festival with *Film No. 5 "Smile"* on November 14, 1968. The album serves as the soundtrack to this film, in which Yoko and John directed cameraman William Wareing to capture their superimposed faces in the process of turning, laughing, speaking, and staring. Halfway through the film, the scene shifts to John and Yoko facing each other against a blue sky with clouds. They kiss in excruciating slow motion, occasionally hugging and caressing each other's hair. Hearing Yoko's cries and John's electronic improvisation as a backdrop to this intense scene, one becomes acutely aware that they intended their musical performances to reveal the thoughts, experiences, personal histories, and dreams they brought to their sexual and spiritual encounter. Only by separating sounds as free-flowing thoughts from visions of bodily union could Yoko express the "vibrations" of "the kind that were between [her and John]."[35] "There wasn't any point in just making love, secretly and everything," Yoko commented, "we had to make a film which had the same vibrations as making love."[36]

Yoko's desire to explore the imaginary music of the mind by acting on the silent presence of the female body marks much of her artwork from the early 1960s onward. Very early on, she realized that she could make the conceptual reality of her artwork into "concrete 'matter'" only by "asking others to enact it," thereby preventing the artwork from remaining in the realm of the imaginary.[37] In one of her most famous performance pieces, *Cut*, from 1964, for example, she established a firm yet theatrically fictional presence by sitting immobile, mute, and elegantly dressed on a stage, with an expression of resolve mixed with deep sorrow on her face. Audience members had been instructed to approach her and use the scissors positioned close to her body in order to cut a snippet out of her dress. As they began climbing on stage and cutting away at her clothing, the theatrical illusion broke, leaving everybody acutely aware that Yoko's inert and inexpressive bodily mass was actually very real. Here, as elsewhere, Yoko created ambiguity between fiction and reality and enabled audience participation by removing her own agency and conscious will, transforming her body into a weighted mass upon which people could project their most forbidden and violent fantasies.[38] John Jones remembered that "the powerful and inescapable thoughts of public rape" rendered spectators in *Cut* "hardly able to cut at all."[39] Yet all the while Yoko refused to be victimized, preferring to understand her role as "a form of giving that has a lot to do with Buddhism."[40] "If women put themselves in a situation where they are demanding their rights," she argued, "they put themselves in the position of beggars. If we are really going to change society, we have to be in a position where we can *give*."[41] Her body did not exist as an island unto itself but rather was implicated in human existence through its capacity to engage the imagination or be violated and destroyed by it. In Kristine Stiles' words, Yoko "created a confrontational language of interaction in order to emphasize the process of cleaving through to a knowledge of interior substance," in this way "augment[ing] participants' ability to cut through to the hidden sources of Being where questions of human will, purpose, destiny, and teleology coincide with considerations of God."[42]

Like *Cut*, the film *Two Virgins* functioned as conceptual mirror, diverting spectators' gazes away from the viewed or heard objects toward the active inner workings of their own desires and feelings about love, sexuality, and interracial heterosexual relationships. The sounds on the album were likewise "unfinished music . . . a process. The unfinished part that's not in the record—what's in you, not what's in the record—is what's important."[43] Yoko defined such unfinished processes as specifically female: "That is why my works are always unfinished, because my art is an ever-changing process just like life itself. I think it is a very masculine quality to state that something is ready: 'Here it is.' As soon as something becomes a status symbol, in me awakens the desire to tear it down and destroy it."[44] In the spirit of the counterculture, Yoko hoped such self-reflection would inspire active participation and subsequent transformation of consciousness. When *Two Virgins* was premiered with *Film No. 5 "Smile,"* the audience indeed did react by playing music, performing, putting microphones and other objects in front of the screen, yelling slogans, and sitting on the edge of the stage. Although Yoko hoped that audiences would "realize good through [such] acts of visualization," this was not always the case.[45] Roger Ebert erroneously remembered John cupping Yoko's breasts in this film, for example, and misunderstood its mood as best captured by an audience member who said that "in an indescribable way, the shape and feel of a girl's breasts are exactly like her personality."[46] Such relentlessly sexist attitudes were common to many American youth movements of the late 1960s, and foreign to Yoko's egalitarian vision.

Two Virgins as an album, film, and image celebrates Yoko's and John's rebirth as equal creative musicians, born of an originating creative act. In reality, however, Yoko and John did not feel that equal. John frequently felt the need to exert his control over Yoko, for example, and thus continued to argue that *Two Virgins* had been his idea: "Paul had Mary Hopkins, George had Jackie Lomax, so I wanted to do something with Yoko."[47] At other times, he claimed that he had originally intended to photograph Yoko alone nude.[48] And by 1969, he even regretted that he had not conceived her: "I don't like the idea of her being born in somebody else's womb. That's one of my great jealousies. It's a drag that she was in somebody else's womb, but I can't do anything about it."[49] Yoko had likewise not always felt emotionally equal to John. When she had first met him, she had felt on the verge of dissolving, for example, and had described him as the "mountain" she could lean on in order to "materialize" herself.[50]

In spite of their insecurities and anxieties, Yoko and John chose not to thematicize their gender and racial inequality in their art. Instead, they emphasized their symbolic equality through "imaginary shaping of memory" and "self-construction of remembered events."[51] And so they imaginatively recalled the night on which they had created *Two Virgins* in such a manner as to emphasize and celebrate their rebirth as equal musician-artists through their first communal, sexual experience of making music together. In so doing, they went against the Beatles' fans and critics, who accepted and even admired the sexual exploits of male rock stars but expected rock wives to secure the institution of heterosexual marriage by remaining sexually and emotionally faithful, and clothed.[52] They also went against Paul McCartney and Derek Taylor, who showed their allegiance to such discriminatory views of sexual relations in the texts they chose for the album's jacket. McCartney spoke of "the long struggle to prove *he* was a saint" (ignoring Yoko), while Taylor chose chapter 2, verses 21–25 from Genesis, in which Woman is created from the rib of Adam—a passage that can be problematic for feminists and that seems to deny Yoko's equal rights as a composer on the album.[53]

The idea of the sonic equality and fusion of the sexes to which John and Yoko gave birth on *Two Virgins* came to its first full fruition in the piece "Cambridge 1969," which takes up the entire first side of their second album *Unfinished Music No. 2: Life with the Lions* (May 1969). Recorded on 2 March 1969 during an international avant-garde jazz workshop at Lady Mitchell Hall in Cambridge, England, this twenty-six-and-a-half-minute work documents Yoko's and John's first attempt to fuse their musical beings, as they fused their images in *Two Virgins*, by melding the sounds of Yoko's voice and the feedback of John's electric guitar in an extended free improvisation. Here, for the first time, Yoko establishes her woman's voice as the utter sonic equivalent to John's electric guitar by producing an oscillating vocal sound that inspires and coaxes John's electronic feedback, resulting in a mutually inspired give and take of abstract sounds. In one electrifying moment, Yoko takes control of the shrieking female screams that had assured women's subjugation as the desiring fans of Beatlemania. By bringing this explosion of female sonic expression on stage, she topples the traditional hierarchy of 1960s pop, turning John Lennon into the subjugated, desiring male whose electric guitar shrieks with the yearning screams of fandom.

Paradoxically, the explosive sexual and musical revolution of *Two Virgins* and "Cambridge 1969" became an aesthetic impasse for Yoko and John. Feeling "suffocated" by the abstract mind games encouraged by her conceptual music, Yoko began searching for a more embodied female musical presence, which could stand on its own without visual accompaniment. Influenced by the Beatles' recording sessions at Abbey Road, which she had sat in on since May 1968, she returned to her fundamental idea that music needed rhythm, and that the most natural rhythm possible for all human beings was the heartbeat, as it revealed itself in rock and roll.[54] On *Unfinished Music No. 2*, she and John dramatically reintroduced the heartbeat as the expression of their embodiment by including as an individual track the taped heartbeat of the fruit of their union, their unborn child, whom Yoko miscarried in November 1968. As if stunned by the very power of the rhythm of life to interrupt their conceptual reveries, Yoko and John allowed this recording to stand on its own as a five-minute track. They had found a way to make their musical voice embodied as it had not been on *Two Virgins*, thereby defining a state of physically being in the world that was in their eyes "universal" and not dependent on identity politics, gender, or race.

Having established their corporeal presence, Yoko and John felt free to explore ever more imaginative means of expressing their feminine and masculine halves. On their *Wedding Album* (October 1969), for example, they investigate the expressive potentialities of the male and female voice as such by saying each other's names to each other for over twenty-two and a half minutes. Motivated in their late-night session by a great deal of humor and wit, they journey back and forth through the broad range of emotions they have for each other, against the backdrop of a human heartbeat that establishes their embodied state. We hear screaming, anger, questioning, recognition, jubilation, fear, whispering, love, kissing, affection, crying, pleading, sexual orgasm, eating, teasing, imitation, and chewing—a gamut of emotions and actions that again mirrors the build-up and release of energy of intercourse in order to tell us about a sonic relationship between aurally equal male and female principles.

As 1969 drew to a close, Yoko and John began to emerge from the cocoon of their early love, gaining an independence from each other that was reflected in their desire to create more distinguished and rhythmically differentiated female and male sonic personas. Although Yoko did not discuss it, her performances indicated that she was beginning to see the beat of rock and roll, or the heartbeat, as symbolically male, and thus as contrary to her feminine being. By approaching this music in these gendered, rather than racial, terms, she implicitly challenged Eldridge Cleaver's much-discussed claim of 1968 that the beat of rock and roll belonged to the black people.[55] Yoko prioritized gender over racial politics, abandoning her earlier, *Two Virgin* fantasy of being able to fuse with John through music in favor of constructing for herself an independent feminine musical identity that could hold its ground in opposition to his rock and roll. She first confronted his musical world with her feminist voice on 11 December 1968, when she participated with John in a jam session with the Rolling Stones in *The Rolling Stones Rock and Roll Circus*. She more explicitly attempted to balance the male-dominated sound of rock with her female presence when she joined John and the Plastic Ono Band (with Eric Clapton, Klaus Voorman, and Alan White on drums) on 13 September 1969 at the Toronto Rock 'n' Roll Revival concert.[56] The video of the later concert begins with a tribute to the masculine lineage of rock and roll in the form of performances by Lennon's idols Bo Diddley, Jerry Lee Lewis, Chuck Berry, and Little Richard. Shots of a dancing back-up woman with a tambourine for Bo Diddley and of Hells Angels driving into Toronto on their motorcycles remind the viewer of the macho gender stereotypes that characterized 1960s rock. Yoko begins her feminist disruption of this rock-and-roll

scene by entering a white bag during Eric Clapton's guitar solo on "Blue
Suede Shoes" and continues it by inserting sonic foreign bodies into the
blues and rock basis of Lennon's "Yer Blues" and "Cold Turkey." Such
confrontations between avant-garde and rock-and-roll practices, and
between guitar heroes and their "women," rarely took place in the late
1960s and thus appear fantastically courageous, even today.[57] Yoko
most forcefully asserts her conscious female presence in front of her
hostile public in her own songs "Don't Worry Kyoko" and "John," in
which she constructs feminine musical identity through her unrelenting
expression of female desire, by improvising on her emotions toward her
daughter Kyoko and lover John, over the Plastic Ono Band's repeated
riffs. Throughout, Yoko sings "out of tune" on purpose as a means of
resisting the expectations and resolutions associated with the established
practice of tonality. Her consistent practice of purposefully not rhyming
her lines or matching them to the musical phrases prevents her audiences
from ignoring her. Precisely choosing her pitches so that they cut through
the musical fabric being improvised by her fellow players, Yoko creates
disruptive sonic events that overpower even a great guitar hero like Eric
Clapton, whose playing at that time was widely identified as the epitome
of a virtuostic electric guitar style associated with white, male virility.
When Yoko responds with force to the feedback created by John, Eric
Clapton, and Klaus Voorman at the end of this concert, they react by
forsaking their instruments and smoking a cigarette before abandoning
the stage, as if acknowledging Yoko's sonic victory. For usurping their
power, she would remain the unsung hero of Clapton, Lennon, and
underground fans, yet unforgiven by the rock establishment.

By the time of their dual album project of 1970 (*Yoko Ono/Plastic
Ono Band* and *John Lennon/Plastic Ono*), Yoko and John had realized
that their gendered sonic identities had become too distinct to be fused
through an act of sexual music making. Their more individuated "male"
and "female" voices now expressed themselves increasingly not only in
terms of sheer sound but also in words and musical practice, on separate
albums with utterly egalitarian covers. Gender and racial differences
were no longer on the surface of their fused spiritual state but rather were
part of their identities as two separate individuals who begin to act out
their sexual politics in a much more directly oppositional dialogue.
Throughout 1969, John had gradually returned to the rock and roll with
which he had always defined his male sexuality (albeit now influenced by

feminism), whereas Yoko, more explicitly than ever before, aligned her symbolically female sounds with the musical practices of free jazz, as she had come to know them through saxophonist Ornette Coleman, who himself challenged racial and gender hierarchies in his dressing style, attitudes, and playing.[58] By the summer of 1969, free jazz was emerging in Europe as the most intense cultural expression of the black community's struggle for equality, reflecting the political militancy of exiled Afro-Americans whose musical politics offered an alternative to the neutralizing, integrative rock-and-roll harmony of festivals in the United States such as Woodstock. Inspired by the pan-African music festival in Algiers in July 1969, many Afro-American musicians had left the United States to pursue free jazz interests in Paris, especially around the BYG record label.[59] Like Yoko, these free jazz artists wanted to express spontaneously what was happening around them and inside themselves, seeking thereby to bring about social and historical change. In the words of Malcolm X, improvising in jazz gave "the black man the liberty to create: He could invent a society, a social system, an economic system, a political system different than any that exists and ever has existed on earth."[60] By crossing over into free jazz, Yoko allied her feminist project with the black movement, adopting a stance common in the late 1960s. Through her free improvisation she politicized her music, creating a possible sonic world for women—an imagined place where their desires could be voiced and given attention within the rock-and-roll world of men.

On the album *Yoko Ono/Plastic Ono Band*, Yoko and John experiment with various ways of engaging free jazz and rock and roll in a female–male dialogue that moves beyond mythical archetypes into the realm of language. "Why," the first track, for example, opens with the frantic Yoko-like scream of John's guitar over a powerful dance bass-and-drum track by Klaus Voorman and Ringo Starr. Now aware that her own irregular and thus "conceptual" rhythms tended to become dangerously abstract on their own, Yoko is careful here to ground them: "Conceptual rhythm I carry on with my voice," Yoko commented, "which has a very complicated rhythm even in 'Why,' but the bass and the drum is the heartbeat. So the body and the conceptual rhythms go together."[61] Within seconds, Yoko responds to John's shouts and guitar screams, allowing her voice to emerge organically out of the electronic fray, before articulating the word "why" through the sonic substance of her primal cry. Refashioned into the contours of a word, her abstract sounds cease to exist for themselves in the world, as Cage and others believed avant-garde sounds should, and become charged with historical and political meaning, expressing through constantly varied repetitions over repeated harmonic riffs Yoko's existential desire to be. John responds with some of the best improvised playing he ever recorded.[62] Yet his jamming style is distinctly different from Yoko's, focused less on rhythmic variety and more on the rich electric guitar sounds he can produce to match Yoko's vocal utterances within a minimalist context rooted in rock and roll.[63] "A lot of the music was really free-form," John remembered. "I would just sort of follow her on guitar, or set a rhythm and she would say, 'I like that. I can do this over that.' She would select from my limited playing and decide what she wanted to use, or I'd give her a lick and she'd just howl."[64] Although still unified as polar gender opposites within "John & Yoko," their collaborative roles have shifted: John wavers between improvising as Yoko's sonic equal and accompanying her with his rock and roll (on "Why Not" and "Touch Me," for example), while she stops performing on his tracks completely, replacing her active music making with spiritual and musical advising in the studio. Also, whereas John composed each of his classic rock-and-roll songs carefully, Yoko improvised almost her entire album in one all-night session, marking her ethnic Otherness in relation to John by drawing on an ever wider variety of musical traditions. In Ornette Coleman's words, Yoko used "the sounds of all the ethnic cultures of the present civilizations," in order to define herself as "a real global artist."[65]

By 1971, Yoko and John had almost entirely abandoned their "John & Yoko" notion of living fused lives in superimposed musical universes. On *Fly* and *Imagine*, their separate albums of this year, they shifted their focus by exploring the presence of polar opposites (female/male, East/West) within themselves. Yoko made this project explicit by designing *Fly* as a double album, with a first record containing symbolically "masculine" rock and roll (with far less involvement from John) and a second record based on symbolically "female" avant-garde/free jazz experimentation, and further subdivided into tracks expressing the yang principle, or "delicateness of Male" ("Airmale"), and those expressing yin, or "the aggressiveness of female," ("You" and, to a lesser extent, "Fly").[66] The manner in which Yoko represented the female and male indicated that after three years in the pop music business and public eye, she was far less convinced of the social equality of men and women in the society in which she lived. Whereas the track "Airmale" and Lennon's film *Erection*, to which it served as a soundtrack, depicted the male as a constructive, busy, success-oriented principle, for example, "You" and "Fly" (the latter as both soundtrack and film) portrayed the female as victimized, suffocating, and in pain.

Going back to the existential roots of her early art, Yoko defines female existence on *Fly* no longer as desire itself (as she had frequently done in her early work with John) but rather as its *frustration* in male-dominated society. The reception she had received as John Lennon's wife had hurt her to the point of stifling her ability to express herself as a woman:

> What I learned from being with John is that the society suddenly treated me as a woman, as a woman who belonged to a man who is one of the most powerful people in our generation. And some of his closest friends told me that probably I should stay in the background, I should shut up, I should give up my work and that way I'll be happy. . . . Because the whole society started to attack me and the whole society wished me dead, I started to accumulate a tremendous amount of guilt complex, and as a result of that I started to stutter. I consider myself a very eloquent woman, and also an attractive woman all my life and suddenly because I was associated to John that I was considered an ugly woman, an ugly Jap who took your monument or something away from you. That's when I realized how hard it is for women, if I can start to stutter, being a strong woman and having lived thirty years by then, learn to stutter in three years in being treated as such, it is a very hard road.[67]

Yoko reacts to such abuse and violation by seeking on *Fly* to efface her female body, refashioning her voice electronically into an automata, like the ones designed by her old Fluxus friend Joe Jones and used on this album. The distancing effect resulting from such a removal of agency and emotion is evident on tracks such as "Telephone Piece," in which Yoko replaces the gutteral, unplugged presence of her female singing voice with a symbolic representation of it in the form of her own recorded answering machine message, indicating her presence only as absence. On "Fly" and other tracks, she returns to her voice, yet contains it by choking her very efforts to make sounds, suffocating her vocal desires to the point that they become desperate gasps. She later compared her feeling of helplessness to that of a fish on a cutting board, tormented because it was out of water: "I'm breathing hard because I'm out of oxygen. I want to be killed because living is painful. I want to be cut up with a knife. That's the vision I have of myself."[68] In the accompanying film *Fly*, Yoko even more acutely pinpoints her feelings of helplessness by filming an invasive fly as it skirts, buzzes, and picks its way across every detail of the utterly still, immobile, and even comatose surface of a female body. By robbing the represented woman's body of its expressive capacity for active response, Yoko allows for a displacement of emotion and sensation: viewers finds themselves feeling the physical irritation of the probing, buzzing fly and sensing an almost irresistible urge to shoo the pesky nuisance away. In this manner they share intimately in Yoko's humiliation in the face of violation, experiencing firsthand how it may have felt to be her in the late 1960s. The feeling of stifled self-expression is exacerbated by the acute disjunction between silent film image and vocal soundtrack, especially when the fly begins to probe the mute mouth of the passive female to the accompaniment of Yoko's wrenching and choked vocal expressions of female pain. Yoko's cry, so often misunderstood, becomes the eerily detached expression of an excruciating pain caused by male physical violation. As John Lennon commented, "[H]er pain is such that she expresses herself in a way that hurts you—you cannot take it."[69]

Strengthened by the existential struggle of *Fly*, Yoko felt ready to embrace the world of rock and roll on her own. On her next album, *Approximately Infinite Universe*, she would begin to sing. Abandoning the vocalizations that would remain her trademark, she embraced the world of popular music, creating one of the first classic albums of second-wave feminism.

In the "John & Yoko" project, Yoko and John had attempted through conceptual, visual, and musical means to project and thus help realize positive visions of heterosexual relationships based on racial and gender equality. Wary of the idealizing effects of mass media, they had struggled to keep their dialogue truthful, by allowing it to reflect all the different, and even difficult, stages of their relationship. Together, Yoko and John had found their voice (*Two Virgins*), witnessed its suffering (*Plastic Ono Band*), explored its existential needs (*Imagine* and *Fly*), and gained their independence. By 1972, they had lost their innocence, realizing that their struggle for equality was going to require of them a much more activist, independent stance as a couple. When Yoko returned to collaborating with John on *Double Fantasy* (1980), both had changed, developing a dialogue based not on absolute equality but rather on the reversal of traditional male and female roles. Remarkably, in spite of fierce opposition and John's brutal death, Yoko has never stopped fighting for the utopic vision of gender and racial equality that she and John dreamed up one romantic dawn in the spring of 1968. "You better start feeling the truth. I'm gonna be around for quite a while," Yoko screamed out to her audience during a concert tour in Japan in 1974. The sixties generation, and all those afterwards, are deeply fortunate that she is.

NOTES

I am grateful to Richard Joly, Eric Lewis, Katherine Rosenblatt, Kristine Stiles, Lloyd Whitesell, and the editors of this volume for their very helpful information and comments on this essay.

1. See *Rolling Stone* 1, 1, 9 November 1967, 1, 3.

2. Gillian G. Gaar, *She's a Rebel: The History of Women in Rock and Roll*, preface by Yoko Ono (New York: Seal Press, 1992), 101.

3. See Kevin Concannon and Reiko Tomii, "Chronology: Exhibitions, Concerts, Events, etc.," in *Yes: Yoko Ono*, ed. Alexandra Munroe, with Jon Hendricks (New York: Japan Society and Harry N. Abrams, 2000), 306–35.

4. See the unidentified article by Jud Yalkut, included in "This Is Not Here: Zeitungen zur Ausstellung," assembled by John Lennon and Peter Bendry, in the possession of Yoko Ono and included in the exhibition "Yoko Ono Film Works Filme Seen and Unseen," Neue Gesellschaft für Bildende Kunst, Berlin, Germany, 14 June–6 July 2003.

5. *Grapefruit* was first published in Tokyo in 1964 by Wunternaum Press. The British, American, and German editions followed in 1970. For a complete list of editions, see *Yes: Yoko Ono*, 337.

6. Yoko Ono, "The Feminization of Society," *New York Times*, 23 February 1972, 41; rpt. as program notes for the CD *Approximately Infinite Universe* (1972; Rykodisc, 1997).

7. Barbara Haskell and John G. Hanhardt, *Yoko Ono: Arias and Objects* (Salt Lake City: Peregrine Smith Books, 1991), 11.

8. See *Rolling Stone* 1, 22, 23 November 1968, insert between pp. 1 and 8.

9. Jann S. Wenner, "The Ballad of John and Yoko," in *Yes: Yoko Ono*, 60.

10. Kristine Stiles, "Unbosoming Lennon: The Politics of Yoko Ono's Experience," *Art Criticism* 72 (Spring 1991): 23.

11. Ono, "Feminization of Society."

12. Wenner, "Ballad of John and Yoko," 60.

13. Haskell and Hanhardt, *Yoko Ono*, 81.

14. Yoko Ono, "Feeling the Space," *New York Times*, 24 August 1973, 33; rpt. in the program notes to *Walking on Thin Ice: Compliation* (Rykodisc 1992).

15. bell hooks, "The Dancing Heart: A Conversation between Yoko Ono & bell hooks" September 1997, online at www.papermag.com/magazine/mag_97/mag/sep97/yoko/yoko.htm, accessed 7 June 2002.

16. On Yoko's involvement with existentialism, see Alexandra Monroe, "Spirit of YES: The Art and Life of Yoko Ono," in *Yes: Yoko Ono*, 15. See also Kristine Stiles, "Being Undyed: The Meeting of Mind and Matter in Yoko Ono's Events," in *Yes: Yoko Ono*, 149.

17. Yoko Ono, quoted in *The Ballad of John and Yoko*, ed. Rolling Stone (New York: Doubleday & Co., 1982), 71. Yoko created her first "bag piece" in 1964; see *Yes: Yoko Ono*, 162–65.

18. Yoko Ono, quoted in "Greenwich Village, March 18, 1965," included in Lennon and Bendry, "This Is Not Here."

19. Alan W. Watts, *The Two Hands of God: The Myths of Polarity* (New York: Collier, 1963).

20. John Lennon, quoted in Brian Cullman and Vic Garbarini, with Barbara Graustark, *Strawberry Fields Forever: John Lennon Remembered* (New York: Bantam, 1980), 87.

21. Joan Rothfuss, commentary to "Destruction in Art Symposium (DAS), 1966," in *Yes: Yoko Ono*, 168.

22. John Lennon, quoted in Jonathan Cott, "Two Virgins," *Rolling Stone* 28, 1 March 1969, 20.

23. John discusses this issue in *John and Yoko: The Interview* (6 December 1980), BBC Radio Collection, BBCD 6002.

24. Cott, "Two Virgins," 20.

25. Yoko frequently commented on her affinity for Berg's *Lulu*. See, for example, Robert Palmer, "On Thin Ice: The Music of Yoko Ono," included as program notes in the *Ono Box* (Rykodisc 1992).

26. John Lennon, quoted in Jonathan Cott, "Yoko Ono and Her Sixteen-Track Voice," *Rolling Stone* 78, 18 March 1971, 25; rpt. in *Ballad of John and Yoko*, 123.

27. For recorded examples of Yoko's collaborations with Toshi Ichinayagi, see Kuri Yoji, *AOS* (1964) and *Tragedy on the G-String* (1969), on *The Manic Age* (Montvale, N.J.: Laserdisc Corporation of America, 1986).

28. Jill Johnston, "Life and Art," *Village Voice*, 7 December 1961; rpt. in *Yes: Yoko Ono*, 312.

29. See Joy Press, "A Life in Flux," *Wire* 146, April 1996, 18–24.

30. Haskell and Hanhardt, *Yoko Ono*, 28.

31. Yoko Ono, quoted in Barbara Graustark, "Yoko: An Intimate Conversation," *Rolling Stone* 353, 1 October 1981, 15.

32. See Klaus Hübner, *Yoko Ono: "Leben auf dunnem Eis"* (Munich: Ego & List, 1999), 21–22; and "Yoko Ono," in *The Guests Go in to Supper*, ed. Melody Sumner, Kathleen Burch, and Michael Sumner (Oakland, Calif.: Burning Books, 1986), 172–73.

33. John Lennon, quoted from an interview with Marshall McLuhan, in Ritchie York, "John, Yoko and Year One," *Rolling Stone* 51, 7 February 1970, 19.

34. Yoko Ono, quoted in Daniel Rothbart, "The Dragon Lady Speaks: An Interview with Yoko Ono" (2002), online at http://nyartsmagazine.com/66/ono.htm, accessed 6 June 2002.

35. Yoko Ono, "On Film No. 5 & Two Virgins" (22 October 1968), in *Grapefruit: A Book of Drawings and Instructions* (New York: Simon & Schuster, 1970; rpt., 2000), n.p.; originally printed as "Yoko Talks about It," *Rolling Stone* 24, 21 December 1968, 15.

36. Yoko Ono, quoted in an unidentified article by Jud Yalkut, included in Lennon and Bendry, "This Is Not Here."

37. Yoko Ono, "Kyokosha no gen," *SAC Journal* 24 (May 1962), translated into English by Yoko Ono as "The World of a Fabricator," in *Yes: Yoko Ono*, 285.

38. According to Yoko's notes, *Cut* can be performed by a man or a woman. See Yoko Ono, "Nine Concert Pieces for John Cage, 15 December 1966," in *Yes: Yoko Ono*, 279. I know of only one occasion when *Cut* was performed by men, in September 1966, when two men were cut out of a sack.

39. John Jones, "Meeting Yoko Ono," in *The Lennon Companion: Twenty-Five Years of Comment*, ed. Elizabeth Thomson and David Gutman (New York: Schirmer, 1987), 142.

40. Yoko Ono, quoted in "1968 Interview with Tony Elliot from Time Out Magazine," online at http://ccub.wlv.ac.uk/~fa1871/yoko.html, accessed 6 July 2002.

41. Yoko Ono, quoted in Graustark, "Yoko," 100.

42. Stiles, "Being Undyed," 148.

43. Yoko Ono, quoted in Cott, "Two Virgins," 20.

44. Yoko Ono, quoted in "Yoko Ono in Helsinki," online at http://www.kaapelo.fi/aiu/helsinki.html, accessed 6 July 2002.

45. Yoko Ono, quoted in Monroe, "Spirit of YES," 12.

46. See Roger Ebert, "Cinema," *Rolling Stone* 24, 21 December 1968, 15.

47. John Lennon, quoted in "Ringo's Right: We Can't Tour Again," *New Musical Express*, 7 June 1969, 3; rpt. in *New Musical Express Originals* 1, 1 (2002): 132.

238 | TAMARA LEVITZ

48. See Jonathan Cott, "The Rolling Stone Interview: John Lennon," *Rolling Stone* 1, 22, 23 November 1968, 14; rpt. In *Ballad of John and Yoko*, 94.

49. John Lennon, quoted in "Bore, Fool or Saint: John Just Wants to Be Loved," *New Musical Express*, 20 December 1969; rpt. in *New Musical Express Originals* 1, 1 (2002): 140.

50. Yoko Ono, quoted in Cott, "Yoko Ono and her Sixteen-Track Voice," 26; and Graustark, "Yoko," 15.

51. These terms are used by Anthony Elliot in *The Mourning of John Lennon* (Berkeley: University of California Press, 1999), 72–74.

52. Ibid., 82.

53. See *The Beatles Anthology* (San Francisco: Chronicle Books, 2000), 302.

54. See Cott, "Yoko Ono and Her Sixteen-Track Voice," 24; and Roy Carr, *New Musical Express*, 7 October 1972, rpt. in *Instant Karma* 20 (February/March 1985), online at http://www.instantkarma.com/balladissue20.html. accessed 15 March 1999. On Yoko's interest in the heartbeat before 1968, see Stiles, "Unbosoming Lennon," 28.

55. See Eldridge Cleaver, *Soul on Ice* (New York: Dell, 1968).

56. *The Rolling Stones Rock and Roll Circus*, dir. Michael Lindsay-Hogg (ABKCO Films, New York, 1995); and *Live Rock and Roll Revival, Toronto*, dir. D. A. Pennebaker (HBO Video, New York, 1988); released as a DVD by Pioneer Entertainment in 2002 under the title *John Lennon: Sweet Toronto (1969)*.

57. See Jon Wiener, "Pop and Avant-Garde: The Case of John and Yoko," *Popular Music and Society* 22, 1 (Spring 1998): 1–13.

58. See David Ake, *Jazz Cultures* (Berkeley: University of California Press, 2001).

59. See Thurston Moore and Byron Coley, program notes, in *Jazzactuel: A Collection of Avant Garde/Free Jazz/Psychedelia from the BYG/Actuel catalogue of 1969–1971* (Snapper Music, Charly Licensing Aps, 2001: SNAJ 707 CD).

60. Malcolm X, excerpt from a speech given on 28 June 1964, Organisation of Afro-American Unity, quoted in Frank Kofsky, *Black Nationalism and the Revolution in Music* (New York: Pathfinder Press, 1970), 65–66.

61. Yoko Ono, quoted in Cott, "Yoko Ono and Her Sixteen-Track Voice," 24.

62. See Palmer, "On Thin Ice."

63. One can gain considerable insight into the nature of Yoko and John's rock-free jazz dialogue by comparing it with Yoko's collaboration with Ornette Coleman on the same album, or with the free-jazz jamming of electric guitarist Sonny Sharrock and Linda Sharrock, whose vocal practice at times bears a striking resemblance to Yoko's. See Sonny and Linda Sharrock, *Monkey Pockie Boo* (Actuel 37, 22 June 1970); and *Black Woman* (Vortex 2014, October 1968 and May 1969).

64. John Lennon, quoted in *The Playboy Interviews with John Lennon and*

Yoko Ono: The Final Testament, interviews by David Sheff, ed. G. Barry Golson (New York: Berkley Books, 1981), 229.

65. Ornette Coleman, quoted in notes to Ono, *Walking on Thin Ice*.

66. Yoko Ono, "Fly—A Double Album, 1971," in *Yes: Yoko Ono*, 284.

67. Yoko Ono, "Bonus Track: 'I Learned to Stutter/Coffin Car," on Yoko Ono, *Feeling the Space* (1974; Rykodisc 1997).

68. Yoko Ono, "My Love, My Battle" (in Japanese), *Bungei Shunju* (1974); quoted in Jerry Hopkins, *Yoko Ono* (New York: Macmillan, 1986), 191.

69. John Lennon, quoted in Graustark, "Yoko," 15.

12

"Hanoi Jane" Lives
The 1960s Legacy of Jane Fonda

Barbara L. Tischler

Reflecting on her life on the cusp of sixty in 1997, Jane Fonda decided to compile a film portrait that would present the various personas that comprise her productive life. Looking for a central image or defining theme, she asked, "Am I simply a chameleon that changes color according to the times and the men in my life?"[1] A simple response to this question is a resounding "Yes!" but Fonda's life-long search for an individual identity is far more nuanced. In an attempt to find and be herself, she successfully escaped the "Lady Jane" image of her privileged childhood. Later in life, she embraced the "Workout Queen" image that projected physical and emotional health, and she describes herself today as content with her life as a single woman and with her newfound Christian faith. But this immensely talented and complex creative woman has been unable to distance herself from a moment of antiwar activism that led to accusations of treason in the 1970s.

For many Americans, Fonda will always be "Hanoi Jane." Thirty years and more after her notorious trip to Hanoi, where she excoriated American military policy and lionized the Vietcong, Fonda cannot seem to transcend that label.

Fonda's quest for herself replicated that of many American women in the second half of the twentieth century, although her talent, celebrity, and financial resources allowed her to try on a number of identities, some of which she now regrets. Talent and money notwithstanding, Fonda embraced the characters cast for her by men (particularly her father and first husband), responded to the political turmoil and cultural energy of the late 1960s, and eventually, in the wake of the New Feminism, sought a more authentic version of herself.

There was little in Jane Seymour Fonda's early upbringing that pointed to later political activism, much less charges of treason. Born in New York City on December 21, 1937, to actor Henry Fonda and New York socialite Frances Seymour Brokaw, Fonda had a privileged but turbulent childhood that was marred by distant treatment from her father and her mother's mental illness. Frances's confinement to a mental hospital was precipitated by Henry Fonda's announcement that he was leaving her for a younger woman. Mental illness in the 1950s was often kept secret, particularly by people in public life, and suicide was a taboo subject for most Americans. In 1950, when Jane was only twelve years old and her brother Peter was ten, their mother committed suicide by slitting her own throat.

Although Fonda experienced some happy times with her brother, she remembers her father as distant and uncommunicative. Thinking it best to "protect" his children from the truth about their mother's death, Henry concocted the story that Frances had had a heart attack in the hospital. Jane learned the truth a year later when a friend read the story in a magazine.[2] Jane and her brother had no opportunity to grieve for their mother—she had been "put away" at the time of her mental illness, and her death simply represented the end of the family as the children had known it.

Throughout her adolescence and until her involvement in the fitness craze of the 1970s, Fonda suffered from bulimia, a disease that was not recognized or understood in affluent post–World War II America. Looking back on that experience in 2001, Fonda noted that, for twenty-five years, "I could never put a forkful in my mouth without feeling fear. . . . I've been bulimic and anorexic for 25 years of my life."[3] Like many women in the 1950s and 1960s, Fonda assumed that her condition was her own fault, rather than a disorder born out of the social pressures of her life and her own self-critical desire for perfection. That perfection was realized, according to the standard wisdom of the time, in a "36-24-36" figure, an ideal that most women could never achieve. For Fonda, the same drive to be in control of her body and her image led to success as well as disease.

"Lady Jane," as she was called, exhibited little early interest in acting. She made a minor appearance with her father in an Omaha Community Theatre charity production of *The Country Girl* in 1954. In the mid-1950s, Fonda earned a reputation at Vassar College as a "sophisticated delinquent" who broke as many rules as she could but did so with panache. She left Vassar after two years to travel to Paris and then returned to New York to study with Lee Strassberg at the Actors' Studio. Fonda responded to the demands of Strassberg's Method, which called for actors not simply to learn their parts but to live them. Author Peter Braunstein noted that it was in the Actors' Studio that Fonda "mastered the two elements that would make her such an effective harbinger and exemplar of her times—empathy and exhibitionism. The technique that allowed her intuitively to appropriate someone else's subjectivity for the purposes of a screen role would later enable her to conform to, and inhabit, the changing configurations of American culture—to 'become' the culture, as it were."[4]

Fonda soon appeared on Broadway as a cheerleader in *Tall Story,* a role that she re-created in Hollywood opposite Tony Perkins in 1960. The 1960s saw her in a perky sex kitten role in *Period of Adjustment* and as a "bad girl" in *Walk on the Wild Side* (both 1962). She won a Golden Globe Award as Most Promising Newcomer for her work in *Sunday in New York* in 1963. She then jumped the Hollywood ship in favor of the more adventurous filmmaking of the French avant-garde. Fonda gained considerable notice for her nearly nude appearance in *La Ronde* (1964), directed by her lover and first husband, Roger (Plemiannikov) Vadim. Vadim, who had previously been married to Brigitte Bardot, had helped to mold that actress's sex queen image in the 1950s. While Fonda at the time was certainly more of an ingenue than Bardot, she was enticed by the sexuality, artistic freedom, and apparent daring of the "French style" directors. She was particularly drawn to Vadim, observing later in her life that

> I needed someone to teach me how to be a woman and I was stupid enough—no, I take that back—superficial enough to think that Vadim would do it. And he taught me a lot, but it's a certain version of womanhood.[5]

Compared to American movies that often featured safely sexual characters and stories with happy endings, French film of the mid-1960s represented the cutting edge of sexuality. Fonda established herself in both cultural realms, playing hedonistic and sexually daring characters in Paris while portraying safe female characters in Hollywood.

While movie critic Judith Crist decried the nudity in Vadim's *The Game Is Over (1966),* Hollywood's *Cat Ballou* (1965) helped make Jane Fonda a star. Her big screen success was followed by *Any Wednesday* (1966); *Barefoot in the Park,* with Robert Redford (1967); and *They*

Shoot Horses, Don't They? (1969), which established Fonda as a serious dramatic actress and earned her an Academy Award nomination.

Fonda's work with Vadim later in the 1960s continued to project her image of uninhibited sexuality. In the campy comedy *Barbarella* (1968), Fonda plays a "five star double-rated astronautical aviatrix" who wears outlandish costumes and Nancy Sinatra go-go boots, in marked contrast to the madcap comedic persona in *Cat Ballou*. Director Vadim called the film "a kind of sexual Alice in Wonderland of the future." Writing about a revival showing of the film in 1996, *San Francisco Chronicle* critic Edward Guthmann gushed,

> Hell, what's not to like about set designs that look like someone's acid-induced science project, or a series of breast-enhancing Space Queen outfits that make the 29-year old Fonda resemble a dishy mutation of Judy Jetson, Buster Crabbe and Charo?

With a forgettable plot, the focus was on Fonda's gorgeous body and big blonde hair, along with her uncanny ability to survive an encounter with vampire dolls, a space ship crash, and an evil queen. The film was sexy and fun. Commenting on the comedic talent that was not fully realized in Fonda's career, critic Guthmann wrote:

> It's sad to note that Fonda rarely did comedy after "Barbarella," and eventually fell into a rut of playing noble, uplifting bores. Politics gave her a sense of identity and made her an effective standard-bearer for women, but the self-righteousness that followed—compounded by the distractions of a lucrative aerobics dynasty—brought death to a brilliant career.[6]

The sex goddess of *Barbarella* was largely a creation of Roger Vadim. By 1968, Fonda was beginning to tire of what she called "the world of Roger Vadim, with my blond hair and falsies." Realizing that her marriage was disintegrating, Fonda returned from Paris to the United States. Once home, she became aware of the changes that were being wrought by the civil rights, antiwar, and countercultural movements that had attracted the attention of many Americans. She had been out of touch with politics for most of her life, but the persistence of these three social movements made such distance less tenable by 1968.

Not having experienced the development of a political persona as

Fig. 12.1. Jane Fonda as an intergalactic sex queen in the 1968 film *Barbarella*.

many young Americans did throughout the 1960s, Fonda began what was for her a new life as a politically active person. Energized by a new relationship with, and eventually a new marriage to, activist Tom Hayden, she jumped into her new role as energetically as any Method actor. From the events that followed, it appears that Fonda was susceptible to the draw of radical politics, as exemplified in Hayden's participation in major social movements of the time, and that she accepted the verities of the antiwar movement, along with those of the American Indian Movement and the Black Panther Party, uncritically.

The period following the 1968 Tet Offensive was frustrating for the antiwar movement, as the conflict itself seemed intractable. Disruptions at the Chicago Democratic Convention in 1968 by activists intent on "bringing the war home" had neither stopped the war nor prevented the election of Richard Nixon. The public heard year-long reports of wrangling at the Paris Peace Talks over the shape of the negotiating table. Students began to think twice about participation in civil disobedience on campus after the shooting of four students at Kent State University in

May 1970. The event demonstrated that if hurling rocks or obscenities in the general direction of the National Guard could be dangerous, walking to class could be deadly. At the same time, the president was promising "Vietnamization" and "peace with honor," while American soldiers continued to kill and die in the jungles of Vietnam. GI resistance in the field emerged as victory proved elusive. Soldiers understood that while the president had declared it was no longer their war, they were still expected to obey orders to fight. Many expressed their anger and frustration with the phrase "Nobody wants to be the last guy to die in Vietnam."[7]

Shortly after her return to the United States, Fonda was arrested with a group of Native Americans who had attempted to take over Fort Lawton, an Army installation near Seattle. She demonstrated her support for the Black Panther Party by posting bail for a member arrested on gun charges and by describing Panther leader Huey P. Newton as "the only man I've met that I would trust as the leader of this country" at a speech to students at Michigan State University on November 22, 1969, the sixth anniversary of the assassination of John F. Kennedy. In the same speech in East Lansing, Fonda told her student audience, "I would think that if you understood what communism was, you would hope, you would pray on your knees that we would someday become communist."

In March 1971, after a visit to activist Angela Davis in jail, Fonda called for civil disobedience as part of an antiwar action planned for May in Washington, D.C., and San Francisco. The demands of the broad-based antiwar coalition included a withdrawal of U.S. troops from Vietnam, a government-guaranteed annual income for a family of four on welfare, and the freeing of American "political prisoners." Such demands were standard fare as the antiwar movement became more radicalized. It was also common to find highly visible celebrities involved in the movement to end the war. But Fonda's statements expressed a more revolutionary perspective than those of other Hollywood stars who occasionally participated in marches and antiwar rallies. Her attachment to Hayden and his politics influenced her political perspective.

Fonda saw herself as a revolutionary, and she pursued the cause with high energy. At the same time that the Hollywood Women's Press Club awarded Fonda its "Sour Apple Award" for representing the film industry in what the club saw as a negative light, she received her first Academy Award for her brilliant dramatic portrayal of a prostitute being stalked by a killer in *Klute* (1971).

In February 1971, Fonda supported the Winter Soldier Investigation, sponsored by Vietnam Veterans Against the War, in which GIs offered their testimony at hearings in Detroit regarding wartime atrocities and war crimes. That year also saw a massive May Day demonstration in Washington. As the summer approached, Fonda joined forces with *Klute* co-star Donald Sutherland, singers Holly Near and Country Joe McDonald, writer Jules Feiffer, and director Mike Nichols to produce a satirical antiwar revue at the Haymarket Square GI Coffeehouse in Fayetteville, North Carolina, just outside Fort Bragg.

The show, FTA—"Fox Trot Alpha," "Free the Army," "Fun, Travel, and Adventure" (the satirical name of a GI antiwar newspaper published at Fort Knox, Kentucky), or, in the parlance of the antiwar movement, "Fuck the Army"—had its genesis, according to McDonald, in an unlikely place:

> In 1971, my daughter Seven Ann's mother, Robin Menken, became friends with Jane Fonda. Jane sent her daughter Vanessa [Vadim] to the Blue Fairyland Nursery School in Berkeley. The Blue Fairyland was run by the leftist commune the Red Family. I worked in the nursery school as a volunteer and Seven went there for several years. So Jane Fonda became a regular in our lives at the time.

Once written and rehearsed, the show made the rounds of GI coffeehouses, including ones in Mt. Home, Idaho, and Killeen, Texas, in addition to Fort Bragg.[8] The show also made a tour of Hawaii, the Philippines, and Okinawa that was filmed in 1972 by Francine Parker.

The FTA show provided an alternative to the apolitical entertainment that more traditional Hollywood stars had historically provided to the troops abroad. Fonda declared that it was disconcerting to see that Bob Hope, Martha Rae, and other companies comprised only of stars who supported the war had cornered the market on GI entertainment and were the only entertainers allowed by the military brass to speak with military personnel on base in the United States and in Vietnam. Not surprisingly, the military brass maintained a tight control over the entertainment provided to U.S. forces.

When the FTA troupe proposed to present its debut performance at Fort Bragg, the commanding officer, Lieutenant General John J. Tolson III, declared the show to be "detrimental to discipline and morale."[9] Five hundred GIs attended the show at the Haymarket Square coffeehouse off base. Their reactions were mixed, many saying that they had hoped to see the sexy "Barbarella" rather than the newly politicized Fonda singing lyrics such as

> Nothing could be finer
> Than to be in Indochina
> Making mo-o-ney

sung to the tune of the old standard "Carolina in the Morning."

Coming to political consciousness in her mid-thirties rather than as a young student, Fonda seemed eager to compress all her political energy into support for as many radical causes as she could find. She told *Life* magazine:

> I never felt politics touched my life. But as a revolutionary woman, I'm ready to support all struggles that are radical.[10]

It may have been Fonda's celebrity, her intensity, or the content of her naive but revolutionary pronouncements that frightened the military brass, the State Department, and members of Congress who were quick to cry "treason." She was no ordinary entertainer hoofing and singing for the troops. Her message of resistance tapped into a deeply felt and growing antiwar sentiment among general enlisted personnel and officers in Vietnam. Nearly sixty-four thousand members of the armed forces saw the FTA show on its Pacific tour, a fact that was not ignored by a variety of authorities. As the tour made its way through the Pacific, reporter Vivian Gornick observed:

> It became clear, even to me, that indeed the F.T.A. was surrounded, wherever it went, by agents of the CID, the OSI, the CIA, the local police, [and] the various investigative agencies of the countries that it visited. In fact, one of the most incredible elements in the entire Asian tour of the F.T.A. was the miracle of frightened attention that it received from the U.S. military. . . . Men were confined to base, "riot" conditions were declared, GIs were photographed.[11]

Other members of the FTA troupe, Donald Sutherland, Holly Near, and Country Joe McDonald, were sharply criticized for their antiwar sentiments, but none was vilified as was Fonda. Whether she had been influenced by the radicalism of the moment (as had composer Leonard Bernstein and a few other chic celebrities) or was not only acting the part of a revolutionary but living it (as Lee Strassberg had taught her to do for all her roles), Fonda's radicalism carried with it passion, intensity, and at least momentary sincerity. In addition, Fonda violated the law by traveling to North Vietnam. It is not at all surprising that her every move attracted government attention.

Even before Fonda's involvement in the FTA shows and the July 1972 trip to Hanoi, she and Students for a Democratic Society/Chicago Seven activist Tom Hayden, who fathered her second child while she was still married to Vadim and who would soon become her second husband, provided financial support to the Indochina Peace Campaign (after which she would later name her film production company, IPC). The group also raised funds and support for the United Farm Workers and the presidential campaign of George McGovern. But it was Fonda's trip to Vietnam that earned her the hatred of millions of Americans.

Americans who protested their country's participation in an undeclared war in Vietnam did so in a variety of ways and with a variety of focal points. Sending American troops to the other side of the world for purposes that seemed distant from the interests of the American people at home provided an impetus for some who wrote letters, marched in mass demonstrations, and even burned draft cards. Humanitarian concerns for Vietnamese civilians motivated many, as did the increasing shrillness of the United States' political support for repressive or inept Vietnamese regimes. Very few Americans took the radical steps of traveling to Vietnam or supporting North Vietnam's National Liberation Front and the communist cause that had been most effectively articulated by Ho Chih Minh.

The release of the *Pentagon Papers* in 1971, after a Supreme Court battle between the U.S. government and the *New York Times,* confirmed that policy-makers in the State Department supported selective bombing of dikes. The logic was that such targeted bombing would ruin the rice crop and cause starvation, creating an opportunity for the United States to use food aid as a bargaining tool at the Paris peace negotiations. In contrast, a massive campaign of bombing population centers would rally support for the North, both in Vietnam and in the international community.[12]

In July 1972, Jane Fonda traveled to North Vietnam to create a documentary film about the everyday realities of the war in the city of Hanoi. She also filmed craters and bomb damage to dikes that the U.S. government had denied existed. She had crossed the line from protest and antiwar activism to activities that drew the attention of the State Department and prowar veterans groups, just as her domestic appearances and speeches had already attracted the attention of the FBI. U.S. citizens were not permitted to travel to Vietnam, and Fonda's arrival in Hanoi from Moscow saw her wearing pajama-like clothing similar to that worn by the Vietcong. Fonda's documentary contradicted official U.S. government pronouncements, which made her evidence suspect in the minds of many. Further, her activities in Hanoi provided aid and comfort to an enemy of the United States, in the eyes of her critics.

Why did Fonda risk her liberty, not to mention her successful Hollywood career, in the name of an unsophisticated, if sincere, concept of revolutionary action? Fonda's trip to North Vietnam, and her public visits with high-ranking Vietnamese officials with whom the U.S. government was not communicating publicly, provided legitimacy to an enemy cause. Her visits to local villages and a prisoner-of-war camp were designed to portray the heroic struggles of the Vietnamese peasants and give credence to the notion that American prisoners were being treated humanely, despite evidence to the contrary. Her speeches on Radio Hanoi reminded many of the work of the legendary Tokyo Rose. Most damning for many Americans were the visual images of Fonda's visit, in particular a series of images that showed her fraternizing with North Vietnamese soldiers and looking through the sight of an enemy anti-aircraft gun. For Americans, this portrait crossed traditional gender lines, but in North Vietnam, it was common for women to participate in the war effort on an equal footing with men.

Possible explanations for Fonda's actions focus on two interconnected themes in her life: her ongoing search for an identity of her own through the men and events that surrounded her, and her training and instincts as a Method actor. Like many American women in the 1960s who were struggling for their own personal and political liberation, she found that decades of conditioning to seek approval from men were hard to shake. One biographer described Fonda in this period as "malleable" and "ready to find her relevance in the use others could make of her."[13] Seeking approval and finding it in her craft as an actress, Fonda immersed herself in the radical sixties *Zeitgeist*, in effect transforming herself into a North Vietnamese peasant and soldier in the face of American military might and power in the world. Peter Braunstein observed:

> All the earmarks of her actress training came into play; a radical immersion in the subject experience resulting in profound empathy, followed by an exhibitionist portrayal of this newly adopted perspective.[14]

There was only one problem: Fonda had completely lost touch with her audience. Her North Vietnamese hosts were interested only in the propaganda value of her visit, and the Americans who had flocked to see her Hollywood films were appalled. Even the antiwar movement didn't know what to do with her. She was "out there" as a good Method actor should be, but she lacked an understanding of the ramifications of her actions. Perhaps Fonda expected to be praised for her politics. Instead, she was vilified for committing what many saw as treason.

What was the content of the speeches that earned Fonda the sobriquet "Hanoi Jane"? Transcripts reveal two distinct audiences in Vietnam—the general population, who might be inspired by the words of an American celebrity, and American military personnel, those on active duty, who might be influenced not to fight; plus POWs, who could be encouraged to cooperate with their captors. One of the speeches she recorded for Radio Hanoi invoked places, events, and people that would be familiar to a Vietnamese audience. In this speech, Fonda and her North Vietnamese speech writers articulated three important themes—the North Vietnamese people are hard-working, civilized, and courageous; American bombing targets innocent civilians; and the American war effort will never triumph over the people of North Vietnam. She described her visits with people from all walks of life:

> workers, peasants, students, artists and dancers, historians, journalists, film actresses, soldiers, militia girls, members of the women's union, writers.
>
> I visited the (Dan Xuac) agricultural co-op, where the silk worms are raised and thread is made. I visited a textile factory [and] a kindergarten in Hanoi. The beautiful Temple of Literature was where I saw traditional dances and heard songs of resistance. I also saw unforgettable ballet about the guerrillas training bees in the south to attack enemy soldiers. The bees were danced by women and they did their job well.

But this was no ordinary sightseeing chronicle. Fonda went on to connect her hosts with American culture:

> In the shadow of the Temple of Literature, I saw Vietnamese actors and actresses perform the second act of Arthur Miller's play, "All My Sons," and this was very moving to me—the fact that artists here are translating and performing American plays while US imperialists are bombing their country.

Fonda did not mention the controversial subject of Miller's play—the cheating on defense contracts by a manufacturer during World War II, and his patriotic son's suicidal response. Fonda went on to highlight the contrast between the beautiful culture of Vietnam and the ugliness of war brought on by American bombing:

> I cherish the memory of the blushing militia girls on the roof of their factory, encouraging one of their sisters as she sang a song praising the blue sky of Vietnam—these women, who are so gentle and poetic, whose voices are so beautiful, but who, when American planes are bombing their city become such good fighters. I cherish the way a farmer, evacuated from Hanoi, without hesitation, offered me, an American, his best individual bomb shelter while US bombs fell nearby. The daughter and I, in fact, shared the shelter wrapped in each other's arms, cheek against cheek. It was on the road back from Nam Dinh, where I had witnessed the systematic destruction of civilian targets—schools, hospitals, pagodas, the factories, houses, and the dike system.

Fonda further told her audience that her observations gave the lie to President Nixon's pronouncements of an end to the war.

When she addressed American soldiers and sailors, Fonda made a number of accusations that were designed to illustrate the impact of the war, specifically the bombing, on innocent civilians. She also offered a political analysis of the war in the context of American imperialism in language that would sound familiar to more politically sophisticated participants in the antiwar movement. Speaking to American soldiers as well as a broader audience, her charges included the use of chemical bombs and toxic chemicals; the secret intention to turn Vietnam into a "neocolony"; and the cynical use of the war by the Nixon administration as a last desperate gamble to stay in office in 1972. Finally, she said,

> I think Richard Nixon would do well to read Vietnamese history, their poetry, and particularly the poetry written by Ho Chih Minh.[15]

Fonda's remarks about her visit with American prisoners of war contributed the most to what has become a "Hate Fonda" movement that shows little signs of losing its energy thirty years after her visit to Hanoi. Her comments made the meeting with men who had been shot down by anti-aircraft fire and were subject to torture sound like a normal conversation in a normal world.

> This is Jane Fonda speaking from Hanoi. Yesterday evening . . . I had the opportunity of meeting seven U.S. pilots. . . . They are all in good health. We had a very long talk, a very open and casual talk. We exchanged ideas freely. They asked me to bring back to the American people their sense of disgust of the war and their shame for what they have been asked to do.
>
> . . . They asked me to bring messages back to their loved ones, telling them to be as actively involved in the peace movement as possible, to renew their efforts to end the war. . . . They assured me that they have been well cared for. They listen to the radio. They receive letters. They are in good health.[16]

Aside from the condescending tone, Fonda damaged her credibility by accepting the North Vietnamese version of the prisoners' condition as healthy and positive.

Not surprisingly, former prisoners and the general public at home responded with fury, both at Fonda's comments and at the fact that she went to North Vietman in the first place while Americans were still fighting and dying there. Former POW Sam Johnson wrote of his own reactions to Fonda's visit to his prison camp:

> Our camp guards and the commander were overjoyed to have a celebrity of her status come over and align herself with their "humane cause." I'll never forget seeing a picture of her seated on an antiaircraft gun, much like the one that had shot my plane out of the air and given seven years of my life to the North Vietnamese prison system. I stood in front of her photograph in a quiz [interrogation] room and stared in disbelief until the twisting in my gut made me turn away.[17]

Hostile reactions were not confined to former service personnel. The Manchester *Union-Leader* demanded that Fonda be tried for treason. Many Americans agreed with the paper that if Fonda were convicted, she should be shot. A few members of Congress hoped to amend the 1950 McCarran Internal Security Act to make travel to enemy nations a felony. But in the absence of a congressional declaration of war, there were legal debates as to whether the United States was really at war. In addition,

Fonda could not be prosecuted for an offense committed before Congress had made her actions explicitly illegal. With little interest in such legal wrangling, veterans and former POWs vilified "Hanoi Jane" in their publications and, later, on numerous Web sites. For the general public, the issue seemed to fade.

Why was Jane Fonda able to avoid the lasting public punishment that veterans hoped to inflict on her through angry words, protests at her film locations, and talk of boycotting her films? The answer transcends the legal difficulty of pinning a "traitor" label on "Hanoi Jane." It lies in the struggles of the political moment and a subtle shift away from a culture of toleration for protest to a more conservative moment that reached its zenith with the election of Ronald Reagan in 1980.

Fonda traveled to Hanoi in July 1972. When she returned, the nation was just waking up to the events of June 17 of that year, when security guard Frank Wills discovered duct tape over a lock on the door of the Democratic National Committee headquarters at the Watergate Hotel in Washington, D.C. The events of the next few years were truly remarkable. For example, Americans learned the meaning of new terms: "dirty tricks," plumbers, and CREEP, the Committee to Re-Elect the President. Watergate was no longer just a hotel and office complex—the name had come to signify political corruption and a lack of trust in government. With the resignation of a sitting vice president, Americans learned the Latin phrase *nolo contendere*. They learned that the president taped his official White House conversations and then erased them. And the same president could resign the highest office in the land, receive a pardon from his successor without having been convicted, and re-emerge in the public mind as an elder statesman who had "done some good things."

Jimmy Carter won the White House in 1976 on a platform of unity, healing, and human rights. No one wanted to hear any more about Watergate, and the political pundits declared that the Democrats could have beaten the hapless Gerald Ford by running an aardvark.

The years after Fonda's return were characterized by a politics of exhaustion. Sixties radicalism, never the motivating force of a majority of Americans in the first place, declined after Kent State. Post-Watergate politics gave us corruption, popular cynicism, the "Me" Generation, the soap opera of Patty Hearst, and the cultural deadness of disco. Americans turned inward, and Fonda simply laid low. In 1973, she married activist Tom Hayden, and they both re-cast their political vision in terms more like the Jeffersonian Port Huron Statement than the rhetoric of the Chicago Seven.

By the mid-1970s, a new, re-invented version of Jane Fonda emerged. Much of the public that identified with her more "mature" politics embraced Fonda's new image. Peter Braunstein noted that Fonda now called herself not a revolutionary but a "progressive Democrat." He observed:

> This repositioning was consistent with the new ambitions of former sixties radicals who now sought a place in the "system," be it electoral or corporate.

Her husband Tom Hayden even bought a suit and ran in California (unsuccessfully) for the Senate in 1976, with the slogan "The radicalism of the 1960s is becoming the common sense of the 1970s."[18] Hayden's campaign called itself the Campaign for Economic Democracy. He and Fonda raised funds for their political work by forming a new film production company, IPC, which few in Hollywood or elsewhere knew stood for Indochina Peace Campaign.

IPC's first film, the successful Vietnam War film *Coming Home* (1987), cast Fonda as a military wife who had never questioned the values of her husband or the society and culture in which she lived. Her character expresses her independence in terms of a love relationship rather than politics. She falls in love with a disabled veteran who also happens to have been transformed into an antiwar activist. Her preference of lovers can be interpreted as a choice about the politics of the war, particularly given the response of her straight-arrow husband, whose feeling of betrayal is represented by his suicide at the end of the film. Fonda got it right—audiences in the heyday of the "Me" decade wanted to forget about Vietnam, not re-fight the war on film.

In her IPC career, Fonda was fortunate to produce an apparently apolitical issue film just before that issue hit the headlines. In 1979, she starred in and co-produced *The China Syndrome*, about an accident at a nuclear power plant that led to a "melt-down" of the dangerous materials used to produce power for the public. The real-life accident at the Three Mile Island nuclear power plant in central Pennsylvania hit close to home, not only for people who lived near the Susquehanna River region, where the plant was located, but throughout the nation, where Americans began to raise questions about the safety of the power source that had promised relief from the reliance on foreign oil that had created so much economic and political havoc during the oil crisis of the early 1970s. *The China Syndrome*, in spite of Fonda's apparently apolitical character, became a highly political film because of its timeliness. It was another vehicle for Fonda's extraordinary acting talent.

In addition to luck, the IPC venture saw a degree of calculation, particularly in the production of *Nine to Five* (1980), a film that tackled the issues that women face in the workplace every day, such as limited opportunity and sexual harassment. Far from a serious consideration of the plight of women office workers, the film utilized visual comedy and one-liner comebacks to highlight the intelligence and humanity of women who are treated as second-class citizens, or worse, as "girls" in a working world that needs their talents and their savvy.

The year 1980 brought in Ronald Reagan and a "get government off our backs" rejection of both the liberalism of the late 1960s and the hedonistic self-absorption of the latter part of the 1970s. President Jimmy Carter's aceticism, his blue sweater, and his serious commitment to human rights made him a man not of his time.[19] Ronald Reagan ran on a platform that promised a return by the United States to preeminent political and military leadership in the world, and his wife Nancy promised a return of elegance and alcohol to White House parties. The self-reliance, with the implication that there would be no government help to rely on, of Nancy Reagan's "Just Say No" solution to the problem of drugs in American society also ushered in new political and personal priorities. Government and society were there to help those who helped themselves, and Jane Fonda was in the forefront of the newest self-help crusade.

Fonda the Workout Queen was the woman of the eighties. She was well into middle age, but that did not stop her from maintaining her body in top youthful form, thanks to years of exercise and dance training, along with a personal obsession with being thin as a victim of bulimia. When she was called upon to do a back flip off a dock in *On Golden Pond*, she learned the stunt herself rather than have someone else do it. Her workouts, peppered with encouragement and advice, reached women who had learned that liberation brings stress, and she promised a body that looked like hers and an inner self that would be at peace. In books, on audiotapes, and in the new videotape format, her workouts were a tremendous success, and the financial gains from the workout empire helped finance Tom Hayden's election to the California State Assembly in 1982.

But the surprising success of the workout enterprise did not bring about a realization of Fonda's dream of an identity of her own. Indeed, her divorce from Tom Hayden and marriage to media mogul Ted Turner seemed to mark yet another phase in Fonda's quest for identity. Just as Fonda the Sex Kitten had seemed anomalous when perched astride an anti-aircraft gun in North Vietnam, so too did the former political activist and feminist look odd doing the "Tomahawk Chop" with her husband at Atlanta Braves games. Fonda's attraction to Turner was, no doubt, a highly personal matter, but the fact remains that each had lost a parent to suicide and each had earned considerable praise and criticism in a highly public life.

Jane Fonda in the twenty-first century is thrice divorced and in the midst of yet another phase of her life. As a born-again Christian, she has embraced a commitment to faith that seems to fit the times. She continues to support good works as she did during her marriage to Turner, when his resources could match her commitment.[20] She describes her life as a "quest for growing up. . . . I had to invent myself, and I used men to do it."[21]

Today, Web sites abound that feature negative commentary from veterans and others who will not let the "Hanoi Jane" image fade into the back pages of history. In a 1988 interview with Barbara Walters for *20/20*, Fonda had an opportunity to apologize to her detractors:

> I would like to say something, not just to Vietnam Veterans in New Eng-land [some of whom were protesting at the site of her film shoot, attempting to shut down the production] but to men who were in Viet-nam, who I hurt, or whose pain I caused to deepen because of things I said or did. I was trying to end the killing and the war, but there were times when I was thoughtless and careless about it and I'm very sorry that I hurt them. And I want to apologize to them and their families.[22]

It is clear from the volume of anti-Jane material on the Internet that the apology has not been accepted. Jane Fonda may have found redemption with the movie-going public that identified with her apolitical characters, who found themselves in highly charged political situations and nearly always did the "right" thing; and she has certainly found success with her holistic approach to fitness and health, which has brought her wealth and even more celebrity than the accident of her birth or the quality of her talent. But for many Americans, she will always be "Hanoi Jane."

NOTES

1. Peter Braunstein, "Ms. America: Why Jane Fonda Is a Mirror of the Nation's Past Forty Years," *American Heritage* (July–August 2001); online at http://www.americanheritage.com/AMHER/2001/05msamerica.shtml

2. Ibid.

3. *Jane Fonda*, online at http://www.swingingchicks.com/jane_fonda.htm.

4. Braunstein, "Ms. America."

5. Ibid.

6. Edward Guthmann, "1969 'Barbarella' Is a Romp with a Babe," *San Francisco Chronicle*, September 13, 1996.

7. On GI resistance, see Barbara L. Tischler, "Breaking Ranks: GI Antiwar Newspapers and the Culture of Protest," in *Vietnam Generation* 2, 1 (1990): 20–50.

8. Online at http://www.countryjoe.com/backroom.htm.

9. "Left Face," *New Republic,* March 31, 1971, 9.

10. "Nag, Nag, Nag: Jane Fonda Has Become a Nonstop Activist," *Life*, April 23, 1971, 51.

11. Vivian Gornick's remarks are quoted in J. Hoberman, "GI Jane," *Village Voice*, May 2–8, 2001; online at http://www.villagevoice.com/issues/0118/hoberman/php.

12. See the *Pentagon Papers as Published by the New York Times* (New York: Quadrangle Books, 1971), 4:43; and Mary Hershberger, *Traveling to Vietnam: American Peace Activists and the War* (Syracuse: Syracuse University Press, 1998): 208.

13. The remarks of Peter Collier are cited in Henry Mark Holzer and Erika Holzer, "How 'Hanoi Jane' Betrayed America," *Insight*, March 2, 2002; online at http://www.insightmag.com/main.cfm/include/detail/storyid/195014.html.

14. Braunstein, "Ms. America."

15. See Holzer and Holzer, "How 'Hanoi Jane' Betrayed America."

16. Ibid.

17. Ibid.

18. Braunstein, "Ms. America."

19. But the Nobel committee's awarding of the coveted Peace Prize for his work on behalf of those who most need his insistence on freedom and justice, both during his administration and in the two decades since he left office, suggests that history will treat Carter more kindly than did the American electorate in 1980.

20. Fonda supported the Georgia Campaign for Adolescent Pregnancy Prevention. She also gave $12 million to Harvard University's School of Education to support programs for the study of women and girls.

21. Braunstein, "Ms. America."

22. Fonda's apology is reprinted online at http://geocities.com/fateymike/jane.html.

PART IV

Connect

13

"I Feel the Earth Move"

Carole King, Tapestry, *and the Liberated Woman*

Judy Kutulas

From its first distinctive piano chords to its final reinterpretation of "Natural Woman," Carole King's 1970 release, *Tapestry*, marked something new in the music business. Its achievements went beyond its measurable successes, its massive sales and multiple Grammy awards. *Tapestry* reflected both a shift in the music business and a larger social transformation. King was a singer-songwriter, one of a group of musicians, both male and female, who sang about the impact of the 1960s revolutions. Like that of James Taylor, Paul Simon, Jackson Browne, and Carly Simon, her music was personal and immediate. Together, these artists helped young people negotiate the social and cultural fallout of the 1960s. As the first woman in the singer-songwriter group to make it big, King sang directly to a changed demographic of young single women about their new experiences and feelings. She provided one model that young women might embrace, a "natural woman," as the song said, modern, liberated, and attuned to her own spiritual and sexual needs. *Tapestry* updated popular notions of the ideal woman, centering her in a universe she dominated and defined by her womanliness.

The world into which Carole King (then Carol Klein) was born in 1941 ascribed decided limits on women's roles. Although the Second World War briefly opened up opportunities for women, by the time King reached school age, those opportunities disappeared amid post-war concerns about women's power and Communism. Americans protected themselves against both by channeling women into the home and nuclear families, where their responsibilities were to nurture and serve.[1] King, who grew up middle-class and Jewish in Brooklyn, New York, was raised in a larger social atmosphere that discouraged girls from taking risks, imagining careers, or being independent. Americans also valued education, and one of the unresolved contradictions of what Betty Friedan called the feminine mystique was that women, destined mainly for the home, attended college in record numbers.[2] King, like other middle-class girls of her generation, went to college, in her case, Queens College.

College was the last fling before adulthood for a generation that married young and settled quickly into responsibilities such as mortgages and diapers. In 1950s America, teens became a constant source of social concern because they adhered to peer values more than parental ones. They were also big business, possessing as they did the money and leisure to consume cars, sodas, movies, and, particularly, rock and roll.[3] Rock and roll excited King, giving her a way of escaping into worlds beyond her limited horizons. At Queens College, much to her parents' dismay, she gravitated toward a musical crowd and became friends with aspiring musician Neil Sedaka (who wrote "Oh, Carol!" in her honor). She briefly attempted a musical career, recording a few novelty tunes, including "Oh, Neil!" in response to Sedaka, but quickly passed through the portal to adulthood, marrying and dropping out after only a year. Her new husband, chemistry student Gerry Goffin, must have looked like a steadying influence to her parents, a good catch who would steer her away from her dreams of making music. Instead, she influenced him. Before long, Sedaka introduced King to Don Kirchner, who arranged for her and Goffin to join his and Al Nevin's music publishing firm, Aldon Music.

King and Goffin were like a lot of young couples in the early 1960s. Early marriage was the norm, if not a guarantee that young couples wanted immediately to replicate their parents' lives. Materially, they wanted more than their parents had. Often, the allure of new houses, shiny station wagons, and matching furniture tempted girls into marriage. Young couples wanted more satisfying marriages, too, aspiring to egalitarian relationships built on complementary gender roles. Young women looked at their mothers and saw, as Wini Breines noted, "models to avoid," martyred and boring.[4] Eager to save up for houses and cars and also happy to stay in the public sphere a little longer, many teenage brides worked until they started having children. Thus, when King joined Aldon Music, it was hardly an act of rebellion, especially since her job was to back up Goffin's lyrics with tunes. Working on their music at first at night, after "Will You Love Me Tomorrow" hit the charts in 1960, King and Goffin quit their day jobs (she as a secretary, he as a chemistry lab assistant) and headed for Aldon's offices, next door to the center of the music business, the Brill Building.

The Brill Building stood for a particular kind of music. It was not the home of original rock and roll, which was based in African-American forms, Southern styles, and working-class white performers such as Elvis Presley and Jerry Lee Lewis. Original rock was raw, publicly associated with sex and juvenile delinquency. By the time Goffin and King joined the Brill Building milieu, its early rebelliousness had been tamed. Dick Clark harnessed its energy, smoothed its rough edges, and produced softer-sounding singers with cute, mainstream looks. Don Kirchner "master-minded the takeover of rock by the songwriters,"[5] who wrote tunes he then assigned to his stable of artists, marketing them relentlessly and scrupulously managing their images. Singers had little control over their product. At Aldon Music, teams of writers—often male-female pairs— composed pop songs rather than hard rock, music that "spanned the yawning stylistic gap between the sleek, sophisticated Tin Pan Alley era and the rock epoch."[6] As Gerry Goffin explained, to reach the main-stream teen market, songs could not be "too adult, too artistic, too correct. You should shy away from anything too deep or too happy."[7] This was music about teen "romantic fiction, . . . first meetings, hasty partings, finding love, losing friends."[8] Its themes and stories, in short, were safely rebellious, allowing teens to try on different identities while, in the end, reinforcing the gendered status quo.

In the romantic world of teen music, as well as in most teens' lived experiences, boys called the shots in relationships, although girls were not entirely without power. Different listeners heard different messages in songs. Teenage boys learned they were desirable and desired, so desired they could often misbehave. Girls, groomed for little else besides finding a guy, settling down, and raising a family, learned the paramount impor-tance of making good romantic choices. Bad choices limited their futures. But bad choices made for more interesting songs, allowing teenage girls a vicarious walk on the wild side. The stereotype of the good girl who falls hard for the "bad" boy appears often in Goffin/King songs. Some bad boys turned out to be good, which reinforced girls' faith and revealed parents' fallibility. But, more commonly, as titles such as "What I Gotta Do to Make You Jealous," "I Can't Stay Mad at You," and "Is This What I Get for Loving You" suggest, boys were not particularly amenable to reform, and girls' role in relationships was to suffer, worry, cry, and tolerate what they could not change.

Even though such songs seemed to paint a dismal picture of love for teenage girls, their drama, urgency, implied sexuality, and passion hinted at lives different from girls' mothers'. Goffin and King wrote for the branch of the music business that had sanitized rock by eliminating its overt sexuality with songs about first dates, first kisses, good girls and bad boys, all set to sappy strings. But, in truth, the sexual revolution was just around the corner, teenage culture was already changing, and teen songs reflected girls' sexual angst.[9] One of the most famous Goffin/King songs, "Will You Still Love Me Tomorrow," served up female desire in ballad form, coyly using a catch phrase to imply an act not directly identified. The female voice is not concerned about her reputation or what her parents will think. She feels sexual longing but worries about whether she's being taken advantage of by a boy who merely wants to score. In an era when nearly half of all females had sex before marriage,[10] the song hardly told a shocking story for teenagers. Hearing something girls debated quietly voiced publicly, though, was thrillingly illicit, particularly since it was not something parents wanted to hear. Equally important was the song's characterization of passion. Phrases such as "the magic of your sighs" suggested feelings so powerful they would overtake logic, reason, and social convention. For teenage girls, this kind of passion was intoxicating. "Will You Still Love Me Tomorrow" promised love so dramatic and special that it would transform their adult lives and distinguish them from their mothers' more mundane ones. In a world where selfless wife-and-mother was the normal female path, passion, romance, and drama empowered girls by promising them fulfillment too.

Yet, ironically, King herself well knew the reality behind the romantic teenage drama of the songs she helped write. She was a working mother to daughters Louise and Sherry. Nearly a third of all mothers worked in 1960, with little social accommodation of their needs.[11] King was lucky, because her career carried more family clout than the normative female role did. She could afford to employ a series of housekeeper/nannies (including Little Eva, before she was discovered by King and Goffin and recorded their song "The Loco-Motion"). She got to dress in smart career-woman suits and style her thick, curly hair into a neat pageboy. She made as much money as her husband did. Whether working or not, however, mothers bore the brunt of domestic responsibilities. King was no exception. She was invisible, a behind-the-scenes facilitator both at home and on the job. Her occasional forays into recording and performing went nowhere. She could not travel and did not like to perform live. As a "kind of plain-looking girl"[12] with what was then considered an "ethnic" nose and sometimes-unruly hair, she did not fit the stereotype of the perky, blond, WASP female performer, like Lesley Gore or Shelly Fabres. In the music business, as at home, her role was to support and be subservient, but never to be the center of attention.

Indeed, King worked in an industry where males counted for more than females, both as musicians and as audience. Those in charge of the business were almost all male. They had certain prejudices and assumptions about their work. They branded girls fans but boys true aficionados of the rock-and-roll genre. The distinction is critical, for the female audience was stereotyped in consumer terms while boys held the higher status of defining taste. Producers considered young girls' interest to be transitory and fickle, based "less in music than in chat and clothes and possessions and pictures,"[13] all the props of teen idols. Rock was about leisure and discretionary income. Girls had less leisure than boys because they were housewives-in-training. They had less pocket money too. After a few years spent enjoying fantasies about Dion or Fabian or Ricky Nelson, they switched to real boys and spent their money on clothes and makeup. Once married, they had neither spare cash nor leisure.[14] Female performers, who accounted for nearly a quarter of all Top Twenty hits in the 1960s,[15] were attractive to female listeners, but men controlled their packaging and seemed to think they needed a hook or style, as in the case of the glamorous Supremes, the cute Dixie Cups, or, in cultural critic Susan Douglas's great phrase, the "eat-my-dirt, in-your-face, badass" Shangri-Las.[16] While King co-wrote songs that often articulated a female voice in the early 1960s, she had little control over the larger business that objectified, stereotyped, and undervalued women.

In the second half of the 1960s, the once-successful King and Goffin partnership did less well, both professionally and personally. Music changed. The British invasion sent a number of U.K. artists to the top of the American charts, including the Beatles, the Rolling Stones, the Kinks, the Who, the Hollies, and the Yardbirds. A series of hard-rocking American artists such as Jefferson Airplane, the Doors, and Jimi Hendrix followed. These performers wrote their own songs without much control by producers. Sex, once only politely hinted at in songs, was right out there in the open in Jim Morrison's lyrics, Mick Jagger's hips, and Janis Joplin's aching voice. The rock revolution of the late 1960s encouraged musicians to write their own songs. The result was often harsh or shocking social, political, or cultural commentary, not the kind of soft, sweet songs that were King and Goffin's specialty. "Go Away Little Girl," a 1966 composition of theirs, seemed antiquated and silly when juxtaposed against the Beatles' "Eleanor Rigby" or the Stones' "Mother's Little Helper," both released the same year. After 1965, they had fewer and fewer big hits. Increasingly, less-prestigious artists performed their songs. Peggy Lipton of *Mod Squad* fame recorded three of the ten Goffin/King songs recorded in 1968. The Monkees, a producer-created pop band that did not even play its own instruments, recorded two others. King and Goffin were no longer cutting-edge. In the late sixties, they left the Brill Building scene, striking out on their own label, Tomorrow Records. Meanwhile, their marriage fell apart. King took their two daughters and moved to Los Angeles in search of "a new identity."[17]

King was not alone in feeling the need to reinvent herself. As the music scene suggested, teen culture was in flux, reflecting turbulent times. The general social upheaval triggered by the war in Vietnam left much of the country questioning traditional values and beliefs. Many young people rebelled against authority figures of all kinds—parents, teachers, political leaders. Although there had always been tensions between generations, by 1968 there was so much suspicion between parents and their children that it had a name: the generation gap. The younger generation was anti-authoritarian about lifestyle issues as well. Traditional social institutions, from the corporation to marriage, no longer appealed. Young people embraced the counterculture, with its emphases on self-awareness and living in the moment, while rejecting its opposite, the Establishment. The women's movement raised questions about women's roles, investing the quiet dread many girls felt as they looked at their mothers' lives with broader political meaning. Given all the changes going on around her, it is hardly surprising that Carole King no longer felt comfortable in a relatively traditional marriage or in the male-dominated, corporate world of the Brill Building.

King, like other young women, felt liberated from the confines of women's traditional roles by the 1960s revolutions. With liberation came all sorts of new choices. She made one when she left her marriage. She made another when she gave up the Brill Building for the Los Angeles folk-rock scene. Folk rock had far more musical respectability and authenticity than the pop songs King and Goffin wrote together. As King began making more choices on her own, she faced down some of her performing fears. In 1968, she joined a trio called The City, featuring Danny "Kootch" Kotchman of James Taylor's Flying Machine and Charles Larkey of the Fugs. Kotchman played guitar and Larkey bass, while King wrote the songs, played the piano, and sang vocals. The City struggled, mostly because King struggled with authority and voice. She had never before written the words and felt uncomfortable being the most dominant member of the group. Her insecurities came through in The City's music. The group's sound was forced, trapped somewhere between the poppishness of Goffin/King music and a more hip sensibility. "The main problem with The City," one analyst commented, "was that nobody was willing to take the initiative and push toward the front. Carole's personality should dominate, . . . but she hesitates."[18] Urged by a new friend she met through Kotchman, James Taylor, King decided to go solo at the end of the decade.

The musical world she entered as a solo artist was in significant disarray. The Beatles, who had long shaped musical trends, broke up in 1970. The doors opened for novelty, with nearly 56 percent of Top Ten hits that year by new artists.[19] FM radio, broadcast in stereo, started growing in college markets, offering relief from the Top Forty playlist and bringing a much wider variety of music to listeners.[20] Youth determined trends, thanks in part to the demographic bulge of the baby boom (which gave them market clout) but also because political and social upheaval had weakened traditional authority. As teens entered their twenties, they continued to listen to rock, broadening and age-differentiating the market in complicated ways. Whether in their teens or twenties, though, members of the baby boom generation identified with rebellion, an identity musicians happily supported, freed finally from the last constraints of impresarios like Ed Sullivan or Don Kirchner. Songs got longer, contained more explicit sexual and drug references, and openly expressed disapproval of American politics. A new style of performer emerged in the early 1970s: the singer-songwriter. The singer-songwriter wrote his or her own songs and performed them with stripped-down musical background, often just a piano or guitar. The style was "intimate, confessional, and 'personal,' . . . with precise, semi-autobiographical lyrics and moderate amplification." The primary audience for singer-songwriter music was what *Rolling Stone* journalists later called "proto-yuppies," white, middle-class, college-educated young people with personal experiences rooted in the late 1960s. Singer-songwriters were "the recording superstars of the 1970s."[21]

Singer-songwriters existed without the slick packaging of record producers. Their success rested on their ability to establish themselves as authentic voices, not on cosmic matters such as war or politics but on lifestyle. For the previous generation, there was really only one middle-class ideal, the one symbolized by picket fences and stay-at-home wives. But after the collapse of authority in the late 1960s, there were many more possibilities for how to live one's life, each fraught with complicated political, moral, and cultural significance. As the women's movement famously declared, the personal was political. King's rejection of pack-aged pop in favor of a more authentic, personal sound was part of a quest for personal and musical integrity fueled by the counterculture, just as her choice to step from behind the scenes and onto the stage solo reflected a changed sense of what a woman could do or be. Like her admirers, King was confused about who she was; but she had the advantage of being slightly older than most of her audience, with more experience, and the luxury of money and time to figure out her priorities and needs. She was well placed to be a voice for a particular generation of women.

King had many audiences, but young women were her biggest and most loyal fan base. Like King, they grew up with one set of expectations, only to discover their trajectories altered by the 1960s revolutions. Their horizons were wider, their possibilities endless; but they had few role models to suggest how they might behave or feel. Raised to be wives and mothers, increasing numbers of them were alone, a status once stigma-tized with words such as *old maid* or *spinster*. Many forces transformed the spinster and the old maid into the far more glamorous single woman. The sexual revolution, the counterculture, and the women's liberation movement reshaped her identity; but it was her consumer status that made the single woman a coveted market segment. Housewives were prime spenders on family necessities, such as detergent and frozen peas and socks. As women delayed before marrying, divorced more, and held jobs, their consumer status changed. They bought luxuries for themselves, personal products, and new convenience goods, such as single-serving packaged meals, running shoes, and hair dryers. They quickly became the most valuable market segment of the consumer culture.[22] The post-1960s female consumer was too mature to buy David Cassidy posters and too hip to buy Barry Manilow records. She gravitated to images of women full of "the vulnerability of growing and struggling into the role of a strong woman,"[23] like wavery-voiced Mary Richards (*The Mary Tyler Moore Show*) or earnest Alice Hyatt (*Alice Doesn't Live Here Anymore*).

Although James Dickerson has argued that the 1970s represented the worst decade for female rock performers in absolute numbers,[24] the reality was more complex. King, without realizing it, was poised to tap into this new market of female consumers.

Her second solo venture, 1970's *Tapestry*, represented something different in the music business, an album that spoke directly to young women. This is not to say King did not also appeal to men, for she did; but her album enjoyed its greatest resonance with women. Its cover helped explain why. To a generation used to reading the political significance of album covers (thanks to *Sergeant Pepper's Lonely Hearts Club Band*), *Tapestry's* cover trumpeted its distinctiveness. *Tapestry* was all about a particular kind of woman. In the cover photo King sits, looking considerably younger than her twenty-nine years. Her hair is wild and natural. She wears jeans and has bare feet. She seems simultaneously comfortable and vulnerable, small, fragile, but at home with her surroundings. Later in the decade, the disco divas would be out and prowling for what Donna Summer called "hot stuff." But King looks content being alone in her home, her cat and her tapestry to keep her busy. King represented a kind of ideal counterculture woman, and *Tapestry* invited young women to define their own safe, comfortable spaces within the evolving counterculture ideal.

Tapestry was a very mainstream album that marketed women's possibilities without offending other audiences. It made no overt references to feminism, and neither did King publicly. Instead, she embodied a muted feminism that straddled the counterculture and the women's liberation movement, an apolitical, somewhat essentialist stance that validated and celebrated women's differences from men. It vested women's stereotypic qualities—nurture and community—with new value, acknowledging women's roles as household producers and mothers but also forefronting female sexuality. Sitting on her window seat, working on her tapestry, King represented the thoughtful hippie woman or the earth mother. Earth mothers cooked (organically), made gardens bloom, took care of children, yet the experiences were vested with a different set of symbols than those of the classic June Cleaver mom of the 1950s. The earth mother was much more attuned to her own needs, in touch with her feelings, and sexually free. A martyr she was not.[25] She was, as the song said, a natural woman, but not the same natural woman as a decade before.

At the center of the earth mother's appeal to women was her sexual empowerment. The very first song on *Tapestry*, "I Feel the Earth Move,"

Fig. 13.1. The cover of King's album, *Tapestry*, reflects the qualities that made it so popular with young women, particularly its intimacy and earthiness. *Courtesy of Epic Records*

invoked the promise of female sexual fulfillment, playing with a phrase that stood for female orgasm. So many 1960s love songs cast females in the passive role, as indicated by the word *me* (object) rather than *I* (subject). "Does he love me, I want to know," asked the "Shoop, Shoop Song." "You just keep me hangin' on," complained the Supremes. Even King's classic asked, "Will you still love me, tomorrow?"[26] But in "I Feel the Earth Move," the female singer is the subject, and a deliriously happy subject at that. "I just lose control, down to my very soul," she declares. The focus is on the feelings and experience, not the lover. Few songs so effectively expressed the upside of the sexual revolution from the female perspective, with its promises of unbridled joy and physicality.

If, as historian Beth Bailey has persuasively argued, sexual interactions throughout much of the 1950s and 1960s were based on an economy of scarcity and a woman's responsibility was to protect her virtue,[27] then "I Feel the Earth Move" reflected a very different sensibility that sex is natural, normal, a set of desirable, exciting feelings and orgasmic sounds ("ooh, baby"). The song articulated the counterculture's emphasis on sex as a physical experience. Susan Douglas suggests that the girl groups of the early 1960s functioned as forums for debating sexual attitudes ("Are you really going out with him?" asks one of the Shangri-Las in "The Leader of the Pack") and supporting girls wronged by their men.[28] King and other 1970s women liberated sex from that kind of analysis, moving them closer to the counterculture's sexual ideal. Tomorrow is not part of the equation in "I Feel the Earth Move." Its love is in the present tense.

The love King sang about—and that experienced by many young women in the decade—was not the eternal, transcendental feeling captured in previous generations of love songs. If men thought the point of the sexual revolution and the counterculture was "more sex,"[29] women were more ambivalent. Raised to believe that true love lasted forever and that giving in to men's sexual demands devalued them as marriage material,[30] many women suspected that free love exploited them as women. And, indeed, the sexual revolution and the counterculture initially established a sexual dynamic predicated on men's needs and desires. The 1970s, however, redefined that dynamic to better suit women, and King was part of that cultural work. Her "It's Too Late" represented a very different view of love than teen pop songs offered. Here no one has cheated, but there is no happy ending either. Instead, "something inside has died, and I can't hide, and I just can't fake it." The song's version of love is realistic and detached. Love comes, love goes; even though she's "glad for what we had and how I once loved you," the romance is over and the singer knows she needs to move on. Love's capriciousness and its limited lifespan became a theme in 1970s culture, ranging in expression from Woody Allen's film *Annie Hall*, to Paul Simon's "Fifty Ways to Leave Your Lover." The idea echoed through sitcoms such as *Rhoda* and *The Mary Tyler Moore Show* and movies such as *The Way We Were* and *Coming Home*. It was the principle that drove the no-fault divorce craze of the late 1970s. King's was an early expression of something that would become a larger social trend. Love and romance, once the key elements determining a woman's adult life, became merely one part of a larger, fuller life. The sentiments expressed in "It's Too Late" were consistent with the women's movement's urgings that women find careers, have a variety of experiences, and live their lives for themselves and not for others.

Indeed, one of the most important themes running through *Tapestry* is the idea of being alone. Cheating boyfriends or bad boys do not make love melancholy in these songs; distance and separation do. But even if being apart from the one you love is depressing, King's lyrics make clear that what separates lovers or sours relationships is personal growth, and that growth is a dynamic, positive, natural thing. In "So Far Away," for example, she asks "Doesn't anybody stay in one place anymore?" even as she asserts that there are "so many dreams I've yet to find." King's music taps into the counterculture's value of being on the road, of travel as a means of self-discovery and awareness. The idea dates way back, of course, but it was generally a male prerogative, something Holden Caulfield or Jack Kerouac or Bob Dylan did. Even in the hippie communes of the 1960s, women were usually along as wives and mothers, cooking brown rice and birthing babies in tipis. In "Home Again" and "Way over Yonder," King claims the right to wander and explore for women as well as men, putting a womanly twist on it sometimes by adding a man at home waiting ("nobody else knows how to comfort me tonight"), but not always. King is honest about the experience of being alone, of searching for something: for women raised in the 1950s and 1960s, it was hard and scary, and it hurt. "I won't be happy till I see you alone again, till I'm home again and feeling right," she sings in "Home Again." However painful it is to be out there doing what the guys have been doing, though, *Tapestry* proceeds from the assumption that such personal growth is desirable and necessary. Despite the occasional more retrograde song ("Where You Lead," for instance), the album helped romanticize loneliness and separation for women, contributing to the place where the counterculture and the women's movement converged in their validation of self-discovery, self-awareness, and independence in women.

King's earth mother was liberated, independent, sexual, and self-aware, but also domestic. The home in the cover photo was *her* home, paid for by her earnings as a songwriter. Women in the 1950s went from their parents' homes to their husbands', with maybe a brief sojourn in a dormitory or sorority house to separate the two. Women in the 1970s were more likely to live on their own or with roommates. There were few models for how to live alone, and few other popular cultural spaces where living alone might be lauded as desirable for women. Meanwhile, thanks to the 1970s emphasis on lifestyle (as opposed to economic success in a bad economic decade), how those spaces looked, like how one wore one's hair or whether one wore jeans and sandals or skirts and hose, became a form of self-expression. Thus, the tiny details of *Tapestry*'s cover—the India print curtains in the window, the bare feet, the bare wood of the window seat—were all parts of a lifestyle revolution that let young women acknowledge difference and identity. Domestic at her core, King's earth mother was not domestic in the same ways as her listeners' mothers were. She was worldly-wise and independent, casual and organic, confident to establish her space on her own terms. The identity she modeled, both on the cover and in the songs within, forged new ground for women by being about something more than love, romance, and then husband and family. *Tapestry* is about the many, sometimes contradictory pieces of a modern woman's liberated identity.

In many ways, what is most modern about this lifestyle is what it lacks—formality, structure, commercialism, and, most important, a man. Although in "Where You Lead" home is wherever her lover wants it to be, in the rest of the songs and on the cover of *Tapestry*, the lover is an optional accessory. When she is lonely, she longs to see her lover's "face at my door," but the door is hers and life goes on without him. King sings about sex and relationships and transitory romance, never about diamond rings or white wedding dresses. Only about half the songs on the album are about romance. One of the more popular songs, "You've Got a Friend," emphasizes the joys of friendship, not romance. And, perhaps because King's good friend James Taylor made a big-selling recording of the same song, when most listeners heard it, the kind of friendship they imagined was between a man and a woman, an interaction not traditionally commemorated in songs and not common in most women's lives until the 1970s. *Tapestry* was one of the first albums to really open up the range of appropriate subjects for female singers, just as the persona King modeled suggested there were other aspects to a woman's life than wife and mother. "The sweet-tasting good life" centered on women making their own choices, free from the constraints of previous roles. King celebrated both the joys and the fears that came with that liberation, the sexual freedom, the independence, the loneliness, the need to be strong, and the desire to be taken care of. While other artists would pick up her themes later in the decade, and often say them louder and with less hesitation and ambivalence, her songs were out there first.

Certainly, within the genre of singer-songwriter music, *Tapestry* was such a phenomenon that it paved the way for other female singers and, to a degree, set the agenda for their albums. Joni Mitchell's *Blue* (1971) picks up similar themes, scattering images of lovers separated, of love affairs gone sour, and of women on their own. Carly Simon's *No Secrets* (1973) and *Hotcakes* (1974) look at the many parts of women's lives, including childhoods, relationships with other women, and the realities of marriage. Simon, then married to King's old friend James Taylor, posed for the cover of *Hotcakes*, which like *Tapestry* features the artist at a window, while visibly pregnant. Even Joan Baez's 1975 release, *Diamonds and Rust*, was her least-political album, one full of lost lovers and women living alone. As the decade progressed, the images of love and romance became more fractured and the women seemed, like Baez, to be going it increasingly alone. Throughout the 1970s, female singers sang about striking out on their own, forging new relationships, struggling, and succeeding. Even as the earth mother symbolized by King or Simon faded and was replaced by the more sexually assertive, less homebody disco diva, liberation, independence, and self-sufficiency remained the qualities women's music emphasized.[31]

Meanwhile, *Tapestry*'s success forced King to think about her own life as a modern woman. She was suddenly thrust into a very public spotlight. The album was released in May 1970 and a month later was the top-selling record in the country, a position it held for the next fifteen weeks. Four of its twelve songs were Top Ten hits. King was the first woman to win the Grammy Awards "grand slam"—album of the year, record of the year ("It's Too Late"), song of the year ("You've Got a Friend"), and best pop vocal performance by a woman. James Taylor scored a number one hit of his own with her "You've Got a Friend," and Quincy Jones's instrumental version of "Smackwater Jack" won the Grammy for best pop instrumental performance. King faced the daunting prospect of topping *Tapestry*'s success.

Traditionally, artists have marketed albums with tours, encouraging sales and preparing the audience for new releases. King had other priorities, actually being an earth mother, not alone in her Laurel Canyon home (the one featured on *Tapestry*'s cover) with her daughters by Goffin and a new husband, former band-mate Charles Larky. She had never liked performing live anyway, so she retreated to the studio, helping her musical family, playing piano on Taylor's *Mud Slide Slim* album, and writing songs for her *Tapestry* background singer, Merry Clayton. She followed *Tapestry* barely a year later with *Music*, which one biographer described as "a blatant but largely successful attempt to recreate the magic formula" of *Tapestry*.[32] Its most successful song, "Sweet Seasons," barely made it into the *Billboard* Top Ten. *Rhymes and Reasons* followed in November 1972 and *Fantasy* in 1973. The former was "in much the same vein"[33] as the other albums, while the latter failed to do what King did best: connect intimately with her audience by singing about shared personal experiences. Only one song, "You Light Up My Life," became an enormous hit, not for King but for pop singer Debbie Boone. As King tired of fame, *Tapestry*'s moment passed, hard rock revived, disco emerged, and punk exerted its influence. Women remained an important consumer audience for music, but with more possibilities catering to more tastes, they were not so easily a single audience for only one kind of music.

The larger social transformation that *Tapestry* helped popularize was one that promised women freedom and independence. With those choices, however, came responsibility. For King, personal integrity meant being "a singer" rather than "a star with a capital S"[34] while, in appropriately seventies fashion, being focused on lifestyle. Three years after *Tapestry*'s release, her *Current Biography* entry described her as "a contented homebody [who] drives her children to and from school in her battered white Volkswagen and enjoys preparing meals for her family." But King was no June Cleaver homebody; she practiced yoga, wore jeans, and fed her family sushi.[35] Her romantic life also mimicked the songs she sang about the transience of love. She has married four times. Her third husband, Rick Evers, died of a heroin overdose. After his death (1978), she left Los Angeles for rural Idaho, embraced a cause (environmentalism), and wrote and performed a popular album of children's songs, *Really Rosie*. Her primary interest has been her family, including the two daughters that have followed in their mother's footsteps, Louise Goffin and Sherry Goffin Kondor.

Tapestry remains a landmark album, still one of the best-sellers of all time. In 1999 it was reissued as a CD, and in 1995 the entire album was recorded, in song order, by famous fans, including Celine Dion and Rod Stewart, as *Tapestry Revisited*. Its release coincided with a Lifetime television network special on the making of the album and a home video featuring Carole King concert footage. "Where You Lead" is the theme song for *The Gillmore Girls*, a recent TV comedy-drama about a mother and daughter. King continues to speak out occasionally on environmental and parenting issues. These days, she uses a Web site (www.caroleking. com) to sell her music and put forth her ideas and beliefs. But King's contribution to modern culture extends beyond these smaller landmarks. *Tapestry* helped to demolish traditional assumptions about women and popular music. Following its success, record companies and radio programmers could no longer believe that the female audience counted for less, and that its notions of love were girlish, romantic, and virginal.[36] King helped give voice to a new post-1960s liberated female persona: sexy, sexual, hip, and independent, but womanly and domestic. *Tapestry* evokes the exhilaration of being on the cusp of a brave new world for women of a certain age.

NOTES

1. Elaine Tyler May, *Homeward Bound: American Families in the Cold War Era* (New York: Basic Books, 1988), p. 10.

2. Betty Friedan, *The Feminine Mystique* (New York: Dell, 1963; reprint, 1983), chap. 7.

3. "A Young $10 Billion Power: The U.S. Teen-Age Consumer Has Become a Major Factor in the Nation's Economy," *Life*, August 31, 1959, pp. 78–84; and Thomas Hine, *The Rise and Fall of the American Teenager: A New History of the American Adolescent Experience* (New York: Harper Perennial, 1999), chap. 12.

4. On materialism and marriage, see May, *Homeward Bound*, chap. 7. On gender roles in 1950s marriages, see Jessica Weiss, *To Have and to Hold: Marriage, the Baby Boom and Social Change* (Chicago: University of Chicago Press, 2000), pp. 17–19. On girls and their mothers in the 1950s, see Wini Breines, *Young, White, and Miserable: Growing Up Female in the Fifties* (Chicago: University of Chicago Press, 1992; reprint, 2001), p. 77.

5. David Szatmary, *A Time to Rock: A Social History of Rock 'n' Roll* (New York: Prentice Hall, 1987; reprint, 1996), p. 70.

6. Harry Sumrall, *Pioneers of Rock and Roll: 100 Artists Who Changed the Face of Rock* (New York: Billboard Books, 1994), p. 234.

7. As quoted in Szatmary, *Time to Rock*, p. 76.

8. Simon Firth, *Sound Effects: Youth, Leisure, and the Politics of Rock 'n' Roll* (New York: Pantheon, 1981), p. 33.

9. On the sexual revolution, see Beth Bailey, *From Front Porch to Back Seat: Courtship in Twentieth-Century America* (Baltimore: Johns Hopkins University Press, 1988; reprint, 1989), pp. 81–82. On teen songs and sexual angst, see Susan Douglas, *Where the Girls Are: Growing Up Female with the Mass Media* (New York: Random House, 1994), chap. 4.

10. May, *Homeward Bound*, p. 120.

11. On working women's guilt, see Weiss, *To Have and to Hold*, pp. 65–67.

12. Mitchell Cohen, *Carole King: A Biography in Words and Pictures*, ed. Greg Shaw (New York: Sire Books, 1976), p. 7.

13. Firth, *Sound Effects,* p. 226.

14. Ibid., pp. 232–33.

15. James Dickerson, *Women on Top: The Quiet Revolution That's Rocking the American Music Industry* (New York: Billboard Books, 1998), p. 242.

16. Douglas, *Where the Girls Are*, p. 86. See also Ruth Scovill, "Women's Music," in *Women's Culture: The Women's Renaissance of the Seventies*, ed. Gayle Kimball (Metuchen, N.J.: Scarecrow Press, 1981), p. 150.

17. As quoted in *Current Biography Yearbook* (New York: H. W. Wilson Company, 1974), p. 202.

18. Cohen, *Carole King,* 32.

19. See Richard Peterson and David Berger, "Cycles in Symbol Production: The Case of Popular Music," in *On Record: Rock, Pop, and the Written Word*, ed. Simon Frith and Andrew Goodwin (New York: Pantheon, 1990), chart, p. 146.

20. Susan Douglas, *Listening In: Radio and the American Imagination from Amos 'n' Andy and Edward R. Murrow to Wolfman Jack and Howard Stern* (New York: Random House, 1999), pp. 267–70.

21. The quotations and descriptions come from Ed Wards, Geoffrey Stokes, and Ken Tucker, *Rock of Ages: The Rolling Stone History of Rock and Roll* (New York: Rolling Stone Press, 1986), p. 471 (first two quotations); and Michael Fink, *Inside the Music Industry: Creativity, Process, and Business* (New York: Schirmer Books, 1996), p. 20.

22. Bonnie Dow, *Prime-Time Feminism: Television, Media Culture, and the Women's Movement since 1970* (Philadelphia: University of Pennsylvania Press, 1996), p. xx. Although most research has been done on women as a target market for television advertisers, their elevated status as a valuable market segment applies equally well to other popular cultural venues.

23. Scovill, "Women's Music," p. 155.

24. Dickerson, *Women on Top*, 125. He calculates that male performers had 77 percent of the Top Twenty hits during the decade and female performers only 23 percent (as compared to 76 versus 24 percent the decade before and 69 versus 31 percent the decade after).

25. Bruce J. Schulman, *The Seventies: The Great Shift in American Culture, Society, and Politics* (New York: Free Press, 2001), pp. 171–76; Lauri Umansky, *Motherhood Reconceived: Feminism and the Legacies of the Sixties* (New York: New York University Press, 1996), pp. 63–75.

26. Barbara Bradby suggests that girl-group songs were more complex, being about both fantasy and reality. See her essay "Do-Talk and Don't Talk: The Division of the Subject in Girl-Group Music," in Frith and Goodwin, eds., *On Record*, pp. 340–68.

27. Bailey, *From Front Porch to Back Seat*, pp. 77–96.

28. Douglas, *Where the Girls Are*, pp. 97.

29. Barbara Ehrenreich, Elizabeth Hess, and Gloria Jacobs, *Re-Making Love: The Feminization of Sex* (New York: Anchor Press/Doubleday, 1986), p. 74.

30. Bailey, *From Front Porch to Back Seat*, p. 95.

31. See Judy Kutulas, "'You Probably Think This Song Is about You'": The Women's Movement and Women's Music from Carole King to the Disco Divas," in *Disco Divas: The Women's Liberation Movement and Popular Culture in the 1970s*, ed. Sherrie Inness (Philadelphia: University of Pennsylvania Press, 2003), pp. 172–93.

32. Cohen, *Carole King*, p. 38.

33. Martin Strong, *The Great Rock Discography* (New York: Times Books, 1994; reprint, 1998), p. 440.

34. *Current Biography*, p. 203.

35. Ibid., p. 203.

36. Firth, *Sound Effects*, p. 233.

14

Sonia Sanchez
"Fearless about the World"

Michelle Nzadi Keita

In the 1960s, African Americans organized, voted, faced fire hoses, and bled under police batons as they demanded their full rights as citizens. They also wrote. Writing proved vital to their insistence on being reckoned with *as human beings* by much of the country.

African American women, moreover, had to break the silence imposed by their place at the bottom of the bottom, the "double jeopardy" of being black and female described by writer Frances Beale.[1] They faced a formidable challenge: Laws had to be changed and written; notions of racial and gender identity subjected to question, dispute, and redefinition; an entire culture re-imagined. This radical reshaping of American culture would demand radical shifts in ways of seeing, knowing, and marking self and others.

Who would capture the emotional forces guiding this transition? It would take more than manifestos or task force reports for African American women to be seen in an authentic way. It would take artists willing to breathe power into muffled voices. Sonia Sanchez was one such artist.

Alabama-born as Wilsonia Benita Driver in 1934, Sanchez lost her mother, Lena, at age one. Her grandmother then became the maternal figure who, by her example as church deaconess, allowed her granddaughter to learn "how to listen to women gathering to take care of business" and to hear the "fruitful, quiet, beautiful sound of women's voices, women's concern for each other. . . . You wanted to be like those women, the way they were able to resolve things."[2] What Sanchez gained from her grandmother's voice and presence would shape her identity profoundly: "She let me be my wild self, my tomboyish self, and that was good for me. . . . She let me run outside without restrictions, so therefore

279

I have never feared anything. And I think when you write you've got to be fearless about yourself, about the world."[3] Sanchez attributes her early sense of safety and respect to her grandmother, who "knew [Sanchez] was different" and encouraged others, as well, to "'just let her be.'"[4]

At six, when her grandmother died, Sanchez began to stutter. Instead of talking, she wrote notes and poems in secret. After a series of temporary arrangements, the family migrated to New York City when Sanchez was nine. A profuse reader, she attended public schools, where she excelled—in part, she has said, because the academic discipline of her early southern schooling instilled in her an attitude that her father reinforced.[5] Throughout adolescence she absorbed and observed Harlem, with its uneasy mix of hope and peril, gradually learning to walk "with razorblades between her teeth."[6]

After receiving a B.A. in political science from Hunter College in 1955, Sanchez took graduate courses at New York University. A workshop there with poet Louise Bogan provided her with a place to develop as a creative writer, studying poetic form and craft. Bogan's course catalyzed a group of writers, including Sanchez, who continued to meet independently throughout the late 1950s. Consequently, Sanchez began to publish in literary journals such as the *Minnesota Review* and the *Transatlantic Review*.[7]

As 1959 became 1960, Sanchez met poet-playwright Amiri Baraka (then LeRoi Jones) at the Five Spot, a Greenwich Village jazz club, for the first time. In an unpublished interview, Sanchez recalled that "Baraka called out to me, 'Sanchez, I hear you're a poet. I'm editing this anthology . . . why don't you send me some work?'" Weeks passed before Sanchez, who saw herself as an apprentice, realized he was serious. She recalls, "Baraka would introduce me [by saying] 'Here's Sonia Sanchez, she's a poet.' So I was named, and in a sense, when you're named, you become that which you're named. . . . So I began to think of myself as a poet, and began that serious work of writing and sending work out."[8]

A member of the New York branch of the Congress of Racial Equality (CORE) in the early 1960s, Sanchez received her activist training on picket lines, demanding open housing from Long Island developers and negotiating African American employment from trade unions. She speaks with satisfaction about a tense standoff between CORE picketers and New York police. When Harlem Hospital sought to build an extension using union workers, CORE refused to disband its picketing unless blacks were allowed into the union. Negotiations wore into the early morning hours, but ultimately CORE succeeded; black workers were admitted, among them Sanchez's brother, Wilson Driver, an electrician.[9]

CORE was a pivotal experience for Sanchez, feeding the will to confront injustice and re-imagine power that her poems reveal. Through her activist work with CORE, Sanchez met Malcolm X. After hearing one of his street-corner speeches, she remembers her first words to him, spoken in awe: "Mr. X, I didn't quite agree with everything you said." Not the least bit offended, Malcolm answered her prophetically. "He looked at me with those eyes, so gentle and loving, and said 'But you will one day, my sister.'"[10]

As the mid-1960s approached, the phrase "Black Power" elicited an evolving black consciousness that intersected with the Civil Rights movement. CORE engaged in a struggle "between people who wanted to get whites out [of Civil Rights work] and those who wanted them in," Sanchez says.[11] Drawn to black nationalism through the ideas of Malcolm X and Baraka's network of artists, Sanchez shifted her focus away from CORE, which viewed Malcolm X "as a racist."[12] With this shift, Sanchez's life took a direction that would guide her for decades. In 1964 she turned her energies toward community art and youth, working with Harlem Youth Opportunities Unlimited (HARYOU-ACT) and the Black Arts Repertory Theatre/School (BART/S) to organize cultural events including plays, poetry readings, and discussions.[13]

This association drew her into the nexus of the Black Arts movement— a cultural revolt that redefined African American arts and literature with brash ferocity. The poems and essays of Baraka and late playwright-poet Larry Neal advanced its theory; the political and social activism of numerous artists such as poets Askia M. Toure and Haki Madhubuti energized its range of concerns.[14] This was a movement not motivated simply to express but also to establish a different worldview, an ideology grounded in expression. It described "Black Art" as art that spoke "directly to the needs and aspirations of Black America."[15] It took a position "radically opposed to any concept of the artist that alienates him from his community."[16] Consequently, Sanchez found her focus as a poet-activist.

As a woman within this movement, Sanchez occupied a unique place. Her poetry, containing what scholar Kalamu Ya Salaam calls a "word arsenal" of "hyperbole, name calling (wolfing, the dozens), double entendre and . . . profanity,"[17] established a voice and stance roundly categorized as militant (a label that persisted long after the sixties). Salaam describes her sixties-era poems as "brief, razor sharp, and full of scorn and invective for 'white America.'"[18] Indeed, Sanchez displayed a style that set her apart from many of her contemporaries, male and female. Her work also demonstrated a tangible example of Neal's call for the "Black artist [to] address himself to . . . reality in the strongest terms possible."[19]

In 1965, after the death of Malcolm X and the closing of BART/S, Sanchez left New York. Working with Baraka, playwrights Ed Bullins and Marvin X, and poet Sarah Fabio, she helped found the first Black Studies program at San Francisco State College (now University) in 1966. Sanchez says that her efforts were motivated in part by her college experience, during which she "never, ever, ever . . . [saw] anything about [Blacks] that was positive." She taught in San Francisco until 1969 and ended that year in a teaching position at the University of Pittsburgh.[20]

As the decade drew to a close amid increasing anti-war protests, the emergence of women's movement, the assassinations of Martin Luther King and Robert Kennedy, and riots in American cities, Sanchez gained prominence. Her voluminous Afro, aggressive poetics, and activist work made her an emblem of powerful black womanhood. Through the *Journal of Black Poetry* and *Negro Digest,* her poems reached a wider African American community. *Drama Review* published her play "The Bronx Is Next" in 1968. In the coming years, she would also write the plays "Sister Son/ji," "Uh Huh, but How Do It Free Us?" "Malcolm/ Man Don't Live Here No Mo'," and "I'm Black When I'm Singing, I'm Blue When I Ain't."[21] Participation in the Black Arts movement led to her inclusion in anthologies by both independent black presses and mainstream white publishers. By the time Broadside Press, an independent black press responsible for bringing attention to several notable poets, published her first book in 1969, Sanchez had already become a recognizable poetic voice of sweeping change and vision.

A girl with faintly budding breasts in a simple school dress appears on the cover of Sanchez's first volume, *Homecoming.* On inky black bare feet, she treads lightly, but her posture is deliberate and poised. In one hand she hoists a spear. Drawn by a Black Panther Party artist known only as Emory, the image may reflect anti-colonial revolutions then underway in southern and West Africa, struggles in which children played distinct roles, instances in which a school girl and a warrior could be one and the same. This initial image suggests that Sanchez intends to combine the familiar and the unexpected in the service of change, that women in her poems will live, speak, and establish presence. The young woman warrior indicates that change is likely to be radical and aggressive, to compel action, to—in some way or another—unsettle.

The poems in *Homecoming* comment on the social landscape of the United States in the 1960s. The slim volume raises a range of fundamental issues, ignited by the times, bound by a common idea of power: economic, political, cultural, personal. The poems voice black pride but do not romanticize or deny harsh reality. The poet draws from political leaders as well as the music black consumers buy. Further, she unearths some of the decade's sexual politics of race, evoking a counterpoint to the sexual revolution underway at the time. She launches an assault on the sense of American cultural hegemony that led Black Arts movement theoretician Larry Neal to advocate "a radical reordering of the western cultural aesthetic."[22] But the voice that inhabits these poems also recognizes the diversity of roles African American women have played: as teachers, wives, and mothers; as mainstays of the Civil Rights movement; as community organizers, artists, and intellectuals. It examines the community at close range, as does Toni Cade's pivotal anthology *The Black Woman*, in which Fran Sanders questions how the black woman feels about her relationship to "the new breed of Black man";[23] Abbey Lincoln wonders "[w]ho will revere the Black woman";[24] and Toni Cade analyzes contraception as a potential tool of both genocide and self-empowerment.[25]

Homecoming addresses the matter of black female expressive power as Sanchez unsettles the public silence black women historically employed as a survival tool. The volume announces her as a poet willing to reach into the inner stores of anger, abandonment, pain, celebration, love, and sexuality, qualities that African American women held in reserve. In general, these were emotions black women rarely disclosed publicly, or perhaps even privately at that point in time, in an effort to embody responsibility, accommodate family and community needs above their own, and transcend the history of rape and exploitation they inherited through American slavery.

Historically, African American women have striven for a "ladylike" public presence, often through women's clubs and church activities, to create a dignity for themselves that they were not granted by American society. Women in Sanchez's poems, however, are freed from such constraints through language and subject matter. "The poets of the day could not just stay introspective," Sanchez explains. "This was a period when we called white people a lot of names and cussed them out a lot. But it was also a period when we began to say that we had to move beyond cussing out white folk and . . . do the work we needed to do for our survival."[26]

The speaker in one of two poems titled "to all sisters" asks, in anaphoric lines, "what a white woman got?"[27] Each time in the monologue (which could also be read as a call-and-response dialogue), the speaker answers her own question, as in the first stanza: "cept her white pussy / always sucking after blk/ness."[28] Sanchez suggests a self-affirming posture black women may choose as an alternative way to evaluate themselves when confronted with the recurrent presumption of white female superiority. She takes aim at white female beauty as an emblem of mythic American beliefs: purity, success, sexual allure. She seeks to stabilize the self-esteem of women whom those beliefs devalued. Overtly, in its blunt challenge and use of vulgarity, the poem reveals the probability of pent-up frustrations within black women and offers psychological relief from them.

In a companion poem on this entwined issue of race and sex, "to all brothers," the speaker addresses a contentious subject: a black woman's sense of rejection by black men. Sanchez subtly castigates those men who allow white women to "in/tegrate [their] / blackness" and the women themselves, who "will say out/right / baby I want / to ball you."[29] The poem demonstrates a lifted silence about centuries-old emotional pain and divisions having much to do the systemic oppression of enslaved black people. The speaker's voice is raw with this cultural knowledge, calling for accountability by men at large and yet indicating the black woman's active sense of abandonment. It underscores some of the dialogues and debates triggered by the ideological clash between pro-integrationist Civil Rights groups and black nationalists, some of whom advocated separatist platforms. Sanchez further questions views of the black family as espoused by Muslims and cultural nationalists-both of whom accepted submissive roles for women. She tempers the interracial ideals so closely bound to the 1960s with this unapologetic observation, made by a "sister" who "knows / and waits."[30] This sister uses her liberated tongue to free other women from the notion that, in a decade of change, they must continue to mumble or hold their silence about what they perceive to be true.

By advancing such woman-centered views in her poems, Sanchez challenges sexism within the society at large, and by implication, within the Black Arts movement and other such community-based initiatives. She was, in her own words, "one of the few female[s] on the circuit with mostly male poets" and, thus compelled, "brought issues of women and children, love and respect when men were always talking in general terms about changing the country."[31] The poems of *Homecoming* bear her out; women's voices assess a wide range of concerns, and do so with an equally wide emotional scope. Fearless and faithful, the speaker of "poem at thirty" offers her hand to the "black man / stretching scraping,"[32] while the simply titled "poem" seeks to affirm black eighth-graders' beauty.[33] However, "to a jealous cat" readily questions and rebukes notions of heterosexual manhood as grounds for controlling women.[34]

Sanchez's work thus becomes a late 1960s response to Civil Rights activist Pauli Murray's retrospective observation that "despite the crucial role which Negro women . . . played [during the Civil Rights movement] in the struggle . . . the aspirations of the black community [were] articulated almost exclusively by black males," with "very little public discussion of the problems, objectives, or concerns of black women."[35]

Romanticism abounded in the late 1960s as to the meaning of the term *revolutionary*. Did revolutionary black women work alongside men as equals in organizing for social change? Did they limit themselves to home, providing a domestic foundation and raising babies for the revolution? Did they follow or challenge existing leadership or establish their own? Toni Cade, in scrutinizing the question of gender roles, cites a

> dangerous trend in some quarters of the Movement to program [the Black woman] into a cover-up, shut-up, lay-back-and-be-cool obedience role . . . that supposedly neutralizes the acidic tension . . . between Black men and Black women.[36]

Frances Beale similarly calls for a redefined "understanding of traditional personal relationships between man and woman" as revolutionary behavior, noting that these relationships often oppress women. In stating that "[t]o die for the revolution is a one-shot deal; to live for the revolution means taking on the more difficult commitment of changing our day-to-day life patterns,"[37] Beale underscores Sanchez's vision. By writing from a woman-centered point of view, Sanchez was waging womanist revolution.

In allusions to capitalism, racism, class politics, and genocide, Sanchez chooses epithets usually directed to women and deflects them to a larger, recontextualized target. America becomes a "white whore," a "white son of / a bitch," and a "country of sheep," as well as a place of "gents / and /

gigolos . . . , liars / and / killers . . . , dreamers /and drunks."[38] The speaker thrusts, threatens, snatches the reader by the shoulder. She curses, spits, and laughs over the carcass of an America seen as dying but still dangerous. In "for unborn malcolms," a steely voice calls for retribution for the murder of Malcolm X:

> git the word
> out that us blk/niggers
> are out to lunch
> and the main course
> is gonna be his white meat.
> yeah.[39]

In short, Sanchez articulates rage, the rage of suffering and loss, unaccountable and unrecognized over centuries, on the part of black Americans as a group, and black women in particular. Her strident poems exorcise and purge. Equally important, they present a precise picture of the various ways such a population might protest for change. Contemporaneous critic Richard Barksdale recognized that "like other Black poets in other times, these new Black poets are merely being responsive to the conditions under which they have had to live and write."[40] Because Sanchez lived and wrote from the particular vantage point of a black woman, her work is a document of black women's rage.

Yet if, through Sanchez, women often sang dissonant scales, they could also sing harmoniously. Sanchez's classic poem "black magic" testifies that black men and women can and do love each other. Their bond contains a mystical, powerful joy. The voice of a loving woman asserts sexual delight directly to her lover in a way that affirms them both: "black / magic is your / touch / making / me breathe."[41] This black woman's voice is a rare literary experience—unashamed of desire, liberated from appeasing white America, and aloof to stereotypes of the black woman as the hypersexual, unrapeable whore. Sanchez extended a message of coexistence and hope, despite the looming ideological struggles to define black manhood and womanhood in the late 1960s.

As clearly as Sanchez articulated rage, she spoke of love and collectivity. Using innovative language, transgressive urgency, distinct tone, and social critique, she redefined love as a source of power, rather than a distraction without political meaning. Love, she asserted, is not always a

Fig. 14.1. Sonia Sanchez in 1966, reading poetry at a workshop held at the Countee Cullen Library in New York City. *Photo reprinted with permission of Sonia Sanchez*

personal luxury. Struggle may also be sweet. And the power of love, its personal and political strength as a force for black liberation, transcended heterosexual romance. Love, redefined, could and must include both relationships among women and a healthy regard for self.

With a focus and embrace that few others could match in the late 1960s, Sanchez named the collective power of African American women as a potent agent for change. This belief in transformation is dramatized by "summer words of a sistuh addict," in which a young girl states that

> the first day i shot dope
> was on a sunday.
>   i had just come
>   home from church
> got mad at my motha
> cuz she got mad at me. u dig?[42]

An unidentified "someone," a sensitive presence, raises, for the young woman and for readers, the possibility of hope through a startling question:

> sistuh.
> did u
> finally
>   learn how to hold yo/mother?[43]

With this question ringing in the background, the poem closes with the image of a supportive group, reinforcing that hope with singing.

In the end, after rage, love, and communion, Sanchez did not pretend to know all the answers. This reckoning is ultimately part of the ultimate return to self and origins that marks the title poem of her volume, a collection that powerfully signals the close of a powerful decade. She saw and cited the complexity of the black world, having lived among "all those hide and/seek faces peeling with freudian dreams."[44] In "homecoming," the speaker represents a generation—those children of southern migrants who crossed the borders into urban cities and northern sites of higher education—who return home from college, as

> Sanchez did, to
> watch all
> the niggers killing
> themselves with . . .
> needles
> that
> cd
> not support
> their
> stutters.[45]

If coming to terms with a transformed self and rejecting degradation solved some problems, it added others, as in "summary," wherein a woman has swallowed pills and wine, wandered in thoughts personal and polemic, and found herself alone, discovering that "one night of words / will not change / all that."[46]

Ultimately, Sanchez propelled the initiatives of the 1960s into the culture with such force because she was not simply writing them but living them. Having grown up in Harlem, she knew firsthand that "it / ain't like they say / in the newspapers."[47] She wrote continuously, not in isolated contemplation but always in concert with motherhood and the need for economic survival. In the late 1960s, Sanchez was married to Etheridge Knight, who spent time in prison before emerging as a notable poet.[48] Knight battled drug addiction for most of his adult life, a battle that certainly impacted on Sanchez and surfaced in her work at the time. While working on the project of developing Black Studies at then San Francisco State College, Sanchez attracted the FBI and was evicted from her apartment. Later, she had consistent difficulty in finding a teaching job after relocating to New York City. By this time she was a divorced single parent, supporting a daughter and two sons.[49] It becomes apparent that the issues that underlie a woman's right to pursue a life of her own choosing wound tough and constant threads through the fabric of Sonia Sanchez's life. This poet knew the underside of struggle. Her poems made clear how much revolution costs and how worth the price it could be if black women—and men—pointed their love and rage toward liberation.

NOTES

1. Frances Beale, "Double Jeopardy: To Be Black and Female," in *Words of Fire: An Anthology of African-American Feminist Thought*, ed. Beverly Guy-Sheftall (New York: New Press, 1995), 146.

2. Sonia Sanchez, personal interview, 30 April 1995.

3. Ibid.

4. Juanita Johnson-Bailey, "Sonia Sanchez: Telling What We Must Hear," *Ms.*, July–August 1998, 53.

5. Sanchez interview, April 1995.

6. Sonia Sanchez, "Present," *I've Been a Woman: New and Selected Poems* (Sausalito: Black Scholar Press, 1978), 55.

7. Sonia Sanchez, personal interview, 10 December 2002.

8. Sanchez interview, April 1995.

9. Sanchez interview, December 2002.

10. Ibid.

11. Ibid.

12. Ibid.

13. Ibid.

14. Houston Baker Jr., "The Florescence of Nationalism in the Sixties and Seventies," in *The Journey Back: Issues in Black Literature and Criticism* (Chicago: University of Chicago Press, 1980), 119.

15. Larry Neal, "The Black Arts Movement," in *African American Literary Criticism, 1773–2000,* ed. Hazel Arnett Ervin (New York: Twayne Publishers, 1999), 122.

16. Ibid.

17. Kalamu ya Salaam, "Sonia Sanchez," in *Dictionary of Literary Biography* 41, *Afro-American Poets since 1955*, ed. Trudier Harris and Thadious M. Davis (Farmington Hills: Gale Research Co., 1985), 297.

18. Ibid.

19. Neal, "Black Arts," 124

20. Sanchez interview, December 2002.

21. ya Salaam, "Sonia Sanchez," 295–96.

22. Neal, "Black Arts," 122.

23. Fran Sanders, "Dear Black Man," in *The Black Woman: An Anthology*, ed. Toni Cade (New York: New American Library, 1970), 73.

24. Abbey Lincoln, "Who Will Revere the Black Woman?" in Cade, ed., *The Black Woman*, 80.

25. Toni Cade, "The Pill: Genocide or Liberation?" in Cade, ed., *The Black Woman*, 164.

26. Zala Chandler, "Voices beyond the Veil: An Interview with Toni Cade Bambara and Sonia Sanchez," in *Wild Women in the Worldwind: Afra-American Culture and the Contemporary Literary Renaissance*, ed. Joanne M. Braxton and Andree Nicola McLaughlin (New Brunswick: Rutgers University Press, 1990), 358.

27. Sonia Sanchez, *Homecoming* (Detroit: Broadside Press, 1969), 27.

28. Ibid.

29. Ibid., 10.

30. Ibid.

31. Sanchez interview, April 1995.

32. Sanchez, *Homecoming*, 11.

33. Ibid., 22.

34. Ibid., 13.

35. Pauli Murray, "The Liberation of Black Women," in Guy-Sheftall, ed., *Words of Fire*, 188–89.

36. Cade, ed., *Black Woman*, 102.

37. Beale, "Double Jeopardy," 154–55.

38. Sanchez, *Homecoming*, 14–15.

39. Ibid., 28.

40. Richard K. Barksdale, "Humanistic Protest in Recent Black Poetry," in *Modern Black Poets: A Collection of Critical Essays*, ed. Donald Gibson (Englewood Cliffs: Prentice-Hall, 1973), 154.

41. Sanchez, *Homecoming*, 12.

42. Sonia Sanchez, *We a BadDDD People* (Detroit: Broadside Press, 1970), 35.

43. Ibid.

44. Sanchez, *Homecoming*, 9.

45. Ibid.
46. Ibid., 15.
47. Ibid., 9.
48. ya Salaam, "Sonia Sanchez," 299.
49. Sanchez interview, December 2002.

15

A Beacon for the People
The Sixties in Dianne McIntyre

Veta Goler

In 1965, writer LeRoi Jones (later known as Amiri Baraka) wrote a poetic essay titled "The Revolutionary Theatre." Turn all their faces to the light, Jones wrote, "[A]nd if the beautiful see themselves, they will love themselves."[1] These words capture what is for some the essence of the American black liberation struggle of the 1960s and 1970s and the sentiment that motivated multifaceted art forms used as tools or weapons in that struggle. There were two fundamental approaches to addressing the oppressive conditions African Americans faced. One approach was to confront white people about individual and systemic racism. The other was to instill pride and hope in black people by "turning their faces to the light" of their own beauty. These two approaches converged in a series of dramatic and long-lasting products of the 1960s: Walls of Respect. Painted on buildings in urban black neighborhoods and business districts, these large murals depicted black heroes and scenes from African American life. Even today, painted legacies of this art movement serve the function of instilling hope and inspiration in residents of black communities.

The first mural, which came to be known as the Great Wall of Respect and established the name for the larger project, was a twenty-by-sixty-foot scene painted on a building in Chicago by a group of revolutionary visual artists. Like the walls that followed, it was designed both to build self-esteem and to stimulate revolutionary action in black people. The wall in Chicago catalyzed a movement that resulted in more than one thousand inner-city murals across the country by 1975.[2] The creation of the first wall quickly became a community event, as residents, political activists, and tourists watched its progress. In addition, as the visual artists worked, musicians, writers, dancers, and singers made their own creative offerings at the site, in support and appreciation of the wall's development.³

Wall artists took the art of painting out of the studio, magnified it, and placed it in the community in a way that allowed artists, politicians, and community members to interact with each other as they engaged the art. The art and the interaction of the people were all part of the black liberation struggle. Similarly, choreographer Dianne McIntyre transformed traditional modern dance movement and choreographic processes. She modified them with her own movement vocabulary, revealed her dancers' effort and intensity, and incorporated new music. Then she placed all this in her studio, on the concert stage, in the theater, and in the streets for artists and members of the community to enjoy. She also opened her studio as a gathering place for artists and others who were interested in engaging each other in creative collaborations and dialogue. Dianne McIntyre, a woman artist whose work grew out of 1960s political activism, exhibits the kind of uplift approach to revolution taken by artists such as those who created the Walls of Respect.

Chronologically and artistically, after Katherine Dunham and Pearl Primus, Dianne McIntyre was the next major African American female modern dance choreographer. Dunham and Primus, pioneers of black modern dance, established internationally recognized dance companies with highly skilled dancers performing repertoires based in Africanist aesthetics. Both women had disbanded their companies by the mid-1960s. It was almost a decade before an African American woman choreographer—Dianne McIntyre—filled the vacancy they left. From 1972 to 1988, McIntyre directed her company and school, Sounds in Motion, in Harlem, New York. Known for her collaborations with jazz musicians, McIntyre is the most important black woman dance artist to emerge from the 1970s. She has developed a distinctive body of work that features an idiosyncratic use of music and a dynamic movement style. Modern dance and African American social dance forms, gesture, performance intensity, and raw energy combine in dance that is both down-home earthy and highly elevated. Today, she is a prolific independent choreographer, creating concert dance and dance theater, and choreographing for theater, television, film, and recording artists.

Born in 1946 in Cleveland, Ohio, McIntyre came of age during the politically charged 1960s. The cultural and political intensity of these times, as well as one of the major movements of the era, the Black Arts movement, shaped McIntyre as a young artist. The Black Arts movement's overarching premise was that art could serve as an effective weapon in the liberation struggle by encouraging self-affirmation, self-determination, and self-support for black people. Movement artists believed that art did not exist for itself but for the sake of the revolution they wished to bring about. They claimed that art was not an elitist endeavor but should serve the masses, and they worked in and from a black aesthetic. The Wall of Respect adhered to these principles, as would McIntyre's choreography.

Modern dance began to develop around the turn of the twentieth century. Initially, European American modern dance pioneers rebelled against the rigid, codified, and—to them—irrelevant genre of ballet. In addition, their work countered what they saw as non-substantive dance in vaudeville and other "popular culture" venues. By the early 1930s, they had worked to create dance that would be considered "serious," American "art." Black choreographers were on a related quest. For them, this meant, in part, actively questioning their goals for the art form and the nature of their subject matter. "What shall the Negro dance about?" was the topic of discussion at a 1933 dance forum.[4] The artists of that generation knew they had to take corrective measures to counter racist and stereotypic images of black people that had been imprinted on the national consciousness during minstrelsy. They also sought to bring forth material from their own lives and culture as worthy of presentation on the concert stage. Thus, dance pioneers Katherine Dunham and Pearl Primus, and the less well known Hemsley Winfield, Edna Guy, and Asadata Dafora, created serious dance that ensured that black thematic material and African-based aesthetics became acceptable for the concert stage.

By the mid-1940s, white mainstream modern dancers had established the art form with specific approaches to choreography and a few well-defined movement vocabularies based on the teachings and theories of a handful of choreographers. Modern dance communicated meaning and emotion through virtuosic technique and the use of sets, costumes, lights, props, and other clearly theatrical elements.

The next generation of African American choreographers, who came to prominence after black concert dance had achieved an initial grounding in the work of Dunham and Primus, also focused on the black experience. Starting from the early 1950s, Donald McKayle and, later, Alvin Ailey, Eleo Pomare, and Rod Rodgers—all men—created work that presented different facets of black life and aesthetics. Although some of their repertories included universalist abstract pieces, much of their work was literal or representational of black experiences. For example, Ailey depicted scenes from the black church and the juke joint, and Eleo Pomare created works that conveyed the anger of black men living in urban decay and pathology.

The politically and culturally turbulent decades that surrounded McIntyre's development into a mature artist were a time when European American dancers, like other artists, were rethinking their concepts of art and its place in the world. Many of them were discarding old, "establishment" ideas about dance. They were creating their own concepts and engaging in new practices regarding what dance was, who could make and perform dances, and where dances could be presented. They sought to democratize dance and thus rejected all signs of elitism, including star systems and virtuosity, as well as messages and emotions in dance. They rejected, in fact, the very idea that dance had to be "about" something. Instead, they employed movement to carry out tasks, performing with a "backstage" demeanor and making dances that communicated simply movement. In other words, they were committed to art for art's sake, a concept antithetical to Black Arts movement sentiments.

McIntyre's unique brand of modern dance developed from her "traditional" training and from "revolutionary" influences she absorbed. As a student at Ohio State University from 1964 to 1969, she studied the early European dance forms—known by dance researchers as "pre-classic" dances—that gave her a strong traditional background in dance composition.[5] One of the things McIntyre loved about Ohio State was studying dance history.[6] She was drawn especially to the dance of indigenous African and Asian societies and was moved by the fact that in these societies, "the dance was not something outside of the necessities of people's everyday lives."[7] Just as Dunham and Primus demonstrated the value of dance in anthropological contexts, McIntyre understood the power of dance to unite a community, heal a community, bring blessings for crops, and contribute to the practical well-being of people.[8] "I realized it would be okay to be a dancer, because in other societies the dances help move forward the vitality of the communities. . . .They had that power, and [the dancers] were taken care of because of that."[9]

This understanding of the importance of dance in other cultures gave McIntyre the permission she needed to pursue a career in dance here, in America. She concluded: "That's when I knew I could go in that direction in this period of revolution."[10] As the political activism of the country escalated near the completion of her degree in 1969, she began to embrace the tenets of the Black Arts movement. After graduating from Ohio State,

McIntyre taught for a year at the University of Wisconsin–Milwaukee. While there, she met Chestyn Everett, a professor in the theater department. Everett is the brother of Ron Karenga—the creator of the African American holiday, Kwanzaa—and, like Karenga, embraced the African American struggle in his work. McIntyre remembers Everett as a brilliant professor and director who included students, faculty, and community members in the black plays and theater collages that he produced. In addition to involving McIntyre as choreographer, dancer, and actor, Everett encouraged her to interact with writers, poets, and other artists, and she began to experience what she refers to as the interweaving of the arts.[11] This exposure to the Black Arts movement excited McIntyre.

When she arrived in New York City in 1970 with her Ohio State University degree and a year's professional experience, she continued her dance education. She took dance classes, worked in dance research at the New York Public Library Dance Collection, and visited nightclubs to listen to jazz, to which she refers as simply "the music." Very quickly, she also became part of the Black Arts movement. Although she did not view herself as a political activist, she interacted professionally and socially with artists whose work was guided by the political principles of the Black Arts movement. Her colleagues were artists involved in various art forms, working as individuals, within disciplinary organizations, and collaborating across disciplines. Characteristic of the ideals of the period, and following the movement's beliefs, there was camaraderie among them and a sense of communal effort. It was considered essential and was standard practice for the various artists to know what other artists in the movement were doing. McIntyre remembers that in the early 1970s, "every poet, playwright, novelist, painter to be known, you knew them. In the early 70s you knew them often personally or you were keeping up with their work."[12] Not only did the artists see themselves as a group—in some ways akin to the artists of the Harlem Renaissance of the 1920s—they also believed that their art had a profound function. According to McIntyre, many artists felt they could not afford the luxury of writing, dancing, or making music about themes they understood as irrelevant to the life of the community. They believed that art should have an elevating effect on black culture.[13]

Of all the artists McIntyre encountered, those who influenced her work most were the musicians. In her ventures to hear "the music," McIntyre was most interested in the new music, the jazz of innovative musicians who came to the forefront in the era after John Coltrane's supremacy,

Fig. 15.1. Dianne McIntyre and Dorian Williams in "A Free Thing II" at Washington Square Church in 1972 with musicians (not pictured) Aiye Niwaju, Will Crittendon, Joe Rigby, Joe Falcon and Steve Reid. *Courtesy of Dianne McIntyre*

from about 1960 to 1967.[14] Many jazz scholars consider Coltrane, one of the most esteemed musicians of African American classical music (jazz), to be a bridge composer between bebop music and avant-garde Free Jazz. Both the rhythmically and harmonically unrestricted Free Jazz and the second Free wave of the late 1960s, with its emphasis on black self-awareness, appealed to McIntyre. She applied in her choreography the transcendent freedom that was a hallmark of this new music. One reason McIntyre resonated with the music so strongly was that its contributions to the struggle for racial equality and cultural freedom were abstracted. McIntyre did not see the music as necessarily angry or defiant. In her view, the music's radical power was in its energy, which opened up new possibilities for the listener. The music's ability to encourage transcendence—the sloughing off of the limitations and bonds of internalized racial oppression—made it subversive.

In an interview with dance writer Jennifer Dunning, McIntyre says that listening to the music live "gives you inspiration, it opens your mind, opens your whole being and gives you this feeling like, yes, I know I can do that paper or . . . I can go get my Ph.D. I can become President. . . . The music has that kind of power."[15] Because of the music, McIntyre adds, "you walk through walls, rise to the highest, do whatever you dream."[16] In reflection on the radical decades, she emphasizes the music's subversive qualities:

> . . . [I]t kind of opened everybody up to a kind of inner freedom. Because when I connected with the musicians at first, I think that was very clearly like the purpose of the music, because it came out of that revolutionary time. Some of it had an anger in it, but more than that, it had like a very uplifting quality. . . . Some of the musicians in that early time felt that that was one of the reasons why it wasn't more popular.[17]

Record producers, club owners, and other music promoters were not daring enough to present the music in certain venues, and musicians felt they could not perform some of the music they wanted in the clubs. McIntyre observes that the radical potential to uplift black people and counter oppression, which the music had, was problematic for the white power structure and the mainstream music industry. Therefore, black musicians were forced to perform in alternative spaces and create their own organizations to record and present their music.

Fortified by a circle of Black Arts movement artists and inspired by the music, McIntyre was poised to make her own contribution to dance and to black uplift. She presented her first choreographic work in New York City in 1971, and in 1972, one of the contributions she made was founding a company of black dancers, Sounds in Motion. Recognizing that white dancers had more options for work in the various companies in the city, and perhaps greater financial freedom, McIntyre decided to hire only black dancers. In itself, this decision constituted a political statement.[18]

During the 1970s, as she began building a repertory, McIntyre contributed to the black freedom struggle and the Black Arts movement by taking the approach of racial uplift in her choreography. Improvisation-based pieces (*A Free Thing I, A Free Thing II*, and *Life's Force*) and dances focusing on the music (*Piano Peace*, with music by piano giants Mary Lou Williams, Art Tatum, and McCoy Tyner; *Deep South Suite*, set to a Duke Ellington composition; and *Shadows*, danced to the music of Cecil Taylor) celebrated African American art forms and creative approaches. Another work in this line was *Poem: A Collage*, which featured the poetry of Mari

Evans, Ed Bullins, Langston Hughes, Norman Jordan, and Margaret Walker, among others. Other choreographic efforts dealt with aspects of African American history (*The Voyage, Free Voices,* and *Up North, 1881*). *Memories, Last Days of the Down Home Boogies,* and *I've Known Rivers* all presented black life and culture. *Smoke and Clouds* was a 1970s piece concerned with revolutionary ideas. For many of these works, McIntyre collaborated with the greatest avant-garde musicians of the era—Max Roach, Oliver Lake, Gary Bartz, Hamiet Bluiett, Cecil Taylor, and Ahmed Abdullah.

McIntyre's solo *Melting Song* was the first piece she choreographed in New York and premiered in the New Choreographers Showcase Concert at Clark Center in 1971. The work was inspired by Chinua Achebe's powerful 1958 novel, *Things Fall Apart.*[19] *Melting Song* is not a literal dance with representational movement but in an abstract way deals with an issue of profound importance in the histories of African Americans and other peoples: cultural purity and change. McIntyre intended to express the essence of something in its pure state, such as the people of a traditional culture, or a pure substance, and to examine what happens when something else is introduced into it.[20] Concerned about the content and the survival of black culture, her question was: Does the purity survive, or does it "melt away"? In the solo, performed primarily in silence, the sounds of loud drills and banging interrupt McIntyre's dancing and cause her more fluid movement to become shaky. She falters and "melts." As she slowly crumbles to the floor, a bell rings seven times. The bell's rings counter the effects of the drills and she begins to unfold—opening her arms and rising from her crumbled position. This shift suggests that change is possible. The dissolution of traditional culture is not inevitable; it can be avoided. The sound of the seventh bell, however, is cut short. In the silence of that interruption, McIntyre pauses and the lights fade. Did she fully open or did she crumble? Her fate—and that of traditional cultures—remains unknown.[21]

Smoke and Clouds, a group piece, was McIntyre's second dance in New York. The work juxtaposes revolutionary energy and complacency. As the piece begins, a recording of "Come on, baby, let the good times roll!" accompanies several couples' slow dancing. Gradually, as if heavily sedated, the dancers slump and fall to the floor; then they get up, suddenly energized, and begin yelling angrily. Their carefree social dancing contrasts with their lethargic weightedness and their karate-like kicks and thrusts. McIntyre weaves a pattern of falling and rising, of apathy, defeat, and resistance, in which the rock-and-roll music, which accompanies the seemingly unconscious slow dancing, is opposed by the traditional African conga drum aligned with the forceful movement of the dancers as they gain more and more strength. As one critic noted, the couples' "successive rises are infused with progressively greater energy, purpose and full-out stretches; each retreat is marked by lessening fear and resignation."[22]

McIntyre's use of music in the piece is significant. During the 1960s and 1970s, rhythm-and-blues and gospel music were associated with the more conservative aspect of the black liberation struggle—the Civil Rights movement—while African music and Free Jazz were associated with the Black Arts movement and more radical forms of protest. The use of the conga drums may express the strength of "pure" folk traditions, yet McIntyre's signifying here does not negate the value of soul music. Her accompaniment selections evoke the metaphoric "dance" African Americans do in finding joy in life despite oppression, without abandoning the struggle against that oppression.

McIntyre's 1974 Union, which was sometimes viewed as "militant" because of its energetic dancing, was also intended as a source of uplift. Originally titled Union for the Streets, Union was structured with the recitation of Margaret Walker's or Langston Hughes's poetry at the beginning of each section, followed by the dancers' movement, which McIntyre describes as flying and soaring. She credits the energy of the dancing as the reason why some viewers interpreted it as "militant," despite the traditional nature of the poems.[23] The political issue treated in this dance was the relationship between individual strength and group solidarity. An abstract work performed in leotards and tights, the piece juxtaposes a series of solos and ensemble work in an expression of solidity and cohesiveness. Along with the Black Arts movement participants, McIntyre viewed communal solidarity as essential for success in the struggle for black liberation.

McIntyre agrees that the political activism expressed and explored in music and other art forms influenced her artistry in very direct ways. At the same time, she denies that her choreography makes explicit social commentary about African Americans' conditions during the era of the 1960s and 1970s, as was expected in the Black Arts movement. Smoke and Clouds, Melting Song, and, later, Triptych and other works do relate to the socio-political situations of African Americans, yet, McIntyre would argue, they do not address these situations in a direct or literal way. McIntyre embraced the energy of the liberation struggle in her choreography of the 1970s in work that is abstract, and that can therefore be about black people and relate to the world and change in general. Her political approach to creating dance was not directed toward attacking white oppression but toward inspiring black uplift.

Just as McIntyre now disputes that her work consciously addressed racist oppression, she also contends that it did not address sexism. Furthermore, McIntyre does not consider herself feminist. She denies that her choreography carried an agenda to dismantle sexist oppression, as some of the women's movement of the era required. "You know, when I was a little girl and I was wanting to create the dances and was just dancing, dancing, I did not think of myself as a black woman. I thought of myself as dance. Usually that is true all the time. Just dance."[24]

McIntyre's intention may not be to speak out with a consciously feminist agenda. Nevertheless, one could argue that she, like the modern dance pioneers of the 1930s and 1940s—white and black women—lived "feminist" lives. Just as Pearl Primus, Katherine Dunham, Martha Graham, Doris Humphrey, and Ruth St. Denis all avoided naming themselves as working specifically for the betterment of women but lived comparatively free and "uplifted" lives, so too has McIntyre. Like these pioneers, she was a director of a company and school, a role historically held by male choreographers and dancers. She has collaborated extensively—and equally—with male jazz composers. Above all, she is on par with a few African American men colleagues as a major choreographer greatly influencing dance since the early 1970s.

There are other direct links between McIntyre's life/work and feminism. Rejecting the concept of art for art's sake suggests that, on some level, she embraced the concept that "the personal is political." Even with her abstract presentation of revolutionary content, through energy, the basis of the abstraction is an appreciation for the realities of the oppressive conditions that she and other black people face and a commitment to facilitating her own and others' transcendence of that oppression through her art. The union of politics and culture is an implication of the feminist dictum that the personal is political. And given the emphasis on racial uplift over gender advancement, which black men and many black women embraced during the 1960s and 1970s, McIntyre's political efforts through her art were perhaps as close as most black women came to feminism. Furthermore, even if not explicitly feminist, an important element of McIntyre's work was her expression of universal feelings through the specificity of African American culture. Her work can be seen, therefore, as a means of uplift for all humanity. In this way, her artistry incorporates the feminist stance of fighting oppression of all kinds and the particular insistence by women of color that feminism must be broad and inclusive.

In addition to contributing to the atmosphere of change through the energy and messages of her choreography, throughout the 1970s and into the 1980s McIntyre provided a place for the community, as she says, "to be." Just as artists, activists, and others gathered at the Walls of Respect sites, so too did they gather at 290 Lenox Avenue, at the corner of 125th Street, in McIntyre's studio. Sounds in Motion became a Harlem institution because of the creative excellence of the company and school, and because the studio served as a gathering place for artists. McIntyre compares Sounds in Motion to salons of the Harlem Renaissance or the Romantic period in Europe, where poets and visual artists and musicians—people from different disciplines—knew each other and would spend time together.

> Well, that was what would happen at our Sounds in Motion studio. People would come there. Sometimes they were in class, sometimes they would be musicians that would just come to sit in and play in the class, and then sometimes they were people just that would come by and we were just talking. It was a kind of gathering place.[25]

McIntyre's studio was not only a place for dance; poetry readings and music performances were also held there, and a couple of seminal black theater companies also moved to 290 Lenox Avenue.[26]

Following the guiding principles of the Black Arts movement that had led to the creation of the Walls of Respect, Sounds in Motion took its art out of the studio and into the street—and the people welcomed them warmly. McIntyre remembers one late-1970s Dancemobile performance in an intimidating area of Harlem referred to as Death Valley. Although it was near her apartment, she rarely had cause to go there. On this occasion, as the musicians played and her company prepared to perform, people surrounded them. "It was one of the biggest crowds we ever had for Dancemobile. I mean, the people were . . . going on and on and on, and all around, all around us. This was one of the most moving experiences I have had in the dance, because they treated us like we were superstars."[27] The response of Death Valley residents to McIntyre and her company indicates that they resonated with her avant-garde performance and were uplifted. The residents saw beauty in the performers—who looked like them—and loved what they saw.

For Dianne McIntyre, powerful influences of the 1960s led to the creative contributions she made through her work in the 1970s. She and other artists believed they could change the world—not just as a passing fad but permanently. Some would do this by decrying injustice, others by presenting black art, life, and culture in all their glory. Paraphrasing LeRoi Jones's lines, McIntyre's approach has been to elevate black people through her choreography so they would turn their faces to the light and love themselves. Her impact on African American people—and dance—is captured in the words of her mother, Dorothy Layne McIntyre: "In the 60s and 70s black people really broke out. We weren't held back any more. . . .The thing is, you had to be really brilliant."[28] McIntyre's brilliance shone the light of and on black people—and others who ventured near. Her Walls of Respect–in–motion inspired them to follow their dreams.

NOTES

1. Larry Neal, *Visions of a Liberated Future: Black Arts Movement Writings* (New York: Thunder's Mouth Press, 1989), 68.

2. Jeff Donaldson, "The Rise, Fall and Legacy of the Wall of Respect Movement," *International Review of African American Art* 15, no. 1 (1998): 22.

3. Ibid., 23.

4. Richard A. Long, *The Black Tradition in American Dance* (New York: Rizzoli, 1988), 18.

5. Jennifer Dunning, interview with Dianne McIntyre, 1 April 2000, 39. Transcript and audio cassette available at the New York Public Library, Jerome Robbins Dance Division.

6. Dianne McIntyre, interview with the author, 17 June 2003.

7. Dunning interview with McIntyre, 1 April 2000, 24.

8. McIntyre interview, 17 June 2003.

9. Dunning interview with McIntyre, 1 April 2000, 24.

10. McIntyre interview, 17 June 2003.

11. Ibid.

12. Ibid.

13. Ibid.

14. Dianne McIntyre, interview with the author, 17 April 1993.

15. Jennifer Dunning, interview with Dianne McIntyre, 8 April 2000, 134.

16. McIntyre interview, 17 June 2003.

17. Dunning interview with McIntyre, 8 April 2000, 134.

18. Ibid., 158.

19. Cinua Achebe, *Things Fall Apart* (Greenwich, CT: Fawcett Publications, Inc., 1959).

20. McIntyre interview, 17 April 1993.

21. McIntyre interview, 17 June 2003.

22. Lillie F. Rosen, "Sounds in Motion," *Dance News* (June 1976): 17.

23. McIntyre interview, 17 June 2003.

24. Dunning interview with McIntyre, 8 April 2000, 165.

25. Dunning interview with McIntyre, 1 April 2000, 85.

26. McIntyre interview, 17 June 2003.

27. Dunning, interview with McIntyre, 1 April 2000, 81.

28. McIntyre interview, 17 June 2003.

16 | Judy Chicago in the 1960s

Gail Levin

In 1960, at the start of a decade when millions of young Americans contested their identities, Judy Chicago turned twenty-one.[1] She was at the age that takes chances, experiments, and delights in what is new. By nature curious, fearless, and bright, she was already committed to a life in art. While taking part in the decade's political battles, she forcefully asserted her identity as an artist who *happened* to be a woman. She succeeded in making herself an influential artist and innovative educator. With varying degrees of deliberateness, Judy Chicago also helped foment a feminist revolution in the art world. Her journey toward synchronized creative and political expression both reflected and enabled the paths of many other women artists of the era.

Chicago's childhood in the Midwest set the stage for her involvement with feminist activism in southern California, where she moved to attend college. Although she would later adopt the surname of her native city, she was born Judith Sylvia Cohen to first-generation Americans. All four of her grandparents were poor Jewish immigrants from Eastern Europe. Growing up in an urban setting, she never experienced or aspired to the life of a suburban housewife. "I was raised with the idea that I could do what I wanted and realize whatever potential I had."[2] Encouraged by her parents, she showed artistic ambition early, excelling in children's classes at the Art Institute of Chicago, which she attended from the age of eight. But the truly shaping experiences of her childhood stemmed from her father's politics.

Arthur Cohen (1909–1953) came of age along with the stock market crash and the beginning of the Great Depression. Like so many of his generation, he questioned the validity of capitalism in Depression-era America and turned instead to the idealism of the Communist Party. Even the Hitler-Stalin Non-Aggression Pact in 1939, the year of his daughter's birth, did not cause him to abandon his party membership. Despite his job working nights at the post office, his family suffered the consequences of the Depression. During the day, Arthur stayed home to care for his young daughter while his wife, May, who had once been a dancer, was employed in social work. Arthur, who was also a labor organizer for the postal workers' union, held a liberal attitude toward women, which appears to have predated the American Communists' acknowledgment that the press and popular culture perpetuated male supremacy by depicting women through negative female stereotypes.[3]

From her father's beliefs, Chicago shaped her own later concern with the rights of women. She writes: "There was an expressed commitment to equal rights for women, something I not only heard stated but saw demonstrated by the way in which my father always made sure to include the women in these lively discussions. Moreover, I saw it manifested in the way he treated me."[4] She recalls: "I was raised amid record parties for various causes, including the Spanish Civil War. People of all races mingled in our second-floor apartment to engage in near-constant political arguments."[5]

Hardship as well as parties colored Chicago's childhood. When, in 1945, at the age of six, she was briefly at home alone with her infant brother, an FBI agent dropped by, only to be chased away by the sudden return of their mother before he could question her about her father's friends and activities.[6] Shortly thereafter, Arthur Cohen was forced to resign from the post office. The tensions of such persecution contributed to a decline in his health. He did not survive surgery to relieve the intense pain caused by an infected ulcer.[7] On July 15, 1953, when she was only thirteen, Judy had to face the death of her father.[8] She sought solace in her love of art. Her mother, despite financial hardships, continued to support Judy's artistic ambitions.

Chicago had won numerous scholarships and honors in her classes at the Art Institute, but she was passed over for their college scholarship. Disappointed, she took the scholarship that her high school awarded her, which was applicable anywhere, and went, in the fall of 1957, to the University of California at Los Angeles. There she could live with her aunt and uncle on her mother's side.[9] Chicago, whose attitude was to take difficult courses "just for the stimulation," told her mother: "I've decided that I can be neither strictly goal or grade oriented, forgetting my basic purpose in college i.e. to become a broadened, enlightened human being, and a sensitive artist."[10]

Already at the beginning of her first semester, Chicago found political activism attractive. This was hardly a surprise, given her family history. She fits the profile of a "red-diaper baby," as the children of Communists have often been called. In his analysis of the New Left, Todd Gitlin described the influence on others of those who grew up "breathing a left-wing air; their sense of being different, touched by nobility and consecrated by persecution, was magnetic; they had a perch from which to criticize."[11] Chicago, like other red-diaper babies, lost no time getting involved on campus. Just as the Civil Rights movement was gearing up, she volunteered to make posters for the National Association for the Advancement of Colored People (NAACP) and soon became the chapter's Corresponding Secretary. She observed that UCLA lacked "Negro professors" and that "Westwood Village, the area immediately surrounding the campus, has no apartments available for Negroes, & there are Barber Shops, restaurants, stores, etc. in this 'elite' neighborhood that won't serve them."[12] Just two years after Rosa Parks had refused to give up her seat to a white man on a bus in Montgomery, Alabama, Chicago eagerly joined the struggle.

When her uncle told Chicago that "Communism is the worst evil man has ever seen," she complained to her mother that he was "too reactionary."[13] Another time, she went to a musical evening to benefit "the Committee for the Protection of the Foreign Born, and primarily to repeal the Walter-McCarran Act."[14] Chicago's political sympathies with powerless minorities echoed those of her father, about whom she wrote her mother from college: "How proud I am to have had a Father such as I did."[15]

Chicago's letters to her mother from college also discuss her focus on existentialist literature and philosophy, an intellectual source for many of the generation of the New Left. This "generation haunted by history," according to Gitlin, "had been taught that political failure or apathy can have the direst consequences; they had extracted the lesson that the fate of the world is not something automatically to be entrusted to authorities. The red-diaper babies among them were often especially eager not to be cowed; their own passivity might confirm their parents' defeats."[16] Having observed her father's undoing, Chicago found Samuel Beckett's *Waiting for Godot* "extremely exciting, funny almost to absurdity, with an underlying current of Existentialist-type philosophy."[17] When she read an "existentialist novel for her French course, she pointed out that "one sees some rebellion against the conformity that so characterizes our time" and further explained: "Existentialism develops from the idea that man is put on earth with no apparent purpose and in Jean-Paul Sartre's words . . . 'Man is condemned to freedom.' This of course, gives man a great many responsibilities—but to himself."[18] Nearly two years later, on the occasion of seeing a production of Albert Camus's *Caligula*, whose work she labeled "French existentialist," she would note that she had been recently reading Jean-Paul Sartre and that she had "read quite of few of his books and he's really something."[19] Gitlin almost describes Chicago when he argues: "All breathed the air of existentialism: action might not avail, but one is responsible for choosing. And so from the dead hand of history, they leaped to a paradoxical conclusion: that history was alive and open."[20] It becomes increasingly clear that Chicago was determined to change history.

Chicago's mother took her daughter's pronouncements from college in stride, commenting: "Judy is just about what expected—20, emancipated half-baked college educated."[21] Neither her daughter's radical politics, her African-American boyfriend, her ambition, nor her decision to live on her own caused a major rift between the two.[22] The mother knew her daughter well and recognized her strengths, confiding in her close friend: "When I think of the many parents who are uneasy because their children do not have a sense of direction, I cannot help but feel that this one has a strong independent spirit."[23] Only her daughter's dropping out of college caused despair: "the waste of a good mind, a good child's potential."[24]

Chicago recalls what became the largest obstacle to her education: "In college I began to run into direct personal attacks upon my right to do what I wanted. But by that time already had a sense of internalized permission to do what I wanted, that most girls don't have."[25] By June 1959, she had fallen in love with Jerry Gerowitz, who, like her, had grown up in a secular Jewish family in Chicago. Not long after announcing to her mother her plan to move into her own studio and paint, she moved in with Gerowitz, who was rather undirected and unemployed; he toyed with the idea of writing and liked to gamble.[26] Out of money, the pair elected to hitchhike to New York in the late summer of 1959, just as her mother and brother were moving to LA, in part to be closer to her.[27]

The young couple lived in "a cockroach-infested apartment on East Sixth Street" in Greenwich Village.[28] Chicago supported herself modestly in New York by working five afternoons a week with preteens at the Henry Street Settlement House, where, as part of her job, she designed and produced costumes for a play.[29] She was fascinated by the neighborhood around Henry Street, which she described as "80% tenement, 20% co-op and public housing. Middle-class, Jewish families mixed with Italians, Negroes, Puerto Ricans who are not quite so middle-class (economically speaking—I do not vouch for anyone's morals!)."[30] She told her mother that she planned "to work from a base of Creative Arts, as I did last year," referring to her part-time job in Los Angeles working with recreation groups for children at a Jewish community center.[31]

Her afternoon jobs left Chicago with all her mornings free to spend in the studio. For the first time, she set up "a structured studio life, working every day from 8AM–2PM."[32] She also sought to continue to study art during the one year she planned to spend in New York. She was disappointed to find that she would have to wait until the following spring to take the entrance exam for Cooper Union, where tuition was free, but wrote to her mother that she could begin at CCNY (City College of New York), Hunter College, or Brooklyn College as early as February. She noted with authority: "Motherwell, one of the leading painters in America, teaches at Hunter, so that has definite possibilities."[33]

Before long, Chicago was pleased to report that she had enrolled in painting, drawing, and composition classes at the New School for Social Research. Her teacher was Social Realist painter Raphael Soyer, a Russian-born Jew who came of age during the 1930s. She described him as "a small, quiet, skinny little man who insists that we must find a 'new-realism,' whatever that means—it obviously excludes non-representational art."[34] Soyer quickly recognized Chicago's exceptional talent and ambition, telling her that she drew so well that she might learn more from working with a print maker than by being in a class.[35] He then set her up with an etcher who had arrived recently from Italy. Although married, the young man made unwanted sexual overtures to his new student, who wanted nothing more from him than lessons in etching—making the latter impossible for her to obtain.[36]

Despite this setback, Chicago soon proclaimed New York her "soul city." She eagerly took in a wide range of cultural events. At the Museum of Modern Art, she especially admired *Guernica*, the monumental painting Picasso produced in 1937 to protest the Germans' brutal bombardment of that Basque town during the Spanish Civil War.[37] She was so moved that she declared that the museum made her entire trip to New York worthwhile. She responded to Frank Lloyd Wright's new Guggenheim Museum building as "a piece of sculpture . . . so great I couldn't believe it."[38] She saw dance performances by both Alwin Nicholais and

Merce Cunningham, the latter with musical compositions by John Cage, Morton Feldman, and Christian Wolff, all of which she referred to as a "remarkable exploration of Dance and Movement." She frequented the theater, seeing a variety of plays, ranging from avant-garde work such as the Living Theatre's *The Connection* and Beckett's *Waiting for Godot* to classics such as Shakespeare's *Henry IV, Part I*. Her favorite films included those directed by Ingmar Bergman, whose rich symbolic content was in vogue.[39]

Chicago's exposure to music in New York ranged from hearing Leonard Bernstein conduct Beethoven and Shostakovich at Carnegie Hall to her companion Gerowitz's attempts at song writing. Among their friends, "singers Paul [Simon] and Art [Garfunkel] who record for Columbia" asked her to design a costume for them after seeing her work on children's play costumes. Not yet famous, they offered her $80 for what she described as "a brilliant design even by my stringent standards" but postponed payment until they made their next record.[40]

By January 1960, Chicago, who had found Soyer too conservative, had hopped on the bandwagon of Abstract Expressionism, the gestural painting style that had emerged in New York during the 1940s and dominated the avant-garde during the 1950s. She wrote to her mother: "I'm sure you've heard the term Abstract Expressionism—well, that's the kind of painting I'm doing. It took a little while for me to learn to see this way, but it's coming slowly. I do believe it is today's way of seeing the world and that is very important."[41] She declared "De Kooning's series of paintings entitled 'Woman,' . . . great. He has one called 'Marilyn Monroe' which kept me laughing for a week."[42]

Some of the women she encountered in the "ritzy-type places" to which the Police Athletic League took children whom she taught art annoyed her to the extent that she complained that they were "T.S. Eliot types who talk about Michelangelo at Cocktail parties. I do believe that one of the things that the emancipation of women has produced, aside from a lot of crazy women, is an abundance of brilliant comments on American womanhood, ranging from Eliot to Lawrence to De Kooning." Chicago's sarcasm may reflect the fact that she already aspired to *be* "Michelangelo," rather than talk about him.

Clearly, it was not with the women but with the men who made the brilliant comments that Chicago identified herself. Already as an undergraduate, she followed her ambition and sought out as friends the most serious students, who then were usually men. She recalled: "They often told me that I was 'different' from other women. I felt a warm glow of pride in my 'specialness' and enjoyed the status that I had as the result of being the only woman they took seriously. . . . I slowly and unknowingly began to absorb the culture's contempt for women, rationalizing my own femaleness, as the men did, by the fact that I was somehow 'different.'"[43] Like many creative and intellectual women of the time, Chicago bought individual success for the price of male supremacy disguised as gender blindness. A hollow bargain, it might have been the only one accessible to her in the early sixties.

This was a critical juncture for Chicago, attuned as she was to cultural change. The previous year, 1959, saw the publication of Norman O. Brown's *Life against Death*, in which he held that repression produced individual neurosis and social pathology. "Art," he wrote, was not "a compromise with the unconscious either in the cognitive or in the libidinal sense"; art, he concluded, "affords positive satisfaction. . . . "[44] Chicago found her art an ideal medium with which to express her feelings directly, including sexuality from a female point of view.

This new expressive freedom would affect Chicago not long after she returned to UCLA in September 1960 and married Gerowitz in 1961. She took many literature and philosophy classes, made Phi Beta Kappa, and graduated from college in 1962. The following year, she began graduate study in art at UCLA. Once again, she had to deal with grief, when her new husband died in an automobile accident on a twisting canyon road near the couple's home. She continued to be known as Judy Gerowitz, for she had taken his surname when it occurred to her that "there seemed to be too many other artists named Cohen."[45]

In graduate school, where she received a teaching assistantship, Chicago's paintings, although abstract, made recognizable references to male and female sexual organs. She described one of these works, *Bigamy*, as having "a double vagina/heart form, with a broken heart below and a frozen phallus above. The subject matter was the double death of my father and husband, and the phallus was stopped in flight and prevented from uniting with the vaginal form by an inert space."[46] This work provoked dismay in her instructors, who were predominantly male. Although the time was the early 1960s, their attitude reflects a powerful residue of the conservative 1950s, when the link between the twin dangers of women's uncontrolled sexuality and atomic power became established and marked popular culture—as seen not only in the use of "bombshell" as the slang term for a sexy woman but also in the naming of abbreviated, two-piece swim suits for the Bikini Islands, where the bomb dropped during testing was said to have been decorated with a photo of a Hollywood sex symbol.[47] Unwittingly, Chicago had exposed the sexist underbelly of the emerging sexual revolution, which initially positioned women as the objects of liberated male libido.[48] Nor did Chicago herself yet have the feminist mindset or lexicon to stake a claim to sexual liberation through artistic expression.

Although her teachers rejected her suggestive biomorphic imagery, Chicago received her master's degree with a double major, in both painting and sculpture, in the spring of 1964. She had obtained special permission for what was an atypical, although challenging, program.[49] Chicago later characterized her attitudes in this period: "I was impatient and ambitious. I wanted to be out there in the world, and I thought I was just as talented as all those men. So I chose a confrontational mode, and it had benefit not only for me but for a lot of other women."[50] At the time, her mother observed how hard her daughter worked, remarking: "She drives and drives and wears herself out."[51]

Chicago's formidable energy and talent had won her a prominent Los Angeles art dealer, Rolf Nelson, who staged her first solo show at his gallery in January 1966.[52] Taking note of his young artist's pronounced Midwestern accent, Nelson began calling her "Judy Chicago." Encouraged by him, she even listed herself that way in the phone book.[53] Through her dealer, she became friends with his brother-in-law, the innovative architect Frank Gehry. He was so taken with Chicago that in June 1966 he visited the summer school class that she taught in sculpture at the University of California at Irvine, and spent nearly two hours talking to her students.[54] She continued to make ends meet by part-time teaching.

With Nelson, Chicago visited the LA artists' bar Barney's Beanery.[55] Hanging out with male artists, whose ambition she shared, Chicago longed to be "one of the boys." She tried to act tough by wearing boots and smoking cigars.[56] Influenced by the "finish fetish" style—characterized by new industrial techniques and unblemished surfaces—that then dominated the LA art scene, she attended auto-body school to learn to spray paint smoothly on metal so that she could more easily fuse color and surface in her own work. In the process, she gained a greater appreciation of the role of craft.[57] Hoping to learn to mold fiberglass, she subsequently took a course in boat building. Her purpose in studying such male-oriented pursuits was not to meet men, for from early 1965 she became involved with sculptor Lloyd Hamrol, whom she had known since undergraduate days at UCLA. The couple lived together intermittently; even in the face of unresolved issues concerning ambition, sexuality, and equality, they continually struggled to make their relationship work.[58]

Chicago made such personal issues taboo in her art of this period. Instead, the abstract sculptures that she produced at this time can best be described as adhering to a formalist aesthetic concentrating on color and form. She turned out minimalist cylinders, beams, and domes. She produced these forms using innovative materials and techniques including fiberglass, lacquered acrylic, and monochrome-painted canvas stretched over a shaped plywood frame. Six different pastel-colored beams, progressively larger in size and made of canvas over plywood, compose Chicago's multi-element minimalist sculpture *Rainbow Pickett* (1965), which she named after the soul singer Wilson Pickett. It was included in the show "Primary Structures" at New York's Jewish Museum in 1966. There, in the company of now well-known male sculptors such as Carl Andre and Ronald Bladen, Chicago's work attracted praise from one of the most prominent critics of the day, Clement Greenberg.[59]

Around this time, Chicago had also begun to produce temporary, collaborative works, for which she began to seek public patronage. Chicago's and Hamrol's collaborative "environments" were reviewed in the *Los Angeles Times*, prompting her mother, the former dancer, to describe one of them with gusto to a friend:

> They built walls of inflated plastic in the old gallery, with 300 lbs. of chicken feathers on the floor. Sure it stinks somewhat, although they are constantly spraying it and dusting it with talcum, but when the room is entered it is truly an experience. Suddenly you are in a sense of timelessness, the walls seem distant. . . . [T]here is an eeriness about it which threatens some people, who won't enter, but once inside—all I felt like doing was arabesques."[60]

A few months later, Chicago's mother described her daughter as "always dreaming up something new," noting that she was "the most self-disciplined person."[61]

Chicago soon created another public event, called *Dry Ice Environment* (1967), on which she collaborated with Hamrol and Eric Orr (1940–1998). They employed thirty-seven tons of dry ice donated by the Union Carbide Company. When the *Los Angeles Times* reviewed her "dry ice sculptural happening," it labeled her a "rambunctious iconoclast" and noted her "rejection of permanence as a valid artistic goal," but went on to quote her conviction: "To retain their creative freedom artists must aim to become the manipulators rather than the victims of technology. Only by moving art out of the studio into the factory and ultimately into all suitable public places can the artist hope to affect society."[62] This expressed commitment to "affect society," following her earlier work in the Civil Rights movement, suggests that she was consciously following her father's teachings, whom she recalled spoke to her just before her thirteenth birthday "about his desire to change the condition of black people in America, to abolish poverty, and to try to make the place he worked more humane."[63] Elsewhere, Chicago commented on the metaphoric nature of her dry ice sculptures, pointing out what would come to be an important aspect of her future work: "The sculptures were a metaphor for the preciousness of life."[64] Similarly, Chicago's collapsing the boundaries of "life" and "art" draws on the emerging countercultural ethos, the Black Arts movement, and other sixties arts movements.

Yet Chicago still shied away from explicit gender or identity politics. When the Lytton Center's show "California Women in the Arts" opened in Los Angeles in the spring of 1968, Chicago was asked why she wasn't in it and replied: "Because I won't show in any group defined as Women, Jewish, or California. Someday when we all grow up there will be no labels."[65] Her contempt for such segregated shows was bolstered by the fact that museums had begun to take note of her growing reputation.

In the spring of 1969, the Pasadena Art Museum gave Chicago a solo show of her recent sculpture of spherical acrylic plastic domes and related drawings in its "experimental" gallery. William Wilson, who reviewed the show for the *Los Angeles Times*, commented: "I did not experience this art as tough, theoretical New York type art. It rather blushes with ample hedonism. . . . [S]haded colors are inseparable from them and finally have the innocent lyricism of a bag of marbles, a pretty lady's beads, or a '36 Ford."[66] *Art in America* reported that Judy Chicago "has spent progressively more time as a rallying point for artists concerned with transient events in outdoor environments. Since 1966 a changing roster of artists has made art of ice, smoke, balloons, skywritings, feathers and other such tangible/intangibles."[67] During this period, many artists were moving away from making salable objects, emphasizing ideas over form, some of which became known as Conceptual Art.

By the late 1960s, as the women's liberation movement exploded all around her, Chicago began to connect sexual expression and gender in her work. With a vocabulary, an analysis, and a movement to bolster her, she now moved quickly toward overtly political art. During this period, she continued to create works of performance art that were outdoors, public, and temporary. She called these "atmospheres." She later described these works as "flares of colored smoke out doors and in the landscape. They're all about the releasing of energy."[68] She also stated that her aim was "to transform and soften (i.e. feminize) the environment."[69] To produce the required smoke devices, she began working with a fireworks company and studying to become a pyrotechnician. She had to abandon this work when the man running the only suitable fireworks company in the area became insistent on having sexual relations with her.[70]

Ironically, at the same moment that she had to fend off unwanted sexual overtures, Chicago was dealing with the expression of her own sexuality through her work: "I was also discovering that I was multi-orgasmic, that I could act aggressively on my own sexual needs. The forms became rounded like domes or breasts or bellies and then they opened up and became like donuts, and then the donuts began to be grasping and assertive. I went from three forms to four and started the *Pasadena Lifesavers*."[71] For this series of abstract paintings on acrylic plexiglass surfaces, produced during 1969 and 1970, she developed color systems in which she tried to create the illusion of forms that "turn, dissolve, open, close, vibrate, gesture, wiggle; all those sensations were emotional and body sensations translated into form and color."[72] Explaining her choice of the name, *Lifesavers*, Chicago later reflected, "[I]n a way they did save my life by confronting head-on that issue of what it was to be a woman." This issue would now move to the forefront of both her consciousness and her activities.

This embrace of her female identity prompted her to change her name legally. On the occasion of her solo show in 1970 at California State College at Fullerton, she posted the following notice, which also appeared on the cover of the show's catalogue: "Judy Gerowitz hereby divests herself of all names imposed upon her through male social dominance and freely chooses her own name *Judy Chicago*."[73] For an announcement of her show sent out by the Jack Glenn Gallery (also in Orange County, California), she took her dealer's suggestion and posed provocatively as a boxer in a ring, with her new name emblazoned on her sweatshirt. The photograph recording this stance left no doubt that Chicago wanted to be perceived as a force to be reckoned with. It not only publicized her show and name change but also appeared as an ad in

Fig. 16.1. Advertisement of Cal State Fullerton Exhibition in *Artforum*, December 1970. *Through the Flower Archives*

the magazine *Artforum* for October 1970. The magazine ran the ad gratis after Philip Leider, the publisher, failed to convince Jack Glenn to pay to run it.[74]

Chicago's catalog featured a dedication to twenty-five women who inspired her, including Abigail Adams, Virginia Woolf, and three whose writing she quoted along with her own brief statement: George Eliot, Sojourner Truth, and Simon de Beauvoir. From Eliot's novel *Daniel Deronda*, published in 1876, she chose words that illuminate the depth of her ambition:

> You can never imagine what it is to have a man's force of genius in you, and yet to suffer the slavery of being a girl. To have a pattern cut out . . .

This is what you must be; This is what you are wanted for; A woman's heart must be of such a size and no larger, else it must be pressed small, like Chinese feet. . . . "[75]

Chicago's own statement reads:

Until the egos of both male and female are valued equally throughout all levels of society, the work of a female artist cannot be clearly perceived or accurately judged. For our standards of judgment and modes of perception arise from a history which is primarily the record of the male, the imagery of the male, and the perceptions of the male."[76]

Male reviewers' responses to her work in these two shows disappointed Chicago, for they failed to make the link to her "femaleness." "I wanted to make a symbolic statement about my emerging position as a feminist," she explained, adding: "I wanted to force the viewers to see the work in relation to the fact that it was made by a woman artist. Now I can see that the years of neutralizing my subject matter made it difficult to perceive the content in my work. Even for women."[77] This misinterpretation took place before there was any general consensus that a woman's point of view might be equally significant to but substantially different from that of a man.

By 1970, when Chicago first went public with her feminist stance, feminist consciousness-raising among women artists had just begun. In New York in 1969, politically active women artists broke off from the Art Workers Coalition to form Women Artists for Revolution (WAR), after they realized that "the rights for women artists always ended up at the bottom of the Coalition's list of demands."[78] The goal of WAR was that 50 percent of all the artists exhibited in New York's galleries and museums be women, and that half of all the city's art school teachers be women. Statistics then suggested that 60 to 80 percent of New York art students were women but that 90 percent of their teachers were men. In the spring of 1970, WAR demanded that New York's Whitney Museum include 50 percent women artists in their biennial exhibition of sculpture, as compared to the usual 5 to 10 percent. On the opening day, protesters placed eggs with the message "50 percent" on the museum's staircases.

Concerned about the plight of women artists and their inability to express their own female perspective in their work, Chicago also decided in 1970 to teach art full time at Fresno State College (now California

State University, Fresno). When asked in 1971 why she left Los Angeles for Fresno, Chicago responded:

> . . . my values and attitudes, my sense of what I could and what I couldn't do were developed in the 50s when I was a teenager. Like the whole advent of the hippies and the revolution and the Left . . . the Panthers, the Blacks; and that it had really changed the nature of our society and our values, I felt that I had built my identity and my art-making as a person— as an artist—on the framework of reality that I had been brought up in, and now that framework had changed. So I wanted some time out, to look around and find out what was appropriate now. I sensed that what I could do now differed from what could be done twenty years ago.[79]

She planned to set up a class entirely composed of women and arranged to teach this class of fifteen students off campus in order to escape "the presence and hence, the expectations of men."[80]

In her attempt to find a direct way for women to express themselves through art, Chicago began working with theater and film and with class discussions to explore the students' feelings and experiences. In explaining her willingness to experiment with these techniques, Chicago also credited "the Women's Movement—new options were opened so that I could actually think about using my talent in a variety of ways which had simply not been possible before."[81] A few years after the Fresno experiment, she reflected:

> I became aware of the Women's Liberation Movement and I immediately understood what that meant . . . I realized that I could actually begin to put out all this information I had about my own struggle, my own perceptions, and I also understood that the structure as it existed in the art world and the world as a whole had no provisions for that kind of information.[82]

Chicago's comprehension of what women artists faced impelled her to teach her students to use tools and develop building and mechanical skills in an attempt to instill in them a sense of independence.[83]

Chicago herself, having taken on enormous responsibility for her students' emotional and professional development, felt the need for support. She turned to another woman artist whose work she respected, and whom she knew professionally: Miriam Schapiro. Sixteen years older than Chicago, Schapiro had left her native New York in 1967, when her husband, Paul Brach, was hired to teach in California. By then, following the birth of the couple's son and only child in 1955, Schapiro had dealt with her struggle to reconcile her dual desires to be both mother and artist. Chosen for the "New Talent Exhibition" at the Museum of Modern Art in 1957, Schapiro had the first of several solo exhibitions the following year at the prestigious André Emmerich Gallery in New York. Yet, because her work in the Abstract Expressionist mode left her discontented, she had begun to search for a more personal style, experimenting in the early sixties with a series of hard-edged shrine paintings that embody female forms such as the egg. Chicago recalled: "I knew who she was—a woman artist who had achieved. I had seen some of her work, and I recognized an affinity between her Ox paintings and Egg paintings and my *Pasadena Lifesavers*."[84]

Chicago invited Schapiro to give a guest lecture at Fresno, where the two women discovered that they shared a wish to change art education for women and decided to teach together the following year. Chicago agreed to move the Feminist Art Program to California Institute of the Arts, a newly founded art school in Los Angeles, where Schapiro taught and her husband was dean. Eight of the women from Fresno transferred to rejoin the program in its new locale.

Schapiro recalls that Brach left it up to her to convince his otherwise all-male art faculty at Cal Arts to approve "the idea of having Judy and me teach a feminist art program, *separating* the women from the men in that coeducational institution and teaching them differently."[85] Schapiro explained: "The prospect of our incipient power was frightening to the men. . . . When Judy insisted on locking the door to the large studio where we worked, rumor flew about the school that we were in that room inciting revolution."[86]

Since the new Cal Arts building in Valencia was not yet ready, Paula Harper, an art historian teaching at the school, suggested that the Feminist Art Program find an old house and transform it for the term project. They located a Los Angeles house on Mariposa Street that was slated for demolition.[87] Chicago and Schapiro collaborated with the twenty-one women students enrolled in their program in turning the borrowed building into a group of installations and a performance space. The aim of the project was to challenge gender stereotypes and "raise consciousness" of ways in which the creativity of women was marginalized and repressed. The result, "Womanhouse," opened to the public from January 30 through February 28, 1972.

Visitors to Womanhouse encountered spaces transformed to examine the expected duties of the housewife. The collaborative flesh-pink *Nurturant Kitchen* featured walls covered with 250 foam-rubber fried eggs that progressively became larger, turning into breasts, suggesting women's role as nurturers and as unrecognized service providers. While Womanhouse was in progress, Chicago realized that "nowhere in the house was there a reference to menstruation," prompting her to add the pristine white *Menstruation Bathroom*, containing a garbage can overflowing with bloody evidence.[88] As she broke every taboo, this room came to serve as a metaphor for restrictions that society imposed on women.

At the time, Chicago commented that Womanhouse "synthesized all female activities and the invisible achievements of women," asserting: "I want to change the world."[89] The entire project called into question the patriarchal division of labor and the notion of "anatomy as destiny," for the women had acquired the manual labor skills required to restore the house and build their environments. These fantasy surroundings also served as a setting for consciousness-raising performances.

The spectacle provoked wide media attention and controversy, attracting, it was said, more than ten thousand visitors during the month it remained open. The time was ripe for feminist activism in the visual arts. Textbooks of art history routinely omitted women from the group of artists surveyed. As Schapiro and Chicago traveled around California, meeting women artists, they found that many of them lacked studios and had resorted to working in their kitchens or dining rooms.[90] As they called women's traditional domesticity into question through Womanhouse, participants of the Feminist Art Program contributed to the development of both installation and performance art, significant trends in contemporary art that continue even today. Two films, one about Chicago's year teaching women at Fresno and another of Womanhouse, helped to circulate the ideas, forms, and performances of the Feminist Art Program.[91]

For Chicago, Womanhouse represented a significant step "in the exposure of female experience and the validating of female experience as subject matter for art."[92] In her autobiography, she recalls that she occasionally joked about how women in the early days of the women's movement lacked their "own forms," explaining: "Therefore we borrowed some, notably from the Civil Rights Movement."[93] Yet Chicago never mentions her early work for the NAACP, recalling only that she met an African-American boyfriend at one of the organization's meetings.[94] When an interviewer in the early 1970s asked Chicago how she saw her own work and if "the female direction" was a lifetime commitment, she responded:

> I think my work as an artist for the last 10 years was very much involved in struggling for my identity as a woman and symbolizing that struggle. The subject matter, the content, of my work has to do with myself, my autobiography, my relationship to the culture and the contradiction I felt between who I was and who society said I was.[95]

Although Chicago has since broadened the scope of her inquiry to include her Jewish heritage, she has kept her earlier focus on autobiography and the status of women.[96]

The Dinner Party, Chicago's monumental collaborative project begun in 1974 and completed in 1979, has become a landmark of the feminist struggle. A multi-media installation that recovers and documents the history of women in Western civilization, *The Dinner Party* is the result of mostly volunteer efforts by over four hundred people to research Chicago's idea and realize her vision. Each of thirty-nine place settings at the triangular table is dedicated to a female figure from myth or history. The ceramic plates are often vulval in form to suggest what women have in common. They underline that women give birth, not only to children but, metaphorically, to ideas. The runners or cloths under the plates contain narrative elements, produced by needlework techniques reflecting the era of each of the figures. The heritage floor in the center of the triangle contains the names of 999 more women.

The Dinner Party now features in nearly every introductory art history textbook on the college level. Recently, it has found a permanent home in the Brooklyn Museum of Art. The gift of the Elizabeth A. Sackler Foundation, *The Dinner Party* will be the centerpiece in a new "Feminist Art Center." Chicago's place in history has thus been secured, following more than two decades of controversy, when anti-feminist critics attacked her work as "vulgar" and she herself feared that her achievement would be erased from history, like that of so many other women artists.

To understand how Chicago became a major communicator of feminist ideas, we have looked at her embrace of the Old Left politics of her father, the New Left battle for Civil Rights, and the sexual revolution of the 1960s. We have seen how she subjected all of these to radical revision from the newly emerging feminist point of view. Her feminist consciousness grew as she reacted to the discrepancy between the male chauvinism she observed and suffered in the art world and the more ideal world she had experienced as a child. Empowered by the countercultural rebellion in general and the women's movement in particular, she began to question the gender bias that she encountered in her life as an artist. She sought and found means to affirm herself and her own identity as a woman artist, which she has communicated to others through her teaching, her writing, and her art.

NOTES

1. For research leading to this article, I am grateful for grants from the National Endowment for the Humanities, the Hadassah International Institute for Research on Jewish Women at Brandeis University, and the Research Foundation of the City University of New York.

2. Judy Chicago, "Woman as Artist," *Everywoman* 2, no. 7, issue 18, May 7, 1971 p. 24.

3. The Communists began to consider the woman question after World War II. By the time Susan B. Anthony II's 1946 "Report on the Status of Women" was excerpted as "Jimcrow against Women," *Worker*, October 20, 1946, p. 11, the Cohens' daughter Judy was already seven years old. See Kate Weigand, *Red Feminism: American Communism and the Making of Women's Liberation* (Baltimore: Johns Hopkins University Press, 2000), p. 117.

4. Judy Chicago, *Beyond the Flower: The Autobiography of a Feminist Artist* (New York: Viking Penguin, 1996), p. 3.

5. Ibid.

6. Judy Chicago, *Through the Flower* (New York: Doubleday and Co., 1975; Penguin Books, 1993), p. 4.

7. See ibid.

8. Arthur M. Cohen died in Michael Reese Hospital of acute intestinal obstruction.

9. Her mother's sister, Dorothy, and her husband, Herman Polin.

10. Judy Cohen to May Cohen, letter of November 4, 1958, Judy Chicago Collection at the Arthur and Elizabeth Schlesinger Library on the History of Women in America, Radcliffe College, Harvard University, Cambridge, Massachusetts. All letters quoted herein are previously unpublished. Hereafter [SLRC].

11. Todd Gitlin, *The Sixties: Years of Hope, Days of Rage* (New York: Bantam Books), p. 67.

12. Judy Cohen to May Cohen, letter of December 7, 1957 [SLRC].

13. Judy Cohen to May Cohen, letters of September 7, 1957, and December 7, 1957 [SLRC].

14. Judy Cohen to May Cohen, letter postmarked November 17, 1957 [SLRC]. The Walter-McCarran Act was the Immigration and Nationality Act of 1952, which, though it for the first time granted Asian immigrants the right to become citizens, also provided for the deportation of non-citizens prosecuted for proscribed political beliefs and associations.

15. Judy Cohen to May Cohen, letter of November 1, 1957.

16. Gitlin, *The Sixties*, p. 84.

17. Judy Cohen to May Cohen and Bob [later Ben] Cohen, n.d. [SLRC].

18. Judy Cohen to May Cohen, letter of March 25, 1958 [SLRC].

19. Judy Cohen to May Cohen, letter of January 20, 1960 [SLRC].

20. Gitlin, *The Sixties*, p. 84.

21. May Cohen to Pearl S. Cassman, unpublished letter of August 23, 1959 [SLRC].

22. Judy Chicago to the author, letter of August 16, 2002, recalls that she thought that her mother was "a hypocrite" when she warned her daughter that an interracial marriage would make for a hard life.

23. May Cohen to Pearl S. Cassman, letter of August 23, 1959 [SLRC].

24. May Cohen to Pearl S. Cassman, letter of January 17, 1960.

25. Chicago, "Woman as Artist," p. 24.

26. Judy Cohen to May Cohen, letter of June 9, 1959 [SLRC].

27. Chicago, *Through the Flower*, pp. 18–19.

28. Chicago, *Beyond the Flower*, p. 14.

29. Judy Cohen to May Cohen, undated letter of 1959 and letter of January 20, 1960, [SLRC].

30. Judy Cohen to May Cohen, letter of March 5, 1959 [SLRC].

31. Judy Cohen to May Cohen and Ben Cohen, letter of September 22, 1959, [SLRC].

32. Judy Chicago to the author, letter of August 16, 2002.

33. Judy Cohen to May Cohen, letter of September 18, 1959 [SLRC].

34. Judy Cohen to May Cohen, undated letter of September 1959 [SLRC].

35. Judy Cohen to May Cohen, letter of December 8, 1959 [SLRC].

36. Judy Cohen to May Cohen, undated letter of January 1960 [SLRC].

37. See Gail Levin, "The Response to Picasso's *Guernica* in New York," *Jong Holland*, no. 2 (1991): 2–11.

38. Judy Cohen to May Cohen, letter of December 12, 1959 [SLRC].

39. Judy Cohen to May Cohen, letter of February 20, 1960 [SLRC].

40. Judy Cohen to May Cohen, letter of May 7, 1960 [SLRC]. Author's interview with the artist, 2002, documents that Chicago does not recall meeting Simon and Garfunkel or even if she ever got paid by the soon-to-be-star folk singers.

41. Judy Cohen to May Cohen, letter of January 30, 1960 [SLRC].

42. Judy Cohen to May Cohen, letter of December 28, 1959 [SLRC].

43. Chicago, *Through the Flower*, p. 28.

44. Normon O. Brown, *Life against Death* (New York: Vintage Books, 1959), p. 65. Chicago, in letter to the author of July 21, 2003, recalls reading this book shortly after its publication.

45. Chicago, *Beyond the Flower*, p. 15.

46. Chicago, *Through the Flower*, p. 33.

47. See Elaine Tyler May, "Explosive Issues: Sex, Women, and the Bomb," in Lary May, ed., *Recasting America: Culture and Politics in the Age of Cold War* (Chicago: University of Chicago Press, 1989), p. 165.

48. See Barbara Ehrenreich, *The Hearts of Men: American Dreams and the Flight from Commitment* (Garden City, NY: Anchor/Doubleday, 1983), pp. 118–19.

49. May Cohen to Pearl S. Casman, letter of April 28, 1964 [SLRC].

50. "Judy Chicago in Conversation with Ruth Iskin," *Visual Dialog* 2, no. 3 (May 1977): 14.

51. May Cohen to Pearl S. Casman, letter of December 15, 1963 [SLRC].

52. See the review "Judy Gerowitz, Rolf Nelson Gallery," *Artforum* 4, no. 8 (April 1966): 14.

53. Chicago, *Beyond the Flower*, p. 16.

54. Judy Gerowitz to May Cohen, letter of June 29, 1966 [SLRC].

55. Barney's Beanery was immortalized by California sculptor Edward Kienholz in a work by that name.

56. Chicago, *Through the Flower*, p. 35.

57. Ibid., p. 36.

58. See ibid., pp. 38–54.

59. Clement Greenberg, *Primary Structures: Younger American and British Sculptors* (New York: Jewish Museum, 1966), no. 17, n.p.

60. May Cohen to Pearl S. Cassman, letter of August 30, 1966 [SLRC].

61. May Cohen to Pearl S. Cassman, letter of January 25, 1967 [SLRC].

62. Judy Gerowitz [Chicago], quoted in Henry J. Seldis, "Technology for Art's Sake," *Los Angeles Times*, p. 16, reviewing an exhibition at the Aesthetic Research Center (ARC), a cooperative in Century City begun by Los Angeles artists who "believe it is time to move out of the studio into the industrial environment."

63. Chicago, *Through the Flower*, p. 9.

64. Judy Gerowitz [Chicago], quoted in "Renowned Artist Has a Studio in Kingsburg," *Kingsburg Recorder*, July 30, 1970, p. 11.

65. Judy Gerowitz [Chicago], quoted on Los Angeles FM on Fine Arts radio, May 1968 [SLRC].

66. William Wilson, "Judy Gerowitz Sculpture in Pasadena," *Los Angeles Times*, May 18, 1969, Calendar, p. 48.

67. Peter Selz, with William Wilson, "Los Angeles: A View from the Studios," *Art in America* (Nov./Dec. 1969): p. 144, 147. Chicago was then called Gerowitz. Together with artists Sam Francis and James Turrell, Chicago "planned to stage a spectacular antiwar demonstration on land, sea and air at Santa Monica Beach, until it was stifled by two thousand police officers." In a letter to the author of August 14, 2002, she maintains that she did not get involved in political activities "because I was committed to struggling through my own ideas in the studio."

68. "Judy Chicago Talking to Lucy R. Lippard," interview of September 1973, *Artforum* (September 1974): 60.

69. Chicago, *Through the Flower*, caption under photograph of *Woman/Atmosphere*, following p. 72.

70. Ibid., p. 58.

71. "Judy Chicago Talking to Lucy R. Lippard," p. 60.

72. Ibid.

73. Chicago, *Through the Flower*, p. 63; Chicago, *Beyond the Flower*, p. 20.

74. Judy Chicago in letter to the author of August 16, 2002.

75. George Eliot, *Daniel Deronda* (1876); for quotation excerpted here, see *Judy Chicago*, California State College, Fullerton, California, 1970, n.p.

76. *Judy Chicago*, California State College, Fullerton, n.p. Also reprinted in Judy Chicago to the editor, *Artforum* 9, no. 7 (March 1971): 8–9.

77. "Judy Chicago Talking to Lucy R. Lippard," p. 61.

78. Quoted in Judith Hole and Ellen Levine, *Rebirth of Feminism* (New York: Quadrangle Books, 1971), p. 366. This source also recounts the activities of WAR. See also Cindy Nemser, "The Women Artists' Movement," *Feminist Art Journal* 2 (Winter 1973–74): 8.

79. Judy Chicago, interviewed by Judith Dancoff, *Everywoman* 2, no. 7, issue 18 (May 7, 1971): 4.

80. Chicago, *Beyond the Flower*, p. 23.

81. "Judy Chicago in Conversation with Ruth Iskin," p. 14.

82. Chicago, interviewed by Dancoff, p. 4.

83. Chicago, *Through the Flower*, p. 73.

84. Judy Chicago, quoted in Norma Broude and Mary D. Garrard, "Conversations with Judy Chicago and Miriam Schapiro," in Norma Broude and Mary D. Garrard, *The Power of Feminist Art* (New York: Harry N. Abrams Publishers, 1994), pp. 66–67.

85. Miriam Schapiro, quoted in Broude and Garrard, "Conversations with Judy Chicago and Miriam Schapiro," p. 75.

86. Ibid.

87. Judy Chicago to the author, letter of August 16, 2002, recalls that the fact that the name Mariposa "means butterfly was not lost on me," for she had already identified the butterfly as a symbol of the vagina and of female identity, which she would use in her atmosphere of 1974 called *A Butterfly for Oakland* and in a series of paintings and drawings in that same period. Chicago and Schapiro also invited three Los Angeles artists to participate in creating Womanhouse: Sherry Brody, Carol Edison Mitchell, and Wanda Westcoast.

88. Judy Chicago, "Menstruation Bathroom 'Womanhouse,'" October 1977, typewritten ms. [SLRC].

89. Judy Chicago, quoted in "Womanhouse Opens," *Los Angeles Free Press*, February 4, 1972.

90. Conversation of the author with Miriam Schapiro, August 1996, East Hampton, New York.

91. See Judith Dancoff, *Judy Chicago and the California Girls* (1970); and Johanna Demetrakas, *Womanhouse* (Phoenix Films, 1974). For the scripts of several performances, see Chicago, *Through the Flower*, Appendix, pp. 207–19.

92. Judy Chicago, "Tape of a Conversation with Judy Chicago," n.d. [1972], interviewer not identified [SLRC].

93. Chicago, *Beyond the Flower*, p. 20.

94. Ibid., p. 13. This omission might reflect her wish not to divert attention from feminism, yet it is ironic because she has suffered unfair attacks by those who claim that she has failed to pay enough attention to African-American women, and by Alice Walker, who complained ("*One* Child of One's Own," *Ms.*, July 1979, reprinted in *In Search of Our Mother's Gardens* [San Diego: Harcourt, Brace, Jovanovitch, 1983]) that her rendition of Sojourner Truth's plate in *The Dinner Party* (1979) was not a vulval image like most of the other plates representing different women. The incorrect implication was that her decision to depict Truth weeping reflects some sort of discrimination on her part.

95. Chicago, "Tape of a Conversation with Judy Chicago."

96. See Judy Chicago, *Holocaust Project* (New York: Penguin, 1993).

About the Contributors

Avital H. Bloch is Research Professor at the Center for Social Research, University of Colima, Mexico. She is the director of the U.S. Studies Program and the coordinator of the M.A. in History. She has written widely on contemporary American women and on the intellectual history of the postwar era and the 1960s.

Julia L. Foulkes is a core faculty member of the New School in New York City, where she teaches history. She is the author of *Modern Bodies: Dance and American Modernism from Martha Graham to Alvin Ailey* and a recent recipient of a postdoctoral fellowship at the David C. Driskell Center for the Study of the African Diaspora at the University of Maryland.

Veta Goler is Associate Professor of Dance and Chair of Drama and Dance at Spelman College. Her research focuses on contemporary African American modern dance artists, particularly women choreographers, as well as the intersection of dance and spirituality in popular culture. Her most recent publication is an essay in *Dancing Many Drums: Excavations in African American Dance History.*

Roxanne Power Hamilton is a poet and performer who lives in San Francisco and teaches poetry, gender studies, and writing at the University of California, Santa Cruz. She received her M.F.A. in Poetry from Cornell University and has taught literature and Women's Studies at Hobart and William Smith Colleges and Colorado College. In 2003 she performed in the first "Transcontinental Poetry Reading" as part of a conference she organized at UC Santa Cruz: "Trans Genre: Poetry and the Inter-Arts." Her poems have been published in numerous journals, and she is currently at work on a book on Anne Waldman.

Michelle Nzadi Keita writes poetry, fiction, and essays. Her collection of poems, *Birthmarks*, was published by Nightshade Press; her work has also appeared in journals, including *Proteus* and *Long Shot Review*, and anthologies, including *Beyond the Frontier: African-American Poetry for the 21st Century*. Keita is a spouse, a parent of two sons, and an assistant professor of Creative Writing and English at Ursinus College.

Jaap Kooijman received his Ph.D. in American Studies at the University of Amsterdam in 1999. Since 2000, he has been Assistant Professor in Media and Culture (formerly Film and Television Studies) at the University of Amsterdam. His writings on American politics and American popular culture have been published in *Presidential Studies Quarterly*, *Velvet Light Trap*, and the *European Journal of Cultural Studies*. Kooijman can be reached through his Website: www.jaapkooijman.nl.

Judy Kutulas is Professor of History and American Studies and Director of Women's Studies at St. Olaf College. She is the author of *The Long War: The Intellectual People's Front and Anti-Stalinism, 1930–1940* and several articles on liberalism, as well as several pieces on gender and popular culture. She is finishing a book on the American Civil Liberties Union, after which she expects to begin a study of seventies popular culture.

Gail Levin is Professor of Art History and American Studies at Baruch College and the Graduate Center of the City University of New York. Her work has been recognized by fellowships from the National Endowment for the Humanities, Yale University, the American Council of Learned Societies, and the Smithsonian Institution, among others. She is the author of many books on twentieth-century art and culture, including *Edward Hopper: An Intimate Biography*. She is currently writing a biography of Judy Chicago.

Tamara Levitz is Associate Professor of Musicology at UCLA, where she teaches classes on a wide range of topics related to the study of twentieth-century music, from the Beatles through Cuban modernism to the European avant-garde. Her publications have focused on historical reassessments of the lives and music of composers Ferrucio Busoni, Kurt Weill, Igor Stravinsky, and John Cage. She is currently completing a book on the complicated interrelations between modern music and dance in Europe and the Americas between the two world wars.

Susan Marie. Maloney, SNJM, Ph.D., teaches at the University of Red-
lands in California in the Religious Studies and Women's Studies departments. Prior to this position, she was chair of the master's program in
Feminist Spirituality at Immaculate Heart College Center in Los Angeles.
She was selected by Anita M. Caspary to be her assistant editor for the
book *Witness to Integrity: The Crisis of the Immaculate Heart Community of California*. Dr. Maloney has authored numerous articles and book
chapters on women in religion. In 1999, she was awarded a Coolidge
Fellowship in New York by the Association of Religion and Intellectual
Life for her work with women in cross-cultural contexts. As president
and board member of the Women, Development and Earth Foundation,
she does international solidarity work that examines the linkage of
women's oppression to religious ideology. Dr. Maloney is a member of
the Sisters of the Holy Names of Jesus and Mary, an international order
of sisters dedicated to the education and empowerment of women and
children.

Judith McDaniel currently works as the Deputy Director of the Southern
Arizona AIDS Foundation. She also teaches courses for the Women's
Studies Department of the University of Arizona. Since, 1988, McDaniel
has been the Literary Executor of the Barbara Deming Archive, housed
at the Schlesinger Women's History Library, Radcliffe. She is writing a
biography of Deming.

Zina Petersen is a medievalist with a specialization in women's issues and
women's devotional literature. She received her Ph.D. from the Catholic
University of America in 1997. A longtime fan of Le Guin's writing, in
1999 she was asked to write the entry on Ursula Le Guin for the *Dictionary of Literary Biography*; she has since claimed a secondary emphasis
in Le Guin's works and speculative literature. She teaches at Brigham
Young University.

James Pipkin is Associate Professor of English at the University of Houston. He is the editor of *English and German Romanticism: Cross Currents and Controversies* and has published articles on Romantic
literature, especially the poetry of William Wordsworth, and various
studies of literature and the other liberal arts. The essay on Huey and
King is related to his current research for a book on sports autobiographies and American cultural studies.

Barbara L. Tischler teaches history and is an Associate Dean at the Horace Mann School in Riverdale, New York. She is the author of *An American Music*, editor of *Sights on the Sixties*, and the author of a number of articles on aspects of 1960s culture and politics.

Susana Torre is an architect, critic, and educator based in New York City. Ms. Torre has taught architectural design and theory at numerous graduate schools of architecture, including Columbia and Yale in the United States and the universities of Sydney (Australia), Buenos Aires (Argentina), and Kassel (Germany). She was chair of architecture programs at Parsons School of Design and Barnard College, and Director of the Cranbrook Academy of Art. Her projects have been published internationally and are included in standard reference works such as *Contemporary Architects and Contemporary Masterworks* by St. James' Press. She has lectured about her work at over two hundred universities worldwide. She first wrote about Mary Otis Stevens in a book she edited, *Women in American Architecture: A Historic and Contemporary Perspective*, published by Whitney Library of Design in 1974. Her own dwelling also lacks interior doors and well-defined rooms.

Lauri Umansky is Professor of History at Suffolk University. She is the author of *Motherhood Reconceived: Feminism and the Legacies of the Sixties* and *Naked Is the Best Disguise* (pseud. Lauri Lewin). She has coedited several other books, including *"Bad" Mothers: The Politics of Blame in Twentieth-Century America*, *The New Disability History: American Perspectives*, and *Making Sense of Women's Lives: An Introduction to Women's Studies.*

Margaret A. Weitekamp earned a Ph.D. in History from Cornell University in 2001. While writing her dissertation, she spent a year in residence at the NASA Headquarters History Office as the 1997 American Historical Association/NASA Aerospace History Fellow. In 2002, she won the Aviation/Space Writers Award from the Smithsonian Institution's National Air and Space Museum. She is the author of *The Right Stuff, the Wrong Sex: The Lovelace Woman in Space Program*. Weitekamp is a curator at the Smithsonian Institution's National Air and Space Museum in Washington, D. C.

Index

Aalto, Alvar, 32, 36; Baker House, 32
Abdullah, Ahmed, 299
Abstract Expressionism, 310, 319;
    painters, 107
Abzug, Bella, 55
Achebe, Chinua. See *Things Fall
    Apart* (Achebe)
Actors' Studio, 242–243
Adams, Abigail, 316
African diaspora, 81, 82, 85, 87–88
Aggiornamento, 184
Ailey, Alvin, 294
Airplane, Jefferson, 108, 265
Air Research and Development Com-
    mand (ARDC), 10
Albany Herald, 208
Aldon Music, 262–263
Algarin, Miguel, 117
Allen, Donald, 99
Allen, Reverend Michael, 108
Allen, Woody. See *Annie Hall* (film)
Amateur Athletic Union (AAU), 49,
    50
American Civil Liberties Union
    (ACLU), 126
American Friends Service Committee
    First Day School, 127
American Institute of Public Service,
    126
American National Exhibition, 16
Americans for Democratic Action,
    126

Amnesty International, 142
Anderson, Laurie, 110
Andre, Carl, 313
Andre Emmerich Gallery, 319
Anfuso, Victor, 18, 19, 21
Angel Hair, 99, 102–103, 105
Annie Hall (film), 271
Architectural Collaborative, The
    (TAC), 33
Armed Forces Induction Center (Oak-
    land, Calif.), 140
Arogundade, Ben, 164
Art Institute of Chicago, 305, 306
Art Workers Coalition, 317
Ashbery, John, 101, 110
Assembly of Unrepresented People,
    134
Atwood, Margaret, 75
Avedon, Richard, 167

Badiane, Mamadou, 85
Baez, Albert Vinicio, 127
Baez, Joan, 126–151, 274
Baez, Joan Bridge, 126–127, 140
Bailey, Beth, 270
Baldwin, James, 94
Ballard, Florence, 154, 162; formed
    the Primettes, 154
Ball, Lucille, *The Lucy Show*, 9
Baraka, Amiri (LeRoi Jones), 90, 91,
    113, 280, 281, 282, 292
Bardot, Brigitte, 217, 243

Barksdale, Richard, 286
Barnett, Marilyn, 60
Barry, Marion, 142
Bartz, Gary, 299
Batista regime, 200–201; supporters, 203
Beale, Frances, 279, 285
Beatles, the, 137, 217, 220, 227, 265, 266, 267; Beatlemania, 228
Beat poetry, 101
Beckett, Samuel, 307, 310
Belafonte, Harry, 127
Belton, Don, 161
Bennington College, 100, 199, 213
Berg, Alban, 223
Bergman, Ingmar, 310
Berkeley Defense League, 114
Berkeley Poetry Conference (1965), 99, 101, 109
Bernstein, Leonard, 248
Berrigan, Phillip and Daniel, 212, 310
Berrigan, Ted, 101, 103, 104–105, 106, 109, 111, 120; *Bean Spasms,* 106; *Memorial Day,* 106
Berry, Chuck, 229
Birdsong, Cindy, 162
Black Arts movement, 81–82, 90–95, 111, 281, 283, 284, 293–295, 296, 298, 300, 302, 314
Black Arts Repertory Theatre/School (BART/S), 90, 281, 282
Black Capitalism, 155
Black Panthers, 114, 245; artist Emory, 282; leader Huey P. Newton, 246
Black Power movement, 90, 91, 136, 164
Bladen, Ronald, 313
Blais, Marie-Claire, 210
Bluiett, Hamiet, 299
Bluth, Betty Jean, 192
Bly, Robert, 110

Boaz, Franz, 83
Bogan, Louise, 280
Bogle, Donald, 166
Boone, Debbie, 275
Borde, Percival, 87
Boston University, 129
Boudin, Kathy, 114
Boyd, Jenny, 217
Brach, Paul, 319
Braddix, Darryl, 91
Braunstein, Peter, 243, 250, 255
Breines, Wini, 262
Breuer, Bessie, 201
Brewster Housing Projects (Detroit), 154, 157
Broadside Press, 282
Brokaw, Frances Seymour, 242
Brooklyn College, 309
Brown, Helen Gurley. See *Sex and the Single Girl*
Brown, H. Rap, 91
Brown, James, 153
Brown, Norman O., 311
Browne, Jackson, 261
Brownstein, Michael, 118
Bullins, Ed, 282, 299
Burkett, Warren, 22
Burritt, Katherine, 197
Burroughs, William, 110, 120

Cade, Toni, 285
Cage, John, 119, 218, 310
Caldwell, Sarah, 40
Cale, John, 103
Camus, Albert, 308
Cannes International Film Festival, 167
Capp, Al, 139
Cardwell, Diane, 158
Carlo, Gian Carlo de, 39
Carlos, John, 51
Carmichael, Stokely, 91, 164

Carnegie Recital Hall, 134, 224
Carpenter, M. Scott, 19
Carroll, Jim, 110
Carson, Johnny, 153, 164; *Tonight Show,* 153
Carson, Rachel. See *Silent Spring*
Carter, Jimmy, 254, 256
Caspary, Anita M., 177–195
Caspary, Jacob, 178
Caspary, Marie Bruch, 178
Cassidy, David, 268
Castro, Fidel, 196, 200–201, 202, 203
Catonsville Nine, 114
Chavez, Cesar, 53
Chicago International Film Festival, 225
Chicago, Judy, 305–326
Chicago Seven, 114
City College of New York (CCNY), 309
City Lights Books, 117
Civilian Aeronautics Authority (CAA), 11
Civil Rights Act (1964), 154–155; Title VII of, 18, 25
Civil Rights movement, 281, 283, 285, 300, 307, 314, 320
Clapton, Eric, 229–230
Clark, Dick, 263
Clark, Tom, 103
Clayton, Merry, 274
Cleaver, Eldridge, 229
Club Mt. Auburn 47, 129
Cobb, Geraldine "Jerrie," 9–28
Cobb, Ty, 47
Cochran, Jacqueline, 15
Codrescu, Andrei, 110
Cohen, Arthur, 305–306
Cohen, John, 131
Cold War, 10, 16, 23, 24, 113, 201, 205

Cole, Doris. See *From Tipi to Skyscraper*
Coleman, Ornette, 231, 232
Coltrane, John, 296–297
Comaneci, Nadia, 46
Committee for Nonviolent Action (CNVA), 114, 196–197, 204, 205, 207, 210
Committee for the Protection of the Foreign Born, 307
Committee of Liaison with Servicemen Detained in North Vietnam, 142
Communist Party, 128
Conceptual Art, 314
Congress of Racial Equality (CORE), 280–281
Coolidge, Clark, 103
Cooper Union, 309
Corso, Gregory, 100, 110, 120
Cott, Jonathan, 223
Cox, Anthony, 218
Crist, Judith, 243
Cunningham, Merce, 310

Dadaism, 218
Dafora, Asadata, 294
Daughters of the American Revolution, 139
Davidson, Bill, 210
Davis, Angela, 167, 246
De Beauvoir, Simone, 316
Debord, Guy, 37; Situationists, 37, 38; theory of the *dérive*, 37–38
Dellinger, Dave, 197, 204, 213
Deming, Barbara, 196–216
Deming, Harold, 197–198
Denis, Ruth St., 301
Dickerson, James, 269
Diddley, Bo, 229
Didion, Joan, 130
Dion, Celine, 275

Di Prima, Diane, 110, 119–120
Dixie Cups, 265
Doors, the, 265
Douglas, Susan, 10, 13, 158, 161, 265, 271
DuBois, W. E. B., 87–88
Duchamp, Marcel, 218
Duncan, Robert, 102
Dunham, Katherine, 81–97, 293, 294, 295, 300
Dunning, Jennifer, 297
Durand, Jean Marie, 85
Dyer, Richard, 153, 166
Dylan, Bob, 132–133, 138–139

Earl, Gabriel, 141
Early, Gerald, 156–157
Ebert, Roger, 226
Echols, Alice, 156
Ecofeminism, 73
Ed Sullivan Show, The, 153, 154, 161, 162
Education Act of 1972, Title IX, 44, 47
Edwards, Harry, 52
Eisenhower, Dwight, 33
Eliot, George, 316
Elizabeth A. Sackler Foundation, 321
Ellington, Duke, 298
Ellison, Ralph, 163
Episcopal Peace Fellowship, 141
Equal Employment Opportunity Campaign, 163
Equal Pay Act, 10
Evans, Mari, 299
Everett, Chestyn, 296
Evers, Rick, 275
Evert, Chris, 58, 59, 60; *Chrissie,* 58

Fabio, Sarah, 282
Fabres, Shelly, 265
Fagin, Larry, 107, 120

Faithful, Marianne, 223
Farina, Mimi (Baez), 133, 140, 142
Farina, Richard (Dick), 133, 137
Fawcett, Mary S., 32
Feiffer, Jules, 247
Feldman, Morton, 218, 310
Feminist Art Program, 320; moved to California Institute of the Arts, 319
Ferlinghetti, Lawrence, 117
Fillman, Jesse R., 40
Fillmore East, 108
Fletcher, Jean Bodman, 33
Flickinger, Donald, 10, 11, 12
Fonda, Henry, 242
Fonda, Jane, 55, 241–258
Ford, Gerald, 254
Four Tops, 153
Franklin, Aretha, 153
Freedom Riders, 207
Free Jazz, 297, 300
Freeman, Jo, 190
Free Speech Movement (FSM), 133
Friedan, Betty, 43, 55, 262; *The Feminine Mystique,* 10, 43
Friends Seminary (New York City), 198
From Tipi to Skyscraper (Cole), 39
Fuller, Buckminster, 29, 30, 32, 39
Fulton, James E., 21
Funk, Wally, 20

Gaar, Gillian G., 217
Gagarin, Yuri, 21
Gakushuin University, 218
Gallup, Dick, 105, 106, 120
Gandhi, Mahatma, 135
Garvey, Marcus, 87
Gaye, Marvin, 153, 166
Gehry, Frank, 312
Gerowitz, Jerry, 308, 310
Gillmore Girls (TV series), 275
Gilruth, Robert, 25

Ginsberg, Allen, 99, 101, 109, 110, 119, 120
Giorno, John, 110, 116; "Dial-a-poem" project, 116; Streetworks, 116
Gitlin, Todd, 183, 307, 308
Gladys Knight and the Pips, 153
Glass, Philip, 110
Gleason, Ralph, 156
Glenn, John, 10, 19, 20, 21, 22
Goffin, Gerry, 262–263, 264, 265, 266, 267
Goffin, Louise, 264, 275
Goldstein, Richard, 160
Goodman, Robert, 30
Gordy, Berry, 155, 156, 158–160, 163, 166, 167; belief in Black Capitalism, 155
Gore, Lesley, 265
Gornick, Vivian, 248
Graham, Lawrence Otis, 155
Graham, Martha, 301
Grateful Dead, 108
Great Depression, 305–306
Great Society, 121
Great Wall of Respect, 292. *See also* Walls of Respect
Greenberg, Clement, 313
Greenhill, Manny, 129
Greenpeace, 73
Gregory, Dick, 53
Gropius, Walter, 32, 33, 34; founder of the German Bauhaus, 34
Gugler, Eric, 31–32
Guthmann, Edward, 244
Guttman, Allen, 60
Guy, Edna, 294

Hagwood, Rod Stafford, 161
Hamill, Dorothy, 46
Hamrol, Lloyd, 312, 313
Harkness, Sarah Pillsbury, 33

Harlem Renaissance, 90, 296, 302
Harlem Youth Opportunities Unlimited (HARYOU-ACT), 281
Harney, Eucharia, 179, 180
Harris, David V., 141
Harrison, Patti Boyd, 217
Hart, Jane, 18, 19; husband Phillip Hart, 18
Harvard University, 39
Haussman, Baron, 31
Hayden, Tom, 245, 249, 254, 255, 256, 257; Campaign for Economic Democracy, 255; elected to California State Assembly, 256
Hearst, Patty, 254
Hendrix, Jimi, 265
Herald Tribune, 201
Herskovits, Melville, 83
Highway Trust Act of 1956, 29
Hirshey, Gerri, 152, 166
Hitler-Stalin Non-Agression Pact, 305–306
Holiday, Billie, 166
Holland-Dozier-Holland, 158
Hollies, the, 265
Holloway, Brenda, 158
Hollywood Palace (TV series), 153
Hollywood Women's Press Club, 246
Hootenanny Show (TV series), 133
Hope, Bob, 247
Hopkins, Mary, 227
House Un-American Activities Committee (HUAC), 133
Housing Act of 1949, 29
Huey, Lynda, 43, 44–45, 47–54, 57, 61, 62, 63, 64
Hughes, Langston, 131, 299, 300
Hullabaloo (TV series), 153
Humphrey, Doris, 301
Humphrey, Hubert H., 164–165
Hunter College, 82, 280, 309
Hurston, Zora Neale, 83

Hyatt, Alice, of *Alice Doesn't Live Here Anymore*, 268

Ian, Janis, 137
Ichiyanagi, Toshi, 218
Immaculate Heart College (IHC), 178, 179, 180, 181–183, 184
Immaculate Heart of Mary Sisters (IHMs), 177–180, 182, 184, 186–195
Indochina Peace Campaign, 249, 255
Institute for the Study of Nonviolence in Carmel, 134, 136
i press, 39, 41; *From Tipi to Skyscraper*, 39; *The Ideal Communist City*, 39; *Word of Variation*, 39

Jack Glenn Gallery, 315, 316
Jack Kerouac School of Disembodied Poetics, 99, 109, 119, 120
Jacobs, Jane, 30
Jagger, Mick, 265
James, C. L. R., 87
James, Henry, 104
James, William, 72
Jetsons, The (TV series), 9
Johnson, Lyndon B., 105, 154, 163–164; Great Society initiatives, 105
Johnson, Sam, 253
Johnston, Jill, 223
Jones, Joe, 233
Jones, John, 226
Jones, Quincy, 274
Joplin, Janis, 108, 223, 265
Jordan, Norman, 299
Jung, Carl, 222

Kahn, Louis, 32, 36
Kaiser, Charles, 160
Kandell, Lenore, 109
Kane, Daniel, 103

Karenga, Ron, 91, 94, 296
Kaufman, Philip. See *Right Stuff, The* (Wolfe)
Kennedy, John F., 10, 15, 47, 49, 246
Kennedy, Robert, 113, 282
Kent, Corita, 181
Kent State University, 245, 254
Khrushchev, Nikita, 16
King, Billie Jean, 43, 44, 54–62, 63, 64
King, Carole, 137, 261–278
King, Coretta Scott, 142
King, Larry, 56
King, Martin Luther, Jr., 53, 93, 127, 128, 132, 136, 142, 154, 160, 163, 164, 206, 282
King George IV, 84
Kingston Trio, 127
Kinks, the, 265
Kirchner, Don, 262, 263, 267
Knight, Etheridge, 288–289
Koch, Kenneth, 113–114
Koch, Stephen, 104
Kondor, Sherry Goffin, 264, 275
Korbut, Olga, 46
Kotchman, Danny, 267
Kroeber, Alfred, 66
Kyger, Joanne, 120

Lake, Oliver, 299
Landau, Jon, 160
Langdon, Harry, 167
Larkey, Charles, 267, 274; of the Fugs, 267
Lawson, James, 206
Leadbelly, 100
Le Fevre, Frances, 100
Le Guin, Theodora, 66
Le Guin, Ursula Kroeber, 65–77
Lennon, John, 217, 218, 219–235
Lester, Richard, 217
Lewis, Jerry Lee, 229, 263

Liberation, 206
Library of Congress National Film Library Project, 199
Life, 24, 25, 34, 54, 167, 248
Life of Riley, The (TV series), 56
Lincoln, Abbey, 283
Lipton, Peggy, 266
Little Red School House, 94
Little Richard, 229
Liquori, Marty, 48
Lomax, Jackie, 227
Lombardi, Vince, 47
LOOK, 12, 157
Los Angeles State College, 56
Los Angeles Times, 313, 314
Lovelace, William Randolph II, 10, 11, 12–13, 15, 18, 25; Lovelace Foundation, 12
Low, George, 19
Lowell, Robert, 104
Lucas, John A., 47
Luce, Clare Boothe, 10, 24
Lynch, Kevin, 32
Lyttle, Brad, 208, 210

Madhubuti, Haki, 281
Malanga, Gerard, 103
Malcolm X, 94, 231, 281, 282, 286
Mamas and Papas, the, 223
Manilow, Barry, 268
Mao, Chairman, 53
Martin, John, 82
Marvin X, 282
Mary's Day, 181, 182, 184
Massachusetts Institute of Technology (MIT), 30, 31–32, 33, 36, 39, 127
Matthews, Herbert, 201
Maxfield, Richard, 218
Mayer, Bernadette, 103, 121
McCarran International Security Act, 253
McCarthy, Mary, 200, 209

McCartney, Paul, 227
McDonald, Country Joe, 247, 248
McGovern, George, 249
McGuire Sisters, the, 156
McIntyre, Dianne, 292–304
McIntyre, Dorothy Layne, 303
McIntyre, James Francis Cardinal, 178, 180, 181–187
McKayle, Donald, 92, 294
McNulty, Thomas, 30, 33, 35, 38, 39
Mead, Margaret, 83
Meigs, Mary, 200
Merwin, W. S., 120
Meyer, Karl, 210
Michigan State University, 246
Middleton, Richard, 160
Millay, Edna St. Vincent, 199
Millay, Norma, 199
Miller, George, chair of House Space Committee, 18
Miller, Sherry, 210
Minh, Ho Chih
Mitchell, Joni, 273
Moffitt, Bill, 55
Moffitt, Randy, 55, 61; pitcher for the San Francisco Giants, 55
"Moisopolon Domo" (Sappho), 100
Monk, Meredith, 120
Monkees, the, 266
Moorman, Charlotte, 218
Morison, Samuel Eliot, 32, 39
Morrison, Jim, 265
Motherfuckers' Soup Kitchen, 114
Motown, 153, 154, 155, 156, 162, 163, 165, 167; *A Bit of Liverpool* (1964 concept album), 157; Artist Development Department, 155
Murray, Paul, 285
Museum of Modern Art, 101, 199, 309, 319
Muste, A. J., 197, 210

Naropa Institute, 119, 120; became Naropa University, 120

Nation, 197, 200, 202, 204, 206

National Aeronautics and Space Administration (NASA), 9, 10, 13–22, 23, 25; House Committee on Science and Astronautics, 18; Project Mercury, 14, 16; and Sputnik, 22

National Association for the Advancement of Colored People (NAACP), 85, 207, 307, 321; *The Crisis* (magazine), 82

National Endowment for the Arts, 121

National Organization for Women, 49

National Youth Administration (NYA), 82

Navratilova, Martina, 59

Neal, Larry, 91, 281–283

Neal, Mark Anthony, 159

Near, Holly, 247, 248

Negritude, 89

Nelson, Rolf, 312

Nemerov, Howard, 100, 101

Nevin, Al, and Aldan Music publishing firm, 262

New American poets, 102, 112–113

New Choreographers Showcase Concert, 299

New Dance Group, 82

New Deal: NYA, 82; WPA, 82

New Left, 111, 307, 321

Newport Folk Festival, 129, 138

New School for Social Research, 309

Newton, Huey P., 246

New Urbanism, 30

New Yorker, 200

New York Public Library Dance Collection, 296

New York Times, 160, 201, 249

New York University, 280

Nicholais, Alwin, 309–310

Nichols, Mike, 247

Nixon, Richard, 16, 39; Watergate scandal, 39

North Vietnam Committee for Solidarity with the American People, 142

Nuyorican Poets Cafe, 117

Oberlin College, 48, 52, 53

Odetta, 127

O'Hara, Frank, 101, 105, 111

Olson, Charles, 99, 101, 102, 111; *The New American Poetry*, 99; "open field poetry," 102, 111; "Projective Poetry" manifesto, 102, 111; "Projective Verse," 99, 102, 107

Omaha Community Theatre, 242

Ono, Yoko, 217–239

Oppenheimer, Joel, 103

Orr, Eric, 313

Owen, Maureen, 109

Padgett, Ron, 105, 106

Paik, Naim June, 218

Painters, New York School, 107

Pan-Africanism, 87, 89

Parker, Francine, 247

Parks, Rosa, 307

Partisan Review, 200

Peace Walkers, 205–208

Peninsula Committee for the Abolition of Nuclear Tests, 127

People, 120

Perfectae Caritatis, 185

Perkins, Tony, 243

Philadelphia Freedoms World Team Tennis, 54

Phillips, Michelle, 223

Picasso, Pablo, 309

Pickett, Wilson, 313

Playboy, 141

Poetry Project, 103, 107, 108–111, 114, 116, 120–121; "Creative Arts for Alienated Youth," 108
Poets, New York School, 99, 101, 103, 104, 105, 113
Pomare, Eleo, 91, 294–295; in *Blues Jungle,* 91
Poor, Anne, 201
Poor, Henry, 201
Pope John XXIII, 184
Pope Paul VI, 185
Pound, Ezra, 107
Powell, Cynthia, 217
Powell, Maxine, 155–156
Prefeminist agitation, 10; fifty-thousand-housewife walkout, 10; first woman astronaut candidate, 9–10
President's Commission on the Status of Women, 10
Presley, Elvis, 263
Primettes, the, 154
Primus, Pearl, 81–84, 86–97, 293, 294, 295, 301
Princess Anne, 156
Princess Margaret, 156
Pritchett, Laurie, 207
Projective Poetry, 103, 111
Project WISE (Women in Space Earliest), 11

Quakers, 100, 198, 205
Quartermain, Ola Mae, 207
Queens College (CUNY), 262

Rae, Martha, 247
Rainer, Yvonne, 218
Ray, Nicholas. See *Rebel without a Cause* (film)
Reagan, Nancy, 256
Reagan, Ronald, 254, 256
Reagon, Cordell, 207
Rebel without a Cause (film), 108

Red Cross, 210
Redford, Robert, 243
Redskins (Washington football team), 21
Reed, Lou, 103, 110
Reed, Rex, 153
Reeves, Martha, 158, 160
Resistance, The (anti-war movement), 140, 141
Reynolds, Melvina, 132
Richards, Bob, 56
Richards, Mary, of *The Mary Tyler Moore Show,* 268, 271
Riggs, Bobby, 44, 55, 61
Right Stuff, The (Wolfe), 11, 20; movie, 11
Rinpoche, Chogyam Trungpa, 119
Roach, Max, 299
Robinson, Ray, 209, 213
Roethke, Theodore, 100
Rogers, Rod, 294
Rolling Stone, 217, 220, 267
Rolling Stones, 137, 229, 265, 266; *The Rolling Stones Rock and Roll Circus,* 229
Rollins, Metz, 206
Roosevelt, Eleanor, 10
Roosevelt, Teddy, 47
Rosen, Ruth, 43, 44
Rosenwald Foundation, 82
Ross, Diana, 152–173
Royal Albert Hall, 133
Rudolf, Wilma, 44
Rukeyser, Muriel, 110

Saarinen, Eero, 32, 36
Sabina, Maria, 99, 118
Sainte Marie, Buffy, 137
Saint-Exupery, Antoine de, 221
Salaam, Kalamu Ya, 281
Sanchez, Sonia, 279–291
Sanders, Ed, 120

Sanders, Fran, 283
Sandperl, Ira, 127, 133, 135
San Francisco State College (now University), 282; Black Studies Program, 282, 289
San Jose State University, 48, 50, 52
San Quentin Penitentiary, 134
Santa Rita Rehabilitation Center, 140
Sarah Lawrence College, 218
Sartre, Jean-Paul, 308
Scarrit College for Christian Workers, 206
Schapiro, Miriam, 319, 320
Scott, Jack, 52–53; *Athletics for Athletes*, 52
Second Vatican Council (Vatican II), 177, 178, 180, 184, 185, 186, 190
Sedaka, Neil, 262
Seeger, Pete, 100, 127, 128, 129, 133
Senghor, Leopold, 89
Seventeen, 47
Sex and the Single Girl (Brown), 51
Sherrod, Charles, 207
Sikelianos, Anghelos, 100
Silberstein, Bob, 167
Silent Spring (Carson), 73
SILO, 100
Silverstein, Harry, 108
Simon, Carly, 261, 273–274
Simon, Paul, 137, 261, 271
Sinatra, Nancy, 244
Smith College, 31, 32
Smith, Patti, 110, 115
Smith, Ronald A., 47
Smith, Tommie, 51, 52
Smokey Robinson and the Miracles, 153
Smothers Brothers Comedy Hour (TV series), 139
Snyder, Gary, 110
Solomon, Maynard, 129, 131

Soviet Union, 15, 18
Soyer, Raphael, 309
Spanish Civil War, 306, 309
Spector, Phil, 163
Sports Illustrated, 54
Stanford University, 46, 127, 141, 179
Starr, Maureen, 217
Starr, Ringo, 231
Stein, Gertrude, 101, 107; *O My Life*, 107
Steinem, Gloria, 55
Stevens, Mary Otis, 29–42
Stevenson, Adlai, 33
Stewart, James, 93
Stewart, Rod, 275
Stile, Kristin, 220, 226
St. Mark's Church, 108, 113, 114, 117; in *East Village Other*, 108
St. Mark's Place, 103, 105, 106, 107, 109, 110
St. Mark's Poetry Project, 98, 99, 103, 107; *The World*, 99, 103, 105, 106, 109
Strassberg, Lee, 242, 248–249
Student Nonviolent Coordinating Committee (SNCC), 164, 207
Students for a Democratic Society (SDS), 134, 164
Sullivan, Ed, 267
Summer, Donna, 269
Supremes, the, 154, 155–158, 161–164, 165, 166, 265; first album, 154
Sutherland, Donald, 247, 248

Taoism, 65, 66, 75
Tao Te Ching, 67
Tatum, Art, 298
Taylor, Cecil, 298, 299
Taylor, Derek, 227
Taylor, James, 261, 267, 273–274; Flying Machine, 267

Taylor, Steven, 110
Taylor, Telford, 142
Temptations, the, 153, 165
Tereshkova, Valentina, 24
Terrell, Tammi, 166
Thiam, Mor, 93
Things Fall Apart (Achebe), 299
Tibetan Buddhism, 118, 120; Buddhist Mahayana vow, 121
Time, 158, 166, 177
Tokyo Rose, 250
Tolson, John J., III, 247
Tompkins Square Park, 108, 114
Tonight Show, 153, 164; host Johnny Carson, 153, 164
Toronto Rock 'n' Roll Revival concert, 229
Toure, Askia M., 281
Towards a Non-Oppressive Environment (Tzonis), 39
Truth, Sojourner, 316
Tubman, William, 81, 87, 88, 89
Turner, Ted, 257
Tyner, McCoy, 298
Tzonis, Alexander. See *Towards a Non-Oppressive Environment* (Tzonis)

Union Carbide Company, 313
United Farm Workers, 249
United Nations, 88
University of Baghdad, 33
University of California (Berkeley), 46, 66
University of Chicago, 82
University of Southern California, 179
U.S. Office of Education, 94

Vadim, Roger, 243–244, 249–250
Vanguard Records, 129
Vassar College, 242
Velvet Underground, 103

Verlaine, Jane, 213–214
Vietnam Veterans Against the War, 247
Vietnam War, 39, 73, 98, 126, 134, 135, 142, 196, 197, 207, 211, 112, 246, 247, 248, 266; *Coming Home* (film), 255
Voas, Robert B., 23
Vogue, 200
Voices, 200
Voorman, Klaus, 229, 230, 231

Wakoski, Diane, 110
Waldman, Anne, 98–125
Waldman, John, 100
Walker, Margaret, 299, 300
Walls of Respect, 292, 293, 294, 302, 303
Wareing, William, 225
Warhol, Andy, 103, 105, 107, 108, 115; and Electric Circus, 108
War Resisters League, 210
Warsh, Lewis, 101, 102, 103, 108, 116
Watts, Alan W., 222
Watusi dancers, 83
Wayne, John, 21
Weavers, The, 127
Webb, James E., 16, 17
Welch, Chris, 164
Wells, Mary, 153
Wenner, Jann, 220
Whalen, Philip, 120
White, Alan, 229
Who, the, 265
Williams, Mary Lou, 298
Williams, William Carlos, 98
Wilson, Edmund, 200
Wilson, Mary, 154, 155, 157, 163; formed the Primettes, 154
Wilson, William, 314
Winfield, Hemsley, 294
Winfrey, Oprah, 161

Winter Soldier Investigation, 247
Wolfe, Tom. See *Right Stuff, The*
   (Wolfe)
Wolff, Christian, 310
Women Airforce Service Pilots
   (WASP), 12, 19
Women Artists for Revolution (WAR),
   317
Women's Liberation movement, 213
Women's Movement, 318
Women's Tennis Association, 57
Women Strike for Peace (WSP), 10,
   142
Wonder, Stevie, 153

Woods, Shadrach, 30
Woodstock Festival, 138
Woolf, Virginia, 316
Works Progress Administration
   (WPA), 82
World War II, 66, 199, 204, 207, 218,
   252
Wright, Frank Lloyd, 309

Young, La Monte, 218

Zaharias, Mildred "Babe" Didrikson,
   46
Zenjoir, Yasuda, 218